CASENOTE® Legal Briefs®

CRIMINAL PROCEDURE

Keyed to Courses Using

Dressler, Thomas, and Medwed's
Criminal Procedure: Principles, Policies, and Perspectives
Eighth Edition

Authored by: Publisher's Editorial Staff

ASPEN PUBLISHING

To contact Customer Service, e-mail customer.service@aspenpublishing.com, call 1-800-950-5259, or mail correspondence to:

Aspen Publishing
Attn: Order Department
1 Wall Street
Burlington, MA 01803

Printed in the United States of America.

1 2 3 4 5 6 7 8 9 0

ISBN 979-8-8890-6552-4

FIFTH AMENDMENT

PRIVILEGE AGAINST SELF-INCRIMINATION

"A person shall not be compelled in any criminal case to be a witness against himself."

CONFESSIONS

An accused's Fifth Amendment's rights are violated when prosecution uses at trial evidence of the accused's own incriminating words that were "deliberately elicited" after commencement of adversarial proceedings in the absence of the defendant's counsel.

CUSTODIAL INTERROGATION

"Custodial interrogation" refers to questioning initiated by law enforcement officers after the person has been taken into custody or otherwise deprived of his freedom in a significant way.

1. Custody: The standard is whether, based upon the totality of the circumstances, and assessed objectively, there was a formal arrest or restraint of freedom of movement of the degree associated with a formal arrest. Objective indicia of custody include, but are not limited to:
   - **a.** Formal arrest.
   - **b.** Prolonged detention.
   - **c.** Demeanor of police officers (e.g., confrontational questioning) and the ratio of officers to suspects. *Thompson v. Keohane*, 516 U.S. 99 (1995).
2. Interrogation: Interrogation is any direct or express questioning about the crime being investigated. *Illinois v. Perkins*, 496 U.S. 292 (1990).

INTERROGATIONS

Miranda v. Arizona, 384 U.S. 436 (1966).

Rule: Any statement, whether inculpatory or exculpatory, made by a suspect as the result of custodial interrogation may not be used against the suspect in a criminal trial, unless it is shown that the police provided procedural safeguards to secure the suspectís Fifth Amendment privilege against self-incrimination.

EXCLUSIONARY RULE

1. Impeachment of defendant: Statements obtained in violation of *Miranda* may be used nonetheless to impeach defendant at trial if he testifies inconsistently with the custodial statement.
2. The "fruit of the poisonous tree" doctrine does not apply to *Miranda* violations.

COERCED CONFESSIONS

1. Rule: A statement obtained by police from a suspect as the result of coercion is inadmissible at trial in violation of the Due Process Clause and the Fifth Amendment privilege against self-incrimination.
2. State action is required (i.e., a government agent, such as police, must be coercing the confession).
3. Factors in determining voluntariness:
   - **a.** Use or threatened use of force;
   - **b.** Use of psychological pressure;
   - **c.** Promise of leniency in exchange for a confession; and
   - **d.** Use of deception to secure a confession. *Spano v. N.Y.*, 360 U.S. 315 (1959).

MIRANDA WARNINGS

1. *Miranda v. Arizona*, 384 U.S. 436 (1966): For a confession to be admissible under the Fifth Amendment privilege against self-incrimination, a person in custody must, prior to interrogation, be informed in substance, that:
   - **a.** He has the right to remain silent;
   - **b.** Anything he says can and will be used against him in court;
   - **c.** He has the right to the presence of an attorney; and
   - **d.** If he cannot afford an attorney, one will be appointed for him if he so desires.
2. The above warning must be given:
   - **a.** When anyone is in custody by a government agent and accused of a crime; and
   - **b.** Prior to an interrogation by the police.

USE OF CONFESSION

Use of confession for impeachment: Statements obtained in violation of the *Miranda* warnings may be used to impeach the defendant's trial testimony but may not be used as evidence of guilt. Subsequent confessions are valid.

WAIVER

1. Waiver: Accused may waive the privilege against self-incrimination and/or right to counsel. Waiver must be:
   - **a.** Voluntary;
   - **b.** Knowing; and
   - **c.** Intelligent. *Moran v. Burbine*, 475 U.S. 412 (1986).
2. Waiver may occur only after the full *Miranda* warnings have been given.
3. Prosecution must prove the validity of a waiver by a preponderance of the evidence.
4. Waiver must be expressly stated or implied by the accused's words or conduct. Exceptions: *Oregon v. Elstad*, 470 U.S. 298 (1985).
   - **a.** Public safety: Need not be given in a situation where there is a threat to public safety.
   - **b.** Covert interrogation: Not required when the suspect is unaware that he is speaking with a law enforcement officer.
   - **c.** Booking questions: Need not be given prior to routine booking questions.

CONFESSIONS

1. Fourth Amendment: "Harmless error test"—voluntariness.
2. Fifth Amendment: Privilege against Compelled Self-Incrimination.
3. Sixth Amendment: Right to Counsel.

RIGHT TO SILENCE

Suspect may enforce this right in any manner and at any time prior to or during questioning by indicating that he wishes to remain silent. Interrogation must then cease. The invocation of this right after receiving Miranda warnings may not be used against the defendant at trial (e.g., prosecution cannot argue that defendant must be guilty because he remained silent during questioning). *Doyle v. Ohio*, 426 U.S. 610 (1976); but see *Fletcher v. Weir*, 455 U.S. 603 (1982).

RIGHT TO ASSISTANCE OF COUNSEL

1. If the accused indicates that he wishes to consult an attorney at any time prior to or during questioning, interrogation must cease.
2. Police may not reinstate communication unless the accused's counsel is present.
3. The cease-interrogation rule does not apply:
   - **a.** Unless the accused's request for an attorney is unambiguous; or
   - **b.** If the accused's request for counsel cannot be reasonably construed as an expression of a desire for assistance in dealing with the custodial interrogation.

GOVERNMENT AGENT

1. A waiver is not applicable in the case of secret interrogations, i.e., the use of an undercover agent to elicit incriminating information.
2. The government must demonstrate the intentional relinquishment or abandonment of a known right or privilege.
3. Once right to counsel attaches, if defendant requests assistance of counsel, deliberate elicitation must cease until the defendant talks with his lawyer or initiates communication.

DELIBERATE ELICITATION

"Deliberate elicitation" occurs when the police: *Massiah v. United States*, 377 U.S. 201 (1964).

1. Intentionally seek to obtain incriminating information from the accused either via formal interrogation or use of an undercover agent;
2. Intentionally create a situation likely to induce the accused to make incriminating statements; or
3. Knowingly exploit an opportunity to confront the accused without council present.

DOUBLE JEOPARDY

IN GENERAL

- Under the Fifth Amendment, a person may not be retried for the same criminal offense once jeopardy has attached.
- Jeopardy attaches in a jury trial at the empaneling and swearing in of the jury.
- In bench trials, jeopardy attaches when the first witness is sworn in.

Double Jeopardy continues on page 4

SEPARATE SOVEREIGNS

The constitutional prohibition against double jeopardy does not apply to trials by separate sovereigns. Thus, one may be tried for the same conduct by both state and federal government or even by two states. However, municipalities are not considered a separate sovereign for the purposes of double jeopardy analysis. *Heath v. Alabama*, 474 U.S. 82 (1985).

Example: A woman is falsely charged with the murder of her husband in the state of Washington. The woman is subsequently convicted of that charge by a vindictive jury. In time, however, she finds out that her husband is alive and well in Louisiana. Based on erroneous legal advice given by a disbarred fellow prisoner, the convicted murderer escapes to Louisiana and kills her husband. The woman is brought to trial in Louisiana. She raises the defense of double jeopardy. Her defense will fail because two sovereigns, in this case, Washington and Louisiana, may try and convict her of the same crime–murder of her husband.

REPROSECUTION

1. After mistrial: *United States v. Perez*, 22 U.S. 579 (1824); *United States v. Dinitz*, 424 U.S. 600 (1976).
   a. Definition: A mistrial is a judicial determination of a trial before a verdict is reached; it is granted on the motion of either party or on the court's own motion that a new trial be held.
   b. Mistrial over the defendant's objection bars prosecution unless there is a "manifest necessity."
   c. Verdict of conviction could be reached but would have to be reversed on appeal due to an obvious procedural error.
   d. Mistrial with defendant's consent: Defendant may not object to re-prosecution.
   e. Exception: the Double Jeopardy Clause bars re-prosecution after a mistrial is declared if the prosecutor or judge intended to provoke the mistrial motion.
2. After acquittal: *Ball v. United States*, 163 U.S. 662 (1896); *Green v. United States*, 355 U.S. 184 (1957).
   a. Definition: Verdict of not guilty by judge or jury or any ruling by a judge that represents a resolution in the defendant's favor of some or all of the factual elements charged.
   b. Rule: Defendant may not be re-prosecuted.
3. After dismissal: *United States v. Scott*, 437 U.S. 82 (1978).
   a. Definition: Judicial termination of a trial before a verdict is reached, but does not involve a resolution of any factual element of the offense charged.
   b. Rule: Re-prosecution after dismissal made on defendant's motion or without objection therefrom is not barred.
4. After conviction: *United States v. Tateo*, 377 U.S. 463 (1964).
   a. Rule: Re-prosecution of a defendant who successfully appeals his conviction on the basis of prejudicial error is not barred.
      i. Exception: Reversal of a conviction obtained on the sole ground that the evidence was insufficient to sustain the guilty verdict.
   b. Multiple punishment: The government is not barred from convicting and imposing punishment on a person in a single proceeding for violation of separate statutory provisions that constitute the same offense if the legislature so permits.
   c. Collateral estoppel: Prosecutor may not re-litigate an issue of ultimate fact in a second prosecution if it has once been determined by a valid and final judgment in the defendant's favor. Test is whether a rational jury could have based its verdict upon an issue other than that which the prosecutor seeks to foreclose from consideration.

ENTRAPMENT

IN GENERAL

1. Entrapment applies when a government agents acts improperly with respect to the defendant. It can be raised either as a defense at trial or as a pretrial motion thereby barring prosecution of the entrapped party. *United States v. Russell*, 411 U.S. 423 (1973).
2. Conduct may be so outrageous in some circumstances to constitute a violation of due process. Jurisdictions employ either a subjective or an objective test.
   a. Subjective test: entrapment is proved if a government agent implants in the mind of an innocent person the disposition to commit the offense and induces its commission so that the government may prosecute. *Sherman v. United States*, 356 U.S. 369 (1958).
   b. Objective test: Entrapment is proved if police conduct falls below commonly accepted standards for the proper use of government power.

TRIAL

RIGHT TO FAIR TRIAL

1. Right to trial by jury. *Duncan v. Louisiana*, 391 U.S. 145 (1968).
   a. Only for "serious" offenses, i.e., those with the possibility of imprisonment for more than 6 months.
   b. No jury trial required for civil contempt. Where no penalty is authorized, if the actual sentence is more than 6 months, the right to a jury trial arises.
   c. No constitutional right to 12 jurors, but there must be at least 6.
   d. No right that the jury verdict be unanimous if there are 12 jurors; for 6-person juries, decision must be unanimous.
   e. Right to have the jury selected from a cross-section of the community
      i. Defendant may contest the fact that a significant segment of the community has been omitted, even if he is not a member of such segment.
      ii. Applies only to venire: there is no right to proportional cross-section of community on the defendant's particular jury.
   f. Prosecution may not use peremptory challenges to exclude potential jurors solely because of race or gender. *Batson v. Kentucky*, 476 U.S. 79 (1986).

RIGHT TO CONFRONT WITNESS

1. Defendant has the right to confront witnesses in a criminal prosecution. This right is not absolute:
   a. Defendant may be removed if he is disruptive.
   b. Defendant is not deprived of his right if he voluntarily leaves the courtroom during the proceedings.
2. Confessions of co-defendants are inadmissible, unless:
   a. References to the defendant can be removed;
   b. The co-conspirator is a witness; or
   c. It is used in rebuttal of defendant's allegation that his own confession was the result of coercion.
3. Statements made at prior judicial proceedings may be admitted if:
   a. Witness is unavailable following a good-faith effort on the part of the prosecution; and
   b. Defendant had an opportunity to cross-examine.

RIGHT TO COUNSEL

1. Right to Appointed Counsel at Trial: "In all criminal prosecutions, the accused shall enjoy the right to…have the assistance of counsel for his defense."
   a. Indigents: Right to counsel does NOT apply in all criminal prosecutions.
   b. Felonies: Defendant has right to counsel in felony criminal trials; the accused is entitled to court-appointed attorney if he cannot afford one.
   c. Misdemeanors: An indigent is entitled to the assistance of counsel in any trial in which a sentence of imprisonment may be imposed.
2. Right of Self-Representation: Must be asserted in a timely fashion or it is LOST; Court may appoint "standby counsel" to take over during trial if necessary.
3. Right to Appointed Counsel on Appeal: The Sixth Amendment is limited to prosecutions. The defendant is entitled to the assistance of counsel under the Fourteenth Amendment Due Process and Equal Protection Clauses for a first appeal but not for subsequent appeals. *Douglas v. California*, 372 U.S. 353 (1963).
4. Right to Effective Representation of Counsel: The Sixth Amendment also requires that counsel provide effective representation of the client. *Strickland v. Washington*, 466 U.S. 668 (1984).
   a. Representation is ineffective if counsel's conduct "so undermines the proper functioning of the adversarial process that the trial cannot be relied on as having produced a just result."
   b. Test:
      i. Deficient representation: Defendant must identify acts or omissions depriving him of effective assistance, based on objective, prevailing norms.
      ii. Prejudice: Defendant must show a reasonable probability that but for such acts or omissions the result would have been different.

About Aspen Publishing

Aspen Publishing is a leading provider of educational content and digital learning solutions to law schools in the U.S. and around the world. Aspen provides best-in-class solutions for legal education through authoritative textbooks, written by renowned authors, and breakthrough products such as Connected eBooks, Connected Quizzing, and PracticePerfect.

The Aspen Casebook Series (famously known among law faculty and students as the "red and black" casebooks) encompasses hundreds of highly regarded textbooks in more than eighty disciplines, from large enrollment courses such as Torts and Contracts to emerging electives such as Sustainability and the Law of Policing. Study aids such as the *Examples & Explanations* and the *Emanuel Law Outlines* series, both highly popular collections, help law students master complex subject matter.

Major products, programs, and initiatives include:

- **Connected eBooks** are enhanced digital textbooks and study aids that come with a suite of online content and learning tools designed to maximize student success. Designed in collaboration with hundreds of faculty and students, the Connected eBook is a significant leap forward in the legal education learning tools available to students.

- **Connected Quizzing** is an easy-to-use formative assessment tool that tests law students' understanding and provides timely feedback to improve learning outcomes. Delivered through CasebookConnect.com, the learning platform already used by students to access their Aspen casebooks, Connected Quizzing is simple to implement and integrates seamlessly with law school course curricula.

- **PracticePerfect** is a visually engaging, interactive study aid to explain commonly encountered legal doctrines through easy-to-understand animated videos, illustrative examples, and numerous practice questions. Developed by a team of experts, PracticePerfect is the ideal study companion for today's law students.

- The **Aspen Learning Library** enables law schools to provide their students with access to the most popular study aids on the market across all of their courses. Available through an annual subscription, the online library consists of study aids in e-book, audio, and video formats with full text search, note-taking, and highlighting capabilities.

- Aspen's **Digital Bookshelf** is an institutional-level online education bookshelf, consolidating everything students and professors need to ensure success. This program ensures that every student has access to affordable course materials from day one.

- **Leading Edge** is a community centered on thinking differently about legal education and putting those thoughts into actionable strategies. At the core of the program is the Leading Edge Conference, an annual gathering of legal education thought leaders looking to pool ideas and identify promising directions of exploration.

Format for the Casenote® Legal Brief

Nature of Case: This section identifies the form of action (e.g., breach of contract, negligence, battery), the type of proceeding (e.g., demurrer, appeal from trial court's jury instructions) or the relief sought (e.g., damages, injunction, criminal sanctions).

Party ID: Quick identification of the relationship between the parties.

Fact Summary: This is included to refresh your memory and can be used as a quick reminder of the facts.

Rule of Law: Summarizes the general principle of law that the case illustrates. It may be used for instant recall of the court's holding and for classroom discussion or home review.

Facts: This section contains all relevant facts of the case, including the contentions of the parties and the lower court holdings. It is written in a logical order to give you a clear understanding of the case. The plaintiff and defendant are identified by their proper names throughout and are always labeled with a (P) or (D).

Issue: The issue is a concise question that brings out the essence of the opinion as it relates to the section of the casebook in which the case appears. Both substantive and procedural issues are included if relevant to the decision.

Palsgraf v. Long Island R.R. Co.

Injured bystander (P) v. Railroad company (D)

N.Y. Ct. App., 248 N.Y. 339, 162 N.E. 99 (1928).

NATURE OF CASE: Appeal from judgment affirming verdict for plaintiff seeking damages for personal injury.

FACT SUMMARY: Helen Palsgraf (P) was injured on R.R.'s (D) train platform when R.R.'s (D) guard helped a passenger aboard a moving train, causing his package to fall on the tracks. The package contained fireworks which exploded, creating a shock that tipped a scale onto Palsgraf (P).

RULE OF LAW
The risk reasonably to be perceived defines the duty to be obeyed.

FACTS: Helen Palsgraf (P) purchased a ticket to Rockaway Beach from R.R. (D) and was waiting on the train platform. As she waited, two men ran to catch a train that was pulling out from the platform. The first man jumped aboard, but the second man, who appeared as if he might fall, was helped aboard by the guard on the train who had kept the door open so they could jump aboard. A guard on the platform also helped by pushing him onto the train. The man was carrying a package wrapped in newspaper. In the process, the man dropped his package, which fell on the tracks. The package contained fireworks and exploded. The shock of the explosion was apparently of great enough strength to tip over some scales at the other end of the platform, which fell on Palsgraf (P) and injured her. A jury awarded her damages, and R.R. (D) appealed.

ISSUE: Does the risk reasonably to be perceived define the duty to be obeyed?

HOLDING AND DECISION: (Cardozo, C.J.) Yes. The risk reasonably to be perceived defines the duty to be obeyed. If there is no foreseeable hazard to the injured party as the result of a seemingly innocent act, the act does not become a tort because it happened to be a wrong as to another. If the wrong was not willful, the plaintiff must show that the act as to her had such great and apparent possibilities of danger as to entitle her to protection. Negligence in the abstract is not enough upon which to base liability. Negligence is a relative concept, evolving out of the common law doctrine of trespass on the case. To establish liability, the defendant must owe a legal duty of reasonable care to the injured party. A cause of action in tort will lie where harm, though unintended, could have been averted or avoided by observance of such a duty. The scope of the duty is limited by the range of danger that a reasonable person could foresee. In this case, there was nothing to suggest from the appearance of the parcel or otherwise that the parcel contained fireworks. The guard could not reasonably have had any warning of a threat to Palsgraf (P), and R.R. (D) therefore cannot be held liable. Judgment is reversed in favor of R.R. (D).

DISSENT: (Andrews, J.) The concept that there is no negligence unless R.R. (D) owes a legal duty to take care as to Palsgraf (P) herself is too narrow. Everyone owes to the world at large the duty of refraining from those acts that may unreasonably threaten the safety of others. If the guard's action was negligent as to those nearby, it was also negligent as to those outside what might be termed the "danger zone." For Palsgraf (P) to recover, R.R.'s (D) negligence must have been the proximate cause of her injury, a question of fact for the jury.

ANALYSIS

The majority defined the limit of the defendant's liability in terms of the danger that a reasonable person in defendant's situation would have perceived. The dissent argued that the limitation should not be placed on liability, but rather on damages. Judge Andrews suggested that only injuries that would not have happened but for R.R.'s (D) negligence should be compensable. Both the majority and dissent recognized the policy-driven need to limit liability for negligent acts, seeking, in the words of Judge Andrews, to define a framework "that will be practical and in keeping with the general understanding of mankind." The Restatement (Second) of Torts has accepted Judge Cardozo's view.

Quicknotes

FORESEEABILITY A reasonable expectation that change is the probable result of certain acts or omissions.

NEGLIGENCE Conduct falling below the standard of care that a reasonable person would demonstrate under similar conditions.

PROXIMATE CAUSE The natural sequence of events without which an injury would not have been sustained.

Concurrence/Dissent: All concurrences and dissents are briefed whenever they are included by the casebook author.

Analysis: This last paragraph gives you a broad understanding of where the case "fits in" with other cases in the section of the book and with the entire course. It is a hornbook-style discussion indicating whether the case is a majority or minority opinion and comparing the principal case with other cases in the casebook. It may also provide analysis from restatements, uniform codes, and law review articles.

Holding and Decision: This section offers a clear and in-depth discussion of the rule of the case and the court's rationale. It is written in easy-to-understand language and answers the issue presented by applying the law to the facts of the case. When relevant, it includes a thorough discussion of the exceptions to the case as listed by the court, any major cites to the other cases on point, and the names of the judges who wrote the decisions.

Quicknotes: Conveniently defines legal terms found in the case.

Note to Students

Aspen Publishing is proud to offer *Casenote® Legal Briefs*—continuing thirty years of publishing America's best-selling legal briefs.

Casenote® Legal Briefs are designed to help you save time when briefing assigned cases. Organized under convenient headings, they show you how to abstract the basic facts and holdings from the text of the actual opinions handed down by the courts. Used as part of a rigorous study regimen, they can help you spend more time analyzing and critiquing points of law than on copying bits and pieces of judicial opinions into your notebook or outline.

Casenote® Legal Briefs should never be used as a substitute for assigned casebook readings. They work best when read as a follow-up to reviewing the underlying opinions themselves. Students who try to avoid reading and digesting the judicial opinions in their casebooks or online sources will end up shortchanging themselves in the long run. The ability to absorb, critique, and restate the dynamic and complex elements of case law decisions is crucial to your success in law school and beyond. It cannot be developed vicariously.

In addition to *Casenote® Legal Briefs*, Aspen Publishing offers the following study aids:

- *Casenote® Legal Briefs*
- *Emanuel® Law Outlines*
- Emanuel® *Law in a Flash Flash Cards*
- Emanuel® *CrunchTime® Series*

Each of these series is designed to provide you with easy-to-understand explanations of complex points of law. Each volume offers guidance on the principles of legal analysis and, consulted regularly, will hone your ability to spot relevant issues. We have titles that will help you prepare for class, prepare for your exams, and enhance your general comprehension of the law along the way.

To find out more about our law school tools for success, visit us at *www.AspenPublishing.com* or e-mail us at *customer.service@aspenpublishing.com*. We'll be happy to assist you.

How to Brief a Case

A. Decide on a Format and Stick to It

Structure is essential to a good brief. It enables you to arrange systematically the related parts that are scattered throughout most cases, thus making manageable and understandable what might otherwise seem to be an endless and unfathomable sea of information. There are, of course, an unlimited number of formats that can be utilized. However, it is best to find one that suits your needs and stick to it. Consistency breeds both efficiency and the security that when called upon you will know where to look in your brief for the information you are asked to give.

Any format, as long as it presents the essential elements of a case in an organized fashion, can be used. Experience, however, has led *Casenote® Legal Briefs* to develop and utilize the following format because of its logical flow and universal applicability.

NATURE OF CASE: This is a brief statement of the legal character and procedural status of the case (e.g., "Appeal of a burglary conviction").

There are many different alternatives open to a litigant dissatisfied with a court ruling. The key to determining which one has been used is to discover *who is asking this court for what.*

This first entry in the brief should be kept as *short as possible.* Use the court's terminology if you understand it. But since jurisdictions vary as to the titles of pleadings, the best entry is the one that addresses who wants what in this proceeding, not the one that sounds most like the court's language.

RULE OF LAW: A statement of the general principle of law that the case illustrates (e.g., "An acceptance that varies any term of the offer is considered a rejection and counteroffer").

Determining the rule of law of a case is a procedure similar to determining the issue of the case. Avoid being fooled by red herrings; there may be a few rules of law mentioned in the case excerpt, but usually only one is *the* rule with which the casebook editor is concerned. The techniques used to locate the issue, described below, may also be utilized to find the rule of law. Generally, your best guide is simply the chapter heading. It is a clue to the point the casebook editor seeks to make and should be kept in mind when reading every case in the respective section.

FACTS: A synopsis of only the essential facts of the case, i.e., those bearing upon or leading up to the issue.

The facts entry should be a short statement of the events and transactions that led one party to initiate legal proceedings against another in the first place. While some cases conveniently state the salient facts at the beginning of the decision, in other instances they will have to be culled from hiding places throughout the text, even from concurring and dissenting opinions. Some of the "facts" will often be in dispute and should be so noted. Conflicting evidence may be briefly pointed up. "Hard" facts must be included. Both must be *relevant* in order to be listed in the facts entry. It is impossible to tell what is relevant until the entire case is read, as the ultimate determination of the rights and liabilities of the parties may turn on something buried deep in the opinion.

Generally, the facts entry should not be longer than three to five *short* sentences.

It is often helpful to identify the role played by a party in a given context. For example, in a construction contract case the identification of a party as the "contractor" or "builder" alleviates the need to tell that that party was the one who was supposed to have built the house.

It is always helpful, and a good general practice, to identify the "plaintiff" and the "defendant." This may seem elementary and uncomplicated, but, especially in view of the creative editing practiced by some casebook editors, it is sometimes a difficult or even impossible task. Bear in mind that the *party presently* seeking something from this court may not be the plaintiff, and that sometimes only the cross-claim of a defendant is treated in the excerpt. Confusing or misaligning the parties can ruin your analysis and understanding of the case.

ISSUE: A statement of the general legal question answered by or illustrated in the case. For clarity, the issue is best put in the form of a question capable of a "yes" or "no" answer. In reality, the issue is simply the Rule of Law put in the form of a question (e.g., "May an offer be accepted by performance?").

The major problem presented in discerning what is *the* issue in the case is that an opinion usually purports to raise and answer several questions. However, except for rare cases, only one such question is really the issue in the case. Collateral issues not necessary to the resolution of the matter in controversy are handled by the court by language known as *"obiter dictum"* or merely *"dictum."* While dicta may be included later in the brief, they have no place under the issue heading.

To find the issue, ask *who wants what* and then go on to ask *why did that party succeed or fail in getting it.* Once this is determined, the "why" should be turned into a question.

The complexity of the issues in the cases will vary, but in all cases a single-sentence question should sum up the issue. *In a few cases,* there will be two, or even more rarely, three issues of equal importance to the resolution of the case. Each should be expressed in a single-sentence question.

Since many issues are resolved by a court in coming to a final disposition of a case, the casebook editor will reproduce the portion of the opinion containing the issue or issues most relevant to the area of law under scrutiny. A noted law professor gave this advice: "Close the book; look at the title on the cover." Chances are, if it is Property, you need not concern yourself with whether, for example, the federal government's treatment of the plaintiff's land really raises a federal question sufficient to support jurisdiction on this ground in federal court.

The same rule applies to chapter headings designating sub-areas within the subjects. They tip you off as to what the text is designed to teach. The cases are arranged in a casebook to show a progression or development of the law, so that the preceding cases may also help.

It is also most important to remember to *read the notes and questions* at the end of a case to determine what the editors wanted you to have gleaned from it.

HOLDING AND DECISION: This section should succinctly explain the rationale of the court in arriving at its decision. In capsulizing the "reasoning" of the court, it should always include an application of the general rule or rules of law to the specific facts of the case. Hidden justifications come to light in this entry: the reasons for the state of the law, the public policies, the biases and prejudices, those considerations that influence the justices' thinking and, ultimately, the outcome of the case. At the end, there should be a short indication of thedisposition or procedural resolution of the case (e.g., "Decision of the trial court for Mr. Smith (P) reversed").

The foregoing format is designed to help you "digest" the reams of case material with which you will be faced in your law school career. Once mastered by practice, it will place at your fingertips the information the authors of your casebooks have sought to impart to you in case-by-case illustration and analysis.

B. Be as Economical as Possible in Briefing Cases

Once armed with a format that encourages succinctness, it is as important to be economical with regard to the time spent on the actual reading of the case as it is to be economical in the writing of the brief itself. This does not mean "skimming" a case. Rather, it means reading the case with an "eye" trained to recognize into which "section" of your brief a particular passage or line fits and having a system for quickly and precisely marking the case so that the passages fitting any one particular part of the brief can be easily identified and brought together in a concise and accurate manner when the brief is actually written.

It is of no use to simply repeat everything in the opinion of the court; record only enough information to trigger your recollection of what the court said. Nevertheless, an accurate statement of the "law of the case," i.e., the legal principle applied to the facts, is absolutely essential to class preparation and to learning the law under the case method.

To that end, it is important to develop a "shorthand" that you can use to make marginal notations. These notations will tell you at a glance in which section of the brief you will be placing that particular passage or portion of the opinion.

Some students prefer to underline all the salient portions of the opinion (with a pencil or colored underliner marker), making marginal notations as they go along. Others prefer the color-coded method of underlining, utilizing different colors of markers to underline the salient portions of the case, each separate color being used to represent a different section of the brief. For example, blue underlining could be used for passages relating to the rule of law, yellow for those relating to the issue, and green for those relating to the holding and decision, etc. While it has its advocates, thecolor-coded method can be confusing and time-consuming (all that time spent on changing colored markers). Furthermore, it can interfere with the continuity and concentration many students deem essential to the reading of a case for maximum comprehension. In the end, however, it is a matter of personal preference and style. Just remember, whatever method you use, underlining must be used sparingly or its value is lost.

If you take the marginal notation route, an efficient and easy method is to go along underlining the key portions of the case and placing in the margin alongside them the following "markers" to indicate where a particular passage or line "belongs" in the brief you will write:

N	(NATURE OF CASE)
RL	(RULE OF LAW)
I	(ISSUE)
HL	(HOLDING AND DECISION, relates to the RULE OF LAW behind the decision)
HR	(HOLDING AND DECISION, gives the RATIONALE or reasoning behind the decision)
HA	(HOLDING AND DECISION, applies the general principle(s) of law to the facts of the case to arrive at the decision)

Remember that a particular passage may well contain information necessary to more than one part of your brief, in which case you simply note that in the margin. If you are using the color-coded underlining method instead of marginal notation, simply make asterisks or checks in the margin next to the passage in question in the colors that indicate the additional sections of the brief where it might be utilized.

The economy of utilizing "shorthand" in marking cases for briefing can be maintained in the actual brief writing process itself by utilizing "law student shorthand" within the brief. There are many commonly used words and phrases for which abbreviations can be substituted in your briefs (and in your class notes also). You can develop abbreviations that are personal to you and which will save you a lot of time. A reference list of briefing abbreviations can be found on page x of this book.

C. Use Both the Briefing Process and the Brief as a Learning Tool

Now that you have a format and the tools for briefing cases efficiently, the most important thing is to make the time spent in briefing profitable to you and to make the most advantageous use of the briefs you create. Of course, the briefs are invaluable for classroom reference when you are called upon to explain or analyze a particular case. However, they are also useful in reviewing for exams. A quick glance at the fact summary should bring the case to mind, and a rereading of the rule of law should enable you to go over the underlying legal concept in your mind, how it was applied in that particular case, and how it might apply in other factual settings.

As to the value to be derived from engaging in the briefing process itself, there is an immediate benefit that arises from being forced to sift through the essential facts and reasoning from the court's opinion and to succinctly express them in your own words in your brief. The process ensures that you understand the case and the point that it illustrates, and that means you will be ready to absorb further analysis and information brought forth in class. It also ensures you will have something to say when called upon in class. The briefing process helps develop a mental agility for getting to the *gist* of a case and for identifying, expounding on, and applying the legal concepts and issues found there. The briefing process is the mental process on which you must rely in taking law school examinations; it is also the mental process upon which lawyers rely in serving their clients and in making a living.

Abbreviations for Briefs

acceptance	acp
affirmed	aff
answer	ans
assumption of risk	a/r
attorney	atty
beyond a reasonable doubt	b/r/d
bona fide purchaser	BFP
breach of contract	br/k
cause of action	c/a
common law	c/l
Constitution	Con
constitutional	con
contract	K
contributory negligence	c/n
cross	x
cross-complaint	x/c
cross-examination	x/ex
cruel and unusual punishment	c/u/p
defendant	D
dismissed	dis
double jeopardy	d/j
due process	d/p
equal protection	e/p
equity	eq
evidence	ev
exclude	exc
exclusionary rule	exc/r
felony	f/n
freedom of speech	f/s
good faith	g/f
habeas corpus	h/c
hearsay	hr
husband	H
injunction	inj
in loco parentis	ILP
inter vivos	I/v
joint tenancy	j/t
judgment	judgt
jurisdiction	jur
last clear chance	LCC
long-arm statute	LAS
majority view	maj
meeting of minds	MOM
minority view	min
Miranda rule	Mir/r
Miranda warnings	Mir/w
negligence	neg
notice	ntc
nuisance	nus
obligation	ob
obscene	obs
offer	O
offeree	OE
offeror	OR
ordinance	ord
pain and suffering	p/s
parol evidence	p/e
plaintiff	P
prima facie	p/f
probable cause	p/c
proximate cause	px/c
real property	r/p
reasonable doubt	r/d
reasonable man	r/m
rebuttable presumption	rb/p
remanded	rem
res ipsa loquitur	RIL
respondeat superior	r/s
Restatement	RS
reversed	rev
Rule Against Perpetuities	RAP
search and seizure	s/s
search warrant	s/w
self-defense	s/d
specific performance	s/p
statute	S
statute of frauds	S/F
statute of limitations	S/L
summary judgment	s/j
tenancy at will	t/w
tenancy in common	t/c
tenant	t
third party	TP
third party beneficiary	TPB
transferred intent	TI
unconscionable	uncon
unconstitutional	unconst
undue influence	u/e
Uniform Commercial Code	UCC
unilateral	uni
vendee	VE
vendor	VR
versus	v
void for vagueness	VFV
weight of authority	w/a
weight of the evidence	w/e
wife	W
with	w/
within	w/i
without	w/o
without prejudice	w/o/p
wrongful death	wr/d

Table of Cases

CHAPTER 1

The Criminal Process: Failures, Choices, and Legitimacy

Quick Reference Rules of Law

Brown v. Mississippi

Convicted murderer (D) v. State (P)

297 U.S. 278 (1936)

NATURE OF CASE: Appeal from murder conviction.

FACT SUMMARY: Brown (D) and others were convicted of murder after they were beaten into confessing to the crime, over their objection that the confessions were coerced.

RULE OF LAW

A confession obtained by inflicting physical pain during interrogation is not admissible against the accused.

FACTS: To elicit murder confessions, the Mississippi police tortured Brown (D) and other African-American men. One defendant was "hanged by a rope to the limb of a tree" three times by a sheriff and subsequently "tied to a tree and whipped," suffering intense pain and agony; later, the same defendant was severely whipped and told the whipping would continue "until he confessed." He confessed. Two other defendants were taken to jail, they were made to strip by the sheriff, and then "they were laid over chairs and their backs were cut to pieces with a leather strap with buckles on it." They too were told the whipping would continue until they confessed; they confessed. At trial, the sheriff admitted the whippings, as did other witnesses. Brown (D) and the other defendants were convicted. They appealed, challenging their conviction on due process grounds in a case of first impression.

ISSUE: Is a confession obtained by inflicting physical pain during the interrogation admissible against the accused?

HOLDING AND DECISION: (Hughes, C.J.) No. A confession obtained by inflicting physical pain during interrogation is not admissible against the accused. The method employed by the interrogating officers to obtain the confessions was a denial of due process. The rack and torture chamber may not be substituted for the witness stand. While states are free to regulate the procedure of their courts in accordance with their own conceptions of policy, such freedom is limited by the requirement of due process of law. In addition, the State's (P) argument that the accused's counsel failed to move for the exclusion of the coerced statements after their introduction has no merit. The duty of the trial court rises above simple procedural rules, particularly when a man is on trial for his life. The trial court was fully aware that there was no additional evidence upon which a conviction could stand. Reversed.

ANALYSIS

Brown v. Mississippi was the first of a long line of confession cases. In the following 20 years, the determining factors for "involuntariness" evolved from "special circumstances" involving physical brutality, upon which the defendant had the burden of proof, to "some" coercive force regardless of the methodology, and finally to a shifting of the burden to the prosecutor, who must show, by a preponderance of the evidence, that no coercion occurred.

Quicknotes

COERCED CONFESSION A statement by a person charged with the commission of a criminal offense acknowledging his or her guilt in respect to the charged offense made when the confessor's free will was overcome as a result of threats, promises, or undue influence, and that is inadmissible at trial.

DUE PROCESS The constitutional mandate requiring the courts to protect and enforce individuals' rights and liberties consistent with prevailing principles of fairness and justice and prohibiting the federal and state governments from such activities that deprive its citizens of life, liberty, or property interest.

Powell v. Alabama

Capital crime defendant (D) v. State (P)

287 U.S. 45 (1932)

NATURE OF CASE: Appeal from convictions for rape.

FACT SUMMARY: Several young black men were convicted of raping two white girls.

RULE OF LAW

In a capital case in which the defendant is unable to employ counsel and is incapable of adequately defending himself, the Due Process Clause requires that effective counsel be appointed for him.

FACTS: Several black men (D) were charged with the rape of two white girls. The defendants were all young, "ignorant and illiterate." They came from other states and had no family or friends in the immediate area. Six days after an indictment and arraignment at which they were not represented by counsel, the youths (D) were tried. Until the morning of the trial, no lawyer had been named to represent them. They were convicted, and the judgment was affirmed by the state supreme court.

ISSUE: In a capital case in which the defendant is unable to employ counsel and is incapable of adequately defending himself, does the Due Process Clause require that effective counsel be appointed for him?

HOLDING AND DECISION: (Sutherland, J.) Yes. In a capital case in which defendant is unable to employ counsel and is incapable of adequately defending himself, the Due Process Clause requires that effective counsel be appointed for him. The record of this case clearly illustrates that from the time of their arraignment until the trial, the defendants did not have the aid of counsel in any real sense. This is often the most critical stage of a criminal trial, during which consultation and investigation must be carried out. The right to a hearing is among the "immutable principles of justice that inhere in the very idea of free government." The right to a hearing has always included the right to counsel, for the right to be heard is often useless unless it includes the right to be heard by counsel; even the intelligent layman is often unable to adequately defend himself. Thus, the failure of the trial court to give the defendants (D) reasonable time and opportunity to employ counsel was a denial of due process. Assuming their inability to secure counsel even if they had been given the opportunity, the failure of the trial court to make an effective appointment of counsel was also a denial of due process. Reversed.

DISSENT: (Butler, J.) If there had been any lack of opportunity for preparation, trial counsel would have applied to the court for a postponement; however, here no such application was made. There was no suggestion at the trial or in the new trial motion that the defendants were denied such an opportunity or were not, in fact, fully prepared. The amended new trial motion contains the first suggestion that the defendants were denied counsel or opportunity to prepare for trial. Such silence requires a finding that the claim is groundless, since if it had any merit there would have been support for it.

ANALYSIS

Powell v. Alabama is the first case to recognize the constitutional right of an indigent defendant to the assistance of court-appointed counsel. Although the *Powell* decision was limited to capital cases, its underlying due process rationale suggested the need for the appointment of counsel generally.

Quicknotes

ARRAIGNMENT The formal charging of an individual with a criminal offense.

CAPITAL CASE An action involving an offense that is punishable by death.

DUE PROCESS CLAUSE Language, found in the Fifth and Fourteenth Amendments to the U.S. Constitution providing that no person shall be deprived of "life, liberty, or property, without due process of law."

INDICTMENT A formal written accusation made by the prosecution to the grand jury under oath, charging an individual with a criminal offense.

Duncan v. Louisiana

Individual convicted of criminal battery (D) v. State (P)

391 U.S. 145 (1968)

NATURE OF CASE: Appeal from criminal conviction in state court for simple battery.

FACT SUMMARY: Duncan (D), who was convicted without the right to a jury trial of simple battery, a crime punishable by a two-year imprisonment and a $300 fine, contended that the denial of a jury trial violated the Sixth Amendment as applied to the states by the Fourteenth Amendment.

RULE OF LAW

The Fourteenth Amendment's Due Process Clause guarantees a right of jury trial in all state criminal cases that, were they to be tried in federal court, would come within the Sixth Amendment's guarantee of a jury trial.

FACTS: Duncan (D), a Black youth, was convicted in Louisiana of simple battery and sentenced to 60 days imprisonment and to pay a fine of $150. Before his trial, Duncan (D) requested a jury trial but his request was denied. Under Louisiana law, a jury trial was guaranteed only in cases where capital punishment or imprisonment at hard labor could be imposed. Simple battery, however, was a misdemeanor punishable with up to two years imprisonment and a $300 fine. After his conviction, Duncan (D) appealed on the basis that denial of a jury trial violated his Sixth and Fourteenth Amendment rights. The United States Supreme Court granted certiorari.

ISSUE: Does the Fourteenth Amendment's Due Process Clause guarantee a right of jury trial in all state criminal cases that, were they to be tried in federal court, would come within the Sixth Amendment's guarantee of a jury trial?

HOLDING AND DECISION: (White, J.) Yes. The Fourteenth Amendment's Due Process Clause guarantees a right of jury trial in all state criminal cases that, were they to be tried in federal court, would come within the Sixth Amendment's guarantee of a jury trial. To determine whether a right extended by the Fifth and Sixth Amendments with respect to federal criminal proceedings is also protected against state action by the Fourteenth Amendment depends on whether the right is part of the fundamental principles of liberty and justice that are at the core of the nation's civil and political institutions, and whether it is a fundamental right that is essential to a fair trial. The right to a jury trial is such a fundamental right that is deeply enshrined in American jurisprudence, as well as the common law, both as a matter of history and current practice. The guarantees of the jury trial in the federal and state constitutions reflect a profound judgment about the way in which law should be enforced and justice administered. A right to jury trial is granted to criminal defendants to prevent oppression by the government, as well as to protect against unfounded criminal charges brought to eliminate enemies and against judges too responsive to the voice of higher authority. Providing an accused with the right to be tried by a jury of peers provides such safeguard against arbitrary law enforcement. Because the nation's commitment to the right of jury trial in serious criminal cases is deep, such right qualifies for protection under the Fourteenth Amendment's Due Process Clause and must be respected by the states. [Reversed.]

CONCURRENCE: (Black, J.) Although the selective incorporation process was here properly applied, the Fourteenth Amendment is intended to make the entire Bill of Rights applicable to the states. The words "No state shall make or enforce any law which shall abridge the privileges or immunities of citizens of the United States" clearly express this intention. There is no more precious "privilege" than to claim the protections of the Bill of Rights. Any reading of "privileges or immunities of citizens of the United States" that excludes the Bill of Rights' safeguards renders the words of this section of the Fourteenth Amendment meaningless. According to Justice Harlan's dissent, the Due Process Clause does not contain a specific and clearly ascertainable constitutional command that judges must obey in interpreting the Constitution. Thus, according to this interpretation, due process does not have a permanent and fixed meaning but may shift in accordance with judges' predilections and understandings of what is best for the country. However, the Constitution, which was intended to limit governmental power, cannot be viewed as endowing judges with such limitless power.

CONCURRENCE: (Fortas, J.) Although the Due Process Clause requires the states to accord the right to jury trial in prosecutions for offenses that are not petty, the practices of the forum states are also relevant. The Supreme Court must not automatically impose on the states all of the ancillary rules that have been, or may hereafter be, developed incidental to the right to jury trial in the federal courts. For example, there is no reason to impose federal requirements regarding jury unanimity on the states. The Supreme Court may well conclude that various features of federal jury practice are not

Continued on next page.

fundamental, so they are not essential to due process of law and, consequently, should not be obligatory on the states. The Due Process Clause requires that state court proceedings assure basic fairness, not that they rigidly and arbitrarily follow the exact pattern of federal proceedings. To find otherwise would transgress fundamental principles of federalism, which requires maximum opportunity for diversity and minimal imposition of uniformity of method and detail upon the states; the Constitution sets up a federal union, not a monolith.

DISSENT: (Harlan, J.) The question presented is whether a state may try non-felony criminal cases before a judge, rather than being required to try such cases before a jury. The answer, based on constitutional history and the history of trial by jury, is that the states have leeway to decide for themselves how such cases should be tried, as long as the procedures used are fundamentally fair. That is all that due process of law requires. Here, notwithstanding that the majority finds nothing unfair about the procedure by which Duncan (D) was tried, nevertheless reverses his conviction by holding that the Fourteenth Amendment applies the Sixth Amendment right of jury trial to the states. The majority's approach, and its reading of history, is "altogether topsy-turvy." First, the Court has never adopted a total incorporation view of the Fourteenth Amendment, and the majority here does not purport to adopt such an absolutist incorporation approach, and second, a selective incorporation approach lacks internal consistency and is flawed because it does not require the Court to determine whether the trial at issue was fundamentally unfair. Instead, the majority merely determines, as a matter of judicial fiat, whether the Sixth Amendment's Jury Trial Clause should be incorporated into the Fourteenth Amendment. However, there is no historical or practical support for using the Fourteenth Amendment to put the states in a constitutional straitjacket with respect to their own development in the administration of criminal or civil law. Likewise, there is no reason to require that the states abide by every federal procedure related to trial by jury. For example, at the federal level, a jury means a jury of 12 individuals. That number, however, is not fundamental to anything: there is no significance except to mystics in the number 12. The same is true of the requirement that there be unanimity—the requirement of which has been abandoned in Britain. Further, the majority's use of the term "fundamental" to describe the right of jury trial is tautological: in the majority's hands, the word does not mean "analytically critical to procedural fairness," but instead it turns out to mean "old," "much praised," and "found in the Bill of Rights." Thus, the majority's definition of "fundamental" turns out to be circular. Moreover, in determining whether there was a denial of fundamental fairness in the case at bar, it must be noted that trial by jury is not the only fair means of resolving issues of fact. Instead, there is a wide range of views on the desirability of trial by jury and on the ways to make it most effective when it is used; there is also considerable variation from state to state in local conditions such as the size of the criminal caseload, the ease or difficulty of summoning jurors, and other trial conditions bearing on fairness. Here, for no good reason, the majority has chosen to impose upon all the states one means of trying criminal cases: it is a good means, but it is not the only fair means, and it is not demonstrably better than the alternatives the states might devise.

ANALYSIS

This case illustrates the doctrine of "selective incorporation" of the Bill of Rights into the Fourteenth Amendment Due Process Clause. Under this doctrine, the Bill of Rights is incorporated by the Due Process Clause only to the extent that the Court decides that the protections and rights therein are so critical to the fundamental principles of due process that they must be upheld against federal and state action. A minority of United States Supreme Court justices (particularly Justices Black and Douglas), however, have argued for total incorporation. Note that the Court has specifically found only two of the guarantees of the Bill of Rights to be nonfundamental. The first is the Fifth Amendment right to indictment by grand jury (some states permit criminal prosecutions to proceed upon the filing of information only). The second is the Eighth Amendment's guarantees regarding bail and fines.

Quicknotes

BILL OF RIGHTS The first ten Amendments to the U.S. Constitution, setting forth individual rights and liberties.

FOURTEENTH AMENDMENT DUE PROCESS CLAUSE Provides that protections mandated by the U.S. Constitution and observed by the federal government are equally applicable, and therefore must be observed by the states.

MISDEMEANOR A crime that does not constitute a felony; generally less severe than a felony and results in lesser punishment.

RIGHT TO JURY TRIAL The right guaranteed by the Sixth Amendment to the U.S. Constitution that in all criminal prosecutions the accused has a right to a trial by an impartial jury of the state and district in which the crime was allegedly committed.

SIXTH AMENDMENT Provides the right to a speedy and public trial by impartial jury, the right to be informed of the accusation, the right to confront witnesses, and the right to have the assistance of counsel in all criminal prosecutions.

CHAPTER 2

Fourth Amendment: An Overview

Quick Reference Rules of Law

Weeks v. United States

Defendant charged with unlawful use of mails (D) v. Federal government (P)

232 U.S. 383 (1914)

NATURE OF CASE: Appeal from conviction for unlawfully using the mails to transport lottery tickets.

FACT SUMMARY: Police officers and a federal marshal (P) seized lottery tickets and other incriminating evidence in a warrantless search of Weeks's (D) house.

RULE OF LAW

Evidence obtained in an unlawful search and seizure by agents of the federal government may not be used against the defendant in a federal prosecution.

FACTS: Police arrested Weeks (D) at work without a warrant; other officers, also without a warrant, went to Weeks's (D) house. A neighbor told them where the key was kept, and they searched Weeks's (D) room and took possession of lottery tickets and various papers, which they turned over to the U.S. Marshal (P). The Marshal (P), also without a warrant, then went to defendant's house and obtained additional evidence.

ISSUE: May evidence obtained in an unlawful search and seizure by agents of the federal government be used against the defendant in a federal prosecution?

HOLDING AND DECISION: (Day, J.) No. Evidence obtained during an unlawful search and seizure by agents of the federal government may not be used against a defendant in a federal prosecution. The Fourth Amendment protects all citizens from unreasonable searches and seizures by federal officials. If evidence seized in violation of the Fourth Amendment may be used against a citizen accused of an offense, its protections are of no value. Reversed.

ANALYSIS

The decision in *Weeks* applies only to the conduct of federal officials; it did not reach the conduct of the state police officers who unlawfully searched Weeks's (D) house. The holding also did not bar state officials from giving illegally seized evidence to federal prosecutors, referred to as the "silver platter" doctrine.

Quicknotes

WRITS OF ASSISTANCE An equitable remedy imposed in order to enforce a previous court judgment ordering the transfer of title to real property.

Wolf v. Colorado

Owner of illegally seized evidence (D) v. State (P)

338 U.S. 25 (1949)

NATURE OF CASE: Appeal from conviction of conspiracy to commit abortion.

FACT SUMMARY: Dr. Wolf (D) was convicted of conspiracy to commit abortion. The conviction rested in part upon evidence seized from his office.

RULE OF LAW

In a prosecution in a state court for a state crime, the Fourteenth Amendment does not forbid the admission of evidence obtained by an unreasonable search and seizure.

FACTS: Appointment books were seized from Dr. Wolf's (D) office. Partly on the basis of this evidence, Dr. Wolf (D) was convicted in a state court of conspiracy to commit abortion. Under Colorado law, evidence seized in an unreasonable search and seizure is admissible against the accused. Had the case been brought in federal court, the evidence would have been inadmissible under the exclusionary rule as being in violation of Dr. Wolf's (D) Fourth Amendment rights.

ISSUE: In a prosecution in a state court for a state crime, does the Fourteenth Amendment forbid the admission of evidence obtained by an unreasonable search and seizure?

HOLDING AND DECISION: (Frankfurter, J.) No. In a prosecution in a state court for a state crime, the Fourteenth Amendment does not forbid the admission of evidence obtained by an unreasonable search and seizure. While the Fourth Amendment's prohibition against unreasonable searches and seizures is incorporated under the due process clause of the Fourteenth Amendment and thus is binding upon the states, the federal exclusionary rule is not binding on the states. The exclusion of illegally obtained evidence is not fundamental to the concept of ordered liberty. It is merely one means of securing compliance with the Fourth Amendment and thus deterring unreasonable searches and seizures. The states are free to fashion other remedies to deter violations of defendants' due process rights, as long as they do indeed provide some means of redress. It is not a departure from the basic standards of individual rights to remand such individuals to the remedies of private action and to such protection as the internal discipline of the police. While it is true that exclusion of such evidence is an effective means of deterring unreasonable searches, the Supreme Court will not condemn a state's reliance upon methods that, if consistently enforced, would be equally effective. Public opinion within the state can be more effectively exerted against the local police than can local opinion be exerted against federal officers. Affirmed.

ANALYSIS

In *Weeks v. U.S.*, 232 U.S. 383 (1914), the United States Supreme Court first held that under the Fourth Amendment, evidence obtained by federal officials by means of an unreasonable search and seizure is inadmissible as evidence in a federal court. Evidence procured by state officials in violation of the Fourth Amendment is also inadmissible in federal court (*Elkins v. U.S.*, 364 U.S. 206 (1960)). In *Wolf*, the Court established two basic propositions: first, the Fourth Amendment's prohibition against unreasonable search and seizure is binding on the states through the Due Process Clause of the Fourteenth Amendment; and second, the rule of *Weeks*, excluding all evidence seized in an unreasonable search, is not commanded by the Fourth Amendment but is a judicially created rule of evidence for federal courts and is, therefore, not binding on the states. Under *Wolf*, then, although unreasonable search and seizure by state officials is unconstitutional, it is permissible for the state courts to use such illegally obtained evidence in state trials if the state has some procedure other than the exclusionary rule to discourage unreasonable searches. Although this case held that the exclusionary rule is not implicit in the Fourteenth Amendment's concept of ordered liberty and fundamental justice, *Mapp v. Ohio*, 367 U.S. 643 (1961), using the same standard, overturned *Wolf* and found that the exclusionary rule was a part of the Fourteenth Amendment and was binding on the states.

Quicknotes

EXCLUSIONARY RULE A rule precluding the introduction at trial of evidence unlawfully obtained in violation of the federal constitutional safeguards against unreasonable searches and seizures.

FOURTEENTH AMENDMENT Declares that no state shall make or enforce any law that shall abridge the privileges and immunities of citizens of the United States. no state shall deny to any person within its jurisdiction the equal protection of the laws.

FOURTH AMENDMENT Provides that persons be secure as to their person and private belongings against unreasonable searches and seizures.

MOTION TO SUPPRESS Motion in a criminal trial to exclude the introduction of evidence i that was unlawfully obtained.

Mapp v. Ohio

Holder of obscene material (D) v. State (P)

367 U.S. 643 (1961)

NATURE OF CASE: Appeal from conviction for possession of obscene material.

FACT SUMMARY: Mapp (D) was arrested and later convicted of possession of obscene material when police without a search warrant forcibly entered her home pursuant to information that a bombing suspect was hiding in the dwelling.

RULE OF LAW

In a prosecution in a federal or state court, the Fourth Amendment (by application of the Fourteenth Amendment) forbids the admission of evidence obtained by an unreasonable search and seizure.

FACTS: When three Cleveland police officers knocked on the door of her house, Mapp (D), upon the telephoned advice of her attorney, refused to admit them without a search warrant. The police had information that a person wanted for questioning regarding a bombing was hiding in the Mapp (D) home. Being refused admission, the policemen forcibly entered, waving a piece of paper they claimed was a warrant, and proceeded to search extensively the second floor and the basement. During the search, certain books, pictures, and photographs deemed to be obscene and unlawful in Ohio (P) were found. Mapp (D) was convicted of their possession, and he appealed, arguing that the search was unlawful because no search warrant had been issued and, thus, the seized material should not have been admitted at trial. The Ohio Supreme Court agreed that the search was unlawful but upheld the conviction on the basis that the materials had not been taken from Mapp's (D) "person by the use of brutal or offensive physical force against" her. The United States Supreme Court granted certiorari.

ISSUE: In a prosecution in a state or federal court, does the Fourth Amendment (by application of the Fourteenth Amendment) forbid the admission of evidence obtained by an unreasonable search and seizure?

HOLDING AND DECISION: (Clark, J.) Yes. In a prosecution in federal or state court, the Fourth Amendment (by application of the Fourteenth Amendment) forbids the admission of evidence obtained by an unlawful search and seizure. For more than 50 years prior to this case, the exclusionary rule has been applied in federal courts. Any forcible and compulsory extortion of one's own testimony or private papers to convict one or to forfeit goods violates the Fourth and Fifth Amendments. If unlawfully seized material could be admitted as evidence, the Fourth Amendment right to be secure against unlawful searches and seizures would be of no value. *Weeks v. United States*, 232 U.S. 383 (1914). Although this Court failed to require application of the exclusionary rule in state courts in *Wolf v. Colorado*, 338 U.S. 25 (1949), the failure to do so there was based on factual considerations not relevant to the constitutional consideration and could not be controlling here. To allow *Wolf* to continue in force would be to grant the right but in reality to withhold its privilege and enjoyment. The purpose of the rule is to deter violation of the right by the only effective way—by removing the incentive to disregard it. If a criminal must go free, it is the law that sets the criminal free. "If the government becomes a lawbreaker, it breeds contempt for law." *Olmstead v. United States*, 277 U.S. 438, 485 (1928). Reversed and remanded.

CONCURRENCE: (Black, J.) Although the Fourth Amendment itself does not expressly require the exclusionary rule, it, together with the Fifth Amendment's ban against self-incrimination, not only justifies the rule, it requires it.

DISSENT: (Harlan, J.) The real issue of this case is whether the Ohio law banning mere possession of obscene material is consistent with the rights of free thought and expression assured by the Fourth Amendment. As for the exclusionary rule itself, the question is whether the individual states should be able to determine the rule's desirability. The Fourteenth Amendment does not allow this court to mold state remedies according to its own notions of how things should be done. What was recognized in *Wolf v. Colorado*, 338 U.S. 25 (1949), was not that the Fourth Amendment *as such* is enforceable against the states as a facet of due process, but the principle of privacy that is at the core of the Fourteenth Amendment.

ANALYSIS

While holding that the exclusionary rule should be applied to the states, the Court noted there was a slow although "significant" trend among the states to adopt it on their own. As stated, the exclusionary rule was applied in federal courts for over 50 years prior to the *Mapp* decision and without significant controversy. The Court sought to put an end to the practice of federal prosecutors taking unlawfully seized evidence to state prosecutors "in the courthouse across the street" to

Continued on next page.

initiate prosecutions they themselves could not bring constitutionally in federal court.

Quicknotes

CERTIORARI A discretionary writ issued by a superior court to an inferior court in order to review the lower court's decisions; the U.S. Supreme Court's writ ordering such review.

EXCLUSIONARY RULE A rule precluding the introduction at trial of evidence unlawfully obtained in violation of the federal constitutional safeguards against unreasonable searches and seizures.

FOURTEENTH AMENDMENT Declares that no state shall make or enforce any law that shall abridge the privileges and immunities of citizens of the United States; no state shall deny to any person within its jurisdiction the equal protection of the laws.

FOURTH AMENDMENT Provides that persons be secure as to their person and private belongings against unreasonable searches and seizures.

CHAPTER 3

Passing the Threshold of the Fourth Amendment

Quick Reference Rules of Law

Katz v. United States

Gambler (D) v. Federal government (P)

389 U.S. 347 (1967)

NATURE OF CASE: Appeal from criminal conviction for transmitting betting information over the phone.

FACT SUMMARY: Katz (D) was arrested for transmitting wagering information by telephone to another state; at his trial the Government (P) introduced recordings of his conversation that were made by attaching a listening and recording device to the outside of a phone booth.

RULE OF LAW

The Fourth Amendment protects a person from search and seizure if, under the circumstances, the person has a justifiable expectation of privacy, regardless of whether an actual physical trespass occurred.

FACTS: Katz (D) was arrested and convicted for transmitting betting information by telephone to another state in violation of a federal statute. At his trial, the Government (P) introduced recordings of phone conversations Katz (D) had made. These recordings were made by attaching a recording and listening device to the outside of a phone booth from which Katz (D) made his calls. There was no search warrant. The Government (P) used this device only after it had made an investigation that indicated that the phone booth was being used to transmit such information, and the Government (P) recorded only conversations that Katz (D) personally had.

ISSUE: Does the Fourteenth Amendment protect a person from search and seizure if, under the circumstances, the person has a justifiable expectation of privacy, regardless of whether an actual trespass occurred?

HOLDING AND DECISION: (Stewart, J.) Yes. The Fourth Amendment protects a person from search and seizure if, under the circumstances, the person has a justifiable expectation of privacy, regardless of whether an actual physical trespass occurred. The Fourth Amendment protects a person's justifiable expectations of privacy and protects people and not places. Whatever a person knowingly exposes to the public, even in his own home, is, therefore, not protected by the Fourth Amendment, but what a person keeps private, even in a public place, may be protected. Earlier cases stated that surveillance without a trespass or seizure of a material object is outside of the Fourth Amendment, and now these cases must be overturned. Even though the phone booth was a public place, and there was no physical trespass (the device was on the outside of the booth), there was a search because the Government (P) violated the privacy upon which Katz (D) justifiably relied. There also is a seizure even though no tangible property was taken because the recording of a statement overheard, even if there is no trespass, is a seizure. The remaining question, then, is whether the Government (P) complied with the constitutional standards of the Fourth Amendment. Although the Government (P) reasonably believed that the phone booth was being illegally used, and its search and seizure was carefully limited both in scope and duration, the action cannot be upheld because there was no search warrant issued. A search warrant is a safeguard in several ways: a neutral magistrate on the basis of information presented determined whether a warrant should issue; the search warrant carefully limits the scope of the search; and the government must report back on the evidence it finds. Without such safeguards, even if the search was in fact reasonable, it cannot be upheld. Reversed.

CONCURRENCE: (Harlan, J.) In order to be protected by the Fourth Amendment, a person must have an actual, subjective expectation of privacy, and the expectation of privacy must be reasonable.

DISSENT: (Black, J.) When the Fourth Amendment was adopted, eavesdropping was a common practice, and if the framers of the Constitution wished to limit that procedure, they would have used appropriate language. This case, then, goes against the plain meaning of the Fourth Amendment that was solely aimed at limiting the practice of breaking into buildings and seizing tangible property. Therefore, wiretapping, which is a form of eavesdropping, is not subject to the Fourth Amendment.

ANALYSIS

Katz rejects the old rule that held that there was no search unless there was a physical trespass and substitutes a new rule based on the defendant's expectation of privacy. One facet of this privacy concept is the place involved – for example, if, unlike Katz (D), the defendant had engaged in conversation in a public place that was audible to others, there would be no search within the meaning of the Fourth Amendment. Also, the privacy concept turns on the action of the defendant. If he had engaged in a loud conversation, even in his own home,

Continued on next page.

that was audible to a person standing outside of his door, there would be no search since the conversation had been exposed by the defendant to the public.

Quicknotes

FOURTH AMENDMENT Provides that persons be secure as to their person and private belongings against unreasonable searches and seizures.

SEARCH AND SEIZURE An inspection conducted in order to obtain evidence to be utilized for the prosecution of a crime and the subsequent taking of such evidence.

TRESPASS Unlawful interference with, or damage to, the real or personal property of another.

WIRETAP A means of acquiring the content of a communication through an electronic or other device.

United States v. White

Federal government (P) v. Narcotics convict (D)

401 U.S. 745 (1971)

NATURE OF CASE: Appeal from the overturning of a criminal conviction for violation of narcotics laws.

FACT SUMMARY: A government informer carrying a concealed radio transmitter engaged in conversation with White (D), and those conversations were simultaneously transmitted to federal narcotic agents. Those agents testified at White's (D) trial as to the conversations they had heard.

RULE OF LAW

The Fourth Amendment does not protect a person from having his conversations with an associate recorded by that associate or transmitted to a recording or listening device located elsewhere.

FACTS: A government informer had engaged White (D) in numerous conversations in a restaurant, White's (D) home, the informer's car, and the informer's house. During these conversations, the informer carried a concealed radio transmitter that transmitted the conversations to federal agents who had a listening and recording device. Additionally, while the conversations were carried on in the informer's house, an agent—with the informer's consent—hid in the kitchen and overheard the conversations. The federal agents did not obtain a warrant or a court order before engaging in this activity. At White's (D) trial, the informer did not testify, but the federal agents testified as to the conversations they had overheard by use of the radio transmitter. White (D) was convicted, but the U.S. court of appeals overturned the conviction, holding that *Katz v. United States*, 389 U.S. 347 (1967), prohibited testimony about the conversations.

ISSUE: Does the Fourth Amendment protect a person from having his conversations with an associate transmitted and recorded by that associate or transmitted to a recording or listening device located elsewhere?

HOLDING AND DECISION: (White, J.) No. The Fourth Amendment does not protect a person from having his conversations with an associate recorded by that associate or transmitted to a recording or listening device located elsewhere. Although *Katz v. United States*, 389 U.S. 347 (1967), stated that the Fourth Amendment protects a person's justifiable expectation of privacy, it didn't hold that a person has a justifiable and constitutionally protected expectation that a person with whom he is talking will not reveal that conversation to the police. And under *Hoffs v. United States*, 385 U.S. 293, no matter how strongly a person trusts an associate, this expectation that the associate will be faithful is not protected by the Fourth Amendment if it turns out that person is a government agent; when a person voluntarily engages in a conversation with another, he risks the chance that the other person will relate the conversation to the police. In a case with very similar facts as this case, *Lee v. United States*, 343 U.S. 747, this Court held that electronic eavesdropping on a conversation with the cooperation of one of the parties is not a violation of the Fourth Amendment. Since the law doesn't protect a person when an associate testifies as to a conversation in which they engaged, there should not be a different result if that same associate, rather than testifying, transmits the conversation to another by use of electronic equipment. Since the associate could testify as to the conversation, the recording serves the same function but with increased reliability and accuracy. Additionally, with a recording, the informant/associate is less likely to later change his story. A different result is not required because the informant did not testify at the trial; the question of whether an act violates the Fourth Amendment is determined at the time of the act and is not changed by later events. Reversed.

DISSENT: (Douglas, J.) The concepts of privacy enshrined in the Fourth Amendment vanish completely when we slavishly allow an all-powerful government, proclaiming law and order, efficiency, and other benign purposes, to penetrate all the walls and doors that men need to shield them from the pressures of a turbulent life around them and to give them the health and strength to carry on. The Court must reaffirm the need for judicial supervision of the use of judicial surveillance, which, uncontrolled, promises to lead into a police state.

DISSENT: (Harlan, J.) The impact of third-party bugging undermines that confidence and sense of security in dealing with one another that is characteristic of individual relationships between citizens in a free society.

ANALYSIS

Katz v. United States, 389 U.S. 347 (1967), held that the Fourth Amendment protects a defendant's justifiable expectations of privacy; whatever a person knowingly exposes to the public is not protected, but whatever a person justifiably considers as private and keeps from public view or hearing is protected. *White*, however, holds that when a person engages in a conversation, he or she does not have a constitutionally protectable

Continued on next page.

expectation that the other party to the conversation will not reveal the conversation to the authorities, either by testifying or by contemporaneously transmitting the conversation to third-party eavesdroppers. This appears to be a sharp limitation on *Katz's* rather broad "expectation of privacy" approach; but, under *Katz*, unless the defendant knowingly exposes a conversation to the public (by speaking too loudly in a public place), the conversation cannot be subjected to electronic surveillance without a warrant or the cooperation of the other party to the conversation.

Quicknotes

EXPECTATION OF PRIVACY Requirement that in order to invoke the Fourth Amendment's protection against unreasonable searches and seizures, the individual must have a reasonable expectation of privacy in respect to the location searched or thing seized.

FOURTH AMENDMENT Provides that persons be secure as to their person and private belongings against unreasonable searches and seizures.

WIRETAP A means of acquiring the content of a communication through an electronic or other device.

Smith v. Maryland

Convicted robber (D) v. State (P)

442 U.S. 735 (1979)

NATURE OF CASE: On writ of certiorari from robbery conviction.

FACT SUMMARY: Using evidence obtained from a pen register, police obtained a warrant to search Smith's (D) home, leading to his eventual conviction for robbery.

RULE OF LAW

The warrantless installation and use of a pen register to record numbers dialed from an individual's home telephone does not violate the individual's legitimate expectations of privacy.

FACTS: McDonough was robbed; she described to police the robber and an automobile she observed near the crime. She later saw the car driving past her house and received obscene and threatening phone calls from a man identifying himself as the robber. The police spotted a man meeting the description McDonough had given them driving in McDonough's neighborhood. The police traced the license plate number and learned it was registered to Smith (D). At the request of the police, but without a warrant or court order, the phone company installed a device called a pen register at its offices to monitor and record numbers dialed from Smith's (D) home. The register revealed that Smith (D) had called McDonough, and on the basis of this and other evidence, police obtained a warrant to search his home. The trial court denied Smith's (D) motion to suppress the evidence derived from the pen register, and he was convicted of robbery. The United States Supreme Court granted review.

ISSUE: Does the warrantless installation and use of a pen register to record numbers dialed from an individual's home telephone violate his legitimate expectations of privacy?

HOLDING AND DECISION: (Blackmun, J.) No. The warrantless installation and use of a pen register to record numbers dialed from an individual's home phone does not violate legitimate expectations of privacy. Users of the telephone must realize that they are conveying information about the numbers they dial to the phone company. They typically realize that the phone company has facilities for recording such numbers for a variety of purposes, including billing, detecting fraud, and identifying obscene callers. The fact that Smith (D) dialed the numbers from his home phone is immaterial; the phone company obtains the information regarding numbers dialed in the same way, regardless of where the phone is located. This Court has held that an individual does not harbor a legitimate expectation of privacy in information he voluntarily turns over to third parties. Affirmed.

DISSENT: (Stewart, J.) The majority distinguishes between the numbers dialed and the content of conversations, in which we have held an individual enjoys an expectation of privacy from surveillance. It is incorrect to say that the numbers dialed are without content, as they can easily reveal the most intimate details of a person's life.

DISSENT: (Marshall, J.) The notion that those who reveal information to third parties assume the risk of disclosure implies choice. It is idle to speak of choice in the context of use of a home telephone, an instrument that has become a necessity in our society, and one for which there is no practical alternative.

ANALYSIS

In response to *Smith*, Congress passed legislation prohibiting the installation of pen registers, except for maintenance and testing, without a court order. Likewise, Congress prohibited seizure of financial institution records without a subpoena or warrant, in response to *United States v. Miller*, 425 U.S. 435 (1976), a case cited by Justice Blackmun in *Smith*.

Quicknotes

CERTIORARI A discretionary writ issued by a superior court to an inferior court in order to review the lower court's decisions; the U.S. Supreme Court's writ ordering such review.

SUBPOENA A court-issued mandate to compel a witness to appear at trial.

WARRANT An order issued by a court directing an officer to undertake a certain act (e.g., arrest or search).

Kyllo v. United States

Resident (D) v. Federal government (P)

533 U.S. 27 (2001)

NATURE OF CASE: Appeal from indictment of growing marijuana.

FACT SUMMARY: Federal agents suspected Kyllo (D) of growing marijuana in his residence and used a thermal scanner to prove he was doing so.

RULE OF LAW

Where the government uses a device that is not in general public use to explore details of the home that would previously have been unknowable without physical intrusion, the surveillance is a "search" and is presumptively unreasonable without a warrant.

FACTS: Federal agents suspected Kyllo (D) was growing marijuana in his home and used a thermal imager to scan the residence. The agents concluded that Kyllo (D) was using halide lights to grow marijuana in his house and a magistrate issued a search warrant on the basis of the thermal scan, tips from informants, and Kyllo's (D) heating bills. Kyllo (D) was indicted and unsuccessfully moved to suppress the evidence. The Ninth Circuit Court of Appeals remanded the case for an evidentiary hearing regarding the intrusiveness of the thermal imaging. The District Court upheld the warrant and affirmed denial of the motion. The Ninth Circuit Court of Appeals affirmed.

ISSUE: Where the government uses a device that is not in general public use to explore details of the home that would previously have been unknowable without physical intrusion, is the surveillance a "search" and presumptively unreasonable without a warrant?

HOLDING AND DECISION: (Scalia, J.) Yes. Where the government uses a device that is not in general public use to explore details of the home that would previously have been unknowable without physical intrusion, the surveillance is a "search" and is presumptively unreasonable without a warrant. Obtaining by sense-enhancing technology any information regarding the interior of a home that could not otherwise have been obtained without physical intrusion into a constitutionally protected area constitutes a search, at least where, as here, the technology in question is not in general public use. This assures preservation of that degree of privacy against government that existed when the Fourth Amendment was adopted. On the basis of this criterion the information obtained by the thermal imaging was the product of a search. The Fourth Amendment draws a firm line at the entrance to the house. Remanded to the district court to determine whether probable cause existed independent of the evidence from the thermal visioning. Reversed.

DISSENT: (Stevens, J.) There is a distinction between "through-the-wall surveillance" that gives the observer direct access to information in a private area and the thought processes used to draw inferences from information in the public domain. The Court has crafted a rule that purports to deal with direct observation of the inside of the home. This case, however, involves indirect deductions from observations of the exterior of the home. It would be far wiser to give legislators an unimpeded opportunity to grapple with prematurely devised constitutional restraints.

ANALYSIS

The United States Supreme Court upholds the test of "reasonableness" set forth in *Katz v. United States*, 389 U.S. 347 (1967), that whether the individual has an expectation of privacy depends on whether society is prepared to recognize such expectation as reasonable. The Court rejects the erosion of Fourth Amendment protection by technological advances, concluding that any such technological "intrusion into a constitutionally protected area" constitutes a search, especially if the product of the use of a device is not available to the general public.

Quicknotes

FOURTH AMENDMENT Provides that persons be secure as to their person and private belongings against unreasonable searches and seizures.

PROBABLE CAUSE A reasonable basis for believing that a crime has been committed.

SEARCH An inspection conducted in order to obtain evidence to be utilized for the prosecution of a crime.

WARRANT An order issued by a court directing an officer to undertake a certain act (e.g., arrest or search).

United States v. Jones

Federal government (P) v. Individual (D)

565 U.S. 400 (2012)

NATURE OF CASE: Appeal from intermediate appellate court decision in favor of the defendant.

FACT SUMMARY: Government agents installed a global-positioning system (GPS) tracking device on the undercarriage of a vehicle owned by Jones (D), who was suspected of trafficking in narcotics, and then monitored the vehicle's movements for a period of 28 days.

RULE OF LAW

The government's installation of a global-positioning system (GPS) device on an individual's vehicle, and the government's use of the device to track the location of that vehicle, constitutes a search under the Fourth Amendment.

FACTS: Government agents installed a global-positioning system (GPS) tracking device on the undercarriage of Jones's (D) vehicle for a period of 28 days. The device was able to track the location of the vehicle to within 50 feet. The district court judge denied Jones's (D) motion to suppress the GPS evidence, and a jury convicted him. The D.C. Circuit Court of Appeals then reversed, finding that the evidence obtained by use of the GPS device without a warrant violated the Fourth Amendment. The Government (P) appealed to the United States Supreme Court.

ISSUE: Does the government's installation of a global-positioning system (GPS) device on an individual's vehicle, and the government's use of the device to track the location of that vehicle, constitute a search under the Fourth Amendment?

HOLDING AND DECISION: (Scalia, J.) Yes. The government's installation of a global-positioning system (GPS) device on an individual's vehicle, and the government's use of the device to track the location of that vehicle, constitutes a search under the Fourth Amendment. The Government (P) argues that no search occurred because Jones (D) had no reasonable expectation of privacy in the area of the vehicle accessed by government agents or in the location of the vehicle on public roads. However, this case need not be analyzed on the reasonable expectation of privacy theory. Instead, the government's physical trespass in the form of attaching a device to one's vehicle constitutes the search. One's private vehicle is protected by the Fourth Amendment's prohibition of unreasonable searches of one's "person, houses, papers and effects." The more general unreasonable expectation of privacy theory did not replace the original trespass to property theory of unreasonable searches. Rather, it is supplemental to the original understanding of the Fourth Amendment. It is enough for this case to focus narrowly on the government's trespass upon Jones's (D) "effects," i.e., his vehicle, to find that a search occurred. Affirmed.

CONCURRENCE: (Sotomayor, J.) The government's physical invasion of Jones's (D) personal property constituted a search. However, this Court may need to utilize the more general reasonable expectation of privacy theory in other cases because many forms of electronic surveillance do not include physical intrusion.

CONCURRENCE: (Alito, J.) The Court should have analyzed this under the broader reasonable expectation of privacy theory rather than the simple trespass to property theory. Reliance on the narrow trespass theory will not provide any guidance to law enforcement for those surveillance cases where there is no physical intrusion. The majority's decision unnecessarily avoids the more important issue of the legality of the use of GPS devices for long-term tracking. If such long-term tracking can be somehow accomplished in the future without having to attach a device on the vehicle, this opinion will offer no guidance. The result is also incongruous. If law enforcement uses police vehicles or helicopters to track a vehicle for a long period of time, that will not result in a Fourth Amendment violation, but attaching a GPS device to the car will. The best solutions to all of these new search and seizure issues arising from technological advances should be devised and enacted by federal or state legislatures.

ANALYSIS

While the judgment in this case was unanimous, the Court was split five to four on how to analyze the use of the global-positioning system (GPS) tracking device. The federal agents' intrusion upon the personal property of Jones (D) was the significant factor in this case. As the concurring justices note, however, the issue remains undecided on how far law enforcement can go with electronic or even Internet searches that do not include a physical intrusion.

Quicknotes

FOURTH AMENDMENT Provides that persons be secure as to their person and private belongings against unreasonable searches and seizures.

SEARCH AND SEIZURE An inspection conducted in order to obtain evidence to be utilized for the prosecution of a crime and the subsequent taking of such evidence.

Carpenter v. United States

Convicted robber (D) v. Federal government (P)

138 S. Ct. 2206 (2018)

NATURE OF CASE: Appeal by convicted robber from affirmance of denial of motion to suppress cellular phone routing data, known as cell-site location information, obtained without a warrant.

FACT SUMMARY: Carpenter (D), who was convicted of several counts of robbery, contended cellular phone routing data, known as cell-site location information, that the Federal Bureau of Investigation (FBI) obtained without a warrant and that showed his cell phone was near robbery locations at the time the robberies occurred, should have been suppressed on the grounds the Government's (P) seizure of that data without a warrant supported by probable cause violated the Fourth Amendment.

RULE OF LAW

An individual has a legitimate expectation of privacy in the record of his or her physical movements as captured through cell-site location information (CSLI), so that the government must generally obtain a search warrant supported by probable cause before acquiring CSLI.

FACTS: Each time a cell phone connects to a cell site, it generates a time-stamped record known as cell-site location information (CSLI). Wireless carriers collect and store this information for their own business purposes. After the Federal Bureau of Investigation (FBI) identified the cell phone numbers of several robbery suspects, prosecutors were granted court orders to obtain the suspects' cell phone records under the Stored Communications Act. Wireless carriers produced CSLI for Carpenter's (D) phone, and the Government (P) was able to obtain 12,898 location points cataloging Carpenter's movements over 127 days—an average of 101 data points per day. Carpenter (D) moved to suppress the data, arguing that the Government's (P) seizure of the records without obtaining a warrant supported by probable cause violated the Fourth Amendment. The district court denied the motion, and prosecutors used the records at trial to show that Carpenter's (D) phone was near four of the robbery locations at the time those robberies occurred. Carpenter (D) was convicted. The Sixth Circuit Court of Appeals affirmed, holding Carpenter (D) lacked a reasonable expectation of privacy in the location information collected by the FBI because he had shared that information with his wireless carriers. The United States Supreme Court granted certiorari.

ISSUE: Does an individual have a legitimate expectation of privacy in the record of his or her physical movements as captured through cell-site location information (CSLI), so that the government must generally obtain a search warrant supported by probable cause before acquiring CSLI?

HOLDING AND DECISION: (Roberts, C.J.) Yes. An individual has a legitimate expectation of privacy in the record of his or her physical movements as captured through cell-site location information (CSLI), so that the government must generally obtain a search warrant supported by probable cause before acquiring CSLI. The location information obtained from Carpenter's (D) wireless carriers was the product of a search. A person does not surrender all Fourth Amendment protection by venturing into the public sphere, since the Fourth Amendment seeks to secure the "privacies of life" against "arbitrary power" of the government. To the contrary, the Court has recognized that what one seeks to preserve as private, even in an area accessible to the public, may be constitutionally protected, and that individuals have a reasonable expectation of privacy in the whole of their physical movements. Thus, when an individual seeks to preserve something as private, and the individual's expectation of privacy is one that society is prepared to recognize as reasonable, official intrusion into that sphere generally qualifies as a search and requires a warrant supported by probable cause. The analysis regarding which expectations of privacy are entitled to protection is informed by historical understandings of what was deemed an unreasonable search and seizure when the Fourth Amendment was adopted. These Founding-era understandings continue to inform the Court when applying the Fourth Amendment to innovations in surveillance tools. The digital data at issue—personal location information maintained by a third party—does not fit neatly under existing precedents but lies at the intersection of two lines of cases. One line of cases addresses a person's expectation of privacy in the person's physical location and movements. See, e.g., *United States v. Jones,* 565 U.S. 400 (2012), in which the Court concluded that privacy concerns would be raised by GPS tracking. The other line of cases addresses a person's expectation of privacy in information voluntarily turned over to third parties. See *United States v. Miller,* 425 U.S. 435 (1976), which held there was no expectation of privacy in financial records held by a bank, and *Smith v. Maryland,* 442 U.S. 735 (1979), which held there was no expectation of privacy in records of dialed telephone numbers conveyed

Continued on next page.

to a telephone company. Allowing Government (P) access to cell-site records—which "hold for many Americans the 'privacies of life,'" *Riley v. California*, 573 U.S. 373 (2014)—contravenes the expectation of privacy, because the time-stamped data provides an intimate window into a person's life, revealing not only the person's particular movements, but through them the person's familial, political, professional, religious, and sexual associations. Given the unique nature of cell phone location records, merely because the information is held by a third party does not by itself overcome the user's claim to Fourth Amendment protection. Moreover, cell phone tracking is remarkably easy, cheap, and efficient compared to traditional investigative tools, and, with just the click of a button, the Government (P) can access each carrier's deep repository of historical location information at practically no expense. Cell-site records raise great privacy concerns, given that cell phones have become almost a "feature of human anatomy," *Riley*, 573 U.S. 373 (2014) (slip op., at 9), in that individuals carry their phones with them at all times, beyond public thoroughfares and into private residences, doctor's offices, political headquarters, and other potentially revealing locales. Accordingly, when the Government (P) tracks the location of a cell phone it achieves near perfect surveillance, as if it had attached an ankle monitor to the phone's user, and it can do so retrospectively to retrace a person's whereabouts, subject only to the (current) five-year retention policies of most wireless carriers. Critically, location information is continually logged for all 400 million devices in the United States, not just those belonging to persons who might happen to come under investigation, so the tracking capacity of CSLI runs against everyone. In other words, whoever a suspect turns out to be, that individual already effectively has been tailed for every moment of every day for five years (unless, of course, the individual does not use a cell phone—which these days is extremely rare). Additionally, the precision of such information is rapidly increasing. For these reasons when the Government (P) accessed CSLI from the wireless carriers, it invaded Carpenter's (D) reasonable expectation of privacy in the whole of his physical movements and was a search. The Government (P) contends that the third-party doctrine governs this case, because cell-site records, like the records in *Smith* and *Miller*, are "business records," created and maintained by wireless carriers. However, there is a world of difference between the limited types of personal information addressed in *Smith* and *Miller* and the exhaustive chronicle of location information casually collected by wireless carriers. The third-party doctrine partly stems from the notion that an individual has a reduced expectation of privacy in information knowingly shared with another. *Smith* and *Miller*, however, did not rely solely on the act of sharing. They also considered the nature of the particular documents sought and limitations on any legitimate expectation of privacy concerning their contents. In mechanically applying the third-party doctrine to this case the Government (P) fails to appreciate the lack of comparable limitations on the revealing nature of CSLI. Nor does the second rationale for the third-party doctrine—voluntary exposure—hold up when it comes to CSLI. Cell phone location information is not truly "shared" as the term is normally understood. First, cell phones and the services they provide are such a pervasive and insistent part of daily life that carrying one is indispensable to participation in modern society. Second, a cell phone logs a cell-site record by dint of its operation, without any affirmative act on the user's part beyond powering up. For these reasons, therefore, the Government (P) must generally obtain a warrant supported by probable cause before acquiring CSLI records. Nonetheless, as with other searches, case-specific exceptions may support a warrantless search of an individual's cell-site records under certain circumstances. One well-recognized exception applies when the exigencies of the situation make the needs of law enforcement so compelling that a warrantless search is objectively reasonable under the Fourth Amendment. Such exigencies include the need to pursue a fleeing suspect, protect individuals who are threatened with imminent harm, or prevent the imminent destruction of evidence. Absent such exigencies, the Government (P) will have to obtain a warrant, and merely because CSLI is gathered by a third party will not render it less deserving of Fourth Amendment protection. Reversed.

DISSENT: (Kennedy, J.) The majority errs in departing from the Court's Fourth Amendment precedent's and principles, and, by doing so, unnecessarily imperils criminal investigations in serious cases, as well as in many routine, but vital, law enforcement operations. The Court should have limited the question it was going to decide to whether the Government (P) searched anything of Carpenter's (D) when it used compulsory process to obtain his cell-site records. *Smith* and *Miller*, which hold that individuals lack any protected Fourth Amendment interests in records that are possessed, owned, and controlled only by a third party, require a negative answer. *Smith* and *Miller* have been criticized as being based on too narrow a view of reasonable expectations of privacy, but those criticisms are unwarranted in this case because of Carpenter's (D) attenuated interest in property owned by another, and because there are sufficient safeguards inherent in the use of compulsory process. Established Fourth Amendment principles, which the majority ignores, require that a person have sufficient connection to the thing or place searched to assert Fourth Amendment interests therein. Thus, property concepts are fundamental to whether a person has such interests

Continued on next page.

that are protected. Moreover, the absence of property interests, or their analogues, can be dispositive of privacy expectations. Thus, where, as in *Smith* and *Miller,* and in this case as well, a third party is the sole owner of the thing or place searched, there is no reason for a defendant to have a reasonable expectation of privacy therein. Second, it is also well-established that the Government (P) may use compulsory process to require persons to disclose documents and other evidence within their possession and control. Although *Smith* and *Miller* would not apply if a third party held Carpenter's (D) property on his behalf, the Government's (P) acquisition of cell-site records falls within the heartland of those precedents. Ultimately, the Court's new, unworkable, standard will allow the cell phone to become a protected medium that dangerous persons will use to commit serious crimes. The Court should have resolved this case by interpreting accepted property principles as the baseline for reasonable expectations of privacy.

DISSENT: (Thomas, J.) The reasonable-expectation-of-privacy test has no place in Fourth Amendment analysis and involves prohibited judicial policymaking. The case at bar should not turn on whether a search occurred, but on whose property was searched, since the Fourth Amendment expressly guarantees individuals the right to be secure from unreasonable searches of "their persons, houses, papers, and effects." By obtaining the cell-site records of cellular carriers, the Government (P) did not search Carpenter's (D) property. He did not create the records, he did not maintain them, he could not control them, and he could not destroy them, nor did the terms of his contracts or any provision of law make the records his; they belonged to the carriers. The Court's precedents, particularly *Katz v. United States,* 389 U.S. 347 (1967), erred by holding that a "search" occurs when the Government (P) violates a person's reasonable expectation of privacy, as that concept is nowhere to be found in, nor derived from, the Fourth Amendment. Historically, at the founding, "search" did not have anything to do with expectations of privacy, and that word then had the same meaning it has today: to look over or through for the purpose of finding something. The word "privacy" does not appear anywhere in the Constitution, let alone the Fourth Amendment, which seeks to secure the right of the people to be secure in certain types of property: houses, papers, and effects. Thus, if privacy is incidentally protected through the securing of property, such attendant protection of privacy does not justify the elevation of privacy as the *sine qua non* of the Fourth Amendment. The Court should reconsider *Katz* and its other precedents in this area—which have been a failed experiment—since the Court has no authority to unilaterally alter the Constitution.

DISSENT: (Gorsuch, J.) The technology we all use today, including smartphones and the internet, means that numerous third parties maintain records about us and, increasingly, for us, and that even our most private documents—those that in the past we would have physically locked up or destroyed—now reside on third-party servers. Although *Smith* and *Miller* teach that the police can review all this material, on the theory that no one reasonably expects any of it will be kept private, no one really believes that premise, if they ever did. To keep *Smith* and *Miller* on the books would reduce Fourth Amendment rights to nearly nothing, since the rule they announced is categorical and does not permit any balancing based on the type of information involved. In other words, once you disclose information to third parties, you forfeit any reasonable expectation of privacy you might have had in it. Numerous scholars, judges, lawyers, and others have concluded that the third-party doctrine of *Smith* and *Miller* is extremely "wrong," since people often do reasonably expect that information, they entrust to third parties, especially information subject to confidentiality agreements, will be kept private. Meanwhile, if the third-party doctrine is supposed to represent a normative assessment of when a person should expect privacy, the notion that the answer might be "never" seems a pretty unattractive societal prescription. Moreover, the Court's given justifications for the doctrine are unpersuasive. One justification is that when people turn over information to a third party, they assume the risk that the information may be revealed to the police. However, even if a person who turns information over to a third party knows of such a risk, it is unclear that the person has somehow assented to bear that risk; knowing about a risk does not mean you assume responsibility for that risk. Another justification involves clarity: once you confide information to others, you know precisely that you have no protection from the Government's (P) prying eyes in that information. However, an opposite rule would be equally clear: third party disclosures never diminish Fourth Amendment protection—so clarity alone cannot justify the third-party doctrine. If *Smith* and *Miller* were jettisoned, that would leave *Katz's* "reasonable expectation of privacy" test. However, *Katz* is also quite problematic, since it finds no support in the language of the Fourth Amendment or the Constitution, and it has never been squarely determined whether the test announced in *Katz* is normative or empirical. If it is supposed to be empirical, then judges, who often fail to reflect public views, should not be the ones deciding the question, and, instead, the legislature should decree what are "the peoples' expectations of privacy." Similarly, if the *Katz* test should be normative, it is again not clear why judges, rather than legislators, should get to determine whether society should be prepared to recognize an expectation of privacy as legitimate.

Continued on next page.

Although judges sometimes may be able to discern and describe existing societal norms, so there might be some occasions where *Katz* can be applied in a principled way, more often than not, *Katz* has produced unpredictable, or even unbelievable, jurisprudence. A third option is to take a more traditional property based Fourth Amendment approach to the issues raised here, rather than relying on a "reasonable expectation of privacy" approach. Under the traditional approach, it is clear if a house, paper, or effect is your property, you have a Fourth Amendment interest in its protection. Thus, the question becomes what kind of legal interest must a person have in something to render it that person's property? First, under the concept of bailment, merely because a third party has access to or possession of your papers and effects does not necessarily eliminate your interest in them. Such a principle of property law could be useful to addressing modern data cases; just because a person entrusts their data (the modern-day equivalent of papers and effects) to a third party does not mean the person loses any Fourth Amendment interest in the data's contents. Second, it is doubtful that complete ownership or exclusive control of property is always a necessary condition to the assertion of a Fourth Amendment right, and that is supported by the common law. Third, positive law may help provide detailed guidance on evolving technologies without resort to judicial intuition, since state, and sometimes federal, law often creates rights in both tangible and intangible things. Fourth, whereas positive law may help establish a person's Fourth Amendment interest, there may be some circumstances where positive law cannot be used to defeat such an interest. In either case, the degree of privacy against Government (P) that existed when the Fourth Amendment was adopted must be preserved. Finally, this constitutional floor may, in some instances, bar efforts to circumvent the Fourth Amendment's protection through the use of subpoenas. Applying these principles here, a person's cell-site data could qualify as the person's papers or effects under existing law. Although the carrier holds the information, the relevant statute (47 U.S.C. §222) provides that a customer's CSLI is customer proprietary network information (CPNI) and gives customers certain rights to control use of and access to CPNI about themselves. Carriers are statutorily forbidden to use, disclose, or permit access to individually identifiable CPNI without the customer's consent, except as needed to provide the customer's telecommunications services. The statute also requires the carrier to disclose CPNI upon affirmative written request by the customer, to any person designated by the customer. Congress even afforded customers a private cause of action for damages against carriers who violate the Act's terms. Plainly, customers have substantial legal interests in this information, including at least some right to include, exclude, and control its use. Those interests might even rise to the level of a property right. Ostensibly, Carpenter (D) could have vindicated his Fourth Amendment rights by invoking the law of property or any analogies to the common law, but instead only relied on "reasonable expectations" arguments. Accordingly, Carpenter (D) may have forfeited his most promising line of argument.

ANALYSIS

As the Court in this case notes, a request for cell-site location information (CSLI) lies at the intersection of two lines of cases. The first addresses a person's expectation of privacy in the person's physical location and movements. Prior to this case, the Court held in *United States v. Jones,* 565 U.S. 400 (2012), that warrantless GPS monitoring of a suspect's vehicle through a tracking device violated the Fourth Amendment, not only because of the Government's (P) physical trespass of the vehicle, but also because of the suspect's related privacy expectations. In the second line of cases, the Court has held that a person has no legitimate expectation of privacy in information the person voluntarily turns over to third parties, even if the information is revealed on the assumption that it will be used only for a limited purpose. Thus, the Government (P) is typically free to obtain such information from the recipient without triggering Fourth Amendment protections. This third-party doctrine has been applied to bank records (*United States v. Miller,* 425 U.S. 435 (1976)) and records of landline telephone companies (*Smith v. Maryland,* 442 U.S. 735 (1979)). In this case, the Court declined to extend this doctrine, given what it found are the unique characteristics of cell phone location records, i.e., the ability to infallibly chronicle a person's location for years. Thus, whether the Government (P) uses its own surveillance technology or leverages the technology of a wireless carrier, an individual maintains a legitimate expectation of privacy in the record of the individual's physical movements as captured through CSLI. Nonetheless, the Court's decision in *Carpenter* is a narrow one and does not disturb the third-party doctrine or call into question conventional surveillance techniques and tools, such as security cameras. Nor does the decision address other business records that might incidentally reveal location information or other collection techniques involving foreign affairs or national security.

Quicknotes

EXPECTATION OF PRIVACY Requirement that in order to invoke the Fourth Amendment's protection against unreasonable searches and seizures, the individual must

Continued on next page.

have a reasonable expectation of privacy in respect to the location searched or thing seized.

FOURTH AMENDMENT Provides that persons be secure as to their persons and private belongings against unreasonable searches and seizures.

PROBABLE CAUSE A reasonable basis for believing that a crime has been committed.

Florida v. Jardines

State (P) v. Marijuana grower (D)

569 U.S. 1 (2013)

NATURE OF CASE: Appeal in action charging an individual with cannabis trafficking, on the grounds that the evidence was the result of an unreasonable search.

FACT SUMMARY: Jardines (D), who was charged with cannabis trafficking on the basis of marijuana plants seized in his home, sought to suppress the plants on the grounds that they were obtained as the result of an unconstitutional search conducted by a detective and a trained drug-sniffing dog.

RULE OF LAW

An investigation by the police of the curtilage of a home with a drug-detecting dog is a search for Fourth Amendment purposes.

FACTS: Police Detective Pedraja received a tip that Jardines (D) was growing marijuana inside his home. On the basis of this tip the police went to the home. Detectives could not see into the home because the blinds were drawn, and they observed no activity around the home. However, Detective Bartelt and his trained drug-sniffing dog approached the home. Bartelt kept the dog on a six-foot leash because he acted erratically when searching. As the dog approached Jardines's (D) front porch, the dog apparently sensed an odor he was trained to detect, and he began "bracketing" and "spinning" around while on the leash. The dog then located the strongest source of the odor and sat at the base of the front door. This indicated that the dog detected the scent of an unlawful drug. Bartelt then returned with the dog to the car, informed Pedraja of the positive alert for narcotics, and Pedraja obtained a warrant to search the residence. The search revealed marijuana plants, and Jardines (D) was charged with trafficking in cannabis. Jardines (D) sought to suppress the plants on the ground that the canine investigation was an unreasonable search. The United States Supreme Court granted certiorari.

ISSUE: Is an investigation by the police of the curtilage of a home with a drug-detecting dog a search for Fourth Amendment purposes?

HOLDING AND DECISION: (Scalia, J.) Yes. An investigation by the police of the curtilage of a home with a drug-detecting dog is a search for Fourth Amendment purposes. When the Government (P) obtains information by physically intruding on persons, houses, papers, or effects, a "search" within the original meaning of the Fourth Amendment has undoubtedly occurred. The curtilage is part of a private home for Fourth Amendment purposes, and the home is first among equals for Fourth Amendment purposes. A person's right to retreat to his or her home would have very little practical value if the State's (P) agents could search side yards and porches for evidence with impunity. There is no doubt here the detectives entered the curtilage, which is the area immediately surrounding and associated with the home. The issue then becomes whether the intrusion into a constitutionally protected area occurred with leave from Jardines (D). It did not. The habits of the country may provide an implicit license to a visitor to approach a home. A front door knocker allows for "solicitors, hawkers and peddlers of all kinds." Officers who have no warrant can knock on a front door and speak with the homeowner—because that is what any private citizen can do. However, there is no customary invitation for a trained police dog to explore the area looking for incriminating evidence. The State (P) relies on this Court's cases finding the subjective intent of the officer is irrelevant. Those cases, however, deal with objectively reasonable searches so the officer's real reason for the search does not vitiate the objective reasonableness. Here, the objective basis for the officer's behavior was to conduct a search and no one believes he had a license to do so. The Court need not consider whether the officers violated Jardines's (D) expectation of privacy under *Katz v. United States*, 389 U.S. 347 (1967), because the officers conducted a search by physically intruding on Jardines's (D) property. The *Katz* reasonable-expectations test adds to, not substitutes for, the property-based understanding of the Fourth Amendment. Affirmed. [The Court affirmed the judgment of the Florida Supreme Court, which had upheld the trial court's decision to suppress the marijuana plants, holding that the detectives had engaged in a Fourth Amendment search unsupported by probable cause.]

CONCURRENCE: (Kagan, J.) The Court treats this case under a property rubric, but it could also have been decided on privacy concerns, as demonstrated by a simple analogy: a stranger comes to your front door but does not knock or say hello while he uses high-powered binoculars to peer through your windows into the furthest corners of your home. He has invaded your reasonable expectations of privacy and exceeded the license you have granted to the public. Here, police approached Jardines's (D) door with a super-sensitive instrument (albeit a living one) deployed to detect things they could not detect unassisted. When a home is being searched, privacy concerns align with property concerns. The expectation that

Continued on next page.

the home will be free from governmental incursions as a matter of property has given rise to the expectation of privacy in the home. Had the case been decided on privacy grounds, the rule used would have been taken from *Kyllo v. United States*, 533 U.S. 27 (2001), where the Court held that "Where, as here, the Government uses a device that is not in general public use, to explore details of the home that would previously have been unknowable without physical intrusion, the surveillance is a 'search' and is presumptively unreasonable without a warrant." Applying that rule here, the detectives conducted a search because they used a "device. . .not in general public use" (a trained drug-detection dog) to "explore details of the home" (the presence of certain substances) that they would not otherwise have discovered without entering the premises. The outcome, contrary to the dissent, does not differ merely because the police used a highly trained dog.

DISSENT: (Alito, J.) The Court's decision relies on trespass law that is nowhere to be found in Anglo-American jurisprudence. The majority finds Bartelt committed a trespass when he engaged in an otherwise lawful visit to Jardines's (D) home but brought his dog, Franky. Trespass law provides no support for such a holding. The police are permitted to "knock and talk." Additionally, even as a matter of expectations-of-privacy, the police are permitted to see, hear, and smell what can be detected from their lawful vantage point, even if abetted by a dog. The majority fails to note that, in fact, Officer Pedreja could detect the smell of marijuana coming from the front door. The majority also fails to note that the detectives, along with Franky, spent very little time at the front of the house, so that their conduct came within the license granted members of the public, i.e., to proceed along a walkway leading to the front door of the house, see if someone is home and not linger unless expressly invited to do so. The Court states Bartelt had the objective purpose of conducting a search. There is no meaningful way to distinguish between the objective purpose of a permitted "knock and talk" and what occurred here. The dog is the difference here. There is not a single case that holds a visitor commits a trespass when accompanied by a dog on a leash. Therefore, the Court's trespass rule today is a newly struck counterfeit. Similarly, there is no expectation of privacy in odors that emanate from a dwelling that can be detected by members of the public where they lawfully stand in accord with the license they have. Justice Kagan, in her concurrence, errs in her interpretation of *Kyllo*, which is best understood as a decision about the use of new technology (dogs have been used by the police for centuries). Her proposed use of *Kyllo* would have a much wider reach. When the police used the thermal imaging device in *Kyllo*, they were on a public street. Therefore, if a dog's nose is just like a thermal imaging device for Fourth Amendment purposes, a search would occur if a dog alerted while on a public sidewalk or in the corridor of an apartment building. And the same would be true if the dog was trained to sniff, not for marijuana, but for more dangerous quarry, such as explosives or for a violent fugitive or kidnapped child. There is no reason to hamper legitimate law enforcement in this way.

ANALYSIS

The Court's decision was a narrow one involving drug-sniffing dogs, but technological advancements continue to change state agencies' ability to collect evidence. The Court acknowledges that officers may approach a private residence for the purpose of speaking with a resident and that they may even gather evidence from that "knock and talk." In the future, officers may have technological advances providing a greater ability to see, hear, and smell. The Court may have to reconsider what constitutes an impermissible intrusion resulting in an impermissible search.

Quicknotes

CURTILAGE The area immediately surrounding a dwelling.

REASONABLE EXPECTATION OF PRIVACY In order to invoke the Fourth Amendment's protection against unreasonable searches and seizures, an individual must have a reasonable expectation of privacy in respect to the location searched or thing seized.

United States v. Karo

Federal government (P) v. Individual indicted on various cocaine distribution and possession charges (D)

468 U.S. 705 (1984)

NATURE OF CASE: Appeal from affirmance of grant of motion to suppress evidence in action charging individuals with conspiring to possess cocaine with intent to distribute, and with the underlying offense.

FACT SUMMARY: Drug Enforcement Administration agents placed a tracking beeper in one of several cans of ether that were allegedly to be used to extract cocaine from clothing with the permission of the cans' owner but did not obtain a warrant to do so. Karo (D), who was indicted along with others for conspiring to possess cocaine with the intent to distribute the cocaine, as well as the underlying offense, moved to suppress the evidence obtained by the Government (P) on the grounds the placement of the beeper inside the can of ether violated his Fourth Amendment rights when the cans were delivered to him, since that constituted a warrantless seizure, among other Fourth Amendment violations.

RULE OF LAW

The installation of a tracking device in a container of chemicals with the consent of the original owner does not constitute a seizure within the meaning of the Fourth Amendment when the container is delivered to a buyer having no knowledge of the presence of the device.

FACTS: Through a Government (P) informant, Muehlenweg, the Drug Enforcement Administration (DEA) learned that Karo (D) and his confederates were planning to use ether to extract cocaine from clothing impregnated with the drug and imported into the United States. A DEA agent obtained the consent of Muehlenweg, who was supplying Karo (D) with the ether in multiple cans, to substitute one can containing a beeper for one of the cans of ether. The DEA then had all cans painted to give them a uniform appearance. The agent had a court order for the installation and monitoring of the device, but not a warrant. Karo (D) and his alleged accomplices were eventually indicted for conspiring to possess cocaine with the intent to distribute the cocaine, as well as the underlying offense. Karo (D) moved to suppress the Government's (P) evidence, on the grounds the placement of the beeper inside the can of ether violated his Fourth Amendment rights when the cans were delivered to him, since that constituted a warrantless seizure when he became the owner of the cans he had purchased from Muehlenweg. The district court granted the motion, the court of appeals affirmed, and the United States Supreme Court granted certiorari.

ISSUE: Does the installation of a tracking device in a container of chemicals with the consent of the original owner constitute a seizure within the meaning of the Fourth Amendment when the container is delivered to a buyer having no knowledge of the presence of the device?

HOLDING AND DECISION: (White, J.) No. The installation of a tracking device in a container of chemicals with the consent of the original owner does not constitute a seizure within the meaning of the Fourth Amendment when the container is delivered to a buyer having no knowledge of the presence of the device. The Fourth Amendment protects against unreasonable searches and seizures conducted without a warrant. The actual placement of the beeper into the can violated no one's Fourth Amendment rights. The can into which the beeper was placed belonged at the time to the DEA, so Karo (D) had no legitimate expectation of privacy in it. The ether and the original cans, on the other hand, belonged to, and were in the possession of, Muehlenweg, who had given his consent to any invasion of those items that occurred. Thus, Muehlenweg's consent was sufficient to validate the placement of the beeper in the can. The court of appeals confirmed this, acknowledging that before Karo (D) took control of the cans, his rights were not violated. Instead, the court of appeals held that the violation occurred at the time the can containing the beeper was transferred to Karo (D). On this point, the court of appeals was wrong. A "seizure" occurs when there is a meaningful interference with an individual's possessory interests. Karo's (D) possessory interest was not interfered with in any meaningful way; at most, the beeper constituted a trespass. If it were held that the presence of a beeper in the can constituted a seizure merely because of its occupation of space, it would follow that the presence of any object, regardless of its nature, would violate the Fourth Amendment. Reversed.

CONCURRENCE AND DISSENT: (Stevens, J.) The attachment of the beeper was a seizure. Karo (D) had the right to exclude the world from his property, and to use it exclusively for his own purposes; by attaching the monitoring device, the Government (P) infringed upon that exclusionary right by converting the property to its own use. Contrary to the majority's conclusion, this constitutes an "interference" with possessory rights, since the right to exclude, which attached as soon as the can Karo (D) purchased was delivered, had been infringed. Such

Continued on next page.

"interference" is also "meaningful" since the character of the property is profoundly different when it contains a tracking device. By attaching the beeper and using the container to conceal it, the Government (P) in the most fundamental sense was asserting "dominion and control" over the property—the power to use the property for its own purposes; such assertion of dominion and control is a "seizure" in the most basic sense of the term.

ANALYSIS

The Court also addressed the issue of when an activated tracking and monitoring device in a closed container violates the privacy interests of a homeowner into whose home the container is moved. In this regard, the Court held that the monitoring of a beeper in a private residence, a location not opened to visual surveillance, violates the Fourth Amendment rights of those who have a justifiable interest in the privacy of the residence. The Court reasoned if a Drug Enforcement Administration (DEA) agent had entered Karo's (D) house without a warrant to verify that the ether was in the house, the agent would have engaged in an unreasonable search within the meaning of the Fourth Amendment. The Court further reasoned that the result is the same where, without a warrant, the Government (P) surreptitiously uses a beeper to obtain information it could not have obtained from outside the curtilage of the house. Thus, the Court ruled, there was no reason in this case to deviate from the general rule that a search of a house should be conducted pursuant to a warrant. Under this holding, although the evidence that the ether was in the house, verified by use of the beeper without a warrant, would have been inadmissible against Karo (D) and would invalidate a resulting search warrant, if critical to establishing probable cause, it was not necessary, in this particular case, to suppress such evidence because the cans of ether had been moved via truck to a storage unit, and the DEA agents had observed the loading of the cans onto the truck. Thus, under the circumstances, the Court concluded that the warrant affidavit, after striking the facts about monitoring the beeper while it was in the searched house, nonetheless contained sufficient untainted information to furnish probable cause for issuance of the search warrant.

Quicknotes

POSSESSORY INTEREST The right to possess particular real property to the exclusion of others.

CHAPTER 4

The Substance of the Fourth Amendment

Quick Reference Rules of Law

		PAGE
1.	*Spinelli v. United States.* If an affidavit to obtain a search warrant is based upon an informer's tip (i.e., hearsay), the affidavit must state why the informer is "reliable" and the "underlying circumstances" from which the informer drew his conclusions, so as to enable an independent magistrate to conclude that the informer's information provides probable cause for the search.	*33*
2.	*Illinois v. Gates.* In issuing a search warrant, an informant's veracity, reliability, and basis of knowledge are closely intertwined issues useful in determining probable cause to believe contraband or evidence is located in a particular place.	*35*
3.	*Payton v. New York.* The Fourth Amendment prohibits the police, absent exigent circumstances, from making a warrantless and nonconsensual entry into a suspect's home to make a routine felony arrest.	*37*
4.	*Lo-Ji Sales, Inc. v. New York.* The Fourth Amendment does not countenance open-ended warrants to be completed while a search is being conducted and items seized, or after the seizure has been carried out.	*38*
5.	*Richards v. Wisconsin.* To justify a "no-knock" entry when executing a search warrant, the police must have a reasonable suspicion that knocking and announcing their presence, under the circumstances, would be dangerous or futile, or that it would inhibit the effective investigation of the crime.	*39*
6.	*Warden v. Hayden.* If pursuant to a valid search a law enforcement officer finds evidence that tends to incriminate a suspect of a crime, although the officer specifically was not searching for that particular type of evidence, the evidence is admissible.	*41*
7.	*Chimel v. California.* Under the Fourth and Fourteenth Amendments, a warrantless search conducted incident to a lawful arrest may constitutionally extend only to a search of the arrestee's person and to the area within the arrestee's immediate control (i.e., the area within which the arrestee might obtain a weapon or destroy evidence).	*43*
8.	*Riley v. California.* A warrant generally is required prior to a law enforcement search of a cell phone seized incident to an arrest.	*45*
9.	*New York v. Belton.* When police have made a lawful custodial arrest of the occupant of an automobile, they may, as a contemporaneous incident of that arrest, search the passenger compartment of the automobile.	*47*
10.	*Arizona v. Gant.* Police may search the passenger compartment of a vehicle incident to an occupant's arrest only if the occupant may have access to the vehicle or if it is reasonable to believe the vehicle contains evidence of the offense for which the occupant was arrested.	*48*
11.	*Whren v. United States.* The temporary detention of a motorist who the police have probable cause to believe has committed a civil traffic violation is consistent with the Fourth Amendment.	*50*
12.	*Chambers v. Maroney.* Where there is probable cause to believe that vehicles are carrying contraband or fruits of the crime, warrantless searches of automobiles are permissible, even where the car itself is seized and held without a warrant for whatever period is necessary to obtain a warrant for the search.	*51*
13.	*California v. Carney.* The "automobile exception" to the warrant requirement applies to motor homes.	*52*

Spinelli v. United States

Gambler (D) v. Federal government (P)

393 U.S. 410 (1969)

NATURE OF CASE: Appeal from conviction of violation of gambling statutes.

FACT SUMMARY: Spinelli (D) was convicted upon evidence seized with a search warrant that was issued based upon an affidavit containing a statement from an anonymous informer and information from agents of the Federal Bureau of Investigation agents.

RULE OF LAW

If an affidavit to obtain a search warrant is based upon an informer's tip (i.e., hearsay), the affidavit must state why the informer is "reliable" and the "underlying circumstances" from which the informer drew his conclusions, so as to enable an independent magistrate to conclude that the informer's information provides probable cause for the search.

FACTS: Spinelli (D) was convicted of violation of gambling statutes based upon evidence seized by the Federal Bureau of Investigation (FBI) under a search warrant. The FBI obtained this warrant based upon an affidavit containing the following information: (1) the FBI had been informed by a reliable informer that Spinelli (D) was using two specific telephones to conduct gambling operations; (2) that Spinelli (D) had been seen entering the apartment in which these two telephones were located; and (3) that Spinelli (D) had a reputation as a gambler. Upon conviction, and affirmance of that conviction by the court of appeals, Spinelli (D) brought a petition of certiorari to the United States Supreme Court challenging the constitutionality of the issuance of the search warrant.

ISSUE: If an affidavit to obtain a search warrant is based upon an informer's tip (i.e., hearsay), must the affidavit state why the informer is "reliable" and the "underlying circumstances" from which the informer drew his conclusions, so as to enable an independent magistrate to conclude that the informer's information provides probable cause for the search?

HOLDING AND DECISION: (Harlan, J.) Yes. If an affidavit to obtain a search warrant is based upon an informer's tip (i.e., hearsay), the affidavit must state why the informer is "reliable" and the "underlying circumstances" from which the informer drew his conclusions, so as to enable an independent magistrate to conclude that the informer's information provides probable cause for the search. Of course, in the absence of a statement detailing how the informer's tip was gathered, a search warrant may still issue if (1) the tip describes the accused's criminal activity in such detail that a magistrate may conclude that it was gained in a reliable manner, *Draper v. United States*, 358 U.S. 307 (1959), or (2) there is sufficient independent corroboration of criminal activity in the affidavit so that a magistrate may conclude that there is probable cause that a crime is being committed. Here, first, the tip is insufficient for the issuance of a warrant. The affidavit neither states why the informer was considered reliable nor how he obtained his information. Second, there is no sufficient corroboration of the tip. The fact that Spinelli (D) entered an apartment with two telephones contains no suggestion of criminal activity by itself, and the fact that Spinelli (D) is known as a gambler is only "suspicion" entitled to no weight. Judgment below reversed.

CONCURRENCE: (White, J.) There are limited special circumstances in which an "honest" informant's report, if sufficiently detailed, will in effect verify itself and in which the magistrate when confronted with such detail could reasonably infer that the informant had gained his or her information in a reliable way. Detailed information may sometimes imply that the informant himself has observed the facts. Suppose an informant with whom an officer has had satisfactory experience states that there is gambling equipment in the living room of a specified apartment and describes in detail not only the equipment itself but also the appointments and furnishings in the apartment. Detail like this, if true at all, must rest on personal observation either of the informant or of someone else. If the latter, we know nothing of the third person's honesty or sources; he may be making a wholly false report. However, it is arguable that on these facts it was the informant himself who has perceived the facts since the information reported is not usually the subject of casual day-to-day conversation. Because the informant is honest, and it is probable that he has viewed the facts, there is probable cause for the issuance of a warrant. The *Draper* approach would reasonably justify the issuance of a warrant in this case, particularly since the police had some awareness of Spinelli's (D) past activities. The majority, however, while seemingly embracing *Draper*, confines that case to its own facts. Pending full-scale reconsideration of that case on the one hand, or of the *Nathanson-Aguilar* cases on the other, I join the opinion of the Court and the judgment of reversal, especially since a vote to affirm would produce an equally divided Court. *Nathanson v. United States*, 290 U.S. 41 (1933), *Aguilar v. Texas*, 378 U.S. 108 (1964).

Continued on next page.

ANALYSIS

This case illustrates the two-pronged *Aguilar* test, 378 U.S. 108 (1964), applicable to affidavits for search warrants based upon hearsay. *Harris v. U.S.*, 404 U.S. 1232 (1971), further specified a situation in which a search warrant may be issued on the basis of hearsay. In *Harris* a warrant was upheld based upon hearsay because the affidavit contained sufficient information to allow the magistrate to determine that there was probable cause for a search warrant. The affidavit contained: (1) the informer's "personal and recent observations" of the accused's criminal activity; (2) the informer's statement that was against his own "penal interest;" and (3) the fact that the officer himself had certain knowledge of the accused's background consistent with the illegal activity alleged. Note, finally, that police do not have to reveal the identity of their informer on a hearing on the issue of probable cause, although they must do so when it is material at trial to establish guilt or innocence.

Quicknotes

AFFIDAVIT A declaration of facts written and affirmed before a witness.

CERTIORARI A discretionary writ issued by a superior court to an inferior court in order to review the lower court's decisions; the U.S. Supreme Court's writ ordering such review.

HEARSAY An out-of-court statement made by a person other than the witness testifying at trial that is offered in order to prove the truth of the matter asserted.

PROBABLE CAUSE A reasonable basis for believing that a crime has been committed.

Illinois v. Gates

State (P) v. Drug smugglers (D)

462 U.S. 213 (1983)

NATURE OF CASE: Appeal from grant of motion to suppress evidence.

FACT SUMMARY: Following the receipt of an anonymous letter detailing the drug-related criminal activities of Gates (D), the Bloomingdale Police Department had a Drug Enforcement Administration agent follow him and then obtain a search warrant on the basis of his observations and the anonymous letter.

RULE OF LAW

In issuing a search warrant, an informant's veracity, reliability, and basis of knowledge are closely intertwined issues useful in determining probable cause to believe contraband or evidence is located in a particular place.

FACTS: An anonymous letter was sent to the Bloomingdale Police Department stating that Gates (D) and his wife made their living as drug dealers and detailing how it was their custom for Mrs. Gates to drive the family car to Florida to be loaded with drugs and for Mr. Gates (D) to then fly down, pick up the car, and drive it back to Illinois. The police put a detective on the case who made arrangements to have surveillance conducted, which indicated Mr. Gates (D) was following the above-described pattern. An agent from the Drug Enforcement Administration (DEA) followed Gates (D) and signed an affidavit that was used in connection with the anonymous letter in obtaining a search warrant for the residence and vehicle of Gates (D). The search uncovered substantial amounts of marijuana. However, the trial court suppressed such evidence on the grounds that the affidavit submitted failed to support a determination of probable cause. In affirming, the Illinois Supreme Court concluded that the anonymous letter had to meet a two-pronged test: first, it had to adequately reveal the "basis of knowledge" of the letter writer (the particular means by which he came by the information given in his report); and second, it had to provide facts sufficiently establishing either the "veracity" of the affiant's informant or, alternatively, the "reliability" of the informant's report in this particular case.

ISSUE: In issuing a search warrant, are an informant's veracity, reliability, and basis of knowledge closely intertwined issues useful in determining probable cause to believe contraband or evidence is located in a particular place?

HOLDING AND DECISION: (Rehnquist, J.) Yes. In issuing a search warrant, an informant's veracity, reliability, and basis of knowledge are closely intertwined issues useful in determining probable cause to believe contraband or evidence is located in a particular place. If, on review, it appears that the magistrate had a substantial basis for concluding that there was such a fair probability, his decision will not be tampered with. Probable cause is a fluid concept, one not readily, or even usefully, reduced to a neat set of legal rules. While the informant's "veracity" and his "basis of knowledge" are two relevant factors to be considered in determining if probable cause existed to issue a search warrant, they should not be given independent status. It is wise to abandon the "two-pronged test" in which, according to this Court's decisions in *Aguilar v. Texas*, 378 U.S. 108 (1964), and *Spinelli v. United States*, 393 U.S. 410 (1969), these two factors were given such independent status. It is better to revert to a totality-of-circumstances analysis, which permits a balanced assessment of the relative weights of all the various indicia of reliability (and unreliability) attending an informant's tip. The veracity of people supplying anonymous tips is by hypothesis largely unknown and unknowable. As a result, such tips would seldom survive a rigorous application of the two-pronged test utilized by the courts below. Yet when supplemented by independent police investigation, such tips frequently contribute to the solution of otherwise "perfect crimes." While a conscientious assessment of the basis for crediting such tips is required by the Fourth Amendment, a standard that leaves virtually no place for anonymous citizen information is not. Applying the totality-of-circumstances analysis to this case, it is clear the judge issuing the search warrant had a "substantial basis" for concluding that probable cause existed to search the Gateses' (D) car and residence. Reversed.

CONCURRENCE: (White, J.) Here, it is undisputed that the anonymous tip, by itself, did not furnish probable cause. The lower court's characterization of the Gateses' (D) activity as totally innocent is dubious. In fact, the behavior was quite suspicious. The critical issue is not whether the activities observed by the police are innocent or suspicious. Instead, the proper focus should be whether the actions of the suspects, whatever their nature, give rise to an inference that the informant is credible and the informant obtained his information in a reliable manner.

DISSENT: (Brennan, J.) If the conclusory allegations of a presumptively reliable police officer are insufficient to establish probable cause, there is no conceivable reason why the conclusory allegations of an anonymous

Continued on next page.

informant should not be insufficient as well. It is no reason for rejecting the rules set forth in *Aguilar* and *Spinelli* that some courts may have employed an overly technical version of those standards.

DISSENT: (Stevens, J.) The activities in this case did not stop when the magistrate issued the warrant. The Gateses (D) drove all night to Bloomingdale, the officers searched the car, found 400 pounds of marijuana, and then searched the house. However, none of these subsequent events may be considered in evaluating the warrant, and the search of the house was legal only if the warrant was valid. The Court's casual conclusion that, before the Gateses (D) arrived in Bloomingdale, there was probable cause to justify a valid entry and search of a private home is not acceptable. No one knows who the informant in this case was or what motivated him to write the note. Given that the note's predictions were faulty in one significant respect and were corroborated by nothing except ordinary innocent activity, it is obvious that the Court's evaluation of the warrant's validity has been colored by subsequent events.

ANALYSIS

The rigidness of some of the lower courts in applying the two-pronged test abandoned by the Court's decision is well-illustrated in *People v. Palanza*, 55 Ill. App. 3d 1028, 13 Ill. Dec. 752, 371 N.E.2d 687 (1978). There, an affidavit submitted to support issuance of a search warrant indicated that an informant of proven and uncontested reliability had seen in a particular premise "a quantity of a white crystalline substance that was represented to the informant by a white male occupant of the premises to be cocaine. Informant has observed cocaine on numerous occasions in the past and is thoroughly familiar with its appearance. The informant states that the white crystalline powder he observed in the above described premises appeared to him to be cocaine." In holding the warrant issued to be invalid, the lower court reasoned "(t)here is no indication as to how the informant or for that matter any other person could tell whether a white substance was cocaine and not . . . sugar or salt."

Quicknotes

AFFIDAVIT A declaration of facts written and affirmed before a witness.

MODUS OPERANDI Characteristic method employed by a criminal in committing a particular crime so as to identify the crime as having been committed by that person.

PROBABLE CAUSE A reasonable basis for believing that a crime has been committed.

Payton v. New York

Home arrestee (D) v. State (P)

445 U.S. 573 (1980)

NATURE OF CASE: Appeal from criminal convictions.

FACT SUMMARY: In appealing their criminal convictions, Payton (D) and Riddick (D) alleged that their warrantless arrests in their respective homes were prohibited by the Fourth Amendment and that the evidence seized pursuant thereto was thus improperly admitted into evidence.

RULE OF LAW

The Fourth Amendment prohibits the police, absent exigent circumstances, from making a warrantless and nonconsensual entry into a suspect's home to make a routine felony arrest.

FACTS: Payton (D) and Riddick (D) both appealed from criminal convictions and based their challenge on the constitutionality of New York statutes authorizing police to enter a private residence without a warrant and without consent to make a routine felony arrest. Both had unsuccessfully moved to suppress the evidence introduced in their individual trials. It had been seized pursuant to precisely such an unconsented-to, warrantless in-home arrest. The convictions were affirmed on appeal.

ISSUE: Does the Fourth Amendment prohibit the police, absent exigent circumstances, from making a warrantless and nonconsensual entry into a suspect's home to make a routine felony arrest?

HOLDING AND DECISION: (Stevens, J.) Yes. The Fourth Amendment prohibits the police, absent exigent circumstances, from making a warrantless and nonconsensual entry into a suspect's home to make a routine felony arrest. That amendment draws a firm line at the entrance to the house in terms that apply equally to seizures of property and to seizures of persons. Absent exigent circumstances, that threshold may not reasonably be crossed without a warrant. This issue is not one that was definitively settled by the common law at the time the Fourth Amendment was adopted. Furthermore, although a majority of states have permitted this type of action, it is a declining trend and is being rejected by most state courts squarely facing the issue. Reversed and remanded.

DISSENT: (White, J.) A rule comporting with the common law, traditional practice in the states, and the history and policies of the Fourth Amendment should be adopted. After knocking and announcing, police could make a daytime entry to arrest without a warrant whenever there is probable cause to believe the one to be arrested committed a felony and is present in the house.

ANALYSIS

By 1931, some 24 of 29 state codes of criminal procedure specifically authorized this type of warrantless entry to arrest, and by 1975, this had grown to 31 of 37. Further indication of the previous acceptance of this practice is the fact that the American Law Institute included such authority in its model legislation in 1931 and again in 1975.

Quicknotes

EXIGENT CIRCUMSTANCES Circumstances requiring an extraordinary or immediate response; an exception to the prohibition on a warrantless arrest or search when police officers believe probable cause to exist and there is no time for obtaining a warrant.

PROBABLE CAUSE A reasonable basis for believing that a crime has been committed.

Lo-Ji Sales, Inc. v. New York

Adult bookstore owner (D) v. State (P)

442 U.S. 319 (1979)

NATURE OF CASE: Appeal in prosecution for violation of state obscenity laws.

FACT SUMMARY: A Town Justice (the Justice), who signed an incomplete warrant to search an adult bookstore owned by Lo-Ji Sales, Inc. (Lo-Ji) (D) for obscene materials, accompanied the police and investigators to the store, and seized numerous items the Justice considered obscene. The warrant was then completed retroactively to list all the seized items. Lo-Ji (D) contended that the warrant and the ensuing search and seizure were unconstitutional violations of the Fourth Amendment.

RULE OF LAW

The Fourth Amendment does not countenance open-ended warrants to be completed while a search is being conducted and items seized, or after the seizure has been carried out.

FACTS: A police investigator purchased two films from Lo-Ji Sales, Inc. (D), an adult bookstore, and took them to the Town Justice (the Justice), who viewed them and concluded they were obscene. Upon a warrant application alleging that "similar" items could be found at Lo-Ji Sales (D), the Justice signed a warrant and accompanied police to the store. However, although the Justice included in the warrant a recital that authorized the seizure of obscene materials, at the time the Justice signed the warrant, no items were listed or described following the recital. Thereafter, the Justice, the investigator, and nine other law enforcement officials entered the bookstore; conducted a search that lasted nearly six hours, covering various areas of the store; and examined and seized numerous films, projectors, and magazines. The seized items were inventoried at a State Police barracks and each item was then listed by the police on the search warrant. The United States Supreme Court granted certiorari in the case.

ISSUE: Does the Fourth Amendment countenance open-ended warrants to be completed while a search is being conducted and items seized, or after the seizure has been carried out?

HOLDING AND DECISION: (Burger, C.J.) No. The Fourth Amendment does not countenance open-ended warrants to be completed while a search is being conducted and items seized, or after the seizure has been carried out. The search warrant at issue in this case and what followed the entry on Lo-Ji Sales, Inc.'s (D) premises are reminiscent of the general warrant or writ of assistance of the eighteenth century, against which the Fourth Amendment was intended to protect. The conclusory statement of the police officer that "similar" materials could be found at the Lo-Ji Sales (D) left it to the discretion of the officials conducting the search to decide what materials were obscene. This is not permitted under the Fourth Amendment. Also not permitted is that a warrant is completed during a search, or after a general search has been carried out. At most, there existed probable cause for the Justice to authorize a search for additional copies of the two films initially obtained by police. Instead, the search began and progressed pursuant to the sweeping, unconstitutional open-ended warrant. In our system of criminal justice, it is believed that a warrant authorized by a neutral and detached judicial officer provides a reliable safeguard against improper searches. Here, however, the Justice did not manifest the requisite neutrality and detachment to support the warrant the Justice issued and signed. To the contrary, the record clearly indicates that the Justice became the leader of the search party and became a de facto police officer, caught up in a police operation. For these reasons, the warrant, the search, and the seizures violated the Fourth Amendment. Our society is better able to tolerate the admittedly pornographic business of petitioner than a return to the general warrant era; violations of law must be dealt with within the framework of constitutional guarantees. [Reversed.]

ANALYSIS

Although Chief Justice Burger criticized the conduct of the Town Justice in accompanying the officers, noting that the warrant requirement of a "neutral and detached judicial officer" was not observed, he also noted that a neutral and detached magistrate does not lose his character as such merely by leaving the magistrate's regular office to be available to law enforcement officers who may wish to seek the issuance of warrants by the magistrate. Here, the difference was that the Town Justice undertook not merely to issue a warrant, but actively participated with the police and prosecution in the warrant's execution.

Quicknotes

PROBABLE CAUSE A reasonable basis for believing that a crime has been committed.

Richards v. Wisconsin

Hotel room drug dealer (D) v. State (P)

520 U.S. 385 (1997)

NATURE OF CASE: Appeal of denial of motion to suppress evidence in felony drug trial.

FACT SUMMARY: Richards (D), under investigation for dealing drugs out of his hotel room, filed a motion to suppress evidence obtained by officers serving a search warrant who he alleges forcibly entered his hotel room without knocking and announcing their presence.

RULE OF LAW

To justify a "no-knock" entry when executing a search warrant, the police must have a reasonable suspicion that knocking and announcing their presence, under the circumstances, would be dangerous or futile, or that it would inhibit the effective investigation of the crime.

FACTS: Officers in Madison, Wisconsin, obtained a warrant to search Richards's (D) hotel room for drugs and related paraphernalia following an investigation that led them to believe that he was dealing drugs out of the hotel room. The officers requested a warrant that would have given them advance authorization for a "no-knock" entry into the hotel room, but the magistrate chose not to include such a provision. An officer dressed as a maintenance worker knocked on Richards's (D) hotel room door, while several plainclothes officers and one officer in uniform stood behind him. When Richards (D) cracked the door open and saw the uniformed officer, he quickly slammed the door closed. The officers announced themselves as police officers, kicked and rammed the door to gain entry, captured Richards (D) as he tried to escape through a window, and confiscated cash and cocaine hidden above the bathroom ceiling tiles. At a pretrial hearing, Richards (D) sought to have the evidence from the hotel room suppressed on the ground that the officers had failed to knock and announce their presence prior to forcibly entering the room. The trial court denied the motion, stating that the officers had reason to suspect from Richards's (D) behavior that he might try to escape or destroy evidence. The Wisconsin Supreme Court affirmed, holding that police in Wisconsin may dispense with the knock-and-announce requirement in all felony drug cases. Richards (D) appealed, and the United States Supreme Court granted review.

ISSUE: To justify a "no-knock" entry when executing a search warrant, must the police have a reasonable suspicion that knocking and announcing their presence, under the circumstances, would be dangerous or futile, or that it would inhibit the effective investigation of the crime?

HOLDING AND DECISION: (Stevens, J.) Yes. To justify a "no-knock" entry when executing a search warrant, the police must have a reasonable suspicion that knocking and announcing their presence, under the circumstances, would be dangerous or futile, or that it would inhibit the effective investigation of the crime. Although felony drug cases may frequently involve one or both circumstances, the Wisconsin court erred in holding that the Fourth Amendment permits a blanket exception to the knock-and-announce requirement for the entire category of criminal activity. A search could be conducted at a time when the only individuals present at a residence have no connection with the drug activity under investigation, or the drugs in question could be of a type that would make them impossible to destroy quickly. Therefore, it is the duty of a court to determine whether the facts and circumstances of a particular entry justifies dispensing with the knock-and-announce requirement. Although the Wisconsin court's blanket exception must be rejected, the officers' no-knock entry into Richards's (D) hotel room did not violate the Fourth Amendment. The circumstances clearly showed that the officers had a reasonable suspicion that Richards (D) might have destroyed evidence if given further opportunity to do so, given the easily disposable nature of the drugs. The fact that the judge issuing the warrant to the officers deleted the portion that would have given the officers permission to enter without knocking is irrelevant at this point. The reasonableness of the officers' decision to enter Richards's (D) hotel room must be evaluated as of the time they entered the room. The Wisconsin court's blanket exception is rejected; however, the judgment is affirmed.

ANALYSIS

The United States Supreme Court was justified in its concern over the establishment of a blanket no-knock rule. When constitutional rights are threatened, even if only minimally, so begins an upward battle on a slippery slope. Nevertheless, the Court upheld the Wisconsin court's judgment and rationale in allowing a no-knock entry given the facts at hand, which should make obtaining no-knock warrants in similar situations easier.

Continued on next page.

Quicknotes

EXIGENT CIRCUMSTANCES Circumstances requiring an extraordinary or immediate response; an exception to the prohibition on a warrantless arrest or search when police officers believe probable cause to exist and there is no time for obtaining a warrant.

KNOCK AND ANNOUNCE Requirement that a police officer must first knock and announce his intention before he enters an individual's home in the execution of a valid warrant.

Warden v. Hayden

State official (D) v. Prisoner/convicted armed robber (P)

387 U.S. 294 (1967)

NATURE OF CASE: [Appeal from reversal of denial of habeas corpus petition filed by prisoner contending that certain evidence admitted at trial should have been suppressed.]

FACT SUMMARY: While in hot pursuit of a suspected armed robber who entered a house, a police officer found clothing in a washing machine that matched the description of clothing the alleged perpetrator had been wearing during the robbery. The suspect, Hayden (P), sought to have this evidence suppressed on the grounds that the officer testified he had been searching for a man or money—not weapons or clothing.

RULE OF LAW

If pursuant to a valid search a law enforcement officer finds evidence that tends to incriminate a suspect of a crime, although the officer specifically was not searching for that particular type of evidence, the evidence is admissible.

FACTS: An armed robber stole money from a cab company and ran. Two cab drivers in the vicinity, attracted by shouts of "Holdup," followed the man to a house. One driver notified the company dispatcher by radio that the man was wearing a light cap and dark jacket and that he had entered the house. The dispatcher relayed the information to police who were proceeding to the scene of the robbery. Within minutes, police arrived at the house in a number of patrol cars. An officer knocked and announced their presence. Mrs. Hayden answered, and the officers told her they believed that a robber had entered the house and asked to search the house. She offered no objection. The officers spread out through the first and second floors and the cellar in search of the robber. Hayden (P) was found in an upstairs bedroom feigning sleep. He was arrested when the officers on the first floor and in the cellar reported that no other man was in the house. Meanwhile, an officer discovered a shotgun and a pistol in a flush tank; another officer who, according to the district court "was searching the cellar for a man or the money," found in a washing machine a jacket and trousers of the type the fleeing man was said to have worn. A clip of ammunition for the pistol and a cap were found under the mattress of Hayden's (P) bed, and ammunition for the shotgun was found in a bureau drawer in Hayden's (P) room. All these items of evidence were introduced against Hayden (P) at trial. [Hayden (P) was convicted of armed robbery. He eventually filed a federal habeas petition, which the district court denied. The court of appeals reversed, and the United States Supreme Court granted certiorari.]

ISSUE: If pursuant to a valid search a law enforcement officer finds evidence that tends to incriminate a suspect of a crime, although the officer specifically was not searching for that particular type of evidence, is the evidence admissible?

HOLDING AND DECISION: (Brennan, J.) Yes. If pursuant to a valid search a law enforcement officer finds evidence that tends to incriminate a suspect of a crime, although the officer specifically was not searching for that particular type of evidence, the evidence is admissible. It is assumed that the search, under exigent circumstances, was valid. Thus, the question is whether the clothing found by the officer who said he was searching for a man or money should be suppressed. Notwithstanding what the officer said, under the circumstances it may be inferred that he was also looking for weapons. The officer's failure to state explicitly that he was searching for weapons, in the absence of a specific question to that effect, is not controlling. The officer knew that the robber was armed, and he did not know that some weapons had been found at the time he opened the machine. In these circumstances, the inference that he was in fact also looking for weapons is fully justified, and the clothing items were correctly admitted into evidence. Reversed.

ANALYSIS

The Court went on to reject what is known as the "mere evidence rule," which postulates that the Fourth Amendment permits only the search and seizure of instrumentalities, fruits of the crime, and contraband, and that mere evidence cannot not be searched or seized. Although the mere evidence rule was still being applied when Hayden (P) was convicted, it had been whittled down over time, and this case is known for having dealt the rule its final death blow. The mere evidence rule had been praised as a valuable protection of individual privacy, and, for example, in *United States v. Poller*, 43 F.2d 911, 914 (2nd Cir. 1930), Judge Learned Hand observed that "limitations upon the fruit to be gathered tend to limit the quest itself." Although the Court in *Hayden* acknowledged that the rejection of the mere evidence rule would potentially "enlarge the area of permissible searches," the Court also relied on

Continued on next page.

the Fourth Amendment's protections, such as requiring warrants based on probable cause, and the requirement that searches and seizures be reasonable, to safeguard the right to privacy. Some critics of this decision have argued that the Court's rejection of the mere evidence rule has led to more intrusive searches by law enforcement agents.

Quicknotes

EXIGENT CIRCUMSTANCES Circumstances requiring an extraordinary or immediate response; an exception to the prohibition on a warrantless arrest or search when police officers believe probable cause to exist and there is no time for obtaining a warrant.

HABEAS CORPUS A proceeding in which a defendant brings a writ to compel a judicial determination of whether he or she is lawfully being held in custody.

Chimel v. California

Convicted burglar (D) v. State (P)

395 U.S. 752 (1969)

NATURE OF CASE: Appeal from burglary conviction on grounds that evidence used in obtaining the conviction was obtained unconstitutionally.

FACT SUMMARY: Police officers, after lawfully arresting Chimel (D) in his house, conducted a warrantless search, over his objections, of his entire house, that produced evidence used to obtain his conviction on two charges of burglary. Chimel (D) contended that the search of his house without a warrant violated the Fourth Amendment.

RULE OF LAW

Under the Fourth and Fourteenth Amendments, a warrantless search conducted incident to a lawful arrest may constitutionally extend only to a search of the arrestee's person and to the area within the arrestee's immediate control (i.e., the area within which the arrestee might obtain a weapon or destroy evidence).

FACTS: Late one afternoon, police officers arrived at Chimel's (D) home with a warrant authorizing his arrest for the burglary of a coin shop. Chimel's (D) wife allowed the officers to enter the house and wait for Chimel (D) to return from work. When Chimel (D) entered his home, the officers arrested him and then conducted a search, over his objection, of his entire three-bedroom house, including the attic, the garage, and a small workshop. During this search, the officers seized a number of coins, several metal tokens, and other objects used subsequently at Chimel's (D) trial to obtain his conviction on two charges of burglary. The state's appellate courts affirmed, concluding that that the search of Chimel's (D) home had been justified, despite the absence of a search warrant, on the ground that it had been incident to a valid arrest. The United States Supreme Court granted certiorari.

ISSUE: Under the Fourth and Fourteenth Amendments, may a warrantless search conducted incident to a lawful arrest constitutionally extend only to a search of the arrestee's person and to the area "within the arrestee's immediate control" (i.e., the area within which the arrestee might obtain a weapon or destroy evidence)?

HOLDING AND DECISION: (Stewart, J.) Yes. Under the Fourth and Fourteenth Amendments, a warrantless search conducted incident to a lawful arrest may constitutionally extend only to a search of the arrestee's person and to the area within the arrestee's immediate control (i.e., the area within which the arrestee might obtain a weapon or destroy evidence). It is assumed that Chimel's (D) arrest was lawful. Thus, the question is whether the warrantless search incident to that arrest of Chimel's (D) entire house likewise was lawful. The Court's precedents regarding such searches have been far from consistent. On one hand, *Harris v. United States*, 331 U.S. 145 (1947), and *United States v. Rabinowitz*, 339 U.S. 56 (1950), have given a broad scope to warrantless searches conducted incident to arrest. Under these cases, anything within the "possession" of the arrestee (as broadly defined to include a search of the arrestee's entire apartment in *Harris* and to include a search of the arrestee's one-room business office in *Rabinowitz*) may be searched at the time of the arrest for the purpose of seizing any evidence connected with the crime(s) for which the arrestee has been arrested. On the other hand, the *Go-Bart Importing Co. v. United States*, 282 U.S. 344 (1931), *United States v. Lefkowitz*, 285 U.S. 452 (1932), and *Trupiano v. United States*, 334 U.S. 699 (1948), line of cases limits warrantless searches incident to arrest. In both *Go-Bart* and *Lefkowitz*, such searches were limited to evidence that was "visible and accessible and in the offender's immediate custody." In *Trupiano*, the Court stated that a search warrant is always required absent some showing of "necessity," and there must be something more of a necessity for a warrantless search than mere arrest. *Rabinowitz* rejected this rule, and, instead, the Court said that the test "is not whether it is reasonable to procure a search warrant, but whether the search was reasonable." The state courts in this case followed *Rabinowitz*. The doctrine announced by *Rabinowitz*, however, can withstand neither historical nor rational analysis, especially when viewed against the background and purpose of the Fourth Amendment—which in large part was a reaction to the general warrants and warrantless searches that had so alienated the colonists and had helped speed the movement for independence. In the scheme of the Fourth Amendment, therefore, the requirement that "no Warrants shall issue, but upon probable cause," plays a crucial part. Accordingly, the burden is upon those seeking an exemption from the warrant requirement to show that it is justified by necessity. Such justification in the case of warrantless searches incident to arrest may extend no further than the arrestee's person and the area within the arrestee's immediate control. It is reasonable for an officer to search the arrestee's person for the officer's own safety, since the arrestee may have concealed weapons, and it is reasonable to search the area within the arrestee's control to prevent the arrestee from reaching a weapon or destroying evidence. However,

Continued on next page.

any extension beyond such an area would lead to the "evaporation" of the Fourth Amendment's right against unreasonable searches and seizures, and there is no constitutional justification for such a warrantless search. The argument that it is reasonable to search a lawfully arrested person in his or her house is based on little more than a subjective view of acceptable police conduct and has no constitutional safeguards or rational limitations. Why, for example, would it be any less reasonable to search the house if the person is arrested on his or her front lawn? Or down the street? Or at work? In effect, such a requirement could nullify the warrant requirement altogether. Here, the search of Chimel's (D) house was far beyond that area considered reasonable—within the arrestee's reach. Therefore, *Rabinowitz* and *Harris* are overruled. As such, the judgment below must be reversed.

DISSENT: (White, J.) At the core of the Fourth Amendment is the concept of reasonableness. Thus, it is reasonable to search an arrestee and items within the arrestee's immediate reach. The justifications that make such a search reasonable obviously do not apply to the search of areas to which the accused does not have ready physical access. This is not enough, however, to prove such searches unconstitutional. The Court has always held, therefore, that when there is probable cause to search, and it is "impracticable" for one reason or another to get a search warrant, a warrantless search may be reasonable. This reasonableness principle is true independently of whether an arrest has been made. Although a search will not be reasonable absent probable cause to believe that seizable items are on the premises, when there are exigent circumstances and probable cause together, a warrantless search may be reasonable. This case provides a good illustration that it is unreasonable to require police to leave the scene of an arrest to obtain a search warrant when they already have probable cause to search a premises, and there is a clear danger that the items for which they may reasonably search will be removed before they return with a warrant. When, as here, the existence of probable cause is independently established and would justify a warrant for a broader search for evidence, precedent should be followed, and the Court should permit such a search to be carried out without a warrant, where, as here, the arrest supplies an exigent circumstance justifying police action before any evidence can be removed. Moreover, the search in the arrestee's presence alerts the suspect to the search, so that the arrestee can immediately seek both judicial determination of probable cause in an adversary proceeding and appropriate redress. Such an approach would not authorize the type of search pursuant to a general warrant against which the Fourth Amendment was intended to guard. It would permit no broader a search than police could conduct with a warrant that would be required if no exigent circumstances were involved. An arrest provides exigent circumstances, however, because the police already have gained entry to the premises to effect the arrest, and because delaying the search to secure a warrant would involve the risk of not recovering the fruits of the crime.

ANALYSIS

The Court acknowledged that another reason it overruled *United States v. Rabinowitz*, 339 U.S. 56 (1950), and *Harris v. United States*, 331 U.S. 145 (1947), was that the warrantless search doctrine under those decisions gave law enforcement officials the opportunity to engage in searches not justified by probable cause, merely by the expedient of arranging to arrest suspects at home rather than elsewhere. As the renowned jurist, Judge Learned Hand, astutely observed, "After arresting a man in his house, to rummage at will among his papers in search of whatever will convict him, appears to us to be indistinguishable from what might be done under a general warrant; indeed, the warrant would give more protection, for presumably it must be issued by a magistrate. True, by hypothesis the power would not exist, if the supposed offender were not found on the premises; but it is small consolation to know that one's papers are safe only so long as one is not at home." *United States v. Kirschenblatt*, 16 F.2d 202 (1926).

Quicknotes

CERTIORARI A discretionary writ issued by a superior court to an inferior court in order to review the lower court's decisions; the U.S. Supreme Court's writ ordering such review.

FOURTH AMENDMENT Provides that persons be secure as to their person and private belongings against unreasonable searches and seizures.

LAWFUL ARREST The lawful deprivation of a person's liberty pursuant to a valid warrant, probable cause that the person has committed a criminal offense, or pursuant to some other authority conferred by law.

Riley v. California

Arrestee (D) v. State (P)

573 U.S. 373 (2014)

NATURE OF CASE: Appeals in consolidated cases challenging the warrantless searches of cell phones of arrestees.

FACT SUMMARY: Police conducted warrantless searches of cell phones of arrestees, who moved to suppress incriminating evidence found during the searches.

RULE OF LAW

A warrant generally is required prior to a law enforcement search of a cell phone seized incident to an arrest.

FACTS: In the first case, police stopped Riley (D) on a traffic violation, searched the car, and arrested him for possession of concealed and loaded firearms. The officer seized Riley's (D) cell phone incident to the arrest and accessed information on the phone. The information showed what appeared to be Riley's (D) affiliation with the Bloods gang. Law enforcement later searched the digital data more thoroughly and found a photograph that led to additional charges against Riley (D). Riley (D) moved to suppress the cell phone evidence as a search in violation of the Fourth Amendment because it was warrantless and there were no exigent circumstances justifying the search, but the trial court denied the motion. Riley (D) was convicted, the California Court of Appeal affirmed, and the California Supreme Court denied review. The United States Supreme Court granted certiorari.

In the second case, a police officer observed Wurie (D) making a drug sale from his car. The officers arrested Wurie (D) and seized two cell phones incident to the arrest. At the station, one phone continually received calls from "My House." The officers reviewed the phone data and found information leading them to Wurie's (D) residence where they secured his apartment, obtained a search warrant, and found drugs and firearms. Wurie (D) was charged and he moved to suppress the cell phone search. The district court denied his motion; Wurie (D) was convicted. [The court of appeals reversed the denial of Wurie's (D) motion and vacated the convictions that resulted from the cell phone search.] The United States Supreme Court granted certiorari and consolidated the two cases.

ISSUE: Is a warrant generally required prior to a law enforcement search of a cell phone seized incident to an arrest?

HOLDING AND DECISION: (Roberts, C.J.) Yes. A warrant generally is required prior to a law enforcement search of a cell phone seized incident to an arrest. The Fourth Amendment generally requires a warrant for law enforcement searches to be reasonable. There are specific exceptions to the warrant requirement, and a search incident to arrest is such an exception. This Court has a trilogy of precedential cases related to such searches. *Chimel v. California*, 395 U.S. 752 (1969), laid the groundwork for analyzing the reasonableness of warrantless searches incident to arrest. *Chimel* held it is reasonable for the arresting officer to search the person and the area within his immediate control for the officer's safety and to prevent concealment or destruction of evidence. An extensive search of an arrestee's home is not reasonable. In *United States v. Robinson*, 414 U.S. 218 (1973), it was held that it is not necessary for officers to conduct a case-by-case adjudication to determine the probability in a particular arrest situation whether an arrestee would have weapons or destructible evidence. Thus, an officer's opening of a cigarette package seized from an arrestee was reasonable even though it was unlikely the package contained a weapon or evidence related to the arrestee's traffic crime. Finally, in *Arizona v. Gant*, 556 U.S. 332 (2009), the Court authorized searches of vehicles when the arrestee is unsecured and within reaching distance of the passenger compartment or when it is reasonable to believe evidence relevant to the crime of arrest might be in the vehicle. The Founders could not have conceived of the technology encased in a modern cell phone, so the Court is left without founding guidance. The Court must balance the privacy interests of the individual with the degree to which the digital data is needed for the promotion of legitimate governmental interests. Here, harm to officers and destruction of evidence are not present risks when searching digital data. Given the unique nature of smart phones and the trove of personal and private data they can contain, a mechanical application of *Robinson* thus cannot be extended to cell phone data searches, although the Government (P) may inspect the physical phone and its case to ensure they do not contain any weapons or anything that could endanger officers. In considering *Chimel* concerns, the cell phone data cannot be used as a weapon against the officer and destruction of evidence on a cell phone, while possible, is neither prevalent nor unpreventable. To the extent that a search of cell phone data might warn officers of an impending danger, e.g., that the arrestee's confederates are headed to the scene, such a concern is better addressed through consideration of case-specific exceptions to the warrant requirement, such as exigent circumstances. The Government (P) also raises the possibility of remote wiping or encryption, but there

Continued on next page.

are ways to get around those possibilities. In any event, law enforcement's remaining concerns about remote wiping or encryption in a particular case might be addressed by responding in a targeted manner to urgent threats of such activity. Although an arrestee has diminished privacy interests, a search of a cell phone is a massive intrusion into a person's private life. A cell phone regularly contains highly private documents, such as financial materials, photographs, records of entire conversations among individuals, and data about the owner's daily life. Moreover, data on the phone can date back for years. In addition, an element of pervasiveness characterizes cell phones but not physical records. A decade ago officers might have occasionally stumbled across a highly personal item such as a diary, but today many of the more than 90 percent of American adults who own cell phones keep on their person a digital record of nearly every aspect of their lives. Further, the information on the cell phone may not only be on the actual cell phone but might be pulled from cloud computing, which is an additional search. Fallback options offered by the Government (P) are flawed and contravene the Court's general preference to provide clear guidance to law enforcement through categorical rules. One possible rule is to import the *Gant* standard from the vehicle context and allow a warrantless search of an arrestee's cell phone whenever it is reasonable to believe that the phone contains evidence of the crime of arrest. That proposal is not appropriate in this context and would prove no practical limit at all when it comes to cell phone searches. Another possible rule is to restrict the scope of a cell phone search to information relevant to the crime, the arrestee's identity, or officer safety. That proposal would again impose few meaningful constraints on officers. It is unlikely someone would have been carrying a phone book, photo album, and video tape on his person, but that is exactly what is contained in a cell phone. It also would invite difficult line-drawing expeditions as law enforcement determined whether letters were pre-digital emails or voicemails were pre-digital telephone slips. While the Court's holding will have an impact on law enforcement's ability to combat crime, the holding is not that the information on a cell phone is immune from search; it is that a warrant is generally required before a search. The warrant requirement is an important component of Fourth Amendment jurisprudence, and warrants may be obtained with increasing efficiency. In addition, although the search incident to arrest exception does not apply to cell phones, the continued availability of the exigent circumstances exception may give law enforcement a justification for a warrantless search in particular cases. Reversed (*Riley*); affirmed (*Wurie*).

CONCURRENCE: (Alito, J.) The search incident to arrest predates the Fourth Amendment by at least a century. Nothing indicates it should be based exclusively on officer safety or destruction of evidence. Nevertheless, that rule should not be mechanically applied to cell phones. The Court balances in favor of privacy interests although that approach leads to anomalies. One person carrying a physical phone log can have that log searched, but the same phone log on a cell phone cannot be searched without a warrant. There is no workable alternative, however. Nonetheless, the question presented here could be reconsidered if either Congress or state legislatures, after assessing the legitimate needs of law enforcement and the privacy interests of cell phone owners, enact legislation that draws reasonable distinctions based on categories of information or perhaps other variables.

ANALYSIS

The United States Supreme Court noted nearly 90 percent of Americans carry a cell phone, and, of those phones a large percentage are "smart" phones containing a massive amount of personal data. A warrantless search of a cell phone is the modern equivalent of an extensive search of a person's home and office and could be considered similar to a wiretap as many people carry around records of their text messages and voicemails. Law enforcement now has to distinguish between physical items (e.g., the cell phone itself as a possible weapon) and the data on those items (e.g., photographs, call logs) for warrant purposes.

Quicknotes

SEARCH INCIDENT TO A LAWFUL ARREST Exception to the requirement of a valid warrant for a search or seizure so long as the officer is lawfully in the location where the evidence is obtained, and it is apparent that the thing seized is evidence.

New York v. Belton

State (P) v. Jacket owner (D)

453 U.S. 454 (1981)

NATURE OF CASE: Appeal from exclusion of evidence.

FACT SUMMARY: After stopping a car for speeding, police, who smelled marijuana smoke in the car, found marijuana on the floor of the car and, after arresting the occupants, searched the pockets of Belton's (D) jacket in the back seat, there finding cocaine.

RULE OF LAW

When police have made a lawful custodial arrest of the occupant of an automobile, they may, as a contemporaneous incident of that arrest, search the passenger compartment of the automobile.

FACTS: Belton (D) and others were traveling on the New York State Thruway at an excessive rate of speed in an automobile. A State Trooper in an unmarked police car pulled the vehicle over and smelled marijuana smoke. He determined that none of the four occupants owned the car. He also noticed an envelope marked "Supergold" on the floor of the car. He arrested the four men and examined the envelope, which contained marijuana. He then searched the back seat of the car, having removed the men to the police vehicle, and unzipped the pocket of Belton's (D) jacket lying there. It contained cocaine. The trial court denied Belton's (D) motion to suppress the cocaine, but the New York court of appeals reversed. The United States Supreme Court granted certiorari.

ISSUE: When police have made a lawful custodial arrest of the occupant of an automobile, may they, as a contemporaneous incident of that arrest, search the passenger compartment of the automobile?

HOLDING AND DECISION: (Stewart, J.) Yes. When police have made a lawful custodial arrest of the occupant of an automobile, they may, as a contemporaneous incident of that arrest, search the passenger compartment of the automobile. No straightforward rule has emerged regarding the proper scope of a search of the interior of an automobile incident to a lawful custodial arrest of its occupants. In *Chimel v. California*, 395 U.S. 752 (1969), this Court held that a search of the passenger compartment of an automobile is justified because it is within the reach of the arrestee, who may reach somewhere within that area to grab a weapon. The jacket in this case was in the passenger compartment of the car, where Belton (D) had just been located and could have had immediate access before he was removed. Reversed.

DISSENT: (Brennan, J.) The Court turns back today on the careful analysis produced by *Chimel v. California* and applies an arbitrary rule extending to recent occupants of automobiles. This rule fails to reflect the policy behind *Chimel*. While in *Chimel* the arrestee was within reach of the area searched at the time of the arrest, Belton (D) in this case was handcuffed in a patrol car while the passenger compartment of the car in which he had been riding was searched. The upholding of this search is a wholesale retreat from this Court's carefully developed search-incident-to-arrest analysis.

DISSENT: (White, J.) This Court's present holding, as applied to luggage, briefcases, or other containers, is too extreme an extension of *Chimel*. Here, searches of luggage, briefcases, and other containers in the interior of a vehicle are authorized even in the absence of any suspicion whatsoever that they contain anything in which the police have a legitimate interest. More judicial caution is called for.

ANALYSIS

The underlying policy for permitting the search of an area within the control of an arrestee was the protection of the arresting officers from the arrestee, who might grab a weapon and attack. A further justification announced in *Chimel v. California* 395 U.S. 752 (1969), was the possibility that the arrestee may quickly reach for and destroy a small piece of evidence. Neither of these reasons is furthered by the *Belton* rule, which squares neither with constitutional law history nor Justice Stewart's own opinion in *Robbins v. California*, 453 U.S. 420 (1981).

Quicknotes

CERTIORARI A discretionary writ issued by a superior court to an inferior court in order to review the lower court's decisions; the U.S. Supreme Court's writ ordering such review.

CONTEMPORANEOUS At the same time.

Arizona v. Gant

State (P) v. Individual (D)

556 U.S. 332 (2009)

NATURE OF CASE: Appeal from state high court decision in favor of defendant.

FACT SUMMARY: Local police arrested Gant (D) for an outstanding warrant for driving without a license. After the police placed Gant (D) in a police vehicle, a subsequent search of Gant's (D) vehicle revealed cocaine and a handgun.

RULE OF LAW

Police may search the passenger compartment of a vehicle incident to an occupant's arrest only if the occupant may have access to the vehicle or if it is reasonable to believe the vehicle contains evidence of the offense for which the occupant was arrested.

FACTS: After receiving a tip that a house was being used to distribute drugs, Tucson police officers approached the house and spoke to Gant (D). The police then left the house and conducted a records-check on Gant (D), which revealed he had an outstanding warrant for driving with a suspended license. The police went back to the house. While they were there, Gant (D) drove into the driveway. Upon recognizing Gant (D), the police immediately arrested him on the outstanding warrant. The arrest took place 10 to 15 feet away from Gant's (D) vehicle. The police then placed Gant (D) in a patrol car and searched his vehicle. The search revealed a handgun and cocaine. At trial, Gant (D) moved to suppress the evidence on the grounds police did not have probable cause for the search. The trial court denied his motion, but the Arizona Supreme Court found the search was unreasonable. The State (P) appealed.

ISSUE: May police search the passenger compartment of a vehicle incident to an occupant's arrest only if the occupant may have access to the vehicle or if it is reasonable to believe the vehicle contains evidence of the offense for which the occupant was arrested?

HOLDING AND DECISION: (Stevens, J.) Yes. Police may search the passenger compartment of a vehicle incident to an occupant's arrest only if the occupant may have access to the vehicle or if it is reasonable to believe the vehicle contains evidence of the offense for which the occupant was arrested. In *New York v. Belton*, 453 U.S. 454 (1981), this Court held that searches incident to arrest may include the interior of a vehicle because of the assumption that the interior includes an area that an arrestee may reach, to either destroy evidence or retrieve a weapon. Over the past 28 years, however, *Belton* has been construed to allow all searches of a motor vehicle incident to an arrest, regardless of whether an arrestee may actually have access to the interior to the vehicle. *Belton* should not be interpreted so broadly. Rather, a search of a vehicle may be conducted only where the arrestee has actual access to the vehicle or if there is reason to believe the vehicle contains evidence related to the offense of the arrest. Here, Gant (D) was already handcuffed and in the patrol car at the time of the search. There was no way he could access the vehicle. Second, the police arrested Gant (D) for driving with a suspended license. The vehicle would not contain any additional evidence related to that offense. Accordingly, the search was unreasonable. Affirmed.

CONCURRENCE: (Scalia, J.) This case concerns only those searches conducted after police make an arrest. There is some fear that the Court's abandonment of *Belton's* bright-line rule may actually invite officers to leave a scene unsecured in order to conduct a search. *Belton* should be overruled in its entirety and the following new rule should be followed. Vehicle searches following arrests are reasonable only when the object of the search is evidence of the crime related to the arrest. Because there could be no evidence related to Gant's (D) arrest in the vehicle, the search of his vehicle was unlawful. The majority opinion will also better protect citizens from possible unlawful searches, which would likely occur if the dissent's view of the case was adopted.

DISSENT: (Breyer, J.) This is not a case of first impression. Principles of stare decisis apply, and the Court should follow the *Belton* rule and find the search reasonable. Circumstances can exist that allow the Court to overrule prior decisions, but none of those circumstances are present here.

DISSENT: (Alito, J.) The *Belton* holding was clear and unequivocal. That case held whenever an officer makes an arrest of a person from a vehicle, the officer may search the passenger compartment of the arrestee's vehicle. The Court adopted that course because it established a bright-line rule that was easily followed by law enforcement. The Court did not limit its holding with reference to when a search was made. This Court should adhere to *Belton* because of law enforcement's reliance on the rule for the past 28 years. Circumstances have not changed since *Belton* that dictate a change in the law, nor has the *Belton* rule become unworkable. For these reasons, this Court

Continued on next page.

is bound by stare decisis. The Court should have found the search of Gant's (D) vehicle reasonable and consistent with the *Belton* rule.

ANALYSIS

This decision limited the holding in *New York v. Belton,* 453 U.S. 454 (1981), regarding the ability to search vehicles incident to arrests. However, Justice Scalia's point regarding the limited applicability of the decision is significant. This decision applies only to searches following arrests. It does not apply to those situations where officers ask an occupant to step out of a vehicle and a search is conducted without an arrest being made. Those types of searches are not implicated here.

Quicknotes

BRIGHT-LINE RULE A legal rule of decision to help resolve ambiguous issues simply and in a straightforward manner, sometimes sacrificing equity for certainty.

PROBABLE CAUSE A reasonable basis for believing that a crime has been committed.

SEARCH INCIDENT TO A LAWFUL ARREST Exception to the requirement of a valid warrant for a search or seizure so long as the officer is lawfully in the location where the evidence is obtained and it is apparent that the thing seized is evidence.

STARE DECISIS Doctrine whereby courts follow legal precedent unless there is good cause for departure.

Whren v. United States

Driver of truck (D) v. Federal government (P)

517 U.S. 806 (1996)

NATURE OF CASE: Appeal challenging determinations that a police search was constitutional under the Fourth Amendment.

FACT SUMMARY: Whren (D) challenged the constitutionality of a police search of his car, wherein narcotics were found, when the police stopped him for a traffic violation.

RULE OF LAW

The temporary detention of a motorist who the police have probable cause to believe has committed a civil traffic violation is consistent with the Fourth Amendment.

FACTS: On June 10, 1993, plainclothes vice-squad officers patrolled a "high drug area" of Washington, D.C. The police saw Whren (D) sitting at a stop sign in a truck for an unusually long time. When the police approached, Whren (D) turned right without signaling and sped off at an "unreasonable" speed. When the police stopped Whren (D), they looked in the car and saw bags of crack cocaine. When Whren (D) was arrested on narcotics charges, he challenged the legality of the stop, stating the police had no probable cause to search the car. Whren (D) claimed the police's reasons for the stop—traffic violations—were pretextual and that in this circumstance, a stricter, "objective officer" rule should govern whether the search was legal. The district court convicted Whren (D) of the narcotics charges and the appellate court affirmed. Whren (D) appealed.

ISSUE: Is the temporary detention of a motorist who the police have probable cause to believe has committed a civil traffic violation is consistent with the Fourth Amendment's prohibition against unreasonable seizures?

HOLDING AND DECISION: (Scalia, J.) Yes. The temporary detention of a motorist who the police have probable cause to believe has committed a civil traffic violation is consistent with the Fourth Amendment. Here, Whren (D) had violated traffic laws and, as such, the police had the right to stop him to give him a citation. The fact that such violations occur routinely does not warrant a different standard as to whether the search was constitutional. Even though the police were plainclothes officers, they still had the right to stop a motorist who violates traffic laws. An officer's motive does not automatically invalidate objectively justifiable behavior under the Fourth Amendment. Intentional discrimination in the application of a law is a Fifth Amendment Equal Protection question, not a Fourth Amendment search and seizure question, and does not apply to the case at hand. Searches are subject to a reasonableness standard, but where probable cause has existed, balancing tests have been applied only where the search and seizure has been extraordinary. Here, the traffic violation warranted the probable cause and the police properly seized the narcotics in plain view. Affirmed.

ANALYSIS

This case highlights certain Fourth Amendment search and seizure issues in the context of automobiles. While the Fourth Amendment usually requires police to obtain search warrants before conducting a search, the easy mobility of automobiles often permits searches without warrants if the police have probable cause to search the vehicle. Occasions where warrantless searches have been allowed involved searches incident to arrest and searches to prevent the loss of evidence. See *Application of Kiser*, 419 F.2d 1134 (8th Cir. 1969); *Carroll v. U.S.*, 267 U.S. 132 (1925).

Quicknotes

AUTOMOBILE STOP A police officer may stop an automobile and conduct a search of the vehicle without a valid warrant if he or she has probable cause to believe the vehicle contains evidence of a crime or contraband.

PROBABLE CAUSE A reasonable basis for believing that a crime has been committed.

Chambers v. Maroney

Robbery suspect (D) v. Court (P)

399 U.S. 42 (1970)

NATURE OF CASE: Appeal from robbery conviction.

FACT SUMMARY: Chambers (D) contended that the search of an automobile taken to the station house after his arrest was invalid.

RULE OF LAW

Where there is probable cause to believe that vehicles are carrying contraband or fruits of the crime, warrantless searches of automobiles are permissible, even where the car itself is seized and held without a warrant for whatever period is necessary to obtain a warrant for the search.

FACTS: Chambers (D) was indicted for robbing two gas stations. Partially because of a witness's statement that one of the robbers was wearing a green sweater and that the robbers were driving a station wagon, Chambers (D) was arrested, and the station wagon was taken to the police station and searched. There was no warrant. Search of the station wagon revealed evidence linking Chambers (D) with the crimes. The materials taken from the station wagon were admitted into evidence. Chambers (D) was convicted, and sentenced to prison. Chambers (D) did not take a direct appeal from these convictions but applied for a writ of habeas corpus. After state and federal appeals courts denied granting the writ, the United States Supreme Court granted certiorari.

ISSUE: Where there is probable cause to believe that vehicles are carrying contraband or fruits of the crime, are warrantless searches of automobiles permissible, even where the car itself is seized and held without a warrant for whatever period is necessary to obtain a warrant for the search?

HOLDING AND DECISION: (White, J.) Yes. Where there is probable cause to believe that vehicles are carrying contraband or fruits of the crime, warrantless searches of automobiles are permissible, even where the car itself is seized and held without a warrant for whatever period is necessary to obtain a search warrant. Automobiles may be searched without a warrant in circumstances where the intrusion would not be permissible for a house. The opportunity to search a car is fleeting since it is movable. Here, the station wagon could have been searched on the spot since there was probable cause to search and it was a fleeting target for a search. Affirmed.

CONCURRENCE AND DISSENT: (Harlan, J.) Seizure of the car for the period necessary to enable the officers to obtain a warrant is the lesser intrusion and, therefore, the more desirable action. The Court's approval of a warrantless search in this instance is not consistent with the Fourth Amendment's mandate of obedience to judicial procedure. This is so where the lesser intrusion is available.

ANALYSIS

This case is in accord with the proposition that the Fourth Amendment is less strict with cars than it is with homes. The movability of the car, the lesser aspect of privacy, and the plain view of the auto on the highway contribute to this.

Quicknotes

CERTIORARI A discretionary writ issued by a superior court to an inferior court in order to review the lower court's decisions; the U.S. Supreme Court's writ ordering such review.

WRIT OF HABEAS CORPUS A proceeding in which a defendant brings a writ to compel a judicial determination of whether he or she is lawfully being held in custody.

California v. Carney

State (P) v. Motor home drug dealer (D)

471 U.S. 386 (1985)

NATURE OF CASE: Appeal from conviction for drug trafficking.

FACT SUMMARY: Carney (D) was accused of trading drugs for sexual favors.

RULE OF LAW

The "automobile exception" to the warrant requirement applies to motor homes.

FACTS: A Drug Enforcement Agency (DEA) agent placed the motor home of Carney (D) under surveillance. When a youth exited the motor home, he was stopped by Williams, a DEA agent. The youth told him that he had received marijuana in return for sexual favors. Williams and other agents searched the motor home and found marijuana and related paraphernalia. Carney (D) was charged with possession for sale. He moved to suppress the evidence as the agents did not have a search warrant. The trial court denied the motion, but the California Supreme Court reversed.

ISSUE: Does the "automobile exception" to the warrant requirement apply to motor homes?

HOLDING AND DECISION: (Burger, C.J.) Yes. The "automobile exception" to the warrant requirement applies to motor homes. The reason for the exception is twofold. Autos are inherently mobile and can be taken away before a warrant is issued. Also, autos, unlike homes, are subject to regulations that lower the owner's expectation of privacy. The motor home here, while having homelike qualities, is also inherently mobile and is subject to the same state licensing as a regular automobile. Therefore, the rationales for the auto exception apply to mobile homes. Reversed.

DISSENT: (Stevens, J.) Where, as here, agents have the element of surprise on their side, and the motor home is parked, the exigencies justifying the auto exception do not apply.

ANALYSIS

While auto searches do not require warrants, probable cause is still necessary. For this reason, the scope of an auto search is limited. It may not be more intrusive than that necessary to obtain the required evidence.

Quicknotes

AUTOMOBILE EXCEPTION Exception to the requirement of a valid warrant; if a police officer has probable cause to believe that a vehicle contains evidence of a crime or contraband, the officer may search the entire vehicle.

EXIGENT CIRCUMSTANCES Circumstances requiring an extraordinary or immediate response; an exception to the prohibition on a warrantless arrest or search when police officers believe probable cause to exist and there is no time for obtaining a warrant.

PROBABLE CAUSE A reasonable basis for believing that a crime has been committed.

United States v. Chadwick

Federal government (P) v. Accused drug trafficker (D)

433 U.S. 1 (1977)

NATURE OF CASE: Appeal from district court judgment dismissing charges of marijuana possession.

FACT SUMMARY: Chadwick (D) and his confederates were arrested by federal narcotics agents; an hour and a half later, their footlocker was opened and found to contain marijuana.

RULE OF LAW

The "automobile exception" permitting warrantless searches of vehicles in certain narrow circumstances does not apply to searches of luggage.

FACTS: Narcotics agents in San Diego observed the suspicious behavior of two persons (D) carrying a footlocker on a train bound for Boston. They alerted agents in Boston, who had a dog sniff the footlocker upon its arrival. The dog indicated the presence of drugs without alerting the owners of the locker. Chadwick (D) then joined the two suspects (D), and they placed the footlocker in the trunk of Chadwick's (D) car. The agents then arrested the three suspects (D) and took possession of the footlocker. An hour and a half later, the agents opened the footlocker and discovered large quantities of marijuana. Prior to their trial for drug possession, Chadwick et al. (D) successfully moved to suppress the marijuana. The Government (P) sought review.

ISSUE: Does the "automobile exception" permitting warrantless searches of vehicles in certain narrow circumstances apply to searches of luggage?

HOLDING AND DECISION: (Burger, C.J.) No. The "automobile exception" permitting warrantless searches of vehicles in certain narrow circumstances does not apply to searches of luggage. Luggage and automobiles are not analogous for Fourth Amendment purposes. Luggage contents are not open to public view, and the expectation of privacy is greater in luggage than in an automobile. Once the footlocker was transferred to the agents' control, there was no longer a danger that it would be moved before a warrant could be obtained. Moreover, the search, occurring more than an hour after the arrest of Chadwick et al. (D), was not incident to their arrest. The judgment is affirmed.

CONCURRENCE: (Brennan, J.) It is not at all obvious that the agents could have legally searched the footlocker had they seized it after the suspects (D) had driven away with it in their car or at the time and place of the arrests.

DISSENT: (Blackmun, J.) A warrant is not required to search any movable object in the possession of a person arrested in a public place. Perverse circumstances control the outcome here. If the agents had waited until the suspects (D) drove away, they could have made the arrest, taken the locker to their office and searched it there. Alternatively, the agents could lawfully have searched the footlocker at the scene of the arrest.

ANALYSIS

The dissent is clearly suggesting that the automobile exception would have applied if the agents had stopped Chadwick's (D) vehicle "on the highway" rather than making the arrest before the car was started. However, a subsequent case, implicitly addressing Justice Blackmun's concerns, held that the warrantless search of the respondent's luggage was not lawful merely because the luggage happened to be in respondent's vehicle when it was stopped on the highway.

Quicknotes

SEARCH INCIDENT TO LAWFUL ARREST Exception to the requirement of a valid warrant for a search or seizure so long as the officer is lawfully in the location where the evidence is obtained and it is apparent that the thing seized is evidence.

California v. Acevedo

State (P) v. Paper bag owner (D)

500 U.S. 565 (1991)

NATURE OF CASE: Appeal from the grant of a motion to suppress.

FACT SUMMARY: Without first obtaining a warrant, police officers searched a closed container that Acevedo (D) placed in his trunk.

RULE OF LAW

Police officers may search closed containers within an automobile without a warrant, pursuant to a valid search of the vehicle.

FACTS: Drug enforcement agents intercepted a package of marijuana being sent to Daza and notified Daza when it arrived at Federal Express. Officers followed Daza when he picked up the package and drove it to his apartment. Acevedo (D) arrived at Daza's apartment and left shortly thereafter carrying a paper bag of the same size as the marijuana package. Acevedo (D) placed the bag in the trunk of his car and started to drive away. The officers stopped him and opened the trunk and the bag and found the marijuana. Acevedo (D) claimed that the search of the bag was illegal. The appeals court agreed, and the State (P) appealed.

ISSUE: May police officers search closed containers within an automobile without a warrant, pursuant to a valid search of the vehicle?

HOLDING AND DECISION: (Blackmun, J.) Yes. Police officers may search closed containers within an automobile without a warrant, pursuant to a valid search of the vehicle. Two previous cases decided by this Court have raised some confusion in this area. In *United States v. Chadwick*, 433 U.S. 1 (1977), the Court held that a closed container placed in a car could not be searched without a warrant when there was probable cause only as to the container. On the other hand, in *United States v. Ross*, 456 U.S. 798 (1982), we found that a warrantless search of an automobile could include a search of containers inside when there was probable cause to search the car. The contradiction between these cases could result in officers conducting more intrusive searches as they seek to generate probable cause to search an entire car rather than just a container within the car. Furthermore, the rule in *Chadwick* has not protected privacy and has confused courts and police officers. It is better to adopt a single clear-cut rule to govern auto searches. Thus, the warrant requirement for closed containers set forth in *Chadwick* is overruled. Reversed.

CONCURRENCE: (Scalia, J.) While the dissent makes the correct point that the new rule will produce anomalous results, the Fourth Amendment does not require a prior warrant for searches; it requires only that the search not be unreasonable. This is the concept that should govern this area of the law.

DISSENT: (Stevens, J.) When the police have probable cause to search a particular container, they can seize that container and have no need to search an entire vehicle. The majority opinion creates a situation in which a search of a container is prohibited while the owner is carrying it in the open, but allowed once the owner has placed the container in a locked trunk.

ANALYSIS

This decision does not eliminate challenges based on an excessive search under the auto exception. A defendant may still claim that a search of other areas of a car was invalid if the officers had probable cause with regard to the container only. Lower courts have not been consistent in interpreting the new rule.

Quicknotes

MOTION TO SUPPRESS Motion in a criminal trial to exclude the introduction of evidence that was unlawfully obtained.

PROBABLE CAUSE A reasonable basis for believing that a crime has been committed.

Horton v. California

Homeowner (D) v. State (P)

496 U.S. 128 (1990)

NATURE OF CASE: Appeal from conviction of robbery.

FACT SUMMARY: When the police searched Horton's (D) apartment for proceeds of an armed robbery, they found weapons used in the robbery lying in plain view.

RULE OF LAW
Inadvertence is not a necessary condition of "plain view" seizures.

FACTS: Walker was accosted by two masked men, who threatened him with weapons and robbed him. Walker identified Horton's (D) voice as that of one of the robbers. A search warrant was issued authorizing a search for the proceeds of the robbery, but not for the weapons allegedly used in the commission of the robbery. While searching Horton's (D) apartment, the police found the weapons in question in plain view and seized them. The trial court refused to suppress the evidence found in Horton's (D) home, and he was convicted of armed robbery. The California court of appeal affirmed, rejecting Horton's (D) argument that suppression of the evidence that had not been listed in the warrant was required because its discovery was not inadvertent. The California Supreme Court affirmed. The United States Supreme Court granted certiorari.

ISSUE: Is inadvertence a necessary condition of "plain view" seizures?

HOLDING AND DECISION: (Stevens, J.) No. Inadvertence is not a necessary condition of "plain view" seizures. Evenhanded law enforcement is best achieved by application of the objective standards of conduct, rather than standards that depend upon the subjective state of mind of the officer. The fact that an officer is interested in an item of evidence and expects to find it in the course of a search should not invalidate its seizure if the search is confined in area and duration by the terms of the warrant or a valid exception to the warrant requirement. The suggestion that the inadvertence requirement is necessary to prevent the police from conducting general searches is not persuasive because that interest is already served by the requirements that no warrant issue unless it particularly describes the place to be searched and the persons or things to be seized. Here, the scope of the search was not enlarged in the slightest by the omission of any reference to the weapons in the warrant. Affirmed.

DISSENT: (Brennan, J.) In eschewing the inadvertent discovery requirement, the majority ignores the Fourth Amendment's express command that warrants particularly describe not only the places to be searched, but also the things to be seized.

ANALYSIS

In *Arizona v. Hicks*, 480 U.S. 321 (1987), police, during the execution of a search, moved stereo equipment that they suspected (but lacked probable cause to believe) was stolen in order to gain access to the serial numbers on the back of the equipment. The United States Supreme Court rejected the argument that the plain view doctrine authorized police to move the stereo equipment. It found that if an object is unrelated to the justification for the search and if police do not have probable cause to seize the object, they cannot use the plain view doctrine as an excuse for meddling with the object.

Quicknotes

AFFIDAVIT A declaration of facts written and affirmed before a witness.

EXIGENT CIRCUMSTANCES Circumstances requiring an extraordinary or immediate response; an exception to the prohibition on a warrantless arrest or search when police officers believe probable cause to exist and there is no time for obtaining a warrant.

PLAIN VIEW Exception to the requirement of a valid warrant for a search or seizure so long as the officer is lawfully in the location where the evidence is obtained and it is apparent that the thing seized is evidence.

Arizona v. Hicks

State (P) v. Accused robber (D)

480 U.S. 321 (1987)

NATURE OF CASE: On certiorari from appellate court decision reversing robbery conviction.

FACT SUMMARY: Police conducted a search of Hicks's (D) apartment, moving stereo equipment in order to observe the serial numbers.

RULE OF LAW

Physically moving a suspicious object in an individual's home to determine if it is incriminating evidence, without probable cause, during an unrelated warrantless search, is violative of the Fourth Amendment.

FACTS: Police entered Hicks's (D) apartment after a bullet was fired through the floor of the apartment, injuring a man below. One of the officers observed expensive stereo equipment that seemed out of place in the shabby surroundings. He moved the equipment in order to observe and record its serial numbers. It was later determined that the serial numbers matched those on equipment taken in an armed robbery, and a search warrant was issued and executed.

ISSUE: Is physically moving a suspicious object in an individual's home to determine if it is incriminating evidence without probable cause, during an unrelated warrantless search, violative of the Fourth Amendment?

HOLDING AND DECISION: (Scalia, J.) Yes. Physically moving a suspicious object in an individual's home to determine if it is incriminating evidence, without probable cause, during an unrelated warrantless search, is violative of the Fourth Amendment. The moving of the turntable constituted an invasion of privacy unrelated to the objectives of the search for the shooter. Although the movement was slight, the difference between looking at a suspicious object in plain view and moving it even a few inches is more than trivial for purposes of the Fourth Amendment. Without probable cause, the officer may not search beyond what is already exposed to view. The judgment of the Court of Appeals of Arizona is affirmed.

DISSENT: (Powell, J.) The distinction between looking at a suspicious object in plain view and moving it a few inches trivializes the Fourth Amendment.

DISSENT: (O'Connor, J.) On reasonable suspicion an object is contraband, officers ought to be permitted to conduct a cursory inspection, such as was done here. Probable cause should be required in order to conduct a full-blown search.

ANALYSIS

Justice Scalia rejected Justice O'Connor's "cursory inspection" theory, saying that such a vague standard would plunge police and judges into a "new thicket of Fourth Amendment law." He indicated that society's interests in privacy and the consistent administration of justice required a bright-line rule.

Quicknotes

CONTRABAND Items that are illegal to have in one's possession or to trade or produce.

PROBABLE CAUSE A reasonable basis for believing that a crime has been committed.

REASONABLE SUSPICION That which would cause an ordinary prudent person under the circumstances to suspect that a crime has been committed based on specific and articulable facts.

SEIZURE Under the Fourth Amendment, the application of physical force to the body of a person, or a show of force or authority, intended to restrain a person's liberty Also, as relates to property, the meaningful interference with an individual's possessory interests in that property. Only "unreasonable" seizures by the government are prohibited by the Fourth Amendment.

Schneckloth v. Bustamonte

Court (P) v. Passenger of car (D)

412 U.S. 218 (1973)

NATURE OF CASE: Appeal of writ of habeas corpus from a trial for theft.

FACT SUMMARY: Evidence obtained by a vehicle search after the driver consented to the search by a police officer was used to convict Bustamonte (D), a passenger in the vehicle.

RULE OF LAW

Whether consent to a search was "voluntary" or was the product of duress or coercion, express or implied, is a question of fact to be determined from the totality of all the circumstances.

FACTS: During the course of a consent search of a car that had been stopped for traffic violations, evidence was discovered that was used to convict Bustamonte (D), a passenger in the car, of unlawfully possessing a check. The police officer who had stopped the car asked the driver if he could search the car and was told, "Sure, go ahead." Evidence from the search (stolen checks found under the rear seat) resulted in Bustamonte's (D) conviction. The officer had initially stopped the car because he noticed that a headlight and the vehicle's license plate light were burned out. Bustamonte (D) brought a petition for habeas corpus. The federal district court denied the petition, and Bustamonte (D) appealed. The Ninth Circuit Court of Appeals vacated the order of the district court and remanded, and the United States Supreme Court granted certiorari.

ISSUE: Is the question whether consent to a search was "voluntary" or was the product of duress or coercion, express or implied, a question of fact to be determined from the totality of all the circumstances?

HOLDING AND DECISION: (Stewart, J.) Yes. Whether consent to a search was "voluntary" or was the product of duress or coercion, express or implied, is a question of fact to be determined from the totality of all the circumstances. Knowledge of the right to refuse consent to a search is one factor to be considered, but the government need not establish such knowledge as the *sine qua non* of an effective, voluntary consent. Two competing concerns must be accommodated in determining the meaning of a "voluntary" consent to a search: the legitimate need for such searches and the equally important requirement of assuring the absence of coercion. The Fourth and Fourteenth Amendments require that a consent to a search not be coerced, by explicit or implicit means, by implied threat or covert force. Furthermore, in examining all the surrounding circumstances to determine if, in fact, consent to a search were coerced, account must be taken of subtly coercive police questions, as well as the possibly vulnerable subjective state of the person who consents. Our decision today is a narrow one. We hold only that when the subject of a search is not in custody and the state attempts to justify a search on the basis of his or her consent, the Fourth and Fourteenth Amendments require that it demonstrate that the consent was in fact voluntarily given, and not the result of duress or coercion, express or implied. Voluntariness is a question of fact to be determined from all the circumstances, and while the subject's knowledge of a right to refuse is a factor to be considered, the prosecution is not required to demonstrate such knowledge as a prerequisite to establishing a voluntary consent. Here, because the California court followed these principles in affirming Bustamonte's (D) conviction, and because the Ninth Circuit Court of Appeals in remanding for an evidentiary hearing required more, its judgment must be reversed.

DISSENT: (Marshall, J.) This Court is authorizing law enforcement personnel to take advantage of lack of knowledge of citizens to achieve by ploy what they could not accomplish by relying only on the knowing relinquishment of constitutional rights. Of course, it would be "practical" for the police to ignore the commands of the Fourth Amendment, if by practicality we mean that more criminals will be apprehended, even though the constitutional rights of innocent people also are ignored. Such advantage is achieved, however, at the cost of permitting the police to ignore constitutional limitations on their conduct.

ANALYSIS

In *Schneckloth*, the United States Supreme Court noted that a strict standard of waiver has been applied to those rights guaranteed to criminal defendants to ensure that they will be accorded the greatest possible opportunity to utilize every facet of the constitutional model of a fair criminal trial. Any trial conducted in derogation of that model leaves open the possibility that the trial reached an unfair result precisely because all the protections specified in the Constitution were not provided. A prime example, said the Court, is the right to counsel since without this right, wholly innocent accuseds face the

Continued on next page.

real and substantial danger that simply because of their lack of legal expertise they may be convicted.

Quicknotes

CERTIORARI A discretionary writ issued by a superior court to an inferior court in order to review the lower court's decisions; the U.S. Supreme Court's writ ordering such review.

COERCION The overcoming of a person's free will as a result of threats, promises, or undue influence.

DURESS Unlawful threats or other coercive behavior by one person that causes another to commit acts he or she would not otherwise do.

EVIDENTIARY HEARING Hearing pertaining to the evidence of the case.

FOURTEENTH AMENDMENT Declares that no state shall make or enforce any law that shall abridge the privileges and immunities of citizens of the United States. No state shall deny to any person within its jurisdiction the equal protection of the laws.

FOURTH AMENDMENT Provides that persons be secure as to their person and private belongings against unreasonable searches and seizures.

SINE QUA NON Without which not; a necessary element or requirement.

WRIT OF HABEAS CORPUS A proceeding in which a defendant brings a writ to compel a judicial determination of whether he or she is lawfully being held in custody.

Georgia v. Randolph

State (P) v. Cocaine suspect (D)

547 U.S. 103 (2006)

NATURE OF CASE: Appeal from the state supreme court's ruling that suppressed an illegal warrantless search.

FACT SUMMARY: Police conducted a warrantless search of a premises based on consent by a co-occupant. When the other occupant arrived at the premises, he refused the warrantless search alleging his Fourth Amendment rights were violated. He subsequently sought to have the evidence excluded.

RULE OF LAW

A physically present co-occupant's stated refusal to permit a warrantless entry renders the warrantless search unreasonable and invalid as to such co-occupant.

FACTS: Scott Randolph (D) and his wife were separated. One morning the wife called the police to report domestic violence and that Randolph (D) had taken away their son. When the police responded, she told the police Randolph (D) was a cocaine user. She gave permission to search the house. Randolph (D) returned to the premises before the search and expressly refused a warrantless search. The police, nevertheless, conducted a search based on the wife's permission and discovered cocaine. Randolph (D) was indicted for possession of cocaine. He moved to suppress the evidence as the product of an illegal warrantless search. The trial court denied the motion; however, the Georgia Court of Appeals reversed the denial. The Georgia Supreme Court affirmed the Court of Appeals, and the State (P) took a writ of certiorari to the United States Supreme Court.

ISSUE: Does a physically present co-occupant's stated refusal to permit a warrantless entry render the warrantless search unreasonable and invalid as to such co-occupant?

HOLDING AND DECISION: (Souter, J.) Yes. A physically present co-occupant's stated refusal to permit a warrantless entry renders the warrantless search unreasonable and invalid as to such co-occupant. The instant case calls for straightforward application of the rule that a physically present inhabitant's express refusal to give the police consent to a search is dispositive as to that occupant, regardless of the consent of any fellow occupant. The record here reveals no indication the consenter (the wife) indicated any need for her protection inside the house that might have justified a police entry into the area where the cocaine was found, nor were any exigent circumstances shown, such as entry to prevent evidence destruction. This case has no bearing on the capacity of the police to protect victims of domestic violence. The undoubted right of the police to enter premises to protect a victim is clear and is not before the Court. In the balancing of competing individual and governmental interests involved with unreasonable searches, a cooperative occupant's invitation to police to enter or search adds nothing as to co-occupants. Accordingly, disputed permission is no match for the Fourth Amendment. Affirmed.

CONCURRENCE: (Breyer, J.) Here, the totality of the circumstances fails to justify abandonment of the Fourth Amendment's long-established hostility to entry by law enforcement officers into a home without a warrant.

DISSENT: (Roberts, C.J.) Today's rule serves not to interpret the Fourth Amendment to protect privacy but rather to afford its protections on a random and happenstance basis. Great is the cost of providing such random protection.

ANALYSIS

As the United States Supreme Court notes in its *Randolph* decision, the constant element in assessing Fourth Amendment reasonableness in consent cases is the great significance given to widely shared social expectations that are naturally influenced by property law but not totally controlled by its rules.

Quicknotes

CERTIORARI A discretionary writ issued by a superior court to an inferior court in order to review the lower court's decisions; the U.S. Supreme Court's writ ordering such review.

EXIGENT CIRCUMSTANCES Circumstances requiring an extraordinary or immediate response; an exception to the prohibition on a warrantless arrest or search when police officers believe probable cause to exist and there is no time for obtaining a warrant.

FOURTH AMENDMENT Provides that persons be secure as to their person and private belongings against unreasonable searches and seizures.

Illinois v. Rodriguez

State (P) v. Apartment owner (D)

497 U.S. 177 (1990)

NATURE OF CASE: Appeal from acquittal for possession of controlled substance.

FACT SUMMARY: Rodriguez (D) was arrested after Gail Fischer gave the police entry to Rodriguez's (D) apartment.

RULE OF LAW

A warrantless entry is valid when based upon the consent of a third party who the police at the time of the entry reasonably believe has common authority over the premises.

FACTS: Rodriguez (D) was arrested in his apartment by the police and charged with possession of illegal drugs. The police gained entry to Rodriguez's (D) apartment with the assistance of one Gail Fischer. Fischer had referred to the residence as "our" apartment. The police did not obtain an arrest warrant for Rodriguez (D) or seek a search warrant for the apartment. After Fischer let them in, the police found cocaine. The officers arrested Rodriguez (D). Rodriguez (D) was charged with possession of a controlled substance. Rodriguez (D) attempted to suppress all evidence seized at the apartment, claiming that Fischer had vacated the apartment several weeks earlier and had no authority to consent to the police entry. The Cook County court found that Fischer was not a usual resident but rather an infrequent visitor. The court rejected Illinois's (P) contention that, even if Fischer did not possess common authority over the premises, there was no Fourth Amendment violation if the police reasonably believed that Fischer possessed the authority to consent. The appellate court affirmed. The United States Supreme Court granted certiorari.

ISSUE: Is a warrantless entry valid when based upon the consent of a third party who the police at the time of the entry reasonably believe has common authority over the premises?

HOLDING AND DECISION: (Scalia, J.) Yes. A warrantless entry is valid when based upon the consent of a third party who the police at the time of the entry reasonably believe has common authority over the premises. Common authority rests on mutual use of property by persons generally having joint access to the premises. In order to satisfy the "reasonableness" standard of the Fourth Amendment, it is not that the magistrate issuing a warrant or the police officer conducting a search always be correct, but that they always be reasonable. Here, the appellate court found it unnecessary to determine whether the officers reasonably believed Fischer had the authority to consent because it ruled as a matter of law that a reasonable belief could not validate the entry. Remanded for reconsideration of this question.

DISSENT: (Marshall, J.) In the absence of an exigency, warrantless home searches and seizures are unreasonable under the Fourth Amendment. The weighty constitutional interest in preventing unauthorized intrusions into the home overrides any law enforcement interest in relying on the reasonable but potentially mistaken belief that a third party has authority to consent to such a search or seizure.

ANALYSIS

A Wisconsin regulation allowing a probation officer to search a probationer's residence without a warrant if there are reasonable grounds to believe the probationer has contraband does not violate the Fourth Amendment. The special needs of the probation system justify departure from the requirements of a warrant and probable cause. *Griffin v. Wisconsin*, 483 U.S. 868 (1987).

Quicknotes

CONSENT A voluntary and willful agreement by an individual possessing sufficient mental capacity to undertake an action suggested by another.

EXIGENT CIRCUMSTANCES Circumstances requiring an extraordinary or immediate response; an exception to the prohibition on a warrantless arrest or search when police officers believe probable cause to exist and there is no time for obtaining a warrant.

EXPECTATION OF PRIVACY Requirement that in order to invoke the Fourth Amendment's protection against unreasonable searches and seizures, the individual must have a reasonable expectation of privacy in respect to the location searched or thing seized.

Terry v. Ohio

Criminal defendant (D) v. State (P)

392 U.S. 1 (1968)

NATURE OF CASE: Review of order denying motion to suppress in prosecution for carrying concealed weapons.

FACT SUMMARY: Terry (D), who was frisked by a police officer, contended that such a procedure could not have been performed absent probable cause to arrest.

RULE OF LAW

Police may stop and frisk an individual who they reasonably suspect may be armed and dangerous, even if probable cause to arrest is not present.

FACTS: McFadden, a police detective of 35 years' experience, was patrolling his beat on foot when he observed Terry (D) and another man repeatedly strolling by a store, looking in, and then walking away. This continued for over ten minutes. McFadden formed the opinion that they were casing the store. He approached them and asked for identification. When their responses proved evasive, McFadden spun Terry (D) against a wall. Frisking him, he found a gun. Terry (D) was charged with carrying a concealed weapon. His motion to suppress was denied, and the Ohio Supreme Court affirmed. The United States Supreme Court granted review.

ISSUE: May police stop and frisk an individual who they reasonably suspect may be armed and dangerous, even if probable cause to arrest is not present?

HOLDING AND DECISION: (Warren, C.J.) Yes. Police may stop and frisk an individual who they reasonably suspect may be armed and dangerous, even if probable cause to arrest is not present. Competing values are at issue here. On the one hand, the rapidly increasing dangerousness on city streets has created the need for flexible responses on the part of law enforcement. On the other hand, the authority of the police to search a person must be limited to situations when probable cause is present for the Fourth Amendment to have any meaning. Superimposed on this analysis is the limited ability of the judiciary to control day-to-day situations on city streets. The exclusionary rule can go only so far in controlling police conduct. When it cannot do so, its reasons for existence cease. The point of departure for analysis is that the Fourth Amendment's reasonableness requirement remains central. The reasonableness of a stop and frisk depends upon weighing the governmental interest in police and bystander security against a possibly armed criminal and every citizen's interest against police interference. This Court believes that a proper balance between these interests is struck by a rule allowing the minimally intrusive stop and frisk for weapons when an officer suspects, on an objectively reasonable level, that a person may be armed and dangerous. Here, Terry's (D) conduct was sufficiently suggestive of intent to rob that McFadden's belief in this regard was reasonable. The stop, therefore, did not constitute a Fourth Amendment violation. Affirmed.

CONCURRENCE: (Harlan, J.) Once circumstances justify a confrontation with a citizen, the right to frisk naturally flows therefrom.

CONCURRENCE: (White, J.) A person cannot be compelled to cooperate if addressed by an officer, and such refusal cannot in itself furnish a basis for arrest, although it may alert the officer to the need for continued observation.

DISSENT: (Douglas, J.) Nothing less than probable cause can justify forcible detention of an individual.

ANALYSIS

The exclusionary rule is found nowhere in the Constitution. It was created by the Court as a prophylactic measure to advance the rights found in the Fourth Amendment. In the present case, the Court reasoned that when the rule could no longer serve its prophylactic purpose, which is believed to be the case here, it should not be imposed.

Quicknotes

FOURTH AMENDMENT Provides that persons be secure as to their person and private belongings against unreasonable searches and seizures.

***TERRY* STOP** A search of a person suspected of intending to commit a crime that is conducted by patting down the clothes of the person; the search must be limited to the reason for which the individual was lawfully stopped.

Dunaway v. New York

Attempted robbery suspect (D) v. State (P)

442 U.S. 200 (1979)

NATURE OF CASE: Review of conviction obtained after custodial interrogation.

FACT SUMMARY: An inmate provided information insufficient to constitute probable cause that Dunaway (D) was involved in an attempted robbery, and police took Dunaway (D) in and held him where he gave incriminating statements after a *Miranda* warning.

RULE OF LAW

Under the Fourth Amendment, a seizure and transport of a suspect against his will is sufficiently intrusive to require probable cause that the suspect has committed a crime.

FACTS: A police officer told a colleague assigned to an attempted robbery case that he had obtained information that Dunaway (D) had committed the attempt. The investigating officer questioned the source but did not obtain sufficient information to have probable cause that Dunaway (D) was involved in the crime. Nonetheless, the officer had Dunaway (D) arrested from the home of a neighbor and brought in for questioning. Dunaway (D) was advised of his *Miranda* rights and then waived counsel and gave incriminating evidence against himself in the absence of any attorney. Dunaway's (D) motions to suppress the statements and sketches he made were denied, and he was convicted. The New York appellate court affirmed, and the United States Supreme Court granted certiorari and remanded the case. On remand, the county court found that the motions should have been granted. The appellate division reversed, and the United States Supreme Court granted certiorari.

ISSUE: Under the Fourth Amendment, is a seizure and transport of a suspect sufficiently intrusive to require probable cause that the suspect has committed a crime?

HOLDING AND DECISION: (Brennan, J.) Yes. Under the Fourth Amendment, a seizure and transport of a suspect against his will is sufficiently intrusive to require probable cause that the suspect has committed a crime. A suspect may be stopped on less than probable cause if the intrusion into his privacy is less than an arrest. But the stop and frisk exception does not apply in this case. The intrusion upon Dunaway (D) was indistinguishable from arrest. He was taken from his neighbor's home into a car and required to go to the station and be interrogated. He was not "free to go," and physical restraint would have been used to prevent him from going. Under the Fourth Amendment, the seizure and transport of a suspect is sufficiently intrusive to require probable cause that the subject has committed a crime. Here, there was no such probable cause, and the conviction based on evidence obtained by this method must be overturned. Reversed.

CONCURRENCE: (White, J.) The key principle of the Fourth Amendment is reasonableness, namely, the balancing of competing interests. If governmental officials are to have practical rules, this balancing must be properly accomplished, not on a case-by-case basis by individual police officers. It is here sufficient that the police conduct is comparable enough to an arrest that the ordinary level of probable cause is necessary before interests of privacy and personal security be required to yield.

DISSENT: (Rehnquist, J.) The defendant voluntarily accompanied the police to the station to answer their questions. Although a police request to come to the station may be an "awesome experience," such fact alone does not indicate that in every occurrence when a citizen agrees to a police request to come to headquarters, there has been a Fourth Amendment "seizure." The issue turns on whether the officer's conduct is objectively coercive or physically threatening, not on the fact that a person might to some degree be intimidated by an officer's request.

ANALYSIS

The stop and frisk exception to the general rule that probable cause is required for an intrusion into a suspect's privacy depends upon a determination of what is an arrest and what is a mere detention. A detention must be brief and not unreasonably inconvenient under the circumstances. When a person is moved against his or her will, an arrest has usually taken place.

Quicknotes

CUSTODIAL INTERROGATION The questioning of a suspect by police while in custody.

PROBABLE CAUSE A reasonable basis for believing that a crime has been committed.

STOP AND FRISK A brief, non-intrusive stop, requiring the police officer to have a reasonable suspicion that a crime has been committed or is contemplated being committed based on specific and articulable facts, and involving a search for a concealed weapon that is conducted by patting down the clothes of the person.

United States v. Mendenhall

Federal government (P) v. Accused drug trafficker (D)

446 U.S. 544 (1980)

NATURE OF CASE: On petition from judgment of court of appeals overturning conviction for drug possession.

FACT SUMMARY: Drug Enforcement Administration agents conducted a search of Mendenhall (D) without a warrant or probable cause based on her apparent consent.

RULE OF LAW

A person is "seized" within the meaning of the Fourth Amendment only when, in light of all the circumstances, a reasonable person would believe she was not free to leave.

FACTS: Mendenhall (D) was observed by agents of the Drug Enforcement Administration (DEA) at the Detroit Metropolitan Airport exhibiting characteristics of persons unlawfully carrying narcotics. The agents stopped her, identified themselves, and asked to see her airline ticket and identification. The ticket and identification bore different names. One agent asked her to accompany him to the airport DEA office. Once at the office, the agent asked Mendenhall (D) if she would consent to a search of her person and handbag. A policewoman arrived and asked Mendenhall (D) to disrobe. Mendenhall (D) removed her clothes, handed two small packages to the policewoman, and was placed under arrest for possessing heroin.

ISSUE: Is a person "seized" within the meaning of the Fourth Amendment only when, in light of all the circumstances, a reasonable person would believe she was not free to leave?

HOLDING AND DECISION: (Stewart, J.) Yes. A person is "seized" within the meaning of the Fourth Amendment only when, in light of all the circumstances, a reasonable person would believe she was not free to leave. Here, the agents approached Mendenhall (D) in public; they wore no uniforms and displayed no weapons. They asked, but did not demand, to see her identification. Our conclusion that no seizure occurred is not affected by the fact that the agents did not expressly tell Mendenhall (D) she was free to go. The judgment is reversed and remanded to the court of appeals for further proceedings.

CONCURRENCE IN PART: (Powell, J.) This Court should not hold that no seizure occurred; rather, that the agents had reasonable and articulable suspicion that Mendenhall (D) was engaging in criminal activity. They therefore did not violate the Fourth Amendment when they stopped her for routine questioning.

DISSENT: (White, J.) The Government (P) never questioned in the lower courts that a seizure occurred. Having failed to convince the court of appeals that the seizure was justified by reasonable suspicion, the Government (P) now seeks reversal here by claiming no seizure occurred. To the contrary, here the accused's Fourth Amendment interests were indeed implicated, and she was undoubtedly "seized" when the DEA agents escorted her from the public area of the terminal to the DEA office for questioning and a strip-search of her person. Such conduct of the DEA agents was in all important respects indistinguishable from a traditional arrest. She was not free to refuse to go to the DEA office and, once inside, was not permitted to leave.

ANALYSIS

As the dissent observes, five justices held that Mendenhall (D) was lawfully stopped and questioned. However, the justices in the majority disagreed fundamentally on their reasoning. Two justices, announcing the opinion of the United States Supreme Court, decided that no seizure had taken place—and thus did not address the issue of whether such a seizure was justified; the other three justices in the "majority" wrote that Mendenhall (D) was properly seized on reasonable suspicion.

Quicknotes

APPARENT CONSENT The manifestation by actions, or by the failure to act, of an agreement of the minds or of the acquiescence by one party to the will of another.

California v. Hodari D.

State (P) v. Running cocaine possession suspect (D)

499 U.S. 621 (1991)

NATURE OF CASE: Review of order suppressing evidence pursuant to a criminal prosecution.

FACT SUMMARY: Hodari (D) sought to suppress contraband tossed away after a police officer came upon him but prior to his personal restraint.

RULE OF LAW

A defendant's rights against unlawful arrest will not operate to suppress evidence found prior to physical restraint.

FACTS: Two police officers came upon several persons, including Hodari (D), acting in a suspicious manner. When they approached, all took flight. Hodari (D) inadvertently ran in the direction of one officer, whom he did not see until he was almost upon the officer. As soon as he saw the officer, he tossed away an object that later proved to be rock cocaine. Charged with possession, Hodari (D) moved to suppress the evidence on the grounds that the evidence was obtained in an unlawful seizure in violation of the Fourth and Fourteenth Amendments. The trial court denied the motion, but the state court of appeal reversed. The United States Supreme Court granted certiorari.

ISSUE: Will a defendant's right against unlawful arrest operate to suppress evidence found prior to physical restraint?

HOLDING AND DECISION: (Scalia, J.) No. A defendant's right against unlawful arrest will not operate to suppress evidence found prior to physical restraint. The Fourth Amendment protects against unlawful seizure. "Seizure," when applied to the person, as it must be in the context of arrest, can refer only to physical restraint. The term "seizure," as it is commonly understood, implies some form of custody or control. Consequently, any evidence found prior to such custody or control cannot be said to be the fruit of an illegal seizure. Here, Hodari (D) had not been placed under physical restraint when he attempted to conceal the incriminating evidence, so the evidence should not have been suppressed. Reversed.

DISSENT: (Stevens, J.) The Court has essentially concluded that the unlawful attempt at an arrest does not implicate the Fourth Amendment. This is at odds with precedent and logic. Here, the show of force on the part of the police officer, constituting an actual chase, made clear that the accused was not free to leave. This Court should insist on greater rewards to society before sacrificing constitutional protections. Today's holding fails to recognize the coercive and intimidating nature of much current-day police behavior.

ANALYSIS

United States v. Mendenhall, 446 U.S. 544 (1980), had held that a person is seized only if a person's freedom of movement is restrained. Hodari (D) argued that the presence of an officer alone could work to constitute such a restraint. The United States Supreme Court disagreed, noting that *Mendenhall* did not say an arrest was necessarily affected when movement is restrained, but rather that an arrest cannot occur absent such restraint. The dissent declared this a distinction without a difference.

Quicknotes

ARREST The lawful deprivation of a person's liberty pursuant to a valid warrant, probable cause that he or she has committed a criminal offense, or pursuant to some other authority conferred by law.

CERTIORARI A discretionary writ issued by a superior court to an inferior court in order to review the lower court's decisions; the U.S. Supreme Court's writ ordering such review.

EXCLUSIONARY RULE A rule precluding the introduction at trial of evidence unlawfully obtained in violation of the federal constitutional safeguards against unreasonable searches and seizures.

SEIZURE Under the Fourth Amendment, the application of physical force to the body of a person, or a show of force or authority, intended to restrain a person's liberty Also, as relates to property, the meaningful interference with an individual's possessory interests in that property. Only "unreasonable" seizures by the government are prohibited by the Fourth Amendment.

Alabama v. White

State (P) v. Cocaine dealer (D)

496 U.S. 325 (1990)

NATURE OF CASE: Review of order reversing conviction for possession of narcotics.

FACT SUMMARY: Acting on an anonymous phone tip, police stopped Vanessa White (D) and searched her car after corroborating her noncriminal behavior predicted by the informant.

RULE OF LAW

Reasonable suspicion can be established with information different in quantity or content than that required to establish probable cause and can arise from information that is less reliable than that required to show probable cause.

FACTS: On the afternoon of April 22, 1987, Officer Davis received an anonymous telephone tip stating that Vanessa White (D) would leave 235-C Lynwood Terrace Apartments at a particular time later that day in a brown Plymouth station wagon with a broken right taillight lens, that she would drive to Dobey's Motel, and that she would be in possession of a brown attaché case containing an ounce of cocaine. Davis proceeded to the apartment and observed White (D) leave the building empty-handed, enter the described station wagon, and drive by a route involving many turns to Dobey's Motel. Davis stopped the vehicle just short of the motel. Pursuant to a consensual search, marijuana was discovered in a brown attaché case found in the car. Three milligrams of cocaine were later found in White's (D) purse. The trial court denied White's (D) motion to suppress, and she was convicted of possession of narcotics. The Court of Criminal Appeals of Alabama reversed the conviction on the grounds that White's (D) detention was unconstitutional. The Supreme Court of Alabama denied the State's (P) petition for writ of certiorari; the United States Supreme Court granted the State's (P) petition for certiorari.

ISSUE: Can reasonable suspicion be established with information different in quantity or content than that required to establish probable cause and can arise from information that is less reliable than that required to show probable cause?

HOLDING AND DECISION: (White, J.) Yes. Reasonable suspicion can be established with information different in quantity or content than that required to establish probable cause and can arise from information that is less reliable than that required to show probable cause. Reasonable suspicion, like probable cause, is dependent upon both the content of information possessed by police and its degree of reliability as determined by the "totality of circumstances" test. The only difference is that the level of suspicion required to establish "reasonable suspicion" is less than that required to establish "probable cause." Although this is a close case, the range of details actually corroborated by the officers imparted some degree of reliability to the informant's other allegations. The caller's ability to predict White's (D) future behavior demonstrated the possession of inside information, in this case White's (D) itinerary, normally restricted to a small number of people. The totality of these facts established the requisite reasonable suspicion to stop White (D). Reversed.

DISSENT: (Stevens, J.) The common activity of leaving one's apartment at the same time every day carrying an attaché case does not establish reasonable suspicion of illegal activity. It is an activity engaged in daily by millions of lawful citizens. Today's decision makes a mockery of the protections of the Fourth Amendment.

ANALYSIS

White presents one of the weakest factual scenarios held to satisfy the reasonable suspicion standard. The majority quoted the statement in *Illinois v. Gates*, 462 U.S. 213 (1983), that "the anonymous [tip] contained a range of details relating not just to easily obtained facts and conditions existing at the time of the tip, but to future actions of third parties ordinarily not easily predicted." The dissent expressed unease with the record's silence on the issue of whether police made any attempt to determine the identity, motivation, and basis of knowledge of the anonymous phone caller.

Quicknotes

CERTIORARI A discretionary writ issued by a superior court to an inferior court in order to review the lower court's decisions; the U.S. Supreme Court's writ ordering such review.

PROBABLE CAUSE A reasonable basis for believing that a crime has been committed.

REASONABLE SUSPICION That which would cause an ordinary prudent person under the circumstances to suspect that a crime has been committed based on specific and articulable facts.

Illinois v. Wardlow

State (P) v. Convicted weapons felon (D)

528 U.S. 119 (2000)

NATURE OF CASE: Appeal from conviction for unlawful use of a weapon by a felon.

FACT SUMMARY: Wardlow (D) sought to suppress introduction of a .38-caliber handgun at trial on the basis that the gun was recovered during an unlawful stop and frisk.

RULE OF LAW

Flight from police is sufficient to support a finding of reasonable suspicion and to justify a police officer's further investigation.

FACTS: Officers Nolan and Harvey were working as uniformed officers in the special operations section of the Chicago Police Department. They observed Wardlow (D) standing next to a building holding an opaque bag. When he saw the officers, he fled. The officers eventually cornered him and conducted a pat-down search for weapons. During the frisk, Nolan felt a hard object and opened the bag to discover a .38-caliber handgun with five live rounds of ammunition. The officers arrested Wardlow (D). The trial court denied Wardlow's (D) motion to suppress, concluding the gun was recovered during a lawful stop and frisk, and convicted Wardlow (D) of unlawful use of a weapon by a felon. The appellate court reversed on the basis Nolan did not have reasonable suspicion sufficient to justify an investigative stop under *Terry v. Ohio*, 392 U.S. 1 (1968). The Illinois Supreme Court agreed.

ISSUE: Is flight from police sufficient to support a finding of reasonable suspicion and to justify a police officer's further investigation?

HOLDING AND DECISION: (Rehnquist, C.J.) Yes. Flight from police is sufficient to support a finding of reasonable suspicion and to justify a police officer's further investigation. This case is governed by this Court's analysis in *Terry*. Nolan and Harvey were among eight other officers in a four-car caravan converging on an area known for drug trafficking. While an individual's presence in an area of expected criminal activity is not sufficient, without more to support a reasonable, particularized suspicion that the person is committing a crime, the officers may take into consideration the relevant characteristics of a location in determining whether the circumstances are sufficiently suspicious to warrant further investigation. Moreover, nervous, evasive behavior—such as Wardlow's (D) unprovoked flight upon seeing the police—is another pertinent factor in determining reasonable suspicion. Thus, Nolan was justified in suspecting Wardlow (D) was involved in criminal activity and in investigating further. Reversed.

CONCURRENCE AND DISSENT: (Stevens, J.) The State (P) asks the Court to announce a per se rule authorizing the temporary detention of anyone who flees at the mere sight of a police officer, while Wardlow (D) asks the Court to adopt the opposite per se rule—that the fact that a person flees upon seeing the police can never justify a temporary investigative stop. While the Court's rejection of both per se rules is appropriate, the testimony of the officer who seized Wardlow (D) does not support the conclusion that he had reasonable suspicion to make the stop.

ANALYSIS

Compare the result in this case with that in *Florida v. J.L.*, 529 U.S. 266 (2000). There the police responded to an anonymous call that a young Black male would be at a particular location, wearing particular clothing, and carrying a gun. While nothing in the youth's behavior aroused suspicion, the police officer frisked him and discovered a gun. The United States Supreme Court held that an "anonymous tip" was insufficient to establish reasonable suspicion justifying the police to make an investigatory stop.

Quicknotes

PER SE By itself; without more; taken alone; not requiring additional evidence for proof; as a matter of law.

REASONABLE SUSPICION That which would cause an ordinary prudent person under the circumstances to suspect that a crime has been committed based on specific and articulable facts.

STOP AND FRISK A brief, non-intrusive stop, requiring the police officer to have a reasonable suspicion that a crime has been committed or is contemplated being committed based on specific and articulable facts, and involving a search for a concealed weapon that is conducted by patting down the clothes of the person.

Maryland v. Buie

State (P) v. Red-suited robber (D)

494 U.S. 325 (1990)

NATURE OF CASE: Review of order reversing denial of motion to suppress in a robbery prosecution.

FACT SUMMARY: A police officer, after having arrested Buie (D) in his residence, searched the basement for possible accomplices.

RULE OF LAW

After an arrest is made in a residence, a search of the house for accomplices requires articulable facts warranting a belief that the presence of an accomplice is likely.

FACTS: An armed robbery occurred in which one of the robbers was wearing a red running suit. Police obtained an arrest warrant for Buie (D). The officers went to his house and entered it. An officer yelled for anyone in the basement to come out. Buie (D) did and was arrested. An officer, who then descended into the basement to check for possible confederates hiding there, instead found a red running suit. Prior to the trial, the court denied Buie's (D) motion to suppress admission of the running suit as evidence. The state court of appeals reversed, holding probable cause for such a search to be required. The United States Supreme Court granted review.

ISSUE: After an arrest is made in a residence, does a search of the house for accomplices require articulable facts warranting a belief that the presence of an accomplice is likely?

HOLDING AND DECISION: (White, J.) Yes. After an arrest is made in a residence, a search of the house for accomplices requires articulable facts warranting a belief that the presence of an accomplice is likely. As an incident to arrest, police may search the house, as a precautionary measure, without a warrant or probable cause. As long as there is some articulable reason for an officer to believe that there might be an accomplice hiding who might pose a threat, a search for such an individ ual is legitimate. [The Court, rather than ruling on the facts of the present case, vacated the appellate court order and remanded for a factual determination of the issue.]

CONCURRENCE: (Stevens, J.) That Buie (D) offered no resistance when he emerged from the basement is somewhat inconsistent with the hypothesis that the danger of an attack by a hidden confederate persisted after the arrest. All the evidence suggests that no reasonable suspicion of danger justified the entry into the basement.

DISSENT: (Brennan, J.) A planned arrest in the home is very different from a *Terry* search, which is an exception to probable cause designed to protect officers from unavoidable confrontations. A protective search of the home is not minimally intrusive, in light of the sanctity of the home. The nature and scope of the search in this case are widely different from a *Terry* search. In light of the "special sanctity of a private residence" and the highly intrusive nature of a protective sweep, police officers must have probable cause to fear that their personal safety is threatened by a hidden confederate of an arrestee before they may sweep through the entire home.

ANALYSIS

The present case can be seen as a fairly direct descendant of *Terry v. Ohio*, 392 U.S. 1 (1968). There, officers were allowed to stop and pat down a suspect on only a reasonable suspicion of wrongdoing. The standard here, although phrased differently, would appear to be essentially the same.

Quicknotes

ACCOMPLICE An individual who knowingly, purposefully, or voluntarily combines with the main actor in the commission or attempted commission of a criminal offense.

PROBABLE CAUSE A reasonable basis for believing that a crime has been committed.

Michigan Department of State Police v. Sitz

State police (D) v. Automobile drivers (P)

496 U.S. 444 (1990)

NATURE OF CASE: Appeal from order prohibiting state's use of sobriety checkpoints.

FACT SUMMARY: When Police (D) began operation of a sobriety checkpoint in Saginaw, Michigan, Sitz (P), a licensed Michigan driver, filed a complaint seeking relief from potential subjection to the checkpoint.

RULE OF LAW

A state's use of highway sobriety checkpoints does not violate the Fourth and Fourteenth Amendments.

FACTS: The Police (D) established a sobriety checkpoint pilot program in 1986. All vehicles passing through a checkpoint would be stopped and the drivers briefly examined for signs of intoxication. In cases where signs were detected, the officer would check the driver's license and registration, and if warranted, would conduct further sobriety tests. If the tests indicated the driver's intoxication, the driver would be arrested. All other drivers would be allowed to resume their journey. The only checkpoint operated under the program was conducted in Saginaw County. The 126 vehicles passing through the checkpoint were delayed an average of approximately 25 seconds. Two drivers were detained for field tests, and one was arrested for driving under the influence. A third driver who drove through without stopping was pulled over and arrested for driving under the influence. Sitz (P), and other Michigan drivers, filed a complaint seeking declaratory and injunctive relief from potential subjection to the checkpoints. The court held that the program violated the Fourth Amendment and the Michigan Constitution. The Michigan Supreme Court affirmed. The United States Supreme Court granted certiorari.

ISSUE: Does a state's use of highway sobriety checkpoints violate the Fourth and Fourteenth Amendments?

HOLDING AND DECISION: (Rehnquist, C.J.) No. A state's use of highway sobriety checkpoints does not violate the Fourth and Fourteenth Amendments. No one can dispute the magnitude of the drunken driving problem and the state's interest in stopping it. Conversely, the measure of the intrusion on motorists stopped briefly at sobriety checkpoints is slight. The motorist can see that other vehicles are being stopped so he is less likely to be frightened or annoyed by the intrusion. The balance of the state's interest in preventing drunken driving, the extent to which this system can reasonably be said to advance this interest, and the degree of intrusion upon individual motorists who are briefly stopped weigh in favor of the state program. Reversed.

DISSENT: (Brennan, J.) Here, by holding that no level of suspicion is required prior to a police stop to prevent drunk driving, the Court subjects the public to police conduct that may be arbitrary or harassing. The public must be protected against even the so-called minimally intrusive seizures in the instant case.

DISSENT: (Stevens, J.) The Court here ignores the interest of the citizen in liberty from seizures that are suspicionless, unannounced, and investigatory. The effect of sobriety checkpoints on traffic safety is extremely small. Any relationship between sobriety checkpoints and the actual reduction in highway fatalities is even less substantial than the negligible effect on arrest rates. A police officer who questions a driver at a checkpoint has almost limitless discretion to detain a driver on the basis of the slightest suspicion.

ANALYSIS

In *Bostick v. State*, 554 So. 2d 1153 (Fla. 1989), the case involved the constitutionality of a police practice of boarding buses and asking passengers at random for permission to search their luggage. The Florida Supreme Court held that boarding a bus during a brief layover and questioning passengers constituted a "seizure" of the person, which, if not based on an articulable suspicion, violated the passengers' rights guaranteed under the Fourth Amendment. The United States Supreme Court, in *Florida v. Bostick*, 501 U.S. 429 (1991), reversed, saying the action did not violate Fourth Amendment rights because no seizure occurred (i.e., passengers were free to leave).

Quicknotes

CHECKPOINT AUTOMOBILE STOP Exception to the requirement that a police officer have a reasonable suspicion that an automobile contains illegal evidence or contraband for automobile stops made at a fixed checkpoint for the purpose of questioning the occupants of the vehicle; however, the officers must have probable cause or consent of the occupants prior to conducting a search of the vehicle.

Continued on next page.

EXPECTATION OF PRIVACY Requirement that in order to invoke the Fourth Amendment's protection against unreasonable searches and seizures, the individual must have a reasonable expectation of privacy in respect to the location searched or thing seized.

FOURTH AMENDMENT Provides that persons be secure as to their person and private belongings against unreasonable searches and seizures.

City of Indianapolis v. Edmond

City (D) v. Class action plaintiffs (P)

531 U.S. 32 (2000)

NATURE OF CASE: Class action challenging constitutionality of vehicle checkpoints.

FACT SUMMARY: Motorists (P) challenged the constitutional validity of city-imposed vehicle checkpoints as violative of the Fourth Amendment's prohibition against unlawful searches and seizures.

RULE OF LAW

Where a vehicle checkpoint program is designed primarily to uncover evidence of criminal wrongdoing, such program constitutes an unlawful search and seizure in violation of the Fourth Amendment.

FACTS: The City of Indianapolis (D) began to operate vehicle checkpoints in an effort to intercept unlawful drugs. Checkpoint locations were selected weeks in advance, based on certain considerations such as area crime statistics and traffic flow. Edmond (P) and Palmer (P) were each stopped at such a narcotics checkpoint. They filed a lawsuit on behalf of themselves and the class of all motorists who had been stopped or were subject to being stopped in the future at the checkpoints. They claimed the roadblocks violated the Fourth Amendment and the search and seizure provision of the state constitution, and they moved for a preliminary injunction. The district court denied, holding the Fourth Amendment was not violated. The court of appeals reversed, and the United States Supreme Court granted certiorari.

ISSUE: When a vehicle checkpoint program is designed primarily to uncover evidence of criminal wrongdoing, does such program constitute an unlawful search and seizure in violation of the Fourth Amendment?

HOLDING AND DECISION: (O'Connor, J.) Yes. When a vehicle checkpoint program is designed primarily to uncover evidence of criminal wrongdoing, such program constitutes an unlawful search and seizure in violation of the Fourth Amendment. Our checkpoint cases have recognized only limited exceptions to the general rule that a seizure must be accompanied by some measure of individualized suspicion. When law enforcement authorities pursue primarily general crime-control purposes at checkpoints such as these, such stops may be justified only because of some measure of individualized suspicion. Because the primary purpose of the program was indistinguishable from its general interest in crime control, the checkpoints violate the Fourth Amendment. Affirmed.

DISSENT: (Rehnquist, C.J.) The program at issue here complies with previous decisions regarding roadblock seizures. It is constitutionally irrelevant that the law enforcement also hoped to intercept narcotics.

DISSENT: (Thomas, J.) Prior decisions compel upholding the program at issue here, although those cases may not have been correctly decided. A program of indiscriminate stops of individuals not suspected of wrongdoing is not consistent with the intent of the Fourth Amendment.

ANALYSIS

The Fourth Amendment requires that searches be "reasonable" in order to be held valid. A search is presumptively unreasonable if there is a lack of probable cause. A special category of searches is excluded from the reasonable requirement where they are required to serve "special needs, beyond the normal need for law enforcement." The United States Supreme Court has upheld such special needs as border control and sobriety checkpoints, while rejecting discretionary, suspicionless spot checks of drivers' licenses and registrations. The constitutionality of any such program is based on a balancing test between the interests at stake and the program's effectiveness.

Quicknotes

CERTIORARI A discretionary writ issued by a superior court to an inferior court in order to review the lower court's decisions; the U.S. Supreme Court's writ ordering such review.

FOURTH AMENDMENT Provides that persons be secure as to their person and private belongings against unreasonable searches and seizures.

PROBABLE CAUSE A reasonable basis for believing that a crime has been committed.

SEIZURE Under the Fourth Amendment, the application of physical force to the body of a person, or a show of force or authority, intended to restrain a person's liberty Also, as relates to property, the meaningful interference with an individual's possessory interests in that property. Only "unreasonable" seizures by the government are prohibited by the Fourth Amendment.

CHAPTER 5

Remedies for Fourth Amendment Violations

Quick Reference Rules of Law

PAGE

1. *Rakas v. Illinois.* A car passenger has no legitimate expectation of privacy as to the car so that the passenger cannot object to a search of the car or to the introduction of evidence thereby obtained. *72*

2. *Minnesota v. Carter.* An overnight guest in a home may claim the protection of the Fourth Amendment, but one who is merely present with the consent of the householder may not. *73*

3. *Mapp v. Ohio.* In a prosecution in a federal or state court, the Fourth Amendment (by application of the Fourteenth Amendment) forbids the admission of evidence obtained by an unreasonable search and seizure. *75*

4. *Silverthorne Lumber Company v. United States.* Knowledge obtained from illegally seized evidence may not be used against a criminal defendant whose Fourth Amendment rights have been violated. *77*

5. *Murray v. United States.* Evidence found for the first time during the execution of a valid and untainted search warrant is admissible if it is discovered pursuant to an independent source. *78*

6. *Wong Sun v. United States.* Statements made by a defendant directly as the result of lawless police conduct are inadmissible against the defendant. *79*

7. *United States v. Leon.* The Fourth Amendment exclusionary rule does not bar the use of evidence obtained by law enforcement officers acting in good faith in reasonable reliance on a facially valid search warrant ultimately found to be unsupported by probable cause. *80*

8. *Hudson v. Michigan.* Violation of the knock-and-announce rule does not require the suppression of all evidence found in a warranted search. *81*

9. *Herring v. United States.* When police mistakes leading to an unlawful search are the result of isolated negligence attenuated from the search, rather than systemic error or reckless disregard of constitutional requirements, the exclusionary rule does not apply. *83*

10. *Davis v. United States.* Searches conducted by the police in reliance upon binding legal precedent existing at the time of the search are not subject to the exclusionary rule. *84*

11. *Jamison v. McClendon.* Qualified immunity shields a law enforcement officer from liability for violating a law where that law has not been "clearly established" beyond debate so that every reasonable officer would have understood that what the officer did violated that law. *85*

Rakas v. Illinois

Auto passengers (D) v. State (P)

439 U.S. 128 (1978)

NATURE OF CASE: Appeal from conviction for armed robbery.

FACT SUMMARY: Rakas (D) was not allowed to object to the introduction of evidence obtained by a search of the car in which he was riding as a passenger and was convicted of armed robbery.

RULE OF LAW

A car passenger has no legitimate expectation of privacy as to the car so that the passenger cannot object to a search of the car or to the introduction of evidence thereby obtained.

FACTS: After hearing a description of the getaway car used in a robbery, police stopped the vehicle in which Rakas (D) was riding as a passenger. A search of the car revealed rifle shells in the locked glove compartment and a sawed-off rifle under the front passenger seat. Contending that the search had been in violation of the Fourth Amendment, Rakas (D) sought to suppress this evidence, but the trial court held he had no standing to make such a motion, and the appellate court agreed. On appeal from his conviction of armed robbery, Rakas (D) argued that anyone at whom a search was "directed" should have standing to contest the legality of that search and object to the admission at trial of evidence obtained as a result thereof.

ISSUE: Does a car passenger have a legitimate expectation of privacy as to the car so that the passenger can object to a search of the car or to the introduction of evidence thereby obtained?

HOLDING AND DECISION: (Rehnquist, J.) No. A car passenger has no legitimate expectation of privacy as to the car so that the passsenger cannot object to a search of the car or to the introduction of evidence thereby obtained. Until now, many decisions in this area have been couched in terms of whether or not a defendant had "standing" to object to the introduction of evidence obtained by an allegedly unconstitutional search, but this was simply another way of addressing what should now be considered the single guiding standard: whether or not the one making the motion to suppress has had his own Fourth Amendment rights infringed upon by the search and seizure he challenges. As measured by the legitimate expectation of privacy standard, the Fourth Amendment protections offered Rakas (D) were simply not involved when the car was searched. He, therefore, has no basis to object to the evidence obtained. Affirmed.

CONCURRENCE: (Powell, J.) The Fourth Amendment clearly distinguishes between a person's expectation of privacy in a vehicle and his expectation when in other types of locations. Here, none of the vehicle's occupants controlled the vehicle or keys. The passengers had no reasonable expectation the car in which they had been riding would not be searched. Their negligible privacy is not similar to the privacy of a person in one's place of abode or who hides in a telephone booth or of a traveler who hides possessions in a container that is locked.

DISSENT: (White, J.) The majority opinion so limits the concept of what is a legitimate expectation of privacy as to make it nearly impossible to have such an expectation without having a property interest in the place searched, and the Fourth Amendment was not intended to protect property interests but privacy interests. It is now open season on automobiles.

ANALYSIS

A number of courts have determined that one's reasonable expectation of privacy is abandoned when one puts the garbage out for collection. Thus, the government is free to rummage through it without obeying the strictures of the Fourth Amendment.

Quicknotes

CERTIORARI A discretionary writ issued by a superior court to an inferior court in order to review the lower court's decision; the U.S. Supreme Court's writ ordering such review.

FOURTH AMENDMENT Provides that persons be secure as to their person and private belongings against unreasonable searches and seizures.

PROPRIETARY INTEREST An owner's interest and rights in property.

Minnesota v. Carter

State (P) v. Household visitors (D)

525 U.S. 83 (1998)

NATURE OF CASE: Appeal from an order holding that an illegal search had occurred.

FACT SUMMARY: When a police officer saw, through a window, people packaging cocaine and later arrested the occupants of the apartment, they alleged that their Fourth Amendment rights had been violated and sought to have the evidence excluded.

RULE OF LAW
An overnight guest in a home may claim the protection of the Fourth Amendment, but one who is merely present with the consent of the householder may not.

FACTS: A confidential informant told the police that when walking by the window of a ground floor apartment, he had seen people putting white powder into bags. The police officer looked through the same window and saw the men and notified headquarters to prepare affidavits for a search warrant. When Carter (D) and Johns (D) left the building, they were arrested while in a motor vehicle, and cocaine was later found in the vehicle and in the apartment. Carter (D) and Johns (D) had never been in that apartment before and had been there for two hours to package the cocaine. Carter (D) and Johns (D) were convicted of state drug offenses. The trial court held that since they were only temporary out-of-state visitors, they could not challenge the legality of the government intrusion into the apartment, and that the police officer's observation through the window was not a "search" within the meaning of the Fourth Amendment. The state supreme court reversed, holding that Carter (D) and Johns (D) did have "standing" because they had a legitimate expectation of privacy in the invaded place, and that the officer's observation constituted an unreasonable "search" of the apartment. Minnesota (P) appealed.

ISSUE: May an overnight guest in a home claim the protection of the Fourth Amendment, but may one who is merely present with the consent of the householder not claim the protection?

HOLDING AND DECISION: (Rehnquist, C.J.) Yes. An overnight guest in a home may claim the protection of the Fourth Amendment, but one who is merely present with the consent of the householder may not. The purely commercial nature of the transaction engaged in here, the relatively short time on the premises, and the lack of any previous connection between Carter (D) and the householder all lead to the conclusion that their situation is closer to that of one simply permitted on the premises, rather than that of an overnight guest. Therefore, any search that may have occurred did not violate their Fourth Amendment rights. Reversed.

CONCURRENCE: (Scalia, J.) This Court would go beyond its proper power were it to restrict the ability of the people to govern themselves by use of the full choice of policy decisions that the Constitution provides them. Whereas it is plausible to regard a person's overnight lodging as at least his "temporary" residence, it is entirely impossible to give that characterization to an apartment that he uses to package cocaine.

CONCURRENCE: (Kennedy, J.) Almost all social guests have a legitimate expectation of privacy, and hence protection against unreasonable searches, in their host's home. In this case, Carter (D) and Johns (D) have established nothing more than a fleeting and insubstantial connection with Thompson's home.

CONCURRENCE: (Breyer, J.) The police officer's observation made from a public area outside the curtilage of the residence did not violate Carter's (D) Fourth Amendment rights. The officer did not engage in what the Constitution forbids, namely, an unreasonable search.

DISSENT: (Ginsburg, J.) The Court's decision undermines not only the security of short-term guests, but also the security of the home resident herself. When a homeowner chooses to share the privacy of her home and her company with a short-term guest, both host and guest have exhibited an actual (subjective) expectation of privacy, and that expectation is one that our society is prepared to recognize as reasonable.

ANALYSIS

Property used for commercial purposes is treated differently for Fourth Amendment purposes than residential property. While Carter (D) and Johns (D) were present in a "home," it was not their home. Only the Dissent argued that a short-term guest in a home should share his host's shelter against unreasonable searches and seizures. Since there was no violation of the Fourth Amendment, the evidence seized by the police was used against Carter (D) and Johns (D).

Continued on next page.

Quicknotes

EXPECTATION OF PRIVACY Requirement that in order to invoke the Fourth Amendment's protection against unreasonable searches and seizures, the individual must have a reasonable expectation of privacy in respect to the location searched or thing seized.

FOURTH AMENDMENT Provides that persons be secure as to their person and private belongings against unreasonable searches and seizures.

SEARCH An inspection conducted in order to obtain evidence to be utilized for the prosecution of a crime.

SEIZURE Under the Fourth Amendment, the application of physical force to the body of a person, or a show of force or authority, intended to restrain a person's liberty Also, as relates to property, the meaningful interference with an individual's possessory interests in that property. Only "unreasonable" seizures by the government are prohibited by the Fourth Amendment.

Mapp v. Ohio

Holder of obscene material (D) v. State (P)

367 U.S. 643 (1961)

NATURE OF CASE: Appeal from conviction for possession of obscene material.

FACT SUMMARY: Mapp (D) was arrested and later convicted of possession of obscene material when police without a search warrant forcibly entered her home pursuant to information that a bombing suspect was hiding in the dwelling.

RULE OF LAW

In a prosecution in a federal or state court, the Fourth Amendment (by application of the Fourteenth Amendment) forbids the admission of evidence obtained by an unreasonable search and seizure.

FACTS: When three Cleveland police officers knocked on the door of her house, Mapp (D), upon the telephoned advice of her attorney, refused to admit them without a search warrant. The police had information that a person wanted for questioning regarding a bombing was hiding in the Mapp (D) home. Being refused admission, the policemen forcibly entered, waving a piece of paper they claimed was a warrant, and proceeded to search extensively the second floor and the basement. During the search, certain books, pictures, and photographs deemed to be obscene and unlawful in Ohio (P) were found. Mapp (D) was convicted of their possession and appealed, arguing that the search was unlawful because no search warrant had been issued and, thus, the seized material should not have been admitted at trial. The Ohio Supreme Court agreed that the search was unlawful but upheld the conviction on the basis that the materials had not been taken from Mapp's (D) "person by the use of brutal or offensive physical force against" her. The United States Supreme Court granted certiorari.

ISSUE: In a prosecution in a state or federal court, does the Fourth Amendment (by application of the Fourteenth Amendment) forbid the admission of evidence obtained by an unreasonable search and seizure?

HOLDING AND DECISION: (Clark, J.) Yes. In a prosecution in federal or state court, the Fourth Amendment (by application of the Fourteenth Amendment) forbids the admission of evidence obtained by an unlawful search and seizure. For more than 50 years prior to this case, the exclusionary rule has been applied in federal courts. Any forcible and compulsory extortion of one's own testimony or private papers to convict one or to forfeit goods violates the Fourth and Fifth Amendments. If unlawfully seized material could be admitted as evidence, the Fourth Amendment right to be secure against unlawful searches and seizures would be of no value. *Weeks v. United States*, 232 U.S. 383 (1914). Although this Court failed to require application of the exclusionary rule in state courts in *Wolf v. Colorado*, 338 U.S. 25 (1949), the failure to do so there was based on factual considerations not relevant to the constitutional consideration and could not be controlling here. To allow *Wolf* to continue in force would be to grant the right but in reality to withhold its privilege and enjoyment. The purpose of the rule is to deter violation of the right by the only effective way—by removing the incentive to disregard it. If a criminal must go free, it is the law that sets the criminal free. "If the government becomes a lawbreaker, it breeds contempt for law." *Olmstead v. United States*, 277 U.S. 438, 485 (1928). Reversed and remanded.

CONCURRENCE: (Black, J.) Although the Fourth Amendment itself does not expressly require the exclusionary rule, it, together with the Fifth Amendment's ban against self-incrimination, not only justifies the rule, it requires it.

DISSENT: (Harlan, J.) The real issue of this case is whether the Ohio law banning mere possession of obscene material is consistent with the rights of free thought and expression assured by the Fourth Amendment. As for the exclusionary rule itself, the question is whether the individual states should be able to determine the rule's desirability. The Fourteenth Amendment does not allow this court to mold state remedies according to its own notions of how things should be done. What was recognized in *Wolf v. Colorado*, 338 U.S. 25 (1949), was not that the Fourth Amendment *as such* is enforceable against the states as a facet of due process, but the principle of privacy that is at the core of the Fourteenth Amendment.

ANALYSIS

While holding that the exclusionary rule should be applied to the states, the Court noted there was a slow although "significant" trend among the states to adopt it on their own. As stated, the exclusionary rule was applied in federal courts for over 50 years prior to the *Mapp* decision and without significant controversy. The Court sought to put an end to the practice of federal prosecutors taking unlawfully seized evidence to state prosecutors "in the courthouse across the street" to

Continued on next page.

initiate prosecutions they themselves could not bring constitutionally in federal court.

Quicknotes

CERTIORARI A discretionary writ issued by a superior court to an inferior court in order to review the lower court's decisions; the U.S. Supreme Court's writ ordering such review.

EXCLUSIONARY RULE A rule precluding the introduction at trial of evidence unlawfully obtained in violation of the federal constitutional safeguards against unreasonable searches and seizures.

FOURTEENTH AMENDMENT Declares that no state shall make or enforce any law that shall abridge the privileges and immunities of citizens of the United States; no state shall deny to any person within its jurisdiction the equal protection of the laws.

FOURTH AMENDMENT Provides that persons be secure as to their person and private belongings against unreasonable searches and seizures.

Silverthorne Lumber Company v. United States

Company (D) v. Federal government (P)

251 U.S. 385 (1920)

NATURE OF CASE: Appeal challenging the use of evidence illegally seized and all knowledge obtained therefrom.

FACT SUMMARY: The Silverthornes (D) contended that physical evidence illegally seized, as well as all knowledge that could be gleaned therefrom, could not be used against them.

RULE OF LAW

Knowledge obtained from illegally seized evidence may not be used against a criminal defendant whose Fourth Amendment rights have been violated.

FACTS: The Department of Justice and the United States marshal illegally seized papers, books, and documents from the Silverthornes' (D) company office while the Silverthornes (D) were under arrest. After their release, the Silverthornes (D) sought the return of everything that had been seized and the district court, finding that the seizure was unconstitutional, granted their request. The Government (P) then sought to use the knowledge it obtained from the illegally seized evidence against the Silverthornes (D), who objected to such use. The United States Supreme Court granted review.

ISSUE: May knowledge obtained from illegally seized evidence be used against a criminal defendant whose Fourth Amendment rights have been violated?

HOLDING AND DECISION: (Holmes, J.) No. Knowledge obtained from illegally seized evidence may not be used against a criminal defendant whose Fourth Amendment rights have been violated. The Government (P) asserts that although it may not use the physical evidence illegally seized, it may use knowledge obtained from that evidence to its advantage against the Silverthornes (D). The Government's (P) position is untenable. Otherwise, the Fourth Amendment would be reduced to a shell. To give the Fourth Amendment proper effect, neither illegally seized physical evidence, nor any knowledge that can be gleaned therefrom, may be used against a criminal defendant. However, the facts that constitute such knowledge are not absolutely shielded from use, and, if the Government (P) can obtain knowledge of such facts from an independent source other than the illegally seized evidence, it may use such knowledge against the defendant. [Judgment reversed.]

ANALYSIS

The holding in this case, articulated by Justice Oliver Wendell Holmes, Jr., is now referred to as the "fruit of the poisonous tree" doctrine. The doctrine, stated in other words, is that the government cannot violate the Fourth Amendment and use the fruits of such unlawful conduct to secure a conviction. The portion of Justice Holmes's opinion stating that the government may, however, use knowledge of facts that it obtains from an independent, untainted source, is known as the "independent source" doctrine.

Quicknotes

FRUIT OF THE POISONOUS TREE Doctrine that evidence obtained as a result of illegal procedures is tainted and is usually inadmissible at trial.

INDEPENDENT SOURCE Pertaining to evidence derived from another source, independent of the evidence obtained with a defective warrant.

Murray v. United States

Driver from warehouse (D) v. Federal government (P)

487 U.S. 533 (1988)

NATURE OF CASE: Appeal from conviction for marijuana possession.

FACT SUMMARY: Murray (D) contended that marijuana seized in his warehouse, initially discovered during an illegal search but subsequently acquired through an independent and lawful search warrant, should be excluded.

RULE OF LAW

Evidence found for the first time during the execution of a valid and untainted search warrant is admissible if it is discovered pursuant to an independent source.

FACTS: Police officers made an illegal warrantless entry into a warehouse where they observed bales of marijuana. Some officers stayed at the warehouse, keeping it under surveillance, while others obtained a search warrant. In seeking the warrant, the officers made no mention of the illegal entry and did not rely on any observations made during the entry. After obtaining the warrant, the officers searched the warehouse and seized the marijuana. Murray (D) and the other defendants unsuccessfully objected to the use of the evidence against them on the grounds that the officers should have told the magistrate of the illegal entry and that the illegal entry tainted the warrant. Following his conviction, Murray (D) appealed.

ISSUE: Is evidence found for the first time during the execution of a valid and untainted search warrant admissible if it is discovered pursuant to an independent source?

HOLDING AND DECISION: (Scalia, J.) Yes. Evidence found for the first time during the execution of a valid and untainted search warrant is admissible if it is discovered pursuant to an independent source. If the officers' decision to seek the warrant was prompted by what they had seen during the initial entry, or if information obtained during that entry was presented to the magistrate and affected his decision to issue the warrant, the search pursuant to the warrant would not have been an independent source. The district court found that the officers did not reveal their warrantless entry or their observations of the marijuana to the magistrate. The Court did not, however, explicitly find that the agents would have sought a warrant if they had not earlier entered the warehouse. This was error; a determination of whether the warrant-authorized search was an independent source of the challenged evidence should have been made. Vacated and remanded.

DISSENT: (Marshall, J.) Here, no demonstrated historical facts are set forth to show that the subsequent warrant search was wholly unaffected by the prior search, which was illegal. In both searches, the same investigators were used, and no effort was first made to acquire a warrant. Today's Court ruling lends itself to easy abuse and provides police encouragement to bypass constitutional requirements.

ANALYSIS

Justice Marshall argued that where the police cannot point to some historically verifiable fact demonstrating that the subsequent search pursuant to a warrant was wholly unaffected by the prior illegal search, a per se rule of inadmissibility should be adopted. It would be difficult for the trial court to verify, or the defendant to rebut, an assertion by officers that they always intended to obtain a warrant, regardless of the results of the illegal search. The testimony of the officers conducting the illegal search is the only direct evidence of intent, and the defendant will be relegated simply to arguing that the officers should not be believed.

Quicknotes

FRUIT OF THE POISONOUS TREE Doctrine that evidence obtained as a result of illegal procedures is inadmissible at trial.

INDEPENDENT SOURCE Pertaining to facts derived from another source, independent of those contained in a defective warrant.

PROBABLE CAUSE A reasonable basis for believing that a crime has been committed.

Wong Sun v. United States

Drug dealer (D) v. Federal government (P)

371 U.S. 471 (1963)

NATURE OF CASE: On certiorari from appellate court judgment upholding conviction for dealing in heroin.

FACT SUMMARY: Wong Sun's (D) co-defendant was unlawfully arrested and made incriminating statements to police.

RULE OF LAW

Statements made by a defendant directly as the result of lawless police conduct are inadmissible against the defendant.

FACTS: Federal agents went to the Chinese laundry operated by Wong Sun's (D) co-defendant, James Wah Toy. Toy told the agent that he was not open for business and to come back. The agent identified himself as a narcotics agent, and Toy ran into his living quarters at the back of the laundry. The agents broke open the door, followed Toy into his bedroom, and arrested him. A search of the premises revealed no narcotics. Toy told the agents that he and another man had been smoking the drug the night before and told him where the other man lived. Toy and two others were indicted on drug charges, and his statements to the agents in his bedroom were admitted against him.

ISSUE: Are statements made by a defendant directly as the result of lawless police conduct inadmissible against the defendant?

HOLDING AND DECISION: (Brennan, J.) Yes. Statements made by a defendant directly as the result of lawless police conduct are inadmissible against the defendant. The court of appeals held there was neither reasonable grounds nor probable cause for Toy's arrest. We have held that physical evidence obtained during an unlawful invasion must be excluded. Today we hold that verbal evidence that derives so immediately from an unlawful entry is no less the fruit of official illegality than the more tangible fruits of unwarranted intrusion. There was no intervening independent act to purge the illegality of its taint; therefore, the judgment of the court of appeals is reversed.

ANALYSIS

Wong Sun (D) made a confession as well, but his confession took place when he voluntarily returned several days after being arraigned to make the statement. Given his independent intervening voluntary act, the United States Supreme Court held that the taint of Toy's unlawful arrest was purged as to Wong Sun's (D) confession.

Quicknotes

EXCLUSIONARY RULE A rule precluding the introduction at trial of evidence unlawfully obtained in violation of the federal constitutional safeguards against unreasonable searches and seizures.

United States v. Leon

Federal government (P) v. Cocaine conspirators (D)

468 U.S. 897 (1984)

NATURE OF CASE: Appeal from order granting motion to suppress evidence.

FACT SUMMARY: The district court held that although the police acted in good faith, they seized evidence showing Leon's (D) involvement in illegal drug activities pursuant to a search warrant that was not based on probable cause, and, therefore, the evidence had to be excluded under the Fourth Amendment.

RULE OF LAW

The Fourth Amendment exclusionary rule does not bar the use of evidence obtained by law enforcement officers acting in good faith in reasonable reliance on a facially valid search warrant ultimately found to be unsupported by probable cause.

FACTS: The Burbank police obtained a facially valid search warrant to search Leon's (D) premises for narcotics. The information in the supporting affidavit was obtained from a confidential informant whose credibility and reliability were not substantiated. The police found narcotics, and Leon (D) was charged with conspiracy to possess and distribute cocaine. The district court granted Leon's (D) motion to suppress the evidence, holding the information in the affidavit was stale and derived from an unsubstantiated source. Therefore, the court held, the warrant was not based on probable cause, and the search was illegal. The court further held that the Fourth Amendment's exclusionary rule required suppression of the evidence even though the police admittedly acted in good faith. The court of appeals affirmed, refusing to recognize a good-faith exception to the exclusionary rule, and the United States Supreme Court granted certiorari.

ISSUE: Does the Fourth Amendment exclusionary rule bar the use of evidence obtained by law enforcement officers acting in good faith in reasonable reliance on a facially valid search warrant ultimately found to be unsupported by probable cause?

HOLDING AND DECISION: (White, J.) No. The Fourth Amendment exclusionary rule does not bar the use of evidence obtained by law enforcement officers acting in good faith in reasonable reliance on a facially valid search warrant that is subsequently found to be unsupported by probable cause. The exclusionary rule is not mandated by the Fourth Amendment. The Amendment contains no provision that expressly precludes the use of illegally obtained evidence. It is a judicially created remedy to deter illegal law enforcement conduct. Because of its deterrent purpose, the rule cannot be justifiably applied to cases in which the police have acted in good faith under a facially valid warrant. Therefore, it is clear that exclusion of evidence must be determined on a case-by-case basis and only where such exclusion furthers the purpose of the exclusionary rule. As a result, the evidence, obtained in good faith, should not have been suppressed. Reversed.

DISSENT: (Brennan, J.) The Court's decision to allow illegally obtained evidence in the prosecution's case-in-chief signals the end of the exclusionary rule. The abandonment of the rule shows the Court sacrificing sound principles of individual rights out of fear and frustration caused by an ever-increasing crime rate. The purpose of the Fourth Amendment was to ensure that such sacrifice not be made. The rule is based on the protection of Fourth Amendment rights, not exclusively on deterring police conduct. The decision, therefore, denies constitutionally protected rights.

ANALYSIS

The Court in this case recognized that the issuance of a facially valid search warrant by a neutral magistrate provides sufficient Fourth Amendment protection against unreasonable searches. The exclusionary rule was viewed as having no deterrent effect on the issuing magistrate. Such judicial officers, therefore, will not, as a result of this decision, have any increased incentive to make a reasoned decision concerning the existence of probable cause to search.

Quicknotes

EXCLUSIONARY RULE A rule precluding the introduction at trial of evidence unlawfully obtained in violation of the federal constitutional safeguards against unreasonable searches and seizures.

FOURTH AMENDMENT Provides that persons be secure as to their person and private belongings against unreasonable searches and seizures.

GOOD-FAITH RELIANCE Honest reliance on the representations of another.

PROBABLE CAUSE A reasonable basis for believing that a crime has been committed.

Hudson v. Michigan

Convicted felon (D) v. State (P)

547 U.S. 586 (2006)

NATURE OF CASE: Appeal of lower court refusal to exclude evidence obtained following a knock-and-announce violation.

FACT SUMMARY: Police (P) entered and searched a home after failing to knock and announce. They found drugs and a firearm in their search, and Booker Hudson (D) moved at trial to exclude the evidence based on the knock-and-announce violation.

RULE OF LAW

Violation of the knock-and-announce rule does not require the suppression of all evidence found in a warranted search.

FACTS: Police (P) entered and searched Booker Hudson's (D) home with a warrant but failed to knock first, and waited only three to five seconds after announcing themselves before entering. Hudson (D) was convicted in state court of possessing cocaine and a firearm. Hudson (D) argued that the evidence against him was seized in violation of the "knock and announce" rule of the Fourth Amendment, which requires the police to knock, announce their presence, and wait 20 to 30 seconds before executing a search warrant, except in exigent circumstances. The trial judge granted Hudson's (D) motion to suppress the evidence on the basis of the knock-and-announce rule. The Michigan Court of Appeals reversed, holding that it was bound by two cases decided by the Michigan Supreme Court that created an "exception" to the suppression of evidence obtained in violation of the knock-and-announce rule when the evidence would inevitably have been discovered.

ISSUE: Does violation of the knock-and-announce rule require the suppression of all evidence found in a warranted search?

HOLDING AND DECISION: (Scalia, J.) No. Violation of the knock-and-announce rule does not require the suppression of all evidence found in a warranted search. Evidence seized in violation of the knock-and-announce rule can be used against a defendant in a later criminal trial without violating the Fourth Amendment, and judges cannot suppress such evidence for a knock-and-announce violation alone. The purpose of the knock-and-announce rule is to protect police officers from surprising residents who might retaliate in presumed self-defense, to protect private property from damage, and to protect the privacy and dignity of residents. The knock-and-announce rule has never purported to protect one's interest in preventing the government from seeing or taking evidence described in a warrant. In addition, the cost of excluding evidence based on knock-and-announce violations would be serious, amounting to providing dangerous criminals with a get-out-of-jail-free card. Affirmed.

CONCURRENCE: (Kennedy, J.) The knock-and-announce requirement protects rights and expectations linked to ancient principles in our constitutional order. The majority opinion does not suggest that violations of the knock-and-announce requirement are trivial or beyond the law's concern. In addition, the decision determines only that in the specific context of the knock-and-announce requirement, a violation is not sufficiently related to the later discovery of evidence to justify suppression.

DISSENT: (Breyer, J.) Settled case law by this Court established that the Fourth Amendment normally requires police officers to knock and announce their presence before entering a dwelling. The majority opinion holds that evidence seized from a home following a violation of this requirement need not be suppressed. As a result, the Court destroys the strongest legal incentive to comply with the Constitution's knock-and-announce requirement. At the very least, eliminating the exclusionary rule from consideration for knock-and-announce violations will cause some government agents to find it less risky to violate the rule.

ANALYSIS

This case is premised on the insufficient connection between the failure by the police to knock and announce and the evidence found in the house, thus rendering exclusion of that evidence based on the violation unjustifiable. The case might stand for a broader application of the rule, which might curb altogether the exclusionary rule based on knock-and-announce violations.

Quicknotes

EXIGENT CIRCUMSTANCES Circumstances requiring an extraordinary or immediate response; an exception to the prohibition on a warrantless arrest or search when police officers believe probable cause to exist and there is no time for obtaining a warrant.

Continued on next page.

FOURTH AMENDMENT Provides that persons be secure as to their person and private belongings against unreasonable searches and seizures.

KNOCK AND ANNOUNCE Requirement that a police officer must first knock and announce his or her intention before entering an individual's home in the execution of a valid warrant.

PROBABLE CAUSE A reasonable basis for believing that a crime has been committed.

Herring v. United States

Individual (D) v. Federal government (P)

555 U.S. 135 (2009)

NATURE OF CASE: Appeal from Eleventh Circuit Court of Appeals in favor of government.

FACT SUMMARY: After receiving information from a neighboring county that Herring (D) had an outstanding warrant against him, police officers in Coffee County arrested Herring (D). A search of his vehicle revealed a gun and illegal drugs. The police then learned the warrant had previously been recalled.

RULE OF LAW

When police mistakes leading to an unlawful search are the result of isolated negligence attenuated from the search, rather than systemic error or reckless disregard of constitutional requirements, the exclusionary rule does not apply.

FACTS: Police in Coffee County investigated whether Herring (D) had any outstanding warrants against him. A search of a neighboring county's database initially revealed that Herring (D) had a warrant against him for failure to appear for a felony charge. Acting on the information, the police officers arrested Herring (D). A search of his vehicle incident to his arrest turned up a gun and illegal drugs. Shortly after the search, police dispatch informed the arresting officers that the warrant had actually been recalled five months earlier and was no longer valid. Federal charges were subsequently brought against Herring (D), and he moved to suppress the evidence from the search on the grounds the arrest and search were in violation of his Fourth Amendment rights. The trial court and the Eleventh Circuit Court of Appeals found that because the mistake was caused by the mere negligence of the police record keeping system, the exclusionary rule did not apply. Herring (D) appealed.

ISSUE: When police mistakes leading to an unlawful search are the result of isolated negligence attenuated from the search, rather than systemic error or reckless disregard of constitutional requirements, does the exclusionary rule apply?

HOLDING AND DECISION: (Roberts, C.J.) No. When police mistakes leading to an unlawful search are the result of isolated negligence attenuated from the search, rather than systemic error or reckless disregard of constitutional requirements, the exclusionary rule does not apply. The mere fact that a search is unreasonable does not mean the exclusionary rule automatically applies. The Court has previously held the rule does not apply when police reasonably relied upon an invalid warrant issued by a court. The only issue here is whether negligence by the police, as opposed to others, will lead to the suppression of evidence. The Court holds that it should not. The exclusionary rule was created to deter police misconduct. The conduct must have a deliberate or indifferent nature to invoke the exclusionary rule. Those circumstances are not present here. An error arising from nonrecurring negligence, as opposed to systemic negligence, does not implicate the concerns the exclusionary rule was designed to protect. Affirmed.

DISSENT: (Ginsburg, J.) The Court's decision may lead to the arrest of innocent persons based upon information that is negligently maintained. Police departments across the country will have little incentive to ensure the accuracy of their warrant databases. The exclusionary rule is the only remedy Herring (D) and others in his situation have. A subsequent lawsuit against the police for wrongful arrest will be barred by qualified immunity. Just as in tort law, the risk of exclusion of evidence would encourage police departments at the state and federal levels to monitor the warrant databases and ensure their accuracy.

ANALYSIS

A debate has ensued over the scope of this five-to-four decision. Some commentators believe the scope is limited to police errors in regard to recordkeeping only. However, others believe police departments may rely on the decision to argue that any of their good-faith mistakes will prohibit the application of the exclusionary rule. It does appear though that the holding concerns only those isolated and negligent mistakes that are "attenuated from the search." The precise contours of this "attenuation" factor have yet to be defined.

Quicknotes

EXCLUSIONARY RULE A rule precluding the introduction at trial of evidence unlawfully obtained in violation of the federal constitutional safeguards against unreasonable searches and seizures.

WARRANT An order issued by a court directing an officer to undertake a certain act (e.g., arrest or search).

Davis v. United States

Individual (D) v. Federal government (P)

564 U.S. 229 (2011)

NATURE OF CASE: Appeal from intermediate appellate court decision in favor of the government.

FACT SUMMARY: Davis (D) was a passenger in a vehicle during a routine traffic stop. After the police arrested Davis (D) for giving a false name, the officers conducted a warrantless search of the vehicle incident to the arrest. The search produced an illegal firearm.

RULE OF LAW

Searches conducted by the police in reliance upon binding legal precedent existing at the time of the search are not subject to the exclusionary rule.

FACTS: During a routine traffic stop, police arrested Davis (D) for giving a false name. After the arrest, police conducted a warrantless search of the vehicle. The search produced a firearm in the pocket of Davis's coat. The Government (P) charged Davis (D) with one count of possession of a firearm by a convicted felon. A jury convicted Davis (D). While his appeal was pending at the Eleventh Circuit Court of Appeals, the United States Supreme Court decided *Arizona v. Gant*, 556 U.S. 332 (2009). *Arizona v. Gant* essentially held that law enforcement officers must demonstrate either a continuing threat to their safety or the need to preserve evidence before conducting a warrantless search of a vehicle incident to an arrest. The Eleventh Circuit Court of Appeals upheld the conviction of Davis (D), however, on the grounds that penalizing the officers for conduct in compliance with existing law at the time of the search would not deter officers from future Fourth Amendment violations. The United States Supreme Court granted Davis's (D) petition for review.

ISSUE: Are searches conducted by the police in reliance upon binding legal precedent existing at the time of the search subject to the exclusionary rule?

HOLDING AND DECISION: (Alito, J.) No. Searches conducted by the police in reliance upon binding legal precedent existing at the time of the search are not subject to the exclusionary rule. The reliance upon the binding precedent must be objectively reasonable. The sole purpose of the exclusionary rule is to deter future Fourth Amendment violations by other law enforcement personnel. Where the suppression of evidence will not yield deterrence, exclusion of the evidence is unwarranted. In addition to deterrence, courts must also weigh the substantial social costs generated by the rule. The deterrence benefits must outweigh the heavy costs of releasing criminals upon the community. The deterrence benefits of exclusion depend upon the culpability of the law enforcement conduct at issue in the case. Where police act deliberately or recklessly, the deterrent value of exclusion is strong. When police act in accordance with an objective good-faith belief in the legality of the search, the deterrence rationale carries much less weight. Here, the officers' search followed prior Eleventh Circuit precedent. However, the *Arizona v. Gant* decision has now made such searches illegal without a warrant. Davis (D) argues that prior precedent requires that the *Arizona* decision be applied retroactively to his case. The Court agrees *Arizona* should be retroactively applied. However, the existence of a Fourth Amendment violation does not mean Davis (D) is entitled to the remedy of exclusion of evidence. The remedy only applies where its purpose, deterrence, is effectively advanced. That is not the case here. Applying the good-faith exception to binding legal precedent as we have here will not prevent judicial consideration of prior Fourth Amendment decisions. This Court will continue to review criminal convictions from the twelve circuit courts of appeal and from the states. Affirmed.

CONCURRENCE: (Sotomayor, J.) The majority is correct that where the officers acted in compliance with binding legal precedence, application of the exclusionary rule will not yield appreciable deterrence. The test for legality of searches remains one, whether exclusion results in deterrence, and two, whether the benefits of exclusion outweigh the costs.

DISSENT: (Breyer, J.) While agreeing that *Arizona* applies retroactively to this case, the majority improperly and implausibly denies Davis (D) the remedy of exclusion to which he is entitled. Under this decision, the Court gives improper weight to the culpability of law enforcement. The majority will now apply the exclusionary rule only where the officers' conduct was deliberate or reckless. This will essentially swallow the exclusionary rule and weaken its deterrent effect.

ANALYSIS

Under the case of *Teague v. Lane*, 489 U.S. 288 (1989), any new constitutional rule must be applied retroactively to all pending state or federal cases that have not been completely resolved.

Quicknotes

EXCLUSIONARY RULE A rule precluding the introduction at trial of evidence unlawfully obtained in violation of the federal constitutional safeguards against unreasonable searches and seizures.

Jamison v. McClendon

Motorist (P) v. Police officer (D)

476 F. Supp. 3d 386 (S.D. Miss. 2020)

NATURE OF CASE: Motion for summary judgment in § 1983 action brought against police officer by motorist for violations of motorist's Fourth Amendment rights.

FACT SUMMARY: Clarence Jamison (Jamison) (P), a Black man, brought suit in federal court against White police Officer Nick McClendon (McClendon) (D) under 42 U.S.C. § 1983, contending that McClendon (D) conducted an unlawful search of Jamison's (P) vehicle that violated his Fourth Amendment rights in several ways. McClendon (D) asserted he was entitled to qualified immunity and moved for summary judgment as to all of Jamison's (P) claims.

RULE OF LAW

Qualified immunity shields a law enforcement officer from liability for violating a law where that law has not been "clearly established" beyond debate so that every reasonable officer would have understood that what the officer did violated that law.

FACTS: Clarence Jamison (Jamison) (P), a Black man, was driving through Mississippi on his way home to South Carolina from Arizona, in a car he had very recently purchased. Police Officer Nick McClendon (McClendon) (D), a White man, pulled Jamison (P) over, because, according to McClendon (D), the temporary tag on Jamison's (P) car was folded over to where McClendon (D) could not see it. McClendon (D) said it had two bolts in it, so it folded up with the pressure of the air hitting it while the car was being driven. Jamison (P) testified, however, that it was not curled up and "had four screws in it." After requesting and receiving Jamison's (P) identifying information, and after receiving a clear background check, McClendon (D) decided to run a criminal history check on Jamison (P) and the car. Before receiving the criminal history report, McClendon (D) returned to the vehicle with the goal of obtaining consent to search it. According to McClendon (D), Jamison (P) consented. According to Jamison (P), McClendon (D) put his hand over the passenger door threshold of Jamison's car and told him to, "Hold on a minute." After making three requests for consent to search the car—which Jamison (P) said he did not give—McClendon (D) placed his hand into the car and patted the inside of the passenger door. McClendon (D) asked again as he moved his arm further into the vehicle and then made a fifth and final request, explaining to Jamison (P) that McClendon (D) had received a call about 10 kilos of cocaine, which was a lie. Apparently, Jamison (P) became frustrated and gave up. He told McClendon (D), "As long as I can see what you're doing you can search the vehicle." McClendon (D) patted Jamison (P) down after he exited the car. With Jamison (P) watching, McClendon (D) searched the entire car. Notwithstanding that McClendon (D) found nothing suspicious, he asked Jamison (P) for permission to deploy his canine. Jamison (P) initially refused, but then relented. The dog gave no indication of anything suspicious. In total, the stop and search lasted nearly two hours. Jamison (P) brought suit in federal court under 42 U.S.C. § 1983, asserting three claims. The first alleged that McClendon (D) violated Jamison's (P) Fourth Amendment rights by "falsely stopping him, searching his car, and detaining him." Jamison's (P) second claim, brought under the Fourteenth Amendment, claims McClendon (D) used race as a motivating factor in the decision to stop him, search his car, and detain him. Jamison's (P) third claim alleged a violation of the Fourth Amendment by McClendon (D) for recklessly and deliberately causing significant damage to Jamison's (P) car by conducting an unlawful search of the car in an objectively unreasonable manner amounting to an unlawful seizure of his property. Jamison (P) sought damages for damage to his vehicle, as well as for psychological harm. McClendon (D) moved for summary judgment, which was granted as to Jamison's (P) Fourteenth Amendment claim for a racially motivated stop, and, on grounds of qualified immunity, as to the claims that McClendon (D) did not have reasonable suspicion to stop Jamison (P). However, the court deferred its ruling on summary judgment as to whether McClendon (D) was entitled to qualified immunity on Jamison's (P) lack of consent and prolonged stop claims, and, additionally, McClendon's (D) initial and renewed motions for summary judgment did not provide any argument as to Jamison's (P) third claim. These matters were taken up by the District Court.

ISSUE: Does qualified immunity shield a law enforcement officer from liability for violating a law where that law has not been "clearly established" beyond debate so that every reasonable officer would have understood that what the officer did violated that law?

HOLDING AND DECISION: (Reeves, J.) Yes. Qualified immunity shields a law enforcement officer from liability for violating a law where that law has not been "clearly established" beyond debate so that every reasonable officer would have understood that what the

Continued on next page.

officer did violated that law. The question presented is whether McClendon (D) violated clearly established constitutional rights of which a reasonable person would have known. A clearly established right is one that is sufficiently clear that every reasonable official would have understood that what the official is doing violates that right, and clearly established law must be particularized to the facts of a case. Thus, while a case need not be directly on point, precedent must still put the underlying question beyond debate, and the clearly established law must come from holdings, not dicta. In determining whether a law is clearly established, courts must pay close attention to the specific context of the case, and not define clearly established law at a high level of generality. Here, a review of the record reveals that McClendon (D) violated Jamison's (P) Fourth Amendment rights by intruding into Jamison's (P) vehicle and conducting an unreasonable search. Also, Jamison's (P) consent for the search of his car was effectively involuntary, so the search violated the Fourth Amendment on those grounds as well. Thus, viewing the facts in the light most favorable to Jamison (P), the question in this case is whether it was clearly established that an officer who has made five sequential requests for consent to search a car, lied, promised leniency, and placed his arm inside of a person's car during a traffic stop while awaiting background check results has violated the Fourth Amendment. The answer is that it was not. A case from the Tenth Circuit Court of Appeals offered by Jamison (P) found that an officer unlawfully prolonged a detention after verifying that a temporary tag was valid and properly displayed, and noted that although a temporary tag is more difficult to read in the dark when a car is travelling on the interstate, that that fact does not make every vehicle displaying such a tag fair game for an extended Fourth Amendment seizure. That case, however, neither is controlling authority, nor representative of "a robust consensus of persuasive authority." Moreover, the case is unavailing here since McClendon (D) was awaiting criminal record (NCIC) results when he began to question Jamison (P), and such questioning while awaiting results from an NCIC check is not inappropriate. Thus, McClendon's (D) initial questioning was not in and of itself a Fourth Amendment violation. Given the lack of precedent that places the constitutional question "beyond debate," Jamison's (P) claim cannot proceed, as McClendon (D) is entitled to qualified immunity as to Jamison's (P) prolonged detention and unlawful search claims. Summary judgment, therefore, is granted to McClendon (D) as to those claims. However, because McClendon (D) failed to make any argument regarding Jamison's (P) claims for intentional and reckless damage to his car that resulted from McClendon's (D) search, McClendon (D) forfeited the resolution of that claim on summary judgment, so that the question of whether to grant or deny summary judgment as to that claim is simply not before the court. Accordingly, the claim will be set for trial.

ANALYSIS

Although Judge Reeves grants qualified immunity to officer McClendon (D), Judge Reeves makes clear that he does so only because he is bound to follow United States Supreme Court precedent, notwithstanding that he believes the doctrine of qualified immunity, as created and applied by the Supreme Court and the lower courts bound by Supreme Court precedent, operates like absolute immunity and serves to insulate police officers from accountability for many forms of abuse and misconduct, including thousands of unjustified police killings. After placing the doctrine of qualified immunity in a detailed historical context, as part of the ebb and flow of civil rights on the one hand, and the White supremacist backlash, terror, and violence in response to emancipationist efforts on the other, Judge Reeves says, "But let us not be fooled by legal jargon. Immunity is not exoneration. And the harm in this case to one man [meaning Jamison (P)] sheds light on the harm done to the nation by this manufactured doctrine." Judge Reeves delineates the history of the doctrine's evolution and concludes that the Supreme Court "has dispensed with any pretense of balancing competing values," i.e., balancing the rights of citizens against the need to protect officers who are required to exercise discretion. Judge Reeves adds that once, qualified immunity protected officers who acted in good faith but now protects all officers, no matter how egregious their conduct, if the law they broke was not "clearly established." He notes that the Supreme Court further increased the standard in 2011, when it added the words "beyond debate," so that for a law to be "clearly established, it must have been 'beyond debate' that the officer broke the law." As the Fifth Circuit Court of Appeals has observed, it does not matter if the conduct at issue shocks the conscience, as long as it cannot be shown that every reasonable officer would understand that what they were doing violated the law. Judge Reeves points out that qualified immunity has sweeping procedural advantages, and, being a question of law, creates a "super-summary judgment" right on behalf of government officials. Judge Reeves also notes numerous critiques of the doctrine. Finally, Judge Reeves concludes by calling on the Supreme Court to "waste no time" in righting "this wrong," since otherwise, by perpetuating the qualified immunity doctrine, the Court is perpetuating "something we all know to be wrong only because we fear the consequences of being right."

Continued on next page.

Quicknotes

FOURTH AMENDMENT Provides that persons be secure as to their person and private belongings against unreasonable searches and seizures.

QUALIFIED IMMUNITY An affirmative defense relieving officials from civil liability for the performance of activities within their discretion so long as such conduct is not in violation of an individual's rights pursuant to law as determined by a reasonable person standard.

REASONABLE PERSON STANDARD The standard of care exercised by one who possesses the intelligence, education, knowledge, attention, and judgment required by society of its members when governing behavior; the standard applies to a person's judgment when determining breach of a duty under the theory of negligence.

REASONABLE SUSPICION That which would cause an ordinary prudent person under the circumstances to suspect that a crime has been committed based on specific and articulable facts.

SEARCH An inspection conducted in order to obtain evidence to be utilized for the prosecution of a crime.

CHAPTER 6

Confessions: The Voluntariness Requirement

Quick Reference Rules of Law

Hector (A Slave) v. State

State (P) v. Burglary suspect (D)

Mo. Sup. Ct., 2 Mo. 166 (1829)

NATURE OF CASE: Appeal from trial court ruling that failed to exclude confessions extorted by use of torture.

FACT SUMMARY: When a burglary suspect, Hector (D), confessed to a crime while being flogged, his attorney argued the confession should be excluded.

RULE OF LAW
A confession not freely given but made under torture should be excluded.

FACTS: Hector (D) was caught "by certain persons" for suspected burglary and flogged all night, screaming under the lash, until he confessed. At one point Hector (D) said if they would stop flogging him, he would go and find the money. Hector's (D) attorney moved to exclude the confession and others on the ground they were not freely and voluntarily made but were extorted by pain and torture. The trial court overruled the motion, and Hector's (D) attorney appealed.

ISSUE: Should a confession not freely given but made under torture be excluded?

HOLDING AND DECISION: (M'Girk, C.J.) Yes. A confession not freely given but made under torture should be excluded. The record revealed Hector (D) was under the lash nearly all night. Of itself, such a circumstance would have been sufficient to cause him to confess to any crime charged. When he did ultimately confess, such confession most probably was to prevent further torture and to gain respite from the pain. The trial court further erred in leaving it to the jury to determine which confessions were voluntary and which were not. As a matter of law, this is a court decision. In this case, all confessions should have been excluded. Reversed.

ANALYSIS

The record in *Hector* indicated that all confessions appear to have been given either during torture, out of fear of torture, or to prevent further torture.

Quicknotes

COERCED CONFESSION A statement of a person charged with the commission of a criminal offense acknowledging his or her guilt in respect to the charged offense that was made when the confessor's free will was overcome as a result of threats, promises, or undue influence, and that is inadmissible at trial.

Brown v. Mississippi

Convicted murderer (D) v. State (P)

297 U.S. 278 (1936)

NATURE OF CASE: Appeal from murder conviction.

FACT SUMMARY: Brown (D) and others were convicted of murder after they were beaten into confessing to the crime, over their objection that the confessions were coerced.

RULE OF LAW

A confession obtained by inflicting physical pain during interrogation is not admissible against the accused.

FACTS: To elicit murder confessions, the Mississippi police tortured Brown (D) and other African-American men. One defendant was "hanged by a rope to the limb of a tree" three times by a sheriff and subsequently "tied to a tree and whipped," suffering intense pain and agony; later, the same defendant was severely whipped and told the whipping would continue "until he confessed." He confessed. Two other defendants were taken to jail, they were made to strip by the sheriff, and then "they were laid over chairs and their backs were cut to pieces with a leather strap with buckles on it." They too were told the whipping would continue until they confessed; they confessed. At trial, the sheriff admitted the whippings, as did other witnesses. Brown (D) and the other defendants were convicted. They appealed, challenging their conviction on due process grounds in a case of first impression.

ISSUE: Is a confession obtained by inflicting physical pain during the interrogation admissible against the accused?

HOLDING AND DECISION: (Hughes, C.J.) No. A confession obtained by inflicting physical pain during interrogation is not admissible against the accused. The method employed by the interrogating officers to obtain the confessions was a denial of due process. The rack and torture chamber may not be substituted for the witness stand. While states are free to regulate the procedure of their courts in accordance with their own conceptions of policy, such freedom is limited by the requirement of due process of law. In addition, the State's (P) argument that the accused's counsel failed to move for the exclusion of the coerced statements after their introduction has no merit. The duty of the trial court rises above simple procedural rules, particularly when a man is on trial for his life. The trial court was fully aware that there was no additional evidence upon which a conviction could stand. Reversed.

ANALYSIS

Brown v. Mississippi was the first of a long line of confession cases. In the following 20 years, the determining factors for "involuntariness" evolved from "special circumstances" involving physical brutality, upon which the defendant had the burden of proof, to "some" coercive force regardless of the methodology, and finally to a shifting of the burden to the prosecutor who must show, by a preponderance of the evidence, that no coercion occurred.

Quicknotes

COERCED CONFESSION A statement by a person charged with the commission of a criminal offense acknowledging his or her guilt in respect to the charged offense that was made when the confessor's free will was overcome as a result of threats, promises, or undue influence, and that is inadmissible at trial.

DUE PROCESS The constitutional mandate requiring the courts to protect and enforce individuals' rights and liberties consistent with prevailing principles of fairness and justice and prohibiting the federal and state governments from such activities that deprive its citizens of life, liberty, or property interest.

Lisenba v. California

Convicted murderer (D) v. State (P)

314 U.S. 219 (1941)

NATURE OF CASE: On certiorari from state supreme court judgment upholding murder conviction.

FACT SUMMARY: Lisenba (a.k.a. James) (D) married a woman, took out a life insurance policy on her, then murdered her in a manner to give the appearance of an accident.

RULE OF LAW

(1) Illegal acts committed in the course of procuring a confession do not automatically render the confession inadmissible as a violation of due process.

(2) All the surrounding circumstances must be evaluated to determine whether the confession was freely and voluntarily made.

FACTS: Lisenba (a.k.a. James) (D) hired Mary as a manicurist in his barbershop and subsequently married her. The marriage was invalid, as James (D) had a living wife. While James (D) and Mary were engaged, he took out a life insurance policy on Mary with himself as the beneficiary. After his earlier marriage was annulled, James (D) and Mary were married in a legal ceremony. Several months later, James (D) and a confederate blindfolded Mary, tied her to a table, and allowed rattlesnakes to bite her. When that did not succeed in killing her, they took her to a pond and drowned her. When James (D) attempted to collect the insurance, an investigation was instituted, resulting in his arrest. He eventually confessed, laying the blame for planning the crime on his confederate. When the prosecution sought to introduce the confession, James (D) moved to exclude it, arguing that he had been deprived of the opportunity to consult counsel and that he had been brought to the district attorney's office for questioning without a valid court order. James (D) also claimed that he had been mistreated by police several days earlier, although at the time he was mistreated he did not confess. The confession was admitted, and James (D) was convicted and sentenced to death.

ISSUE:

(1) Do illegal acts committed in the course of procuring a confession automatically render the confession inadmissible as a violation of due process?

(2) Must all the surrounding circumstances be evaluated to determine whether the confession was freely and voluntarily made?

HOLDING AND DECISION: (Roberts, J.)

(1) No. Illegal acts committed in the course of procuring a confession do not automatically render the confession inadmissible as a violation of due process.

(2) Yes. All the surrounding circumstances must be evaluated to determine whether the confession was freely and voluntarily made.

We are bound to make an independent examination of the record to evaluate James's (D) claim. We disapprove of any mistreatment of James (D) and of any unlawful acts by the state, including the deprivation of counsel. However, James (D) admits that no threats, promises, or acts of violence were employed during the questioning when he made his confession, or for eleven days before then. He displayed self-possession, coolness, and acumen during his questioning and at trial that negates the view that he had so lost his freedom of action that the statements he made were not his. The conviction is affirmed.

DISSENT: (Black, J.) Testimony of the officers was sufficient to indicate the confession was not freely and voluntarily given. The confession that convicted James (D) resulted from coercion and compulsion. Accordingly, it should be reversed.

ANALYSIS

The United States Supreme Court considered not only the circumstances directly surrounding the confession, but also James's (D) subjective traits that would bear on the likelihood of voluntariness. Justice Roberts described James (D) as "a man of intelligence and business experience," as well as noting an apparently similar incident where James (D) had collected double indemnity for the "accidental" death of a former wife. The Court also noted that while James (D) did not have his attorney present when he confessed, he had had a full opportunity in the days before to meet with and be advised by counsel.

Quicknotes

COERCED CONFESSION A statement of a person charged with the commission of a criminal offense acknowledging his or her guilt in respect to the charged offense that was

Continued on next page.

made when the confessor's free will was overcome as a result of threats, promises, or undue influence, and that is inadmissible at trial.

DUE PROCESS The constitutional mandate requiring the courts to protect and enforce individuals' rights and liberties consistent with prevailing principles of fairness and justice and prohibiting the federal and state governments from such activities that deprive its citizens of life, liberty, or property interest.

Spano v. New York

Bar-fighting murderer (D) v. State (P)

360 U.S. 315 (1959)

NATURE OF CASE: Appeal from a conviction for first-degree murder.

FACT SUMMARY: After prolonged interrogation, Spano (D) confessed to murder and was thereafter convicted of murder over his objection that the confession was involuntary.

RULE OF LAW

If a confession is obtained by overbearing the will of the accused, it is involuntary and inadmissible.

FACTS: Spano (D), who was a derivative citizen born in Italy, was 25, a junior high school graduate, and regularly employed. On the day of the shooting in question, Spano (D) was drinking in a bar. The decedent took some of Spano's (D) money from the bar. A fight ensued, and the decedent kicked Spano (D) in the head several times. Later, Spano (D) secured a gun, entered a store where the decedent was frequently found, and shot him to death. Spano (D) then disappeared. Later, Spano (D) informed a friend, Bruno who was a fledgling police officer, that he was giving himself up. Spano (D), accompanied by counsel, turned himself in. Thereafter, the police questioned Spano (D), without his attorney, for over eight hours. Using Bruno to gain his sympathy, Spano (D) was worn down physically and mentally until he finally confessed by answering leading questions in a question-and-answer confession. At the trial, the confession was introduced in evidence over appropriate objections. The jury was instructed that it could rely on it only if it was found to be voluntary. The jury returned a guilty verdict, and Spano (D) was sentenced to death. The New York Court of Appeals affirmed, and the United States Supreme Court granted certiorari.

ISSUE: If a confession is obtained by overbearing the will of the accused, is it involuntary and inadmissible?

HOLDING AND DECISION: (Warren, C.J.) Yes. If a confession is obtained by overbearing the will of the accused, it is involuntary and inadmissible. Spano (D) was a 25-year-old foreign-born man with no past history of law violation or of subjection to official interrogation. Spano (D) was not highly educated and had a history of emotional instability. Spano (D) did not make a narrative statement but was subject to the leading questions of a skillful prosecutor in a question-and-answer confession. He was subjected to questioning by many men. Spano (D) was questioned for virtually eight straight hours. The questioners persisted in the face of his repeated refusals to answer on the advice of his attorney, and they ignored his reasonable requests to contact his attorney. Spano's (D) will was overborne by official pressure, fatigue, and sympathy falsely aroused, and, thus, his confession was involuntary and cannot stand under the Fourteenth Amendment. Reversed.

CONCURRENCE: (Stewart, J.) The Constitution provides an accused the right to assistance of counsel at every stage of the criminal process. Here the police were questioning a suspect in investigating an unsolved crime. When Spano (D) surrendered to the New York authorities, he had already been indicted for first-degree murder. At that time he was constitutionally entitled to be represented by an attorney.

ANALYSIS

The abhorrence of society to the use of involuntary confessions does not turn alone on the inherent untrustworthiness of such confessions. It also turns on the deep-rooted notion the police must obey the law while enforcing the law, that in the end life and liberty can be as much endangered from illegal methods used to convict those thought to be criminals as from the actual criminals themselves. See *Brown v. Mississippi*, 297 U.S. 278 (1936), and *Ashcraft v. Tennessee*, 322 U.S. 143 (1944).

Quicknotes

COERCED CONFESSION A statement of person charged with the commission of a criminal offense acknowledging his or guilt in respect to the charged offense that was made when the confessor's free will was overcome as a result of threats, promises, or undue influence, and that is inadmissible at trial.

CUSTODIAL INTERROGATION The questioning of a suspect by police while in custody.

EXCLUSIONARY RULE A rule precluding the introduction at trial of evidence unlawfully obtained in violation of the federal constitutional safeguards against unreasonable searches and seizures.

CHAPTER 7

Police Interrogation: The Self-Incrimination Clause

Quick Reference Rules of Law

Escobedo v. Illinois

Convicted murderer (D) v. State (P)

378 U.S. 478 (1964)

NATURE OF CASE: Appeal from murder conviction on the grounds that confession was obtained in violation of the Sixth Amendment's right to counsel.

FACT SUMMARY: Escobedo (D), who was interrogated as a suspect in a murder, contended that he was denied his Sixth Amendment right to counsel after he and his attorney were separately denied the opportunity to consult with each other despite their repeated requests to be allowed to do so. The State (P) contended that Escobedo (D) did not have such a constitutional right.

RULE OF LAW

The Sixth Amendment's right to counsel requires that a criminal suspect have the assistance of counsel when, prior to formal indictment, the suspect is interrogated by police for the purpose of eliciting a confession.

FACTS: Escobedo's (D) brother-in-law was shot and killed. Without warrant, Escobedo (D) was arrested and interrogated, but he made no statement to the police and was released pursuant to a state court writ of habeas corpus obtained by his lawyer. Several days later, Escobedo's (D) accomplice told the police that Escobedo (D) had fired the fatal shots. Accordingly, the police again arrested Escobedo (D) and, during transport, told him that his accomplice had implicated him. The police urged Escobedo (D) to confess, but he did not, and instead asked to speak to his attorney. Shortly after Escobedo (D) arrived at police headquarters, his attorney also arrived and repeatedly asked to speak with Escobedo (D) but was repeatedly refused access. The police proceeded to interrogate Escobedo (D), prior to formally indicting him. During the interrogation, which occurred over a period of many hours, Escobedo (D) repeatedly asked to consult with his lawyer, but the police lied to him and told him that his lawyer did not want to see to him. Eventually, he confessed to complicity in the murder. No one advised Escobedo (D) of his right to counsel during the interrogation. Escobedo (D) moved both before and during trial to suppress his incriminating statement, but the motions were denied, and he was convicted of murder. The United States Supreme Court granted certiorari in the case.

ISSUE: Does the Sixth Amendment's right to counsel require that a criminal suspect have the assistance of counsel when, prior to formal indictment, the suspect is interrogated by police for the purpose of eliciting a confession?

HOLDING AND DECISION: (Goldberg, J.) Yes. The Sixth Amendment's right to counsel requires that a criminal suspect have the assistance of counsel when, prior to formal indictment, the suspect is interrogated by police for the purpose of eliciting a confession. Here, Escobedo (D), a layperson, was undoubtedly unaware that under state law an admission of "mere" complicity in the murder plot was legally as damaging as an admission of firing of the fatal shots, so that the guiding hand of counsel was essential to advise Escobedo (D) of his rights in such a delicate situation and at the stage when legal aid and advice were most critical to him. It would exalt form over substance to make the right to counsel, under these circumstances, depend on whether at the time of the interrogation the authorities had secured a formal indictment; here, for all intents and purposes, Escobedo (D) had been effectively charged with murder. Limiting the right to counsel to trial would make the trial no more than an appeal from the interrogation, and the right to use counsel at the formal trial would be a very hollow thing if, for all practical purposes, the conviction was already assured by a pre-trial confession. Precisely because the pre-trial interrogation phase of an investigation is so crucial to the police, that is a stage when the need for legal aid and advice is at its highest, and the Sixth Amendment strikes the balance in favor of the accused to be advised of the privilege against self-incrimination. History teaches that a system of criminal law enforcement that depends on "confessions" will, in the long run, be less reliable and more subject to abuses than a system that depends on extrinsic evidence independently secured through skillful investigation. Moreover, no system of criminal justice can, or should, survive if it comes to depend for its continued effectiveness on the citizens' abdication through unawareness of their constitutional rights. No system worth preserving should have to fear that if an accused is permitted to consult with a lawyer, the accused will become aware of and exercise these rights. If the exercise of constitutional rights will thwart the effectiveness of a system of law enforcement, then there is something very wrong with that system. Accordingly, where, as here, the investigation is no longer a general inquiry into an unsolved crime but has begun to focus on a particular suspect, the suspect has been taken into police custody, the police carry out a process of interrogations that lends itself to eliciting incriminating statements, the suspect has requested and been denied an opportunity to consult

Continued on next page.

with legal counsel, and the police have not effectively warned the suspect of the constitutional right to remain silent, the accused has been denied the constitutionally guaranteed right to assistance of counsel so that no statement elicited by the police during the interrogation may be used against the accused at a criminal trial.

DISSENT: (Stewart, J.) Escobedo's (D) confession was a voluntary one, given during the course of a perfectly legitimate police investigation of an unsolved murder. Such investigations are intended to affect trial—that is their purpose. The majority faults the police for not advising Escobedo (D) of his constitutional rights, but the Court has never required that the police provide such advice. The majority also converts a routine police investigation into a distorted analogue of a judicial trial. It imports into such an investigation constitutional concepts historically applicable only after the onset of formal prosecutorial proceedings. By doing so, the majority perverts those precious constitutional guarantees, and frustrates the vital interests of society in preserving the legitimate and proper function of honest and purposeful police investigation.

DISSENT: (White, J.) The majority incorrectly relies on the Sixth Amendment for the right of an accused against self-incrimination. The Sixth Amendment never was meant to amend or supersede the self-incrimination provision of the Fifth Amendment, and nothing in history, the Constitution's text, or the Court's precedents supports the proposition that an accused has an absolute constitutional right not to answer even in the absence of compulsion. The majority's decision also cannot be squared with other constitutional provisions. The Fourth Amendment permits, where there is probable cause, even compulsory searches of the suspect and the suspect's possessions and the use of the fruits of such searches at trial, all in the absence of counsel. The Fifth Amendment authorizes inquisitorial grand jury proceedings at which a potential defendant, in the absence of counsel, is shielded against no more than compulsory incrimination, and a grand jury witness, who may be a suspect, may be interrogated, and the witness's answers, at least until today's decision, are admissible in evidence at trial. Until the majority's decision here, these provisions have been thought of as constitutional safeguards to persons suspected of an offense. Instead, the only "inquisitions" the Constitution forbids are those that compel self-incrimination. Here, Escobedo's (D) confession was not compelled, and the majority does not hold that it was. Instead, it seems that the majority is concerned with the narrower issue of an unknowing defendant who responds to police questioning because the defendant mistakenly believes that he must and that his admissions will not be used against him. That concern, however, goes to whether a confession was compelled, but, standing alone, the Court's precedents have never placed a premium on ignorance of constitutional rights. If an accused is told he must answer police questioning, and the accused does not know better, it would be very doubtful that the resulting admissions could be used against the accused, because when the accused has not been informed of his rights at all, the Court characteristically and properly looks very closely at the surrounding circumstances. However, here, Escobedo (D) knew full well that he did not have to answer and knew full well that his lawyer had advised him not to answer. Although the majority's rule will not cripple law enforcement efforts, it will make them a great deal more difficult, for unsound, unstated reasons that can find no home in any of the provisions of the Constitution.

ANALYSIS

Two years after *Escobedo* was decided, the United States Supreme Court handed down its landmark decision in *Miranda v. United States*, 384 U.S. 436 (1966). Although the Court reaffirmed its holding in *Escobedo*, it announced a sweeping rule requiring warnings against self-incrimination, grounded in the Fifth Amendment, in the setting of custodial interrogations. The Court seems to have done so because it became clear that the *Escobedo* rule was too imprecise, was not well supported by the Sixth Amendment's text, and, as a practical matter, few suspects had counsel or would know to ask for advice of counsel once they were being interrogated as adversarial suspects, rather than generally, as witnesses.

Quicknotes

COMPLICITY The act of conspiring to, or participating in, the commission of an unlawful act.

EXTRINSIC EVIDENCE Evidence that is not contained within the text of a document or contract, but that is derived from the parties' statements or the circumstances under which the agreement was made.

FIFTH AMENDMENT Provides that no person shall be compelled to serve as a witness against him- or herself, be subject to trial for the same offense twice, or be deprived of life, liberty, or property without due process of law.

FOURTH AMENDMENT Provides that persons be secure as to their person and private belongings against unreasonable searches and seizures.

PROBABLE CAUSE A reasonable basis for believing that a crime has been committed.

Continued on next page.

RIGHT TO COUNSEL Right conferred by the Sixth Amendment that the accused shall be provided effective legal assistance in a criminal proceeding.

SEARCH An inspection conducted in order to obtain evidence to be utilized for the prosecution of a crime.

SIXTH AMENDMENT Provides the right to a speedy and public trial by impartial jury, the right to be informed of the accusation, the right to confront witnesses, and the right to have the assistance of counsel in all criminal prosecutions.

WRIT OF HABEAS CORPUS A proceeding in which a defendant brings a writ to compel a judicial determination of whether he or she is lawfully being held in custody.

Miranda v. Arizona

Coerced confessor (D) v. State (P)

384 U.S. 436 (1966)

NATURE OF CASE: Appeal from convictions for murder.

FACT SUMMARY: In this consolidation of several cases, Miranda (D) and others appealed from their convictions, claiming that their confessions were elicited through violation of their constitutional rights.

RULE OF LAW

The prosecution may not use statements stemming from custodial interrogation of the defendant, unless it demonstrates the use of procedural safeguards effective to secure the privilege against self-incrimination.

FACTS: In *Miranda v. Arizona*, the police arrested Miranda (D) and took him to a special room where they secured a confession. In *Vignera v. New York*, Vignera (D) made oral admissions to the police after interrogation. In *Westover v. United States*, Westover (D) was handed over to the FBI by local authorities after they had detained and interrogated him for a lengthy period. The FBI obtained signed statements from Westover (D). Lastly, in *California v. Stewart*, the local police held Stewart (D) for five days in the station, interrogating him until they secured his inculpatory statement. In none of these cases was the defendant given a full and effective warning of his rights at the outset of the interrogation process. In all the cases, the questioning elicited oral admissions, and in three of them signed statements as well, which were admitted at their trials. Miranda (D) and the others appealed from their convictions on the ground that their admissions were secured through means that violated their constitutional rights.

ISSUE: May the prosecution use statements stemming from custodial interrogation of the defendant where it does not demonstrate the use of procedural safeguards effective to secure the privilege against self-incrimination?

HOLDING AND DECISION: (Warren, C.J.) No. The prosecution may not use statements stemming from custodial interrogation of the defendant unless it demonstrates the use of procedural safeguards effective to secure the privileges against self-incrimination. Prior to any questioning, the person must be warned that he has a right to remain silent, that any statement he does make may be used as evidence against him, and that he has a right to the presence of an attorney. The defendant may waive effectuation of these rights, provided the waiver is made voluntarily, knowingly, and intelligently. Likewise, if the individual is alone and indicates in any manner that he does not wish to be interrogated, the police may not question him. In each of the cases at bar, Miranda (D) and the others were subjected to menacing custodial interrogation without the benefits of any procedural safeguards in derogation of their Fifth Amendment rights against self-incrimination. Reversed.

DISSENT: (Harlan, J.) The decision of the Court today in abandoning its historical case-by-case approach represents poor constitutional law. The Court's new rules are designed to ultimately discourage any confession at all. Such an approach cannot be sustained by constitutional or policy considerations. First, constitutionally, there is no basis for extending the Fifth Amendment to the police station. Historically, the ban against self-incrimination has applied only in criminal proceedings, not in "extralegal" situations, such as interrogations. Furthermore, even if it can be applied to custodial interrogations, it has never been held to forbid all pressures on an accused, as the Court today attempts to do. Similarly, there is no constitutional basis for applying the right to counsel to custodial interrogations. The danger of injustice by allowing an untrained person to defend himself in a technical court situation is the basis for this right, and that rationale is not applicable to custodial situations. Second, in considering policy issues, although it is true that police questioning will inherently entail some pressure on the suspect, until today the role of the Constitution has been to "sift out" only "undue pressure." The inflexible rules today, however, ignore this. Those who use coercive tactics may simply lie in court about having given the required warnings. Nothing is gained and many voluntary confessions will be lost. In conclusion, neither the constitutional interpretations nor the consequences of today's ruling are justifiable.

DISSENT: (White, J.) First, the Fifth Amendment forbids self-incrimination only if it is "compelled." Yet, the Court today has no factual basis for concluding that custodial interrogations are so inherently coercive as to make any statements arising from them, if there is no warning of rights, compelled. In fact, the Court has not examined a single transcript of any police interrogation. Furthermore, even if it is assumed that "all" such interrogations are coercive, the rule adopted today is irrational. If such interrogations are so "coercive," how can a suspect ever voluntarily waive his rights as the Court indicates he can? Second, and more importantly, the Court overlooks

Continued on next page.

the ominous consequences of its decision. Although the Court states that the rule adopted is necessary to preserve the "integrity" of the individual, it overlooks the fact that without effective prevention of crime (or personal violence), there can be no human dignity. The most basic function of any government is to provide for the security of an individual and his property but after today's decision, effective law enforcement will be impaired, both by the fact that more who are guilty may go free and many who could easily explain their innocence will waste police time while waiting for their attorneys.

ANALYSIS

In *Michigan v. Mosley,* 423 U.S. 96 (1975), detectives gave the defendant the *Miranda* warnings and then questioned him about the robbery charges for which he had been arrested. When he said he did not want to be questioned any further, the questioning stopped. A few hours later, after repeating the warnings, other detectives questioned the defendant about a homicide for which he had not been arrested. His answers incriminated him, and he was prosecuted for murder. The United States Supreme Court held that the resumption of questioning, each session being independent of the other and accompanied by warnings, did not violate *Miranda*; that is to say, *Miranda* did not create a per se proscription of indefinite duration.

Quicknotes

CUSTODIAL INTERROGATION The questioning of a suspect by police while in custody.

EXCULPATORY CLAUSE A clause in a contract relieving one party from liability for certain unlawful conduct.

FIFTH AMENDMENT Provides that no person shall be compelled to serve as a witness against himself, be subject to trial for the same offense twice, or be deprived of life, liberty, or property without due process of law.

INCULPATORY EVIDENCE A statement or other evidence tending to show a person's guilt in committing a criminal act.

PER SE By itself; without more; taken alone; not requiring additional evidence for proof; as a matter of law.

New York v. Quarles

State (P) v. Gun owner (D)

467 U.S. 649 (1984)

NATURE OF CASE: Appeal from order to suppress evidence.

FACT SUMMARY: The trial court granted Quarles's (D) motion to suppress a statement he made to police before being given his *Miranda* warnings.

RULE OF LAW

Police need not give *Miranda* warnings where the need for such warnings is outweighed by the need to protect the public safety.

FACTS: Two New York police officers were approached by a woman who said she had just been raped by a large Black man who was armed and who had just entered a supermarket. The police entered the market and apprehended Quarles (D) after a short chase. Officer Kraft frisked him, while three other officers surrounded him and discovered he was wearing an empty shoulder holster. After handcuffing him, Kraft asked Quarles (D) where the gun was. Quarles (D) told him, and after the gun was retrieved, he was placed under arrest and given his *Miranda* rights. In his trial for criminal possession of a weapon, Quarles (D) successfully moved to suppress the gun and the statement on the basis that at the time the statement was made he had not been given his *Miranda* warning. The State (P) appealed, contending the need to protect public safety outweighed the need to protect Quarles's (D) *Miranda* rights, thereby eliminating the need to read them in this case. The court of appeals affirmed, and the United States Supreme Court granted certiorari.

ISSUE: Do the police need to give *Miranda* warnings where the need for such warnings is outweighed by the need to protect the public safety?

HOLDING AND DECISION: (Rehnquist, J.) No. Police need not give *Miranda* warnings where the need for such warnings is outweighed by the need to protect public safety. In this case, the police were placed in a situation where in order to protect the people in the supermarket, they had to find a gun they had reason to believe was in the vicinity of the suspect. Under these circumstances, concern for public safety outweighed Quarles's (D) immediate invocation of his Fifth Amendment right against compelled self-incrimination. Therefore, the evidence should not have been suppressed. Reversed and remanded.

CONCURRENCE AND DISSENT: (O'Connor, J.) *Miranda* is now the law and the Court has not provided sufficient justification for departing from it or for blurring its now clear strictures. Accordingly, the initial statement taken from Quarles (D) should be repressed. A "public safety" exception unnecessarily blurs the edges of the clear line heretofore established and makes *Miranda*'s requirements more difficult to understand. In some cases, police will benefit because a reviewing court will find that an exigency excused their failure to administer the required warnings. But in other cases, police will suffer because, though they thought an exigency excused their noncompliance, a reviewing court will view the "objective" circumstances differently and require exclusion of admissions thereby obtained. The end result will be a fine-spun new doctrine on public safety exigencies incident to custodial interrogation, complete with the hair-splitting distinctions that currently plague our Fourth Amendment jurisprudence.

DISSENT: (Marshall, J.) Quarles (D) clearly was in custody and was interrogated without being advised of his *Miranda* rights. Therefore, the evidence must be suppressed. The questioning of Quarles (D) was coercive. The police questioned him in the middle of the night in the rear of an empty supermarket. His hands were handcuffed behind his back, and he was surrounded by four armed officers. The irony of today's majority decision is that safety of the public can be protected without Fifth Amendment abridgement.

ANALYSIS

This case illustrates the United States Supreme Court's adoption of a public safety exception to the requirement that a suspect in custody be informed of his rights to remain silent and to have counsel present during questioning. Even if the evidence were suppressed under *Miranda v. Arizona*, 384 U.S. 436 (1966), it could be admissible under the inevitable discovery doctrine of *Nix v. Williams*, 467 U.S. 431 (1984).

Quicknotes

CERTIORARI A discretionary writ issued by a superior court to an inferior court in order to review the lower court's decisions; the U.S. Supreme Court's writ ordering such review.

CUSTODIAL INTERROGATION The questioning of a suspect by police while in custody.

Continued on next page.

***MIRANDA* WARNINGS** Specified warnings that must be communicated to a person prior to a custodial interrogation; in the absence of the communication of such warnings, any communications made during the interrogation are inadmissible at trial.

PRIVILEGE AGAINST SELF-INCRIMINATION A privilege guaranteed by the Fifth Amendment to the U.S. Constitution in a criminal proceeding for communications made by an accused and protecting an accused or witness from having to give testimony that may incriminate him- or herself.

STOP AND FRISK A brief, nonintrusive stop requiring the police officer to have a reasonable suspicion that a crime has been committed or is contemplated being committed based on specific and articulable facts and involving a search for a concealed weapon that is conducted by patting down the clothes of the person.

Oregon v. Elstad

State (P) v. Convicted burglar (D)

470 U.S. 298 (1985)

NATURE OF CASE: Appeal from conviction for burglary.

FACT SUMMARY: Oregon (P) appealed from a decision of the Oregon Court of Appeals that reversed Elstad's (D) conviction for burglary, holding that the initial failure of police officers to administer *Miranda* warnings tainted the subsequent confession Elstad (D) made after he had been advised of and waived his *Miranda* rights.

RULE OF LAW

A voluntary, signed confession made after being fully advised of *Miranda* rights is not rendered inadmissible by a prior remark made in response to questioning without benefit of *Miranda* warnings.

FACTS: A witness implicated Elstad (D) in the burglary of a local home. Officers Burke and McAllister went to Elstad's (D) home with an arrest warrant. While McAllister advised Elstad's (D) mother of what was happening, Burke told Elstad (D) that they had a warrant for his arrest and that he felt Elstad (D) had been involved. Elstad (D) replied, "Yes, I was there." He was then transported to sheriff headquarters, where, after being fully advised of his *Miranda* rights, he voluntarily made and signed a confession. At his trial, the trial court excluded the statement made at Elstad's (D) home but admitted the confession. He was convicted, and he appealed. The Oregon Court of Appeals reversed, finding that the confession, though voluntarily made after being warned of his *Miranda* rights, was tainted by the earlier remark that the State (P) conceded was made in violation of *Miranda*. It held the confession inadmissible, and overturned Elstad's (D) conviction, and from this decision, the State (P) appealed.

ISSUE: Is a voluntary, signed confession made after being fully advised of *Miranda* rights rendered inadmissible by a prior remark made in response to questioning without benefit of *Miranda* warnings?

HOLDING AND DECISION: (O'Connor, J.) No. A voluntary, signed confession made after being fully advised of *Miranda* rights is not rendered inadmissible by a prior remark made in response to questioning without the benefit of *Miranda* warnings. A procedural *Miranda* violation differs significantly from a Fourth Amendment exclusionary rule violation, whose purpose to deter improper conduct justifies application of the "fruit of the poisonous tree doctrine." The *Miranda* exclusionary rule serves the Fifth Amendment, and the failure to administer *Miranda* warnings raises a presumption of compulsion; this presumption, however, does not necessarily require that the statement and its fruits are irreparably tainted. If such evidence is to be suppressed, one must consider whether this action will deter improper police conduct or will ensure the truthfulness of the evidence admitted. The statement made in the absence of *Miranda* warnings should be suppressed, but absent any evidence of coercion, the admissibility of subsequent statements should turn solely on whether they were knowingly or voluntarily made. Whatever the reason was that Burke failed to give *Miranda* warnings at the outset, it is clear there was no element of coercion involved and the subsequent waiver of the right to remain silent was made voluntarily and knowingly. The reading of *Miranda* rights at this later stage was complete and should serve to remove the presumption of compulsion. The contention that the police were required to tell Elstad (D) that the earlier remark could not have been used is neither practical nor constitutionally mandated. Reversed.

DISSENT: (Brennan, J.) Most federal courts have rejected the rule adopted today. There should be a presumption that a statement obtained in violation of *Miranda* taints subsequent statements, particularly when the second confession is obtained as a result of confronting the defendant with the earlier illegal confession.

ANALYSIS

Justice Brennan's fears that the present case may be used to obtain confessions may be unfounded. There appears to be a view that few officers are sophisticated enough to make the attempt, and that if an officer is confronted with a suspect who wants to talk, the confession can probably be obtained after giving *Miranda* rights.

Quicknotes

EXCLUSIONARY RULE A rule precluding the introduction at trial of evidence unlawfully obtained in violation of the federal constitutional safeguards against unreasonable searches and seizures.

Continued on next page.

FRUIT OF THE POISONOUS TREE Doctrine that evidence obtained as a result of illegal procedures is tainted and is usually inadmissible at trial.

***MIRANDA* WARNINGS** Specified warnings that must be communicated to a person prior to a custodial interrogation; in the absence of the communication of such warnings, any communications made during the interrogation are inadmissible at trial.

Dickerson v. United States

Bank robber (D) v. Federal government (P)

530 U.S. 428 (2000)

NATURE OF CASE: Appeal from denial of motion to suppress statement based on *Miranda* violation.

FACT SUMMARY: Dickerson (D) sought to suppress a statement he made while in an FBI field office prior to being given his *Miranda* warnings.

RULE OF LAW

When a decision of the Court involves interpretation and application of the Constitution, Congress may not legislatively supersede such decision.

FACTS: Dickerson (D) was indicted for bank robbery and conspiracy to commit bank robbery. Before trial he moved to suppress a statement he made at a Federal Bureau of Investigation (FBI) field office, on the grounds that he had not received *Miranda* warnings before being interrogated. The district court granted the motion, and the Government (P) took an interlocutory appeal to the court of appeals, which reversed, stating that 18 U.S.C. § 3501 was satisfied since the statement was made voluntarily. Dickerson (D) appealed.

ISSUE: When a decision of the Court involves interpretation and application of the Constitution, may Congress legislatively supersede such a decision?

HOLDING AND DECISION: (Rehnquist, C.J.) No. When a decision of the Court involves interpretation and application of the Constitution, Congress may not legislatively supersede such decision. *Miranda* and its progeny govern the admissibility of statements made during custodial interrogation in both state and federal courts. Section 3501 provides that the admissibility of a custodial suspect's statements should depend on whether they are voluntarily made. Prior to *Miranda*, the admissibility of a suspect's confession was evaluated under a voluntariness test. The requirement of voluntariness was based on the Fifth Amendment right against self-incrimination and the Due Process Clause of the Fourteenth Amendment. The Court's decisions in *Miranda*, 384 U.S. 436 (1966), and *Malloy v. Hogan*, 378 U.S. 1 (1964), changed the focus of the due process inquiry. In *Malloy*, the Court held that the Fifth Amendment's self-incrimination clause is incorporated into the Due Process Clause of the Fourteenth Amendment, and this applies to the states. In *Miranda*, the Court recognized that the coercion inherent in custodial interrogation makes it difficult to determine whether a statement is voluntary or involuntary and heightens the risk of self-incrimination. Section 3501 was enacted two years after the decision in *Miranda* and was intended by Congress to overrule the Court's decision in that case. The issue is whether Congress has the constitutional authority to do so. While Congress retains the ultimate authority to modify or set aside any judicially created rules of evidence and procedure that are not required by the Constitution, it may not legislatively supersede the Court's decisions that interpret and apply the Constitution. *Miranda* is a constitutional decision. The Court specifically stated that it was intended "to explore some facets of the problems of applying the privilege against self-incrimination to in-custody interrogation and to give concrete constitutional guidelines for law enforcement agencies and courts to follow." The decision is otherwise replete with references to constitutional rules and standards. *Miranda* announced a constitutional rule that Congress may not supersede legislatively. Reversed.

DISSENT: (Scalia, J.) To justify the majority's result the Court is adopting a significant new, if not entirely comprehensible, principle of constitutional law. The majority has held that statutes of Congress can be disregarded, not only when what they prescribe violates the Constitution, but when what they prescribe contradicts a decision of the Supreme Court. What this means is that the Supreme Court has the power not merely to apply the Constitution but to expand it, imposing what it regards as useful "prophylactic" restrictions upon Congress and the states. "That is an immense and frightening antidemocratic power, and it does not exist."

ANALYSIS

The Court also relies on the principle of stare decisis as weighing heavily against overruling *Miranda*, since *Miranda* warnings have become "embedded in routine police practice to the point where the warnings have become part of our national culture." Justice Scalia rejects such rationale on the basis that the court rules are both "mutable and modifiable" and that they "must make sense."

Quicknotes

DUE PROCESS CLAUSE Language in the Fifth and Fourteenth Amendments to the U.S. Constitution

Continued on next page.

providing that no person shall be deprived of "life, liberty, or property, without due process of law."

***MIRANDA* WARNINGS** Specified warnings that must be communicated to a person prior to a custodial interrogation; in the absence of the communication of such warnings, any communications made during the interrogation are inadmissible at trial.

STARE DECISIS Doctrine whereby courts follow legal precedent unless there is good cause for departure.

Missouri v. Seibert

State (P) v. Murder suspect (D)

542 U.S. 600 (2004)

NATURE OF CASE: Appeal from reversal of a murder conviction.

FACT SUMMARY: Patrice Seibert (D) argued that since her murder confession was obtained by the police technique of interrogating in successive, unwarned and warned phases, known as "question-first," the requirements of *Miranda* were violated.

RULE OF LAW

The police technique of interrogating in successive, unwarned and warned phases violates the requirements of *Miranda*.

FACTS: In questioning Patrice Seibert (D), a murder suspect, the police interrogator employed a widely used interrogation technique known as "question-first," in which the interrogator questions the suspect first, then gives the *Miranda* warnings, and then repeats the questioning until the interrogator obtains the confession or incriminating statement that the suspect has already previously provided. After employing this technique of interrogating in successive, unwarned and warned phases, Seibert (D) confessed to murder prior to her warnings and then again after being given the warnings. The trial court suppressed Seibert's (D) prewarning confession but admitted her postwarning confession. She was convicted of murder. The Missouri Supreme Court reversed, holding that here where the interrogation was "nearly continuous," the second statement was clearly "the product of the invalid first statement and should have been suppressed. Missouri (P) appealed.

ISSUE: Does the police technique of interrogating in successive, unwarned and warned phases violate the requirements of *Miranda*?

HOLDING AND DECISION: (Souter, J.) Yes. The police technique of interrogating in successive, unwarned and warned phases violates the requirements of *Miranda*. *Miranda* addressed interrogation practices likely to disable an individual from making a free and rational choice about speaking and held that a suspect must be "adequately and effectively" advised of the choice the Constitution guarantees. The object of the "question-first" technique here utilized against Seibert (D) was to render *Miranda* warnings ineffective by waiting for a particularly opportune time to give them, after the suspect had already confessed. Just as no talismanic incantation is required to satisfy *Miranda's* strictures, it would be absurd to think that mere recitation of the litany suffices to satisfy *Miranda* in every conceivable circumstance. The issue when interrogators question first and warn later is thus whether the warnings reasonably convey to a suspect her *Miranda* rights. Unless the warnings could place a suspect who has just been interrogated in a position to make an informed choice as to whether to speak, there is no practical justification for accepting the formal warnings as compliance with *Miranda* or for treating the second stage of interrogation as distinct from the first, unwarned and inadmissible segment. By any objective measure applied to circumstances exemplified here, it is likely that if the interrogators employ the technique of withholding warnings until after interrogation succeeds in eliciting a confession, the warnings will be ineffective in preparing the suspect for successive interrogation, close in time, and similar in content. Accordingly, the question-first tactic effectively threatens to thwart *Miranda*'s purpose of reducing the risk that a coerced confession would be admitted. Affirmed.

CONCURRENCE: (Breyer, J.) Courts should exclude the "fruits" of the initial unwarned questioning unless the failure to warn was in good faith.

CONCURRENCE: (Kennedy, J.) Not every violation of *Miranda* requires suppression of the evidence obtained. The scope of the *Miranda* suppression remedy depends on a consideration of whether admission of the evidence under the circumstances would frustrate *Miranda's* "central concerns and objectives."

DISSENT: (O'Connor, J.) Because here the isolated fact of the interrogating officer's intent could not have had any bearing on Seibert's (D) capacity to comprehend and knowingly relinquish her right to remain silent, it could not by itself affect the voluntariness of her confession.

ANALYSIS

As the United States Supreme Court makes clear in *Seibert*, the reason for the increased popularity of the question-first method of interrogation is to obtain a confession the suspect would not make if he or she understood his or her rights at the outset. The underlying police assumption, which is accurate, is that with one confession in hand before the warnings, the interrogator can usually count on getting a duplicate. It is unrealistic, explained the Court, to treat two bouts of

Continued on next page.

integrated and proximately conducted questioning as independent interrogations subject to independent evaluation simply because *Miranda* warnings formally punctuate them in the middle.

Quicknotes

CUSTODIAL INTERROGATION The questioning of a suspect by police while in custody.

***MIRANDA* RULE** A required warning given before any questioning by law enforcement authorities can take place. Individuals in custody receive warnings regarding their privilege against self-incrimination, right to remain silent, and right to be represented by an attorney.

***MIRANDA* WARNINGS** Specified warnings that must be communicated to a person prior to a custodial interrogation; in the absence of the communication of such warnings, any communications made during the interrogation are inadmissible at trial.

Berkemer v. McCarty

Drunk driver (D) v. Court (P)

468 U.S. 420 (1984)

NATURE OF CASE: Appeal of conviction for driving under the influence of alcohol and/or drugs.

FACT SUMMARY: When stopped by a traffic officer, Berkemer (D) admitted prior use of alcohol and marijuana.

RULE OF LAW

Miranda warnings do not have to be given during a routine traffic stop.

FACTS: A highway patrol officer noticed Berkemer (D) driving erratically. He pulled him over and subjected him to a field sobriety test, which he failed. Upon being asked if he had been drinking, Berkemer (D) admitted consumption of alcohol and marijuana. He was then arrested. At trial, his statement was admitted against him over objections that the *Miranda* warnings have to be given during a routine traffic stop.

ISSUE: Do *Miranda* warnings have to be given during a routine traffic stop?

HOLDING AND DECISION: (Marshall, J.) No. *Miranda* warnings do not have to be given during a routine traffic stop. *Miranda* is concerned with the inherently coercive nature of custodial interrogation. A roadside stop differs from custodial interrogation in several respects. First, usually only one or two officers are present. Second, such detentions are usually open to public view. Finally, the duration is generally rather short. For these reasons, the Court finds a routine traffic stop not to be so coercive that *Miranda* is implicated. Affirmed.

ANALYSIS

The United States Supreme Court likened routine traffic stops to the situation in *Terry v. Ohio,* 392 U.S. 1 (1968). In *Terry,* incriminating evidence was found on a person during a "pat down." The Court declined to extend *Miranda* to this situation, holding it not to be inherently coercive.

Quicknotes

CUSTODIAL INTERROGATION The questioning of a suspect by police while in custody.

***MIRANDA* WARNINGS** Specified warnings that must be communicated to a person prior to a custodial interrogation; in the absence of the communication of such warnings, any communications made during the interrogation are inadmissible at trial.

TRAFFIC STOP A police officer may stop an automobile and conduct a search of the vehicle without a valid warrant if he or she has probable cause to believe the vehicle contains evidence of a crime or contraband.

Rhode Island v. Innis

State (P) v. Convict with conscience (D)

446 U.S. 291 (1980)

NATURE OF CASE: Review of reversal of conviction for murder.

FACT SUMMARY: Murder suspect Innis (D) directed police officers, who were driving him to the police station following his arrest, to his hidden murder weapon after listening to the officers discuss the risk of harm to nearby children if the weapon were not found quickly.

RULE OF LAW

The term "interrogation" under *Miranda* refers not only to express questioning, but also to any words or actions on the part of the police (other than those normally attendant to arrest and custody) that the police should know are reasonably likely to elicit an incriminating response.

FACTS: On January 16, 1975, the body of a Providence, Rhode Island, taxicab driver killed by a shotgun blast was found. On January 17, 1975, a taxicab driver at Providence police headquarters identified Innis (D) from a photograph as the man who had used a shotgun to rob him in his taxicab earlier that night. Later that night a police officer spotted Innis (D) standing in the street unarmed, arrested him, and advised him of his *Miranda* rights. Innis (D) stated that he wanted to speak with his lawyer. Patrolmen Gleckman, Williams, and McKenna drove Innis (D) to the police station in a patrol car while other officers searched the arrest scene for the shotgun. En route to the police station, Gleckman expressed his concern to McKenna that a school for handicapped children stood near the arrest scene, and "God forbid one of them might find a weapon with shells, and they might hurt themselves." McKenna concurred in the apprehension expressed by Gleckman. Innis (D) interrupted the conversation to direct the officers to the shotgun, which was hidden nearby. Innis (D) was tried, and convicted of murder. The Rhode Island Supreme Court reversed the conviction on the grounds that the officers' dialogue constituted "subtle compulsion" and was therefore equivalent to interrogation under *Miranda*. The State (P) appealed.

ISSUE: Does the term "interrogation" under *Miranda* refer not only to express questioning, but also to any words or actions on the part of the police (other than those normally attendant to arrest and custody) that the police should know are reasonably likely to elicit an incriminating response?

HOLDING AND DECISION: (Stewart, J.) Yes. The term "interrogation" under *Miranda* refers not only to express questioning, but also to any words or actions on the part of the police (other than those normally attendant to arrest and custody) that the police should know are reasonably likely to elicit an incriminating response. The *Miranda* proscriptions were designed to prevent a combination of interrogation and custody that would "subjugate the individual to the will of his examiner." The police practices that evoked this concern included several that did not involve express questioning (e.g., doctored lineups, positing the guilt of the accused, blaming the victim or society). Interrogation within the meaning of *Miranda* therefore extends to express questioning and its functional equivalent. The functional equivalent standard applies to any words or actions by the police, other than those normally attendant to arrest and custody, that the police should know are reasonably likely to elicit an incriminating response from the suspect. Since *Miranda* is concerned with protecting suspects from coercive police practices irrespective of the underlying intent of the police, reasonableness is determined by an examination of the perception of the suspect rather than the intent of the police. The conversation between the officers constituted neither express questioning nor its functional equivalent. The entire conversation consisted of a few offhand remarks in the form of a dialogue to which no response by Innis (D) was invited. Furthermore, nothing in the record suggests that they should have known that Innis (D) was particularly susceptible to an appeal to his conscience concerning the safety of the handicapped children. Reversed.

CONCURRENCE: (Burger, C.J.) The meaning of *Miranda* is reasonably clear, and the practices of law enforcement have adjusted to its confines. *Miranda* should neither be overruled, disparaged, nor extended.

DISSENT: (Marshall, J.) The Court's definition of "interrogation" is correct but its finding that Innis (D) was not interrogated in this case is wrong. Gleckman's appeal to Innis's (D) conscience was a classic interrogation technique and would have constituted interrogation if it had been directed at Innis (D). The result should not be different because the remarks were nominally addressed to another officer.

DISSENT: (Stevens, J.) From the suspect's point of view, the effectiveness of *Miranda* warnings depends on whether it appears that the police are scrupulously honoring his rights. Therefore, any statement that would normally be understood by the average listener as calling for a response is the functional equivalent of a direct question, whether or not it is punctuated by a question mark.

Continued on next page.

ANALYSIS

Justice Stewart explained that the intent of the police "may well have a bearing on whether the police should have known that their words or actions were likely to evoke an incriminating response." In *Brewer v. Williams*, 430 U.S. 387 (1977), the defendant was a mentally ill and very religious man suspected of killing a missing child. When a police officer mentioned to the defendant that the child would need a "good, Christian burial," the defendant directed police to the child's body. His subsequent murder conviction was overturned on Sixth Amendment grounds, based on the officer's knowledge of the suspect's religious fervor and his susceptibility to appeals based on his religious beliefs.

Quicknotes

CUSTODIAL INTERROGATION The questioning of a suspect by police while in custody.

North Carolina v. Butler

State (P) v. Mirandized confessor (D)

441 U.S. 369 (1979)

NATURE OF CASE: Appeal from a conviction for kidnapping, armed robbery, and felonious assault.

FACT SUMMARY: Butler's (D) conviction for kidnapping, etc. was overturned on the ground that no statement of a person under custodial interrogation may be admitted in evidence against him unless he had explicitly waived the right to the presence of a lawyer.

RULE OF LAW

An express oral or written statement of waiver is not a prerequisite to establishing that a defendant waived his *Miranda* rights.

FACTS: Having been arrested and advised of his *Miranda* rights, Butler (D) was taken to the local office of the Federal Bureau of Investigation (FBI) for interrogation. There, Butler (D) was given the FBI's "Advice of Rights" form. Butler (D) read it and replied that he understood his rights when inquiry was made. However, Butler (D) refused to sign the waiver of rights at the bottom of the form. Butler (D) was informed he need neither speak nor sign the form but that agents would like to talk to him. Butler (D) replied, "I will talk to you, but I am not signing any form." Butler (D) proceeded to make incriminating statements that were used at his trial. In setting aside Butler's (D) conviction, the North Carolina Supreme Court held that *Miranda* required that no statement of a person under custodial interrogation be admitted into evidence against the person unless, at the time the statement was made, the person explicitly waived the right to presence of counsel.

ISSUE: Is an express oral or written statement of waiver a prerequisite to establishing that a defendant waived his *Miranda* rights?

HOLDING AND DECISION: (Stewart, J.) No. An express oral or written statement of waiver is not a prerequisite to establishing that a defendant waived his *Miranda* rights. While silence of a defendant after being advised of his rights cannot alone establish waiver, when coupled with an understanding of his rights and a course of conduct indicating waiver it may support a conclusion that a defendant waived his *Miranda* rights. Although the courts must presume nonwaiver and the prosecution's burden is great to show otherwise, there are some cases in which waiver can clearly be inferred from the actions and words of the person interrogated. Reversed.

DISSENT: (Brennan, J.) *Miranda* refuses to recognize a waiver unless "specifically made" after the appropriate warnings, which would require an "affirmative waiver" in the form of some express written or oral statement.

ANALYSIS

Claims of coerced waiver have now taken the place of the once-popular claims of coerced confession in *Miranda*-type cases. In assessing the "voluntariness" of a waiver, the courts use the same "totality of circumstances" test that was previously used in determining the "voluntariness" of confessions.

Quicknotes

CUSTODIAL INTERROGATION The questioning of a suspect by police while in custody.

KNOWING AND INTELLIGENT WAIVER The intentional or voluntary forfeiture of a recognized right.

Edwards v. Arizona

Accused murder suspect (D) v. State (P)

451 U.S. 477 (1981)

NATURE OF CASE: Review of order affirming admission of incriminating statements in a murder trial.

FACT SUMMARY: After invoking his *Miranda* right to counsel, Edwards (D), without counsel, made incriminating statements during a subsequent custodial interrogation initiated by police.

RULE OF LAW

An accused who has expressed the desire to deal with police only through counsel may not be interrogated by police until counsel has been made available to him, unless the accused initiates further communication with the police.

FACTS: On January 19, 1976, Edwards (D) was arrested on murder charges pursuant to a warrant, and he submitted to questioning at a police station after being informed of his *Miranda* rights. During the course of interrogation, the possibility of a plea bargain was raised. After a brief phone call by Edwards (D) to an attorney, he stated, "I want an attorney before making a deal." The questioning then ceased. On the morning of January 20, a detention officer told Edwards (D) that two detectives wanted to see him. When Edwards (D) replied that he did not want to talk to anyone, the officer advised him that he "had to" talk and brought Edwards (D) to the detectives. The detectives advised Edwards (D) of his *Miranda* rights. Edwards (D), with no counsel present, agreed to talk and to listen to a taped statement made by an accomplice. While listening to the tape, Edwards (D) made statements implicating himself in criminal activity. The trial court held these statements admissible. The Arizona Supreme Court affirmed, finding the statements to have been voluntarily and knowingly made. Edwards (D) appealed.

ISSUE: May an accused who has expressed the desire to deal with police only through counsel be interrogated by police before counsel has been made available to him, if the accused does not initiate further communication with the police?

HOLDING AND DECISION: (White, J.) No. An accused who has expressed the desire to deal with police only through counsel may not be interrogated by police until counsel has been made available to him, unless the accused initiates further communication with the police. This Court has held that a waiver of the right to counsel must constitute a knowing and intelligent relinquishment of a known right or privilege. Where the accused actually invokes the right to counsel, additional safeguards are required to ensure subsequent waivers are valid. Edwards (D) invoked his *Miranda* right to counsel on January 19. The police returned the next day, without making counsel available to Edwards (D), and conducted a custodial interrogation. Because this meeting was initiated not by Edwards (D) but by the police, Edwards's (D) responses to their questions did not constitute a valid waiver of his previously invoked right to counsel. The incriminating statements Edwards (D) made on January 20 were, therefore, inadmissible. Reversed.

CONCURRENCE: (Powell, J.) Once the accused has been provided the requisite warnings, and right to counsel has been requested, whether the suspect still is willing to talk to the authorities without counsel is a factual issue for determination under all the circumstances of the particular case.

ANALYSIS

Michigan v. Mosley, 423 U.S. 96 (1975), requires police to "scrupulously honor" a suspect's assertion of the right to terminate questioning. In contrast to *Mosley, Edwards* states a far stricter bright-line rule. The particular *Miranda* clause invoked by the accused, therefore, determines the standard of review, and often the outcome, of waiver cases.

Quicknotes

BRIGHT-LINE RULE A legal rule of decision to help resolve ambiguous issues simply and in a straightforward manner, sometimes sacrificing equity for certainty.

CUSTODIAL INTERROGATION The questioning of a suspect by police while in custody.

KNOWING AND INTELLIGENT WAIVER The intentional or voluntary forfeiture of a recognized right.

PRIVILEGE AGAINST SELF-INCRIMINATION A privilege guaranteed by the Fifth Amendment to the U.S. Constitution in a criminal proceeding for communications made by an accused and protecting an accused or witness from having to give testimony that may incriminate him- or herself.

Berghuis v. Thompkins

State official (D) v. Convicted criminal (P)

560 U.S. 370 (2010)

NATURE OF CASE: Appeal from reversal of denial of habeas corpus request.

FACT SUMMARY: After Thompkins (P) was advised of his *Miranda* rights, Thompkins (P) did not expressly say he wanted to remain silent, did not want to talk with the police, or wanted an attorney. Eventually, toward the end of a three-hour interrogation during which Thompkins (P) was largely silent, he answered "yes" when asked if he prayed to God to forgive him for the shooting of victim who had died. Thompkins (P) was found guilty of murder, and sentenced to life without parole. In his habeas corpus petition, Thompkins (P) argued that he had invoked his Fifth Amendment right to remain silent, that he had not waived that right, and that his inculpatory statements were involuntary.

RULE OF LAW

(1) A criminal suspect's silence during an interrogation does not invoke his right to remain silent.
(2) A criminal suspect waives his right to remain silent when he knowingly and voluntarily makes a statement to the police.
(3) The police are not required to obtain a waiver of a criminal suspect's *Miranda* rights before interrogating him.

FACTS: After advising respondent Thompkins (P) of his rights, in full compliance with *Miranda v. Arizona*, 384 U.S. 436 (1966), detective Helgert and another officer interrogated him about a shooting in which one victim died. At no point did Thompkins (P) say that he wanted to remain silent, that he did not want to speak with the police or that he wanted an attorney. He refused, however, to sign a written acknowledgment that he had been advised of or understood his *Miranda* rights. He was largely silent during the three-hour interrogation, but near the end, he answered "yes" when asked if he prayed to God to forgive him for the shooting. He moved to suppress his statements, claiming that he had invoked his Fifth Amendment right to remain silent, that he had not waived that right, and that his inculpatory statements were involuntary. The trial court denied the motion, the state's intermediate court affirmed, and the state's highest court denied review. The jury found Thompkins (P) guilty, and he was sentenced to life in prison without parole. The district court denied his subsequent habeas request, reasoning that Thompkins (P) did not invoke his right to remain silent and was not coerced into making statements during the interrogation, and that it was not unreasonable for the state's intermediate appellate court to determine that he had waived his right to remain silent. The court of appeals reversed, holding that the state court was unreasonable in finding an implied waiver of Thompkins's (P) right to remain silent. The United States Supreme Court granted certiorari.

ISSUE:

(1) Does a criminal suspect's silence during an interrogation invoke his right to remain silent?
(2) Does a criminal suspect waive his right to remain silent when he knowingly and voluntarily makes a statement to the police?
(3) Are the police required to obtain a waiver of a criminal suspect's *Miranda* rights before interrogating him?

HOLDING AND DECISION: (Kennedy, J.)

(1) No. A criminal suspect's silence during an interrogation does not invoke his right to remain silent. Thompkins's (P) silence during the interrogation did not invoke his right to remain silent. A suspect's *Miranda* right to counsel must be invoked "unambiguously." If the accused makes an "ambiguous or equivocal" statement or no statement, the police are not required to end the interrogation or ask questions to clarify the accused's intent. There is no principled reason to adopt different standards for determining when an accused has invoked the *Miranda* right to remain silent and the *Miranda* right to counsel. Both protect the privilege against compulsory self-incrimination by requiring an interrogation to cease when either right is invoked. The unambiguous invocation requirement results in an objective inquiry that "avoid[s] difficulties of proof and...provide[s] guidance to officers" on how to proceed in the face of ambiguity. Had Thompkins (P) said that he wanted to remain silent or that he did not want to talk, he would have invoked his right to end the questioning. He did neither and therefore did not invoke his right to remain silent.
(2) Yes. A criminal suspect waives his right to remain silent when he knowingly and voluntarily makes a statement to the police. A waiver must be "the product of a free and deliberate choice rather than intimidation, coercion, or deception" and "made with a full awareness of both the nature of the right being abandoned and the consequences of the decision to abandon it." Such a waiver may be "implied" through

Continued on next page.

a "defendant's silence coupled with an understanding of his rights and a course of conduct indicating waiver." If the State (D) establishes that a *Miranda* warning was given and that it was understood by the accused, an accused's uncoerced statement establishes an implied waiver. The record here shows that Thompkins (P) waived his right to remain silent. First, the lack of any contention that he did not understand his rights indicates that he knew what he gave up when he spoke. Second, his answer to the question about God is a "course of conduct indicating waiver" of that right. Had he wanted to remain silent, he could have said nothing in response or unambiguously invoked his *Miranda* rights, ending the interrogation. That he made a statement nearly three hours after receiving a *Miranda* warning does not overcome the fact that he engaged in a course of conduct indicating waiver. Third, there is no evidence that his statement was coerced. He does not claim that the police threatened or injured him or that he was fearful. The interrogation took place in a standard-sized room in the middle of the day, and there is no authority for the proposition that a 3-hour interrogation is inherently coercive. The fact that the question referred to religious beliefs also does not render his statement involuntary.

(3) No. The police are not required to obtain a waiver of a criminal suspect's *Miranda* rights before interrogating him. Thompkins (P) argues that, even if his answer to Helgert could constitute a waiver of his right to remain silent, the police were not allowed to question him until they first obtained a waiver. However, a rule requiring a waiver at the outset would be inconsistent with precedent holding that courts can infer a waiver "from the actions and words of the person interrogated." Any waiver, express or implied, may be contradicted by an invocation at any time, terminating further interrogation. When the suspect knows that *Miranda* rights can be invoked at any time, he or she can reassess his or her immediate and long-term interests as the interrogation progresses. After giving a *Miranda* warning, police may interrogate a suspect who has neither invoked nor waived *Miranda* rights. Thus, the police were not required to obtain a waiver of Thompkins's (P) *Miranda* rights before interrogating him.

Reversed.

DISSENT: (Sotomayor, J.) Under the majority's decisions, criminal suspects must now unambiguously invoke their right to remain silent—which, counterintuitively, requires them to speak. At the same time, suspects will be legally presumed to have waived their rights even if they have given no clear expression of their intent to do so. Those results are not supported by *Miranda* or subsequent precedent and are inconsistent with the fair-trial principles on which those precedents are grounded. The question whether a suspect has validly waived his right is "entirely distinct" as a matter of law from whether he invoked that right. The questions are related, however, in terms of the practical effect on the exercise of a suspect's rights. A suspect may at any time revoke his prior waiver of rights, or guard against the possibility of a future finding that he implicitly waived his rights, by invoking the rights and thereby requiring the police to cease questioning. Thus, analytically, the first question should be whether Thompkins (P) waived his right to remain silent. Precedent places a heavy burden on the prosecution to show waiver, and the presumption is that the suspect did not waive his rights. Waiver may not be presumed merely because a confession was eventually obtained. Here, the circumstances of the interrogation show that Thompkins (P) never waived his right to remain silent. He never expressly waived that right, and his refusal to sign even an acknowledgment that he understood his *Miranda* rights evinces, if anything, intent not to waive those rights. So did his silence during the interrogation for nearly 3 hours. Essentially, his course of conduct did not manifest waiver. Thus, it is objectively unreasonable to conclude the prosecution met its "heavy burden" of proof on a record "consisting of three one-word answers, following 2 hours and 45 minutes of silence punctuated by a few largely nonverbal responses to unidentified questions." By so concluding, however, the majority turns long-standing *Miranda* precedent on its head and significantly dilutes its protections and lowers the prosecution's hitherto high burden of proof. Because *Miranda* and its precedents perceive custodial interrogation to be inherently coercive, requiring proof of a course of conduct beyond the inculpatory statements themselves is critical to ensuring that those statements are voluntary admissions and not the dubious product of an overborne will. Because Thompkins (P) should prevail on his waiver argument, the issue of whether he invoked his right to remain silent should not have been reached, as it was by the majority. Nonetheless, even as to Thompkins's (P) argument that in any event his conduct invoked his right to remain silent, the majority is wrong in holding that a suspect must expressly invoke that right by speaking. Such a novel clear-statement rule for invocation invites police to question a suspect at length—notwithstanding his persistent refusal to answer questions—in the hope of eventually obtaining a single inculpatory response that will suffice to prove waiver of rights. Contrary to the majority's reasoning, there has been a precedential distinction between protections involving the right to counsel and the right to remain silent. The appropriate rule is that when a suspect's conduct is sufficiently unambiguous as to invocation, the police must

Continued on next page.

scrupulously honor that conduct. While this does not provide a bright-line rule, as does the majority's clear-statement rule, the police nonetheless have been following the prior fact-specific rule for over three decades and no evidence has been presented that the status quo has proved unworkable. The clear-statement rule is also a poor fit for the right to silence, since advising a suspect that he has a "right to remain silent" is unlikely to convey that he must speak (and must do so in some particular fashion) to ensure the right will be protected. By contrast, telling a suspect "He has the right to the presence of an attorney, and that if he cannot afford an attorney, one will be appointed for him prior to any questioning if he so desires," implies the need for speech to exercise that right. Moreover, if a suspect's statements or conduct is ambiguous, it is not an undue burden to have the police ask questions clarifying the suspect's intent, such as "Do you want to talk to us?" Such an approach is a more faithful application of precedents than the majority's clear-statement approach.

ANALYSIS

Prior to this decision, courts had to grapple with doctrinal questions of what it took to make a legally valid invocation of, or waiver of, *Miranda* rights. If a suspect's conduct fell between these extremes, there was also the issue of what was acceptable police conduct. The *Thompkins* decision has seemingly done away with those issues. Now, where the police have given the suspect the proper *Miranda* warnings and the suspect understands those warnings and has not been coerced, until the moment when the suspect clearly invokes one of his or her *Miranda* rights, the police may continue to seek a waiver of those rights, and, even absent a clear waiver, as soon as the suspect says anything to the police, the suspect will be held to have impliedly waived his or her rights.

Quicknotes

FIFTH AMENDMENT Provides that no person shall be compelled to serve as a witness against him- or herself, be subject to trial for the same offense twice, or be deprived of life, liberty, or property without due process of law.

HABEAS CORPUS A proceeding in which a defendant brings a writ to compel a judicial determination of whether he is lawfully being held in custody.

INCULPATORY EVIDENCE A statement or other evidence tending to show a person's guilt in committing a criminal act.

***MIRANDA* RULE** A required warning given before any questioning by law enforcement authorities can take place. Individuals in custody receive warnings regarding their privilege against self-incrimination, right to remain silent, and right to be represented by an attorney.

***MIRANDA* WARNINGS** Specified warnings that must be communicated to a person prior to a custodial interrogation; in the absence of the communication of such warnings, any communications made during the interrogation are inadmissible at trial.

CHAPTER 8

Police Interrogation: The Sixth Amendment Right to Counsel

Quick Reference Rules of Law

Massiah v. United States

Wiretapped narcotics suspect (D) v. Federal government (P)

377 U.S. 201 (1964)

NATURE OF CASE: Review of conviction for narcotics possession.

FACT SUMMARY: While free on bail following his indictment and arraignment, Massiah (D) made incriminating statements to an accomplice who had secretly agreed with the authorities to act as an informer.

RULE OF LAW

After the accused has been indicted, the Sixth Amendment forbids the use at trial of incriminating statements deliberately elicited from the accused by government agents in the absence of counsel.

FACTS: Massiah (D) was arrested, arraigned, and indicted for possession of narcotics. He retained a lawyer, pleaded not guilty, and was released on bail. In the same indictment naming Massiah (D), Colson was charged with conspiracy to sell narcotics. Without Massiah's (D) knowledge, Colson agreed to cooperate with federal agents in their investigation of Massiah (D) and have a radio transmitter installed in his car so that federal agents could overhear conversations taking place there. During one such conversation with Colson, Massiah (D) made incriminating statements. The district court admitted the statements at trial, which resulted in Massiah's (D) conviction. The court of appeals affirmed, and Massiah (D) appealed.

ISSUE: After the accused has been indicted, does the Sixth Amendment forbid the use at trial of incriminating statements deliberately elicited from the accused by government agents in the absence of counsel?

HOLDING AND DECISION: (Stewart, J.) Yes. After the accused has been indicted, the Sixth Amendment forbids the use at trial of incriminating statements deliberately elicited from the accused by government agents in the absence of counsel. Under the Fourteenth Amendment, the right of an accused to counsel in a state criminal adversarial proceeding commences no later than upon indictment of the accused. A contrary ruling might deny an accused "effective representation by counsel at the only stage when legal aid and advice would help him." The Sixth Amendment's specific guarantee of the right to assistance of counsel applies directly to this federal proceeding. The interrogation need not take place in a police station. For the rule to have any efficacy, it must also apply to the indirect and surreptitious interrogation conducted here. This is especially true, since Massiah (D) was more seriously imposed upon in that he did not even know he was being interrogated. The continued investigation of Massiah (D) following his indictment was within Sixth Amendment strictures. The introduction at trial of the incriminating statements deliberately elicited from Massiah (D) by authorities in the absence of his counsel was not. Reversed.

DISSENT: (White, J.) Massiah's (D) right to counsel was not interfered with because Massiah (D) was not prevented from consulting with his counsel, no meetings with counsel were disturbed or spied upon, and preparation for trial was in no way obstructed. The Fifth Amendment prohibits the use at trial of coerced incrimination. The decisive element in Fifth Amendment analysis of incriminating statements is voluntariness. The Court has expressly rejected the argument that admissions are to be deemed involuntary if made outside the presence of counsel. Exclusion is particularly inappropriate here because no evidence was presented of coercion during Massiah's (D) conversation with his partner in crime.

ANALYSIS

In *Massiah*, the United States Supreme Court, for the first time, held that the right to counsel arises prior to trial in a criminal proceeding. The Sixth Amendment right to counsel at trial discussed in *Massiah* must be clearly distinguished from the prophylactic right to counsel during interrogation articulated in *Miranda*, 384 U.S. 436 (1966). In fact, *Massiah*, decided in 1964, preceded *Miranda* by two years.

Quicknotes

CONSPIRACY Concerted action by two or more persons to accomplish some unlawful purpose.

CRITICAL STAGE OF PROCEEDINGS That stage in criminal proceedings when an accused's right to counsel arises or at which some action may be taken that will prejudice later proceedings.

PRIVILEGE AGAINST SELF-INCRIMINATION A privilege guaranteed by the Fifth Amendment to the U.S. Constitution in a criminal proceeding for communications made by an accused and protecting an accused or witness from having to give testimony that may incriminate him- or herself.

Brewer v. Williams

Prosecutor (P) v. Murderer with conscience (D)

430 U.S. 387 (1977)

NATURE OF CASE: Appeal from conviction of murder.

FACT SUMMARY: Williams (D) was convicted of murder based on a confession obtained during a custodial trip.

RULE OF LAW

Police interrogation of an accused/defendant during a critical stage of the proceedings without the presence of known counsel is violative of the Sixth and Fourteenth Amendments.

FACTS: Williams (D), an escaped mental patient, killed a 10-year-old girl. Williams (D) subsequently contacted a lawyer in Des Moines, informed him that he was in Davenport and was willing to surrender to the police in Des Moines who were searching for him. The attorney informed the police, and they sent a car to Waterloo to return him to Des Moines under a warrant issued for his arrest. The attorney informed both the police and his client that under no circumstances was Williams (D) to say anything. Williams (D), in the meantime, had been arrested in Davenport and hired counsel there to represent him at the arraignment on the murder charge. His attorney requested permission to accompany Williams (D) on the trip to Des Moines but was refused. The attorney warned both Williams (D) and the police that there was to be no conversation during the trip concerning the crime as Williams (D) was represented by counsel who had informed him to remain silent. During the first part of the trip Williams (D) repeatedly refused to speak unless counsel was present. One of the detectives then began to play on Williams's (D) religious beliefs pleading with him to reveal the dead girl's whereabouts so that she could obtain a Christian burial. Williams (D) finally revealed the whereabouts of the body after confessing to the crime. Williams (D) appealed the admissibility of his confession after conviction. Williams (D) alleged, among other things, that the tactics used to obtain the confession violated his right to counsel. A habeas petition by Williams (D) was granted, and the Eight Circuit Court of Appeals affirmed.

ISSUE: Is police interrogation of an accused/defendant during a critical stage of the proceedings without the presence of known counsel violative of the Sixth and Fourteenth Amendments?

HOLDING AND DECISION: (Stewart, J.) Yes. Police interrogation of an accused/defendant during a critical stage of the proceedings without the presence of known counsel is violative of the Sixth and Fourteenth Amendments. Those two Amendments grant an accused the right to the presence of counsel during all critical stages of the proceedings. First, this was a critical stage. Williams (D) had a warrant issued for his arrest and had already been arraigned in Davenport on the charge. The police officers knew that he was represented by counsel, that he had been informed not to speak, and that Williams (D) told them he would not speak without counsel present. Williams (D) had pleaded not guilty to the charge. There are no grounds present herein that establish that Williams (D) knowingly, intelligently, and voluntarily waived. The state bears a heavy burden of establishing that once rights have been invoked by the defendant/accused they have been waived. No clear and convincing evidence of such a waiver is present herein. While the crime is abhorrent, a resolute loyalty to the Constitution is imperative. Affirmed.

CONCURRENCE: (Marshall, J.) Good police work is something far different from catching the criminal at any price. It is equally important that the police, as guardians of the law, fulfill their responsibility to obey its commands scrupulously. In the end, life and liberty can be as much endangered from illegal methods used to convict those thought to be criminals as from the actual criminals themselves.

CONCURRENCE: (Powell, J.) Interrogation may be subtle. The thrust of the detective's efforts was to elicit information through the use of psychological techniques. Such interrogation cannot be countenanced once constitutional rights have been invoked absent waiver.

CONCURRENCE: (Stevens, J.) Nothing can restore the life of the dead child herein. However, the rights of even the guilty must be protected.

DISSENT: (Burger, C.J.) After at least five warnings from two attorneys Williams (D) voluntarily led the police to where the body was buried. There was no coercion or threats. Williams (D) was prompted solely on the simple statement by the detective. This constitutes a voluntary waiver of known rights. The exclusionary rule should not be arbitrarily applied to non-egregious police conduct.

DISSENT: (White, J.) The voluntary confession by Williams (D), made without threats or coercion, of a known right is conclusive evidence of a waiver. The very fact that Williams (D) consulted with his attorney as to whether he should speak with the officers in counsel's absence makes his later decision to talk to the police better

Continued on next page.

informed and, if anything, more intelligent. Furthermore, the conduct of the officers did not jeopardize the fairness of Williams's (D) trial or risk conviction of a person who was innocent.

ANALYSIS

Miranda warnings, 384 U.S. 436 (1966), were not required to be given to a grand jury witness and their statements were not entitled to suppression in subsequent perjury trials. *U.S. v. Wong*, 431 U.S. 174 (1977). The same rationale applied to grand jury witnesses who were not informed that they were targets of the investigation. *U.S. v. Washington*, 431 U.S. 181 (1977). *Brewer* could probably have been reversed on *Miranda* grounds on a showing that the confession was involuntary.

Quicknotes

CUSTODIAL INTERROGATION The questioning of a suspect by police while in custody.

FOURTEENTH AMENDMENT Declares that no state shall make or enforce any law that shall abridge the privileges and immunities of citizens of the United States. No state shall deny to any person within its jurisdiction the equal protection of the laws.

KNOWING AND INTELLIGENT WAIVER The intentional or voluntary forfeiture of a recognized right.

RIGHT TO COUNSEL Right conferred by the Sixth Amendment that the accused shall be provided effective legal assistance in a criminal proceeding.

SIXTH AMENDMENT Provides the right to a speedy and public trial by impartial jury, the right to be informed of the accusation, the right to confront witnesses, and the right to have the assistance of counsel in all criminal prosecutions.

Patterson v. Illinois

Individual (D) v. State (P)

487 U.S. 285 (1988)

NATURE OF CASE: Appeal from Illinois Supreme Court in favor of the State (P).

FACT SUMMARY: After being indicted for murder, Patterson (D) voluntarily waived his right to counsel and made statements implicating himself in the murder.

RULE OF LAW

Interrogation of a criminal defendant after indictment does not violate the Sixth Amendment right to counsel as long as the defendant knowingly and voluntarily waives his right to counsel at that stage.

FACTS: Patterson (D) and two others allegedly beat a rival gang member who later died as a result of his injuries. After a jury indicted Patterson (D), Patterson (D) inquired aloud to a police officer as to why another person was not indicted because "he did everything." The police officer then handed a *Miranda*, 384 U.S. 436 (1966), waiver form to Patterson (D), read the form aloud to him, and had Patterson (D) initial the form. The form made Patterson (D) aware of his right to counsel and the consequences of any statement he might make to the police. Patterson (D) then gave a detailed statement to the police officer regarding his involvement with the murder. Later in the same day, Patterson (D) read, signed, and reviewed another *Miranda* form with an Assistant District Attorney assigned to the case. After this, Patterson (D) gave additional damaging statements to the prosecutor. At trial, Patterson (D) moved to suppress. The trial court and the Illinois Supreme Court found the statements were admissible and that Patterson (D) had voluntarily waived his right to counsel. Patterson (D) appealed.

ISSUE: Does interrogation of a criminal defendant after indictment violate the Sixth Amendment right to counsel as long as the defendant knowingly and voluntarily waives his right to counsel at that stage?

HOLDING AND DECISION: (White, J.) No. Interrogation of a criminal defendant after indictment does not violate the Sixth Amendment right to counsel as long as the defendant knowingly and voluntarily waives his right to counsel at that stage. First, Patterson's (D) argument that the police were barred from interrogating him after his indictment is incorrect. Our prior cases have held that once a defendant requests counsel, police cannot interrogate him, unless the defendant initiates further communication. That is precisely what occurred here. Second, Patterson's (D) waiver of his Sixth Amendment right to counsel was valid. For a waiver to be valid, the waiver must be knowing and intelligent. On these facts, Patterson's (D) waiver satisfied those requirements. Twice the State (P) informed Patterson (D) of his right to counsel. Moreover, the forms also informed him that his statements could be used against him. Patterson (D) has also not identified any additional information that the police should have provided to him. Lastly, we hold that the *Miranda* warnings that suffice at the arrest stage also suffice for the interrogations at the postindictment phase. The value of counsel at this questioning phase is of minimal value, as opposed to the right to counsel at the trial stage. Therefore, defendant may validly waive his Sixth Amendment right to counsel at the postindictment phase. Affirmed.

DISSENT: (Blackmun, J.) The Sixth Amendment mandates that the defendant should not be subject to interrogation postindictment. However, I would allow for an exception where the accused further initiates contact with the police.

DISSENT: (Stevens, J.) This Court should make a bright-line rule that once a jury indicts a defendant, the prosecutor who will try the case against the defendant should not be able to question the defendant without the presence of counsel. In civil litigation, once a complaint is filed, it is unethical to contact an opposing party without the presence of the party's attorney. The same rule should apply, with even more force, on the criminal side. The defendant's adversary, the prosecutor, cannot adequately provide the defendant with the advice that he can remain silent if he chooses. After jury empanelment at the trial stage, this Court would no doubt disallow contact between the prosecutor and the defendant. The same should hold true for contacts after the criminal complaint is filed.

ANALYSIS

Note that Justice Blackmun's dissent actually appears to agree with the majority's view that postindictment interrogations are not completely barred. However, in an effort to limit the majority's holding, Justice Blackmun emphasized that he would allow postindictment interrogations only when the accused initiates the further contact. Several state courts have disagreed with this decision on state constitutional grounds.

Continued on next page.

Quicknotes

BRIGHT-LINE RULE A legal rule of decision to help resolve ambiguous issues simply and in a straightforward manner, sometimes sacrificing equity for certainty.

INDICTMENT A formal written accusation made by a prosecutor and issued by a grand jury, charging an individual with a criminal offense.

SIXTH AMENDMENT Provides the right to a speedy and public trial by impartial jury, the right to be informed of the accusation, the right to confront witnesses, and the right to have the assistance of counsel in all criminal prosecutions.

WAIVER The intentional or voluntary forfeiture of a recognized right.

McNeil v. Wisconsin

Multiple-crime suspect (D) v. State (P)

501 U.S. 171 (1991)

NATURE OF CASE: Appeal of convictions for murder and armed robbery.

FACT SUMMARY: McNeil (D) contended that his courtroom appearance with an attorney for the West Allis, Wisconsin, crime constituted an invocation of his *Miranda* right to counsel and that his subsequent waiver during police-initiated questioning regarding the Caledonia crime was invalid.

RULE OF LAW

An accused's invocation of his Sixth Amendment right to counsel during a judicial proceeding does not constitute an invocation of his *Miranda* right to counsel.

FACTS: McNeil (D) was represented by counsel at his arraignment for an armed robbery committed in West Allis, Wisconsin. Later that evening Sheriff Butts questioned McNeil (D) about a murder committed in Caledonia. Butts later questioned McNeil (D) on three other occasions, each time administering *Miranda*, 384 U.S. 436 (1966), warnings to McNeil (D). On every occasion, McNeil (D) signed the *Miranda* waiver form. After confessing to the Caledonia crime, McNeil (D) was charged with and convicted of Caledonia murder and the West Allis armed robbery. He moved unsuccessfully to suppress the incriminating statements he made during the sheriff's questions, claiming his invocation of his Sixth Amendment right to counsel at his West Allis arraignment also invoked his *Miranda* right to counsel for purposes of the Caledonia murder questioning. The motion was denied. McNeil (D) appealed.

ISSUE: Does an accused's invocation of his Sixth Amendment right to counsel during a judicial proceeding constitute an invocation of his Miranda right to counsel?

HOLDING AND DECISION: (Scalia, J.) No. An accused's invocation of his Sixth Amendment right to counsel during a judicial proceeding does not constitute an invocation of his *Miranda* right to counsel. The Sixth Amendment right to counsel is offense-specific. It cannot be invoked once for all future prosecutions; it does not attach until a prosecution is commenced. Because McNeil (D) provided the statements at issue here before his Sixth Amendment right to counsel with respect to the Caledonia offense had been (or even could have been) invoked, that right poses no bar to the admission of the statements in this case. McNeil (D) relies, however, upon a different right to counsel, using a combination of the Fifth Amendment guarantee that no person shall be compelled in any criminal case to be a witness against himself and the Sixth Amendment right to counsel. If McNeil's (D) rule were adopted, most persons in pretrial custody for serious offenses would be unapproachable by police officers suspecting them of involvement in other crimes, even though they never expressed any unwillingness to be questioned. Since the ready ability to obtain uncoerced confessions is not an evil but an unmitigated good, society would be the loser if such a rule were adopted. Affirmed.

DISSENT: (Stevens, J.) In this case, the Court undermines the significance of an accused's right to counsel. Although the opinion will doubtless have only a small effect on existing custodial interrogation procedures, as a theoretical matter, the Court's novel creation of an "offense-specific" limitation on the scope of the attorney-client relationship can only create confusion in the law and undermine the protections that underscore the adversarial system of justice.

ANALYSIS

In response to a comment in the dissent that they prefer an inquisitorial system of justice, the majority pointed out that what makes a system adversarial rather than inquisitorial is not the presence of counsel but rather, the presence of a judge who does not (as an inquisitor does) conduct the factual and legal investigation him- or herself but instead decides on the basis of facts and arguments pro and con adduced by the parties. The majority also stressed that the U.S. system of justice is, and has always been, an inquisitorial one at the investigatory stage, and no other disposition is conceivable.

Quicknotes

ARRAIGNMENT The formal charging of an individual with a criminal offense.

CUSTODIAL INTERROGATION The questioning of a suspect by police while in custody.

RIGHT TO COUNSEL Right conferred by the Sixth Amendment that the accused shall be provided effective legal assistance in a criminal proceeding.

SIXTH AMENDMENT Provides the right to a speedy and public trial by impartial jury, the right to be informed of the accusation, the right to confront witnesses, and the right to have the assistance of counsel in all criminal prosecutions.

CHAPTER 9

Entrapment

Quick Reference Rules of Law

Sherman v. United States

Convicted drug dealer (D) v. Federal government (P)

356 U.S. 369 (1958)

NATURE OF CASE: On certiorari from appellate court judgment upholding narcotics conviction.

FACT SUMMARY: Sherman (D), upon the repeated entreaties of a government informer, supplied the informer with narcotics.

RULE OF LAW

The government may not originate a criminal design and implant it in the mind of an innocent person so that the government may prosecute that person.

FACTS: Sherman (D) met another man at a doctor's office where apparently both were seeking treatment for narcotics addiction. Sherman's (D) acquaintance informed him that he was not responding to treatment and that he was suffering greatly, and he asked Sherman (D) if he knew a source of narcotics. Sherman (D) tried to avoid the issue, but the acquaintance repeatedly prevailed on Sherman's (D) sympathy. Sherman (D) finally obtained a quantity of narcotics, which he shared with his acquaintance. The acquaintance, who turned out to be a government informant, then advised police that Sherman (D) had sold him drugs. Sherman was tried and convicted.

ISSUE: May the government originate a criminal design and implant it in the mind of an innocent person so that the government may prosecute that person?

HOLDING AND DECISION: (Warren, C.J.) No. The government may not originate a criminal design and implant it in the mind of an innocent person so that the government may prosecute that person. In considering whether entrapment has occurred, we look not only to the conduct of government agents, but to the subjective willingness of the defendant to commit the crime. If a person is predisposed to commit an offense, and the government merely affords him an opportunity to do that wrong which he was ready and willing to do, then the conduct of the government does not constitute entrapment. However, in this case, the testimony of the prosecution's witnesses indicate that Sherman (D) was anything but ready and willing, and that only repeated entreaties by the informer, who claimed to be in great suffering, caused Sherman (D) to supply him with narcotics. On that basis, we find that Sherman (D) was entrapped as a matter of law. Conviction reversed.

CONCURRENCE: (Frankfurter, J.) Conduct is not less criminal because it is the result of temptation. The better test for entrapment would focus solely on the conduct of the police. As Justice Holmes wrote, "[F]or my part I think it a less evil that some criminals should escape than that the government should play an ignoble part."

ANALYSIS

In addition to disagreeing with the majority over whether the predisposition of the defendant should be considered in evaluating an entrapment defense, Justice Frankfurter argued that entrapment should be a question of law for the judge, not a jury issue. "It is the province of the court and the court alone," he wrote, "to protect itself and the government from such prostitution of the criminal law."

Quicknotes

CERTIORARI A discretionary writ issued by a superior court to an inferior court in order to review the lower court's decisions; the U.S. Supreme Court's writ ordering such review.

ENTRAPMENT An act by public officers that induces a defendant into committing a criminal act.

QUESTION OF LAW An issue regarding the legal significance of a particular act or event, which is usually left to the judge to ascertain.

Jacobson v. United States

Convicted purchaser of child pornography (D) v. Federal government (P)

503 U.S. 540 (1992)

NATURE OF CASE: On certiorari from appellate court judgment affirming conviction for purchase of child pornography.

FACT SUMMARY: Jacobson (D) was arrested for purchasing materials in violation of child pornography laws, following a lengthy sting operation.

RULE OF LAW

Proof that a defendant possesses certain generalized personal inclinations is not sufficient evidence to prove beyond a reasonable doubt that he would have been predisposed to commit the crime independent of the government's coaxing.

FACTS: Jacobson (D) ordered magazines depicting nude male minors. He later claimed that he was expecting magazines with pictures of young men 18 or older; however, his receipt of the magazines was lawful at the time. Shortly thereafter, the child pornography laws changed. Jacobson (D) was contacted by numerous government agencies pretending to be organizations promoting freedom of expression and sexual freedom and was encouraged to purchase child pornography. After nearly three years of such efforts, Jacobson (D) ordered a magazine called *Boys Who Love Boys*. It was delivered, and Jacobson (D) was arrested, tried, and convicted.

ISSUE: Is proof that a defendant possesses certain generalized personal inclinations sufficient evidence to prove beyond a reasonable doubt that he would have been predisposed to commit the crime independent of the government's coaxing?

HOLDING AND DECISION: (White, J.) No. Proof that a defendant possesses certain generalized personal inclinations is not sufficient evidence to prove beyond a reasonable doubt that he would have been predisposed to commit the crime independent of the government's coaxing. The evidence that Jacobson (D) was ready and willing to commit the offense came only after the government had devoted two and a half years to convincing him that he had or should have had the right to engage in the very behavior proscribed by law. Rational jurors could not say beyond a reasonable doubt that Jacobson (D) possessed the requisite predisposition prior to the government's investigation. The conviction is reversed.

DISSENT: (O'Connor, J.) The enthusiasm with which Jacobson (D) responded to the opportunity to commit the instant crime is sufficient for a reasonable jury to conclude that his predisposition to commit the crime charged since the jury is charged with deciding whether predisposition exists. Here, a jury could reasonably have concluded that Jacobson (D) was not entrapped by the government.

ANALYSIS

The dissent also claimed that the majority was significantly redefining the understanding of predisposition. Justice O'Connor argued that the Court's opinion could be read as holding that government investigators must have a reasonable suspicion of criminal activity before beginning an investigation. Such a requirement, O'Connor said, would prevent the government from advertising the seductions of criminal activity, an essential part of such a sting operation.

Quicknotes

CERTIORARI A discretionary writ issued by a superior court to an inferior court in order to review the lower court's decisions; the U.S. Supreme Court's writ ordering such review.

ENTRAPMENT An act by public officers that induces a defendant into committing a criminal act.

STING OPERATION A method by which police apprehend offenders by posing as criminals.

CHAPTER 10

Eyewitness Identification Procedures

Quick Reference Rules of Law

United States v. Wade

Federal government (P) v. Bank robber (D)

388 U.S. 218 (1967)

NATURE OF CASE: Appeal from conviction for robbery and conspiracy to commit robbery.

FACT SUMMARY: The police arranged a lineup where two witnesses recognized Wade (D) as the robber. Wade's (D) appointed counsel was not present at the lineup.

RULE OF LAW

Once the accused is formally charged in an indictment, an information, a preliminary hearing, or an arraignment, the accused is entitled to have counsel present at a lineup where witnesses seek to identify the perpetrator of a crime.

FACTS: Wade (D) and an accomplice were charged in an indictment with robbing a federally insured bank. Two witnesses told police that a man with a small strip of tape on each side of his face entered the bank and ordered at gunpoint that the witnesses fill a pillowcase with money. The perpetrator drove away with an accomplice who was waiting in a stolen car. Pursuant to the indictment, Wade (D) was arrested on April 2, and counsel was appointed to represent him on April 26. Fifteen days after counsel was appointed, the Federal Bureau of Investigation arranged to have the two witnesses observe a lineup made up of Wade (D) and five or six other prisoners that was conducted in a courtroom of the local county courthouse. Each participant wore tape and said, "Put the money in the bag." Both witnesses identified Wade (D) as the robber. Wade's (D) appointed counsel was not notified of the lineup, nor was he present at the lineup. At the trial, the witnesses identified Wade (D), and on cross-examination the prior lineup was exposed. Wade (D) moved for an acquittal or, alternatively, to strike the witness's identification, on the grounds that the lineup without presence of counsel violated Wade's (D) Fifth Amendment privilege against self-incrimination and his Sixth Amendment right to counsel. The motions were denied, and Wade (D) was convicted. The court of appeals reversed the conviction and ordered a new trial at which the in-court identification evidence was to be excluded on Sixth Amendment grounds.

ISSUE: Once the accused is formally charged in an indictment, an information, a preliminary hearing, or an arraignment, is the accused entitled to have counsel present at a lineup where witnesses seek to identify the perpetrator of a crime?

HOLDING AND DECISION: (Brennan, J.) Yes. Once the accused is formally charged in an indictment, an information, a preliminary hearing, or an arraignment, the accused is entitled to have counsel present at a lineup where witnesses seek to identify the perpetrator of a crime. The confrontation of the accused with witnesses in order to elicit identification evidence is particularly susceptible to innumerable dangers that might deny the accused a fair trial. The lineup is therefore a critical stage of the criminal proceedings. The right of the accused to a meaningful cross-examination is indispensable to a fair trial. There can be a high degree of suggestion inherent in the manner in which the accused is presented to the witnesses, and it would be difficult for the defense to reconstruct the way in which the lineup was conducted. Thus, the issue of identification may be permanently settled at the lineup. As a result, there may be a denial of the right to cross-examination because the conviction may rest on a courtroom identification that is in fact the fruit of a suspect pretrial identification that the accused is helpless to subject to effective scrutiny at trial. As a result, the lineup is a critical stage of the criminal proceedings because of the prejudice that may not be capable of reconstruction at trial and because counsel's presence can often avert prejudice and assure a meaningful confrontation. Because the accused and his counsel should have been notified and because counsel's presence is a prerequisite to the conduct of the lineup absent intelligent waiver, the conviction is vacated and the case remanded to the district court to determine whether the in-court identifications had an independent source or whether the identifications were harmless error. The Court rejects any assertion of a Fifth Amendment violation. Self-incrimination applies only against being compelled to testify against himself or otherwise provide the state with testimonial or communicative evidence. The lineup does not force the accused to be a source of real or physical evidence. Vacated and remanded.

DISSENT: (White, J.) The Court is mistakenly propounding a per se rule based on assumptions of improper police practices and pressures that have a derogatory impact on the right to a fair trial. There is no basis for these assumptions. The mistakes that have occurred in criminal trials are as much the consequence of eyewitness testimony problems as police misconduct. The states should not be impaired in their conduct of the criminal process by per se constitutional rules.

Continued on next page.

ANALYSIS

Under *Wade*, a postindictment lineup requires notice to both the defendant and defendant's counsel, and a lineup cannot be held until counsel is present. The rationale for this decision is the defendant's right of confrontation; by being present at the lineup, counsel will be aware of any prejudicial factors at the lineup and will be able to more effectively attack the credibility of later courtroom identification. The United States Supreme Court also expressly holds that a lineup and requiring a defendant to speak or wear certain items is not a denial of the Fifth Amendment privileges against self-incrimination. Although the opinion does not address itself to the issue, a later case held that the *Wade* protection extends only to postindictment lineups, and the accused does not have a right to counsel at lineups held before he or she is arrested or charged with a crime.

Quicknotes

ACQUITTAL The discharge of an accused individual from suspicion of guilt for a particular crime and from further prosecution for that offense.

PER SE By itself; without more; taken alone; not requiring additional evidence for proof; as a matter of law.

PRETRIAL LINEUP Procedure whereby police officers place an alleged perpetrator of a crime in a line with several other persons for purposes of identification by a witness or victim.

SIXTH AMENDMENT Provides the right to a speedy and public trial by impartial jury, the right to be informed of the accusation, the right to confront witnesses, and the right to have the assistance of counsel in all criminal prosecutions.

Perry v. New Hampshire

Individual (D) v. State (P)

565 U.S. 228 (2012)

NATURE OF CASE: Appeal from decision of the New Hampshire Supreme Court upholding defendant's criminal conviction.

FACT SUMMARY: Police received a call that an African-American man was breaking into vehicles in a parking lot. When police spoke with witness Nubia Blandon, she identified Perry (D) as the man she had seen breaking into the vehicles.

RULE OF LAW

The Due Process Clause does not require a preliminary judicial inquiry into the reliability of eyewitness identification when the identification was not obtained by a suggestive identification procedure employed by law enforcement personnel.

FACTS: At 3: 00 a.m. on August 15, 2008, in Nashua, New Hampshire, police received a call about an African-American man breaking into vehicles in a parking lot. When police arrived at the scene, one officer, Nicole Clay, approached Perry (D) who was holding two radio amplifiers in his hands. Perry (D) denied that he had stolen the amplifiers. Clay then spoke with Nubia Blandon about the incidents. Blandon stated that she had witnessed from her kitchen window an African-American man roaming the parking lot and looking into vehicles. Clay then asked Blandon to describe the person. Blandon pointed through her kitchen window to Perry (D), who was standing with another officer in the parking lot. A month later, when police showed Blandon a photographic array that included a picture of Perry (D), she was unable to identify him. The State (P) charged Perry (D) with one count of theft. Perry (D) moved to suppress Blandon's out-of-court identification of him, because it essentially constituted a one-person lineup. The trial court denied the motion and both Blandon and Clay testified as to Blandon's out-of-court identification. A jury convicted Perry (D), and the New Hampshire Supreme Court affirmed the conviction. The United States Supreme Court granted Perry's (D) application for review.

ISSUE: Does the Due Process Clause require a preliminary judicial inquiry into the reliability of eyewitness identification when the identification was not obtained by a suggestive identification procedure employed by law enforcement personnel?

HOLDING AND DECISION: (Ginsburg, J.) No. The Due Process Clause does not require a preliminary judicial inquiry into the reliability of eyewitness identification when the identification was not obtained by a suggestive identification procedure employed by law enforcement personnel. This Court has developed a two-step analysis to determine whether the Due Process Clause requires suppression of out-of-court identifications tainted by police misconduct. The first step is to determine whether law enforcement employed an identification procedure that was suggestive in nature. If so, the reviewing court must next consider whether the improper identification procedure tainted the resulting identification in a manner that would render it unreliable and therefore inadmissible. Reliability of the eyewitness identification is the linchpin of the analysis. Where the indicators of the witness's ability to make an accurate identification outweigh the corrupting effect of the tainted law enforcement suggestion, the evidence should be allowed. Such indicators include the opportunity of the witness to view the defendant at the time of the crime, the accuracy of the description, and the level of certainty. Perry (D) argues the rule requiring pretrial judicial inquiries should not be limited to those situations involving police conduct. Rather, courts should review all eyewitness identifications any time identification is made under suggestive circumstances. Perry (P) is incorrect. A primary purpose of excluding identification under suggestive circumstances created by law enforcement is to deter police officers from using suggestive lineup and photo arrays. The deterrence rationale does not exist where, as in this case, police engaged in no improper conduct resulting in the identification. Moreover, requiring pretrial judicial review of all such eyewitness testimony would place a large burden on criminal trial courts. The jury, not the judge, traditionally determines the reliability of evidence. Other safeguards protect criminal defendants from unreliable out-of-court statements. Those safeguards include the defendant's ability to cross examine the witness. Eyewitness jury instructions warn the jury to take care when evaluating specific evidence relating to eyewitness identifications. Lastly, the government has the high burden of proving the defendant's guilt beyond reasonable doubt. Accordingly, the introduction of Blandon's out-of-court identification of Perry (D) did not render his trial fundamentally unfair. Affirmed.

DISSENT: (Sotomayor, J.) The majority improperly concludes that the primary purpose of requiring pretrial judicial inquiries into out-of-court identifications is deterrence of improper law enforcement conduct. The primary purpose of the requirement is to ensure

Continued on next page.

reliability of such statements before they are submitted to a jury. By requiring the presence of police action as part of the identification, the majority introduces a mens rea or intent inquiry into the rule. This Court's precedents, however, make no distinction between intentional and unintentional suggestive conduct regarding identification. Here, even though the identification was unplanned, it still involved the police. Lastly, scientific analysis of eyewitness identification revealed, in one study, that 76 percent of convictions overturned due to DNA evidence occurred based on faulty eyewitness identifications. Accordingly, the majority should not limit pretrial judicial inquires to those identifications that involve potential police misconduct.

ANALYSIS

Reliability of evidence is typically within the province of the jury. A criminal defendant can always file a motion to suppress an out-of-court identification (or any other out-of-court statements). Perry (D) was seeking a preliminary evidentiary hearing where the judge would hear from the witness regarding the out-of-court statement. However, the New Hampshire trial court found, as did the United States Supreme Court in this decision, that because police conduct was not suggestive, the reliability of the statement was for the jury to consider.

Quicknotes

DUE PROCESS The constitutional mandate requiring the courts to protect and enforce individuals' rights and liberties consistent with prevailing principles of fairness and justice and prohibiting the federal and state governments from such activities that deprive its citizens of life, liberty, or property interest.

EVIDENTIARY HEARING Hearing pertaining to the evidence of the case.

MENS REA Criminal intent

MOTION TO SUPPRESS Motion in a criminal trial to exclude the introduction of evidence that was unlawfully obtained.

SUBSTANTIVE DUE PROCESS A constitutional safeguard limiting the power of the state, irrespective of how fair its procedures may be; substantive limits placed on the power of the state.

CHAPTER 11

Pretrial Release

Quick Reference Rules of Law

Stack v. Boyle

Alleged conspirator advocating overthrow of government (D) v. Government official (P)

342 U.S. 1 (1951)

NATURE OF CASE: Appeal from affirmance of denial of motion to reduce bail as excessive under the Eighth Amendment.

FACT SUMMARY: Twelve individuals (D), who were indicted and arrested for conspiring to overthrow the federal government by violence or destruction in violation of the Smith Act of 1940, contended that a uniform amount of bail, set at $50,000, was excessive under the Eighth Amendment.

RULE OF LAW

Bail must be set as to each individual defendant in an amount reasonably calculated to assure the presence of the accused at trial.

FACTS: Twelve individuals (D), members of the Communist Party U.S.A., were charged with conspiring to overthrow the federal government by violence or destruction in violation of the Smith Act of 1940. Upon arrest, bail was set as to each petitioner in widely varying amounts—from $2,500 to $100,000. On the motion of the Government (P), bail was fixed in the uniform amount of $50,000 for each (D). In support of their motion, the individuals (D) submitted statements as to their financial resources, family relationships, health, prior criminal records, and other information. The only evidence offered by the Government (P) was a record showing that four persons, with no connections to the individuals (D), had forfeited bail after being convicted under the Smith Act in other proceedings. The individuals' (D) motions to reduce bail and requests for habeas corpus relief were denied by the district court, and the court of appeals affirmed. The United States Supreme Court granted certiorari.

ISSUE: Must bail be set as to each individual defendant in an amount reasonably calculated to assure the presence of the accused at trial?

HOLDING AND DECISION: (Vinson, C.J.) Yes. Bail must be set as to each individual defendant in an amount reasonably calculated to assure the presence of the accused at trial. Federal law unequivocally provides that a person arrested for a non-capital offense must be admitted to bail. This traditional right to freedom before conviction permits the unhampered preparation of a defense and serves to prevent the infliction of punishment prior to conviction. Unless the right to bail is preserved, the presumption of innocence loses its meaning. Any amount of bail that is higher than reasonably calculated to assure the accused's presence is excessive under the Eighth Amendment. The standards used in fixing bail are to be applied in each case to each defendant and must be relevant to assuring the defendant's presence. Therefore, each individual defendant's circumstances must be considered when setting bail. Here, the bail for each accused has been set at an amount much higher than that usually imposed for offenses with similar penalties but without any factual justifications for such action. Thus, such action is arbitrary, and to infer from mere indictment alone the need for an unusually high bail would inject into our own system of government the very principles of totalitarianism that Congress was seeking to guard against in passing the statute under which petitioners have been indicted. If there is a need for bail greater than that normally necessary to ensure the presence of any of the individuals (D) given their circumstances and the seriousness of the charges, the individuals (D) are constitutionally entitled to a hearing. Accordingly, the accused individuals (D) may move for a reduction of bail so that a hearing may be held for the purpose of fixing reasonable bail for each of them.

CONCURRENCE: (Jackson, J.) If the district court set bail primarily based solely on the nature of the accusations, rather than on the difference in circumstances between the different defendants, it clearly violated Rule 46(c) of the Federal Rules of Criminal Procedure. Even on a conspiracy charge, defendants do not lose their separateness or identity. Congress has directed that bail be set with regard to financial ability, character, and relation to the charge, not on unproved charges. Thus, each accused is entitled to any benefits due to a good record, and misdeeds or a bad record should prejudice only those who are guilty of them. The question regarding bail concerns the trustworthiness of each defendant to appear for trial and what security will supply reasonable assurance of that appearance.

ANALYSIS

As the Court emphasized in this case, to be constitutional, the amount of bail must be based on criteria that are relevant to ensuring the accused defendant's presence. The Bail Reform Act of 1984, as amended, 18 U.S.C. §3142(g), lists several factors that courts should consider when setting bail, including: the nature and circumstances of the offense charged, including whether the offense is a crime of violence, a crime of terrorism, or involves a minor victim or a controlled substance,

Continued on next page.

firearm, explosive, or destructive device; the weight of the evidence against the person; the history and characteristics of the person, including the person's character, physical and mental condition, family ties, employment, financial resources, length of residence in the community, community ties, past conduct, history relating to drug or alcohol abuse, criminal history, and record concerning appearance at court proceedings; and whether, at the time of the current offense or arrest, the person was on probation, on parole, or on other release pending trial, sentencing, appeal, or completion of sentence for an offense under federal, state, or local law; and the nature and seriousness of the danger to any person or the community that would be posed by the person's release. In considering the conditions of release, a judicial officer may upon the officer's own motion, or upon the motion of the government, conduct an inquiry into the source of the property to be designated for potential forfeiture or offered as collateral to secure a bond, and must decline to accept the designation, or the use as collateral, of property that, because of its source, will not reasonably assure the appearance of the person as required.

Quicknotes

CONSPIRACY Concerted action by two or more persons to accomplish some unlawful purpose.

EIGHTH AMENDMENT Prohibits the imposition of excessive bail, fines, and cruel and unusual punishment.

United States v. Salerno

Federal government (P) v. Bail seeker (D)

481 U.S. 739 (1987)

NATURE OF CASE: Appeal of reversal of denial of bail pursuant to the Bail Reform Act of 1984 in actions involving numerous criminal charges stemming from alleged organized crime activities.

FACT SUMMARY: Salerno (D) and Cafaro (D), reputed organized-crime heads, were denied bail under the Bail Reform Act of 1984 (the Act) on the grounds that they were dangers to the community. They contended the Act was facially unconstitutional because it permitted the indefinite detention of an individual who had not been convicted of any crime merely on the basis of an unproved indictment.

RULE OF LAW

The Bail Reform Act of 1984, which allows a federal court to detain an arrestee without bail before trial if the court finds the arrestee dangerous to any other person and the community, is not unconstitutional.

FACTS: Salerno (D) and Cafaro (D), alleged organized-crime leaders, were indicted on a number of serious charges, including racketeering and conspiracy to commit murder. On a Government (P) motion based on the Bail Reform Act of 1984 (the Act), the district court held a fully adversarial hearing to determine whether they would be held without bail pending trial. The court denied bail, guided by statutorily enumerated factors, which included the nature and the circumstances of the charges, the weight of the evidence, the history and characteristics of the putative offender, and the danger to the community. The court found that the Government (P) had established by clear and convincing evidence that no condition of release could secure the safety of the community, since it determined that Salerno (D) and Cafaro (D) would likely continue their violent, organized-crime activities if released while awaiting trial, notwithstanding that they presented evidence at the hearing to counter the credibility of the government's (P) witnesses and other evidence. They appealed, arguing that the Act was unconstitutional on its face as a violation of the Due Process Clause of the Fifth Amendment and the Eighth Amendment prohibition against excessive bail. The Second Circuit Court of Appeals struck down the Act on substantive due process grounds, thus avoiding an Eighth Amendment analysis. Although the Second Circuit agreed that pretrial detention could be imposed if the defendants were likely to intimidate witnesses or otherwise jeopardize the trial process, it found that the Act's authorization of pretrial detention on the ground of future dangerousness repugnant to the concept of substantive due process, which the court believed prohibited the total deprivation of liberty simply as a means of preventing future crimes. The Government (P) appealed, and the United States Supreme Court granted certiorari.

ISSUE: Is the Bail Reform Act of 1984 unconstitutional on the grounds it allows a federal court to detain an arrestee without bail before trial if the court finds the arrestee dangerous to any other person and the community?

HOLDING AND DECISION: (Rehnquist, C.J.) No. The Bail Reform Act of 1984 (the Act), which allows a federal court to detain an arrestee without bail before trial if the court finds the arrestee dangerous to any other person and the community, is not unconstitutional. Where a party challenges a statute's facial validity, the party must establish that the statute would not be valid under any set of circumstances. Thus, even if the Act might operate unconstitutionally under some conceivable set of circumstances, that would be insufficient to render it completely invalid. As to Cafaro (D) and Salerno's (D) due process arguments, punishment without trial would violate substantive due process. Merely because a person is detained does not necessarily mean that the Government (P) has imposed punishment. Also, the Act is regulatory, not punitive, since Congress rationally intended regulatory detention to protect the community from dangerous individuals, which unquestionably is a valid regulatory goal, and the incidents of pretrial detention are not excessive in relation to that goal. First, the Act carefully limits the circumstances under which detention may be sought to the most serious of crimes. Second, the arrestee is entitled to a prompt detention hearing, and the maximum length of detention is limited by the stringent time limitations of the Speedy Trial Act, 18 U.S.C. § 3161 et seq. Third, the detainee must be housed in a facility, where possible, that does not house convicts. Thus, contrary to Cafaro (D) and Salerno's (D) argument that no governmental interest may ever outweigh constitutional due process protections where the arrestee presents a demonstrable, serious danger to the community, the government's (P) compelling regulatory interest in safety may outweigh the arrestee's right to liberty. Moreover, there are many examples of situations where the Court has held as much, as in times of war, during deportation proceedings, detention of dangerous juveniles, and other situations where society's interests are at their peak.

Continued on next page.

Although the government's (P) general interest in preventing crime is compelling, even this interest is heightened when the Government (P) musters convincing proof that the arrestee, already indicted or held to answer for a serious crime, presents a demonstrable danger to the community. Under these narrow circumstances, society's interest in crime prevention is at its greatest. So, holding does not minimize the individual's liberty interest but, as the Court's precedents have held, such an interest may be subordinated to the greater needs of society when the Government's (P) interest is sufficiently weighty. The Act also complies with procedural due process requirements by providing for a full-blown adversarial hearing on the issue of detention, and the judge is guided by strictly drawn criteria in determining whether the arrestee would pose a significant danger to society if not detained. The judge must include written findings of fact and the reasons for the judge's decision. The Act's review provisions provide for immediate appellate review of the detention decision. Therefore, these extensive safeguards suffice to repel a procedural due process challenge. Finally, the Eighth Amendment does not require release on bail where Congress has mandated detention on the basis of a compelling interest other than flight; it simply requires that if bail is set that it not be excessive in light of the perceived evil, and it says nothing about whether bail must be available at all. In fact, the Court's precedents reveal that there are limited circumstances, such as in capital crimes, where courts do not need to admit defendants to bail. Reversed.

DISSENT: (Marshall, J.) First, the majority allows the Due Process Clause to be violated by simply redefining punishment as "regulation." It permits a person innocent of any crime to be jailed indefinitely if the Government (P) shows to the satisfaction of a judge that the accused is likely to commit crimes, unrelated to the pending charges, at any time in the future. Such statutes are consistent with the usages of tyranny and emblematic of the police state, and therefore are incompatible with fundamental rights protected by the Constitution. The majority reaches its decision by creating a false dichotomy between the substantive guarantees implicit in the Due Process Clause and the protections afforded by the Eighth Amendment, and then demonstrating that these parts are individually inadequate. It narrows its concept of substantive due process to a right to be free from punishment before conviction. Then, by defining pretrial detention as "regulation," rather than "punishment," the majority magically turns such detention into a constitutional measure by concluding that pretrial detention is not an excessive solution to the problem of preventing danger to the community. Second, a refusal to set bail implicates the Eighth Amendment prohibition against excessive bail since there is no difference between the consequences of setting outrageously high bail and setting no bail at all, i.e., the defendant stays in jail. Because there would be no difference in result, there would have been no need for Congress to have even addressed preventive detention at all since, given that the Constitution is, as emphasized by the majority, silent as to whether bail is available at all, under such a theory, a federal judge constitutionally could simply refuse to set bail at all, regardless of considerations such as flight risk or danger to the community. Thus, the majority's conceptualization of the Eighth Amendment is mere sophistry. Because it seems to recognize this manifest absurdity, the majority seeks to avoid it by saying that perhaps the Bail Clause is addressed only to the courts, and not to Congress, but adds that this issue need not be addressed in this case. What it fails to acknowledge is that the issue was resolved long ago: statutes that purport to accomplish what the Eighth Amendment forbids may not stand. The Amendment provides absolutely no support for the majority's speculation that both courts and Congress are forbidden to inflict cruel and unusual punishments, whereas only the courts are forbidden to require excessive bail. When the majority says that when Congress has mandated detention on the basis of a compelling interest other than prevention of flight, as it has here, the Eighth Amendment does not require release on bail, its conclusion follows only if the "compelling" interest upon which Congress acted is an interest that the Constitution permits Congress to further through the denial of bail. The majority does not ask, as a result of its disingenuous division of its analysis, if there are any substantive limits contained in both the Eighth Amendment and the Due Process Clause that render this system of preventive detention unconstitutional. Third, the Act is an unconstitutional limitation on the presumption of innocence since it allows individuals under indictment for one crime to be imprisoned by the government for crimes not yet committed. The majority's untenable conclusion that the Act is constitutional arises from a specious denial of the role of the Bail Clause and the Due Process Clause in protecting the invaluable guarantee afforded by the presumption of innocence. That presumption is axiomatic and elementary, and its enforcement lies at the foundation of criminal law as viewed through the lens of the Constitution. The beliefs that all are innocent until the state has proved them to be guilty, and that such guilt must be proved beyond a reasonable doubt, are implicit in the concept of ordered liberty. If these same individuals had not been indicted, or had been indicted and acquitted, any imprisonment on the ground that they were "dangerous" would surely be found unconstitutional. Clearly, then, the majority's decision turns an indictment into evidence of future criminal activity, if not for the crime for which the defendant is indicted, and as a justification for imprisonment by the Government (P). However, the detention purportedly authorized by the Act is not authorized by

Continued on next page.

the Government's (P) power to try charges—supported by a finding of probable cause—pursuant to processes of justice that are not evaded or obstructed. Instead, the Act gives the Government (P) coercive powers of authority to imprison upon prediction of future acts, and thus gives rise to the concomitant threat that inevitable abuses of such power pose to the liberties of a free society. This would injure not only the wrongly accused but, ultimately, everyone in American society. The idea that the Bail Clause has a vital role in protecting the presumption of innocence is not novel, and unless the right to bail before trial is preserved, the presumption of innocence, secured only after centuries of struggle, loses its meaning.

DISSENT: (Stevens, J.) There are some circumstances, such as in times of war or where there is absolutely no doubt that an individual will kill others in the immediate future, where an individual's dangerousness may justify a brief detention, but in such cases the danger should be serious enough to warrant detention regardless of whether the person has been indicted, convicted, or acquitted of some other offense. Where, as here, an indictment becomes the prerequisite to emergency detention, the detention unconstitutionally infringes upon the presumption of innocence and the prohibition against excessive bail, as explained by Justice Marshall.

ANALYSIS

The Bail Reform Act of 1984 (the Act) was enacted in response to public fears that the bail system in place at the time had the effect of releasing criminals who would continue to commit crimes while awaiting trial. The concern was particularly acute regarding violent crimes. The concern was not unfounded, and some empirical studies have shown that over 15 percent of homicide arrests involve individuals who were either on active bail or fugitives from bail, and that around 122,000 violent crimes annually could have been prevented had bail been denied to all those charged with a violent crime. See Larry Laudan & Ronald J. Allen, "Deadly Dilemmas II: Bail and Crime," 85 *Chi. Kent L. Rev.* 23 (2010). In the decades since the passage of the Act, society has started to move away from incarceration, and several states and municipalities have reformed their bail laws so that most people charged with misdemeanors and nonviolent felonies will, in most cases be released without cash bail, pending their trials. Such reforms have been shown to reduce jail populations without endangering public safety and have also, as a consequence, eliminated the due process and Eighth Amendment concerns voiced by the dissents in *Salerno* regarding most defendants, while preserving the community protections implemented by the Act respecting violent felonies and certain misdemeanors involving sex offenses and criminal contempt coupled with domestic violence. As *Salerno* and these developments illustrate, balancing safeguards for the community at large with individual liberty is an ongoing and complex endeavor.

Quicknotes

CONSPIRACY Concerted action by two or more persons to accomplish some unlawful purpose.

DUE PROCESS CLAUSE Language in the Fifth and Fourteenth Amendments to the U.S. Constitution providing that no person shall be deprived of "life, liberty, or property, without due process of law."

EIGHTH AMENDMENT Prohibits the imposition of excessive bail, fines, and cruel and unusual punishment.

INDICTMENT A formal written accusation made by a prosecutor and issued by a grand jury, charging an individual with a criminal offense.

CHAPTER 12

Case Screening

Quick Reference Rules of Law

United States v. Armstrong

Federal government (P) v. Drug and firearms violator (D)

517 U.S. 456 (1996)

NATURE OF CASE: Review of dismissal of an indictment for possession of crack cocaine and federal firearms offenses.

FACT SUMMARY: After charges were brought against him for violating federal drug laws, Armstrong (D), alleging that he was selected for prosecution because he was Black, brought a motion for discovery in support of his selective-prosecution claim or for dismissal of the indictment.

RULE OF LAW

A criminal defendant bringing a selective-prosecution claim must make a credible showing of different treatment of similarly situated persons in order to obtain discovery in support of the claim.

FACTS: Armstrong (D) was arrested for violation of federal drug and firearms laws. Armstrong (D) alleged he had been selected for prosecution because he was Black. He filed a motion for dismissal of the charges or for discovery of Government (P) documents regarding the Government's (P) prosecution of similar defendants. The district court granted the discovery motion and dismissed the indictment when the Government (P) would not comply with discovery. The court of appeals reversed but then, upon hearing the case en banc, affirmed the district court's order of dismissal. The United States Supreme Court granted certiorari.

ISSUE: Must a criminal defendant bringing a selective-prosecution claim make a credible showing of different treatment of similarly situated persons in order to obtain discovery in support of the claim?

HOLDING AND DECISION: (Rehnquist, C.J.) Yes. A criminal defendant bringing a selective-prosecution claim must make a credible showing of different treatment of similarly situated persons in order to obtain discovery in support of the claim. Under Federal Rule of Civil Procedure 16, which controls discovery in a criminal case, a defendant must show some evidence of disparate treatment—a showing similar to the requirement under equal protection claims. Here, Armstrong (D) did not make such a showing. Thus, the district court's dismissal of the case was improper. Reversed and remanded.

DISSENT: (Stevens, J.) While the defendant did not make a strong enough showing to merit discovery, the district court did not abuse its discretion in requiring some response from the United States Attorney's Office (P).

ANALYSIS

The United States Supreme Court notes that the test for obtaining discovery for a selective-prosecution claim should be similar to that of an equal protection claim. To successfully pursue an equal protection claim, the claimant must show both a discriminatory effect and a discriminatory purpose. In order to show a discriminatory effect, the claimant must also show that similarly situated persons (but of a different race or religion) were not prosecuted. From this equal protection language, the Court developed the test in this case.

Quicknotes

CERTIORARI A discretionary writ issued by a superior court to an inferior court in order to review the lower court's decisions; the U.S. Supreme Court's writ ordering such review.

DISCOVERY Pretrial procedure during which one party makes certain information available to the other.

EN BANC The hearing of a matter by all the judges of the court, rather than only the necessary quorum.

EQUAL PROTECTION Guarantee under the Fourteenth Amendment to the U.S. Constitution that the government must treat each person or class of persons the same as it treats other persons or classes of persons in like circumstances.

Blackledge v. Perry

State (P) v. Convicted armed assailant (D)

417 U.S. 21 (1974)

NATURE OF CASE: On certiorari from conviction for assault with a deadly weapon with intent to kill or inflict serious bodily injury.

FACT SUMMARY: Perry (D) pled guilty to a felony charge of assault with intent to kill after appealing his misdemeanor assault conviction.

RULE OF LAW

When a defendant invokes a statutory right to a new trial, the prosecution may not bring a more serious charge against him prior to the trial de novo.

FACTS: While imprisoned, Perry (D) became involved in a fight with another inmate. He was convicted of assault with a deadly weapon, a misdemeanor. He then appealed his conviction, exercising a right to trial de novo under North Carolina law. After the filing of appeal but before the trial de novo, the prosecutor charged Perry (D) with the felony of assault with a deadly weapon with intent to kill and inflict serious bodily injury. Perry was tried and convicted.

ISSUE: When a defendant invokes a statutory right to a new trial, may the prosecution bring a more serious charge against him prior to the trial de novo?

HOLDING AND DECISION: (Stewart, J.) No. When a defendant invokes a statutory right to a new trial, the prosecution may not bring a more serious charge against him prior to the trial de novo. The Due Process Clause is not offended by all possibilities of increased punishment upon retrial but only by those that pose a realistic likelihood of prosecutorial vindictiveness. There was no evidence in this case that the prosecutor acted maliciously or in bad faith. However, since the fear of such vindictiveness might discourage defendants from exercising their right to appeal, we hold that no retaliatory motivation need be shown. It is not constitutionally permissible to respond to a defendant who has exercised his statutory right to appeal by bringing more serious charges. The conviction is reversed.

DISSENT: (Rehnquist, J.) The Court's conclusion that the respondent may allege the *Pearce* claim, *North Carolina v. Pearce*, 395 U.S. 711 (1969), in this federal habeas action even though he pled guilty after his petition of a trial de novo means an unnecessary desertion from the principles we have recently stated.

ANALYSIS

On appeal, Perry (D) pled guilty to the felony charges and was sentenced to a term concurrent to the term of imprisonment he was then serving. In dissent, Justice Rehnquist argued that the guilty plea waived Perry's (D) right to contest the felony indictment. However, the majority concluded that a guilty plea did not affect Perry's (D) right to challenge the fundamental corruption of the process by which he was brought into court.

Quicknotes

CERTIORARI A discretionary writ issued by a superior court to an inferior court in order to review the lower court's decisions; the U.S. Supreme Court's writ ordering such review.

DUE PROCESS CLAUSE Language in the Fifth and Fourteenth Amendments to the U.S. Constitution providing that no person shall be deprived of "life, liberty, or property, without due process of law."

TRIAL DE NOVO A new trial of a case conducted as if there had not previously been a trial.

Coleman v. Alabama

Criminal convict (D) v. State (P)

399 U.S. 1 (1970)

NATURE OF CASE: Appeal of a criminal conviction.

FACT SUMMARY: Coleman (D) appealed his conviction, arguing that Alabama's (P) failure to provide him with counsel at the preliminary hearing denied him the Sixth Amendment right to counsel at a critical stage of the prosecution.

RULE OF LAW

A preliminary hearing is a critical stage of a criminal prosecution at which the absence of counsel for the accused might derogate from the accused's right to a fair trial.

FACTS: Following his conviction, Coleman (D) appealed, arguing that Alabama's (P) failure to provide him with counsel at the preliminary hearing denied him the Sixth Amendment right to counsel at a critical stage of the prosecution. The Alabama courts denied that claim because the accused is not required to advance any defenses at the preliminary hearing, and failure to do so does not preclude the accused from every defense he may have at trial. Also, the admission of testimony given at a pretrial proceeding where the accused did not have the benefit of cross-examination by counsel is barred. Coleman (D) appealed.

ISSUE: Is a preliminary hearing a critical stage of a criminal prosecution at which the absence of counsel for the accused might derogate the accused's right to a fair trial?

HOLDING AND DECISION: (Brennan, J.) Yes. A preliminary hearing is a critical stage of a criminal prosecution at which the absence of counsel for the accused might derogate from the accused's right to a fair trial. A preliminary hearing is such a critical stage of prosecution that the "guiding hand" of counsel is needed to protect the indigent against improper prosecution. Skilled cross-examination can expose fatal weaknesses in the state's case, can fashion a vital impeachment tool for use at trial, or can preserve testimony of witnesses who do not appear at trial. Counsel can better discover the case and prepare for trial. Counsel can be influential in arguing on such matters as the necessity for early psychiatric examination or bail. Thus, the conviction is vacated, and the case remanded for determination of whether the failure to appoint counsel for the preliminary hearing was harmless error and, therefore, to decide whether to reinstate the conviction or to order a new trial.

CONCURRENCE: (Black, J.) An accused has the constitutional right to the assistance of counsel at a preliminary hearing since a preliminary hearing is a definite stage of a criminal prosecution. Moreover, adequate representation requires that counsel be present at the preliminary hearing to protect the interests of the client.

DISSENT: (Stewart, J.) The majority at least refrains from turning back the clock by ordering a new preliminary hearing to determine all over again whether there is sufficient evidence against the accused to present the case to the grand jury. Instead, the Court has set aside the convictions and remanded the case for determination whether the convictions should be reinstated or a new trial ordered. This action seems quixotic.

ANALYSIS

Due process and equal protection taken together are one source of the right to counsel. That right is unqualified at trial. Generally, in a proceeding where there is a possibility of adverse findings or consequences to a person, the accused has a right to counsel. These are "critical stages" of prosecution that include custodial police interrogation, noncustodial interrogations after the accused has been formally charged, a postindictment lineup, any appearance at which a plea or any defense must be made, a preliminary hearing, and sentencing.

Quicknotes

CRITICAL STAGE OF PROCEEDINGS The points in a criminal proceeding when the rights and defenses of an accused may be impacted by the absence of counsel.

CROSS-EXAMINATION The interrogation of a witness by an adverse party either to further inquire as to the subject matter of the direct examination or to call into question the witness's credibility.

INDIGENT A person who is poor and thus is unable to obtain counsel to provide defense in a criminal proceeding and for whom counsel must be appointed.

PRELIMINARY HEARING A hearing to determine whether there is sufficient evidence to require the detention of, and requirement of bail for, an individual accused of committing a criminal offense.

SIXTH AMENDMENT Provides the right to a speedy and public trial by impartial jury, the right to be informed of the accusation, the right to confront witnesses, and the right to have the assistance of counsel in all criminal prosecutions.

United States v. Williams

Federal government (P) v. Grand jury indictee (D)

504 U.S. 36 (1992)

NATURE OF CASE: Appeal from dismissal of grand jury indictment.

FACT SUMMARY: When Williams (D) argued that imposition of the disclosure rule applied to the Government (P) prosecutor's failure to disclose substantial exculpatory evidence in his possession to the grand jury, the lower courts agreed with Williams (D) and dismissed the indictment.

RULE OF LAW

A district court may not dismiss an otherwise valid indictment because the government failed to disclose to the grand jury substantial exculpatory evidence in its possession.

FACTS: Williams (D) was indicted by a grand jury. The Government (P) did not reveal to the grand jury that it possessed substantial exculpatory evidence in Williams's (D) favor. Williams (D), in seeking dismissal of the indictment, did not contend that the Fifth Amendment obliged the prosecutor to disclose substantial exculpatory evidence in his possession to the grand jury but argued instead that imposition of the disclosure rule was supported by the courts' "supervisory power." That power has been applied not only to improve the truth-finding process of the trial, but also to prevent parties from reaping benefit or incurring harm from violations of substantive or procedural rules governing matters apart from the trial itself. The lower courts agreed with Williams (D) and dismissed the indictment. This appeal to the United States Supreme Court followed.

ISSUE: May a district court dismiss an otherwise valid indictment because the government failed to disclose to the grand jury substantial exculpatory evidence in its possession?

HOLDING AND DECISION: (Scalia, J.) No. A district court may not dismiss an otherwise valid indictment because the government failed to disclose to the grand jury substantial exculpatory evidence in its possession. While courts' supervisory power may be used as a means of establishing standards of prosecutorial conduct before the courts themselves, it cannot be used as a means of prescribing standards of prosecutorial conduct before the grand jury. Because the grand jury is an institution separate from the courts over whose functioning the courts do not preside, it is clear that as a general matter no such "supervisory" judicial authority exists. It is axiomatic that the grand jury sits not to determine guilt or innocence, but to assess whether there is adequate basis for bringing a criminal charge. To make the assessment, it has always been thought sufficient to hear only the prosecutor's side. As a consequence neither in this country nor in England has the suspect under investigation by the grand jury ever been thought to have a right to testify or to have exculpatory evidence presented. It would make little sense to abstain from reviewing the evidentiary support for the grand jury's judgment while scrutinizing the sufficiency of the prosecutor's presentation. Review of facially valid indictments on such grounds would run counter to the whole history of the grand jury institution, and neither justice nor the concept of a fair trial requires it. Reversed and remanded.

DISSENT: (Stevens, J.) The grand jury is not merely an investigatory body, but also serves as a protector of citizens against arbitrary and oppressive governmental action. It blinks reality to say that the grand jury can adequately perform this important historic role if it is intentionally misled by the prosecutor, on whose knowledge of the law and facts of the underlying criminal investigation the jurors will, of necessity, rely. Unrestrained prosecutorial misconduct in grand jury proceedings is inconsistent with the administration of justice in the federal courts and should be redressed in appropriate cases by the dismissal of indictments obtained by improper methods.

ANALYSIS

As the dissent points out to support its position, the majority cites a number of cases in which it declined to impose categorical restraints on the grand jury. The majority does state, however, that one of its prior decisions, *Bank of Nova Scotia v. United States*, 487 U.S. 250 (1988), makes it clear that the supervisory power can be used to dismiss an indictment because of misconduct before the grand jury, at least where that misconduct amounts to a violation of one of those "few, clear rules which were carefully drafted and approved by the United States Supreme Court and by Congress to ensure the integrity of the grand jury's functions." Since the role of the prosecutor in representing the people is to discover the truth, the withholding of substantial exculpatory evidence from the grand jury does not serve to fulfill that function: an indicted defendant who at trial is not found guilty still suffers severe damage for

Continued on next page.

reputation and incurs significant expense in presenting a defense.

Quicknotes

EXCULPATORY EVIDENCE A statement or other evidence that tends to excuse, justify, or absolve the defendant from alleged fault or guilt.

GRAND JURY A group summoned to investigate, inform, and accuse persons of crimes when sufficient evidence exists to do so.

INDICTMENT A formal written accusation made by a prosecutor and issued by a grand jury, charging an individual with a criminal offense.

CHAPTER 13

Preparing for Adjudication

Quick Reference Rules of Law

PAGE

1. *Hoffman v. United States.* The Fifth Amendment privilege against self-incrimination embraces questions that it can reasonably be said furnish a link in the chain of evidence needed to prosecute for a federal crime. *148*

2. *United States v. Agurs.* If the prosecutor has not made use of perjury intentionally, and if defense counsel has not made a specific request for evidence, the defendant is entitled to a new trial only if evidence withheld by the prosecutor actually creates a reasonable doubt of guilt in the mind of the reviewing judge. *149*

3. *Smith v. Cain.* Evidence is material to a defendant's guilt or innocence when there is a reasonable probability that had the evidence been disclosed, the result of the matter would have been different. *151*

4. *Arizona v. Youngblood.* Absent bad faith, failure by the police to preserve potentially exculpatory evidence does not violate due process. *152*

5. *Williams v. Florida.* The notice-of-alibi rule is not violative of the Fifth and Fourteenth Amendments by compelling a defendant to be a witness against himself. *153*

6. *State v. Reldan.* More than a mere allegation of prejudice must be offered to warrant an order for separate trials of properly joined offenses. *155*

7. *Barker v. Wingo.* The determination of whether a defendant has been deprived of his Sixth Amendment right to a speedy trial must be made on a case-by-case basis by balancing the following four factors: (1) length of delay, (2) reason for delay, (3) the defendant's assertion of the right to a speedy trial, and (4) prejudice to the defendant. *156*

8. *Barker v. Wingo.* The determination of whether a defendant has been deprived of the Sixth Amendment right to a speedy trial must be made on a case-by-case basis by balancing the following four factors: (1) length of delay, (2) reason for delay, (3) the defendant's assertion of the right to a speedy trial, and (4) prejudice to the defendant. *156*

Hoffman v. United States

Individual held in criminal contempt (D) v. Federal government (P)

341 U.S. 479 (1951)

NATURE OF CASE: Appeal from a finding of criminal contempt.

FACT SUMMARY: Hoffman (D) asserted the Fifth Amendment in refusing to answer questions before a federal grand jury and was taken before a federal district court where he was held in criminal contempt and sentenced to five months imprisonment. The Third Circuit Court of Appeals affirmed, and Hoffman (D) appealed to the United States Supreme Court.

RULE OF LAW

The Fifth Amendment privilege against self-incrimination embraces questions that it can reasonably be said furnish a link in the chain of evidence needed to prosecute for a federal crime.

FACTS: When called before a special federal grand jury convened to investigate a wide variety of federal crimes, Hoffman (D) was asked questions, some of which he answered but several of which he refused to answer, asserting the Fifth Amendment on the grounds that, while standing alone the answers might not have incriminated him of a federal offense, his answers might reasonably have furnished a link that could have led prosecutors to evidence he had committed one or more crimes. The district court rejected Hoffman's (D) argument and ordered him to answer the questions under penalty of criminal perjury. The Third Circuit Court of Appeals affirmed, and Hoffman (D) appealed to the United States Supreme Court.

ISSUE: Does the Fifth Amendment privilege against self-incrimination embrace questions that it can reasonably be said furnish a link in the chain of evidence needed to prosecute for a federal crime?

HOLDING AND DECISION: (Clark, J.) Yes. The Fifth Amendment privilege against self-incrimination embraces questions that it can reasonably be said furnish a link in the chain of evidence needed to prosecute for a federal crime. Such protection, however, must be confined to instances where the witness, as here, has reasonable cause to apprehend danger from a direct answer. The lower court should have considered, in connection with several of the questions, that the chief occupation of some persons about whom Hoffman (D) was asked involved evasion of a variety of federal criminal laws. The questions asked could easily have required answers that would "forge links in a chain of facts" imperiling Hoffman (D) with conviction of a federal crime. Three of the questions, if answered affirmatively, would establish contacts between Hoffman (D) and another person at a time when such other person was eluding the grand jury. Hoffman (D) could reasonably have sensed the peril of prosecution for federal offenses ranging from obstruction of justice to conspiracy. The judge who ruled on the privilege had himself impaneled the special grand jury. Reversed.

ANALYSIS

In *Hoffman,* the United States Supreme Court is clear to express its viewpoint that the immediate and potential evils of compulsory self-disclosure transcend any difficulties that the exercise of the privilege may impose on society in the detection and prosecution of crime.

Quicknotes

GRAND JURY A group summoned to investigate, inform, and accuse persons of crimes when sufficient evidence exists to do so.

PRIVILEGE AGAINST SELF-INCRIMINATION A privilege guaranteed by the Fifth Amendment to the U.S. Constitution in a criminal proceeding for communications made by an accused and protecting an accused or witness from having to give testimony that may incriminate him- or herself.

United States v. Agurs

Federal government (P) v. Individual convicted of second-degree murder (D)

427 U.S. 97 (1976)

NATURE OF CASE: Appeal from decision of United States Court of Appeals for the District of Columbia overturning defendant's conviction for second-degree murder.

FACT SUMMARY: After Agurs (D) was convicted of second-degree murder, defense counsel discovered that her victim had a prior criminal record that may have bolstered Agurs's (D) legal defense that she acted in self-defense during the confrontation.

RULE OF LAW

If the prosecutor has not made use of perjury intentionally, and if defense counsel has not made a specific request for evidence, the defendant is entitled to a new trial only if evidence withheld by the prosecutor actually creates a reasonable doubt of guilt in the mind of the reviewing judge.

FACTS: Agurs (D) and James Sewell rented a hotel room. At that time, Sewell was carrying on his person a large Bowie knife and another knife strapped to his leg. After a brief sexual encounter, Sewell left the room and returned a short time later. Agurs (D) may have removed $360 in cash from Sewell's wallet while he was absent from the room. Shortly after Sewell's return, employees of the hotel heard Agurs (D) scream for help. When the employees arrived at the room, Sewell was on top of Agurs (D), but Agurs (D) was holding a knife by the handle. Sewell was bleeding from the chest and hands. After the employees separated the two, Agurs (D) departed the scene. Sewell died at the hospital from multiple stab wounds to his chest and abdomen. Agurs (D) turned herself in to the police the next day. A jury convicted Agurs (D) of second-degree murder. Three months later, defense counsel filed a motion for a new trial. He had discovered that Sewell possessed a criminal record that the prosecution had failed to disclose to the defendant. Sewell's prior record included a guilty plea for assault and two guilty pleas for carrying a deadly weapon. Defense counsel argued in the motion for a new trial that the evidence would have bolstered Agurs's (D) defense of self-defense at trial. The District Court denied the motion, but the United States Court of Appeals for the District of Columbia Circuit reversed by finding the criminal record was material to Agurs's (D) defense. Accordingly, the prosecution should have disclosed the evidence because a jury may have returned a different verdict. The United States Supreme Court granted the Government's (P) application for review.

ISSUE: If the prosecutor has not made use of perjury intentionally, and if defense counsel has not made a specific request for evidence, is the defendant entitled to a new trial only if evidence withheld by the prosecutor actually creates a reasonable doubt of guilt in the mind of the reviewing judge?

HOLDING AND DECISION: (Stevens, J.) Yes. If the prosecutor has not made use of perjury intentionally, and if defense counsel has not made a specific request for evidence, the defendant is entitled to a new trial only if evidence withheld by the prosecutor actually creates a reasonable doubt of guilt in the mind of the reviewing judge. In *Brady v. Maryland,* 373 U.S. 83 (1963), this Court held that suppression by the prosecution of evidence favorable to the accused upon request violates due process when the evidence is material to the defendant's guilt or innocence. The issue in this case is whether the prosecution has a duty to disclose exculpatory evidence when there has been no request for evidence or a general request for all exculpatory evidence. The further inquiry is to decide the standard of materiality that gives rise to such a duty. The rule of *Brady* applies in three situations. First, a defendant is entitled to a new trial if the prosecutor utilizes perjured testimony and is aware of it. Second, the rule applies where defense counsel makes a specific request for evidence and the prosecution fails to produce the evidence. An example is the existence of prior statements given by the defendant or other witnesses. The third situation arises when there has been no request at all by defense counsel or merely a general request for all "*Brady*" evidence or all exculpatory evidence. The Constitution does not demand that the prosecution turn over its entire file to defense counsel. The proper standard of materiality relates to the standard of guilt, which is beyond a reasonable doubt. Accordingly, if the omitted evidence creates a reasonable doubt that otherwise did not exist, the omission will constitute constitutional error requiring a new trial. The trial court reviewed the evidence of Sewell's criminal record and found it not material to Agurs's (D) defense of self-defense. That finding was properly based upon the inconsistency between Agurs's (D) claims of self-defense and the fact that she had no cuts or bruises on her body, while Sewell had multiple stab wounds. In addition, the jury was already aware of Sewell's potentially violent nature, evidenced by his carrying two knives on his person at the time of

Continued on next page.

the incident. Accordingly, the prosecution's failure to disclose Sewell's prior criminal record to the defense did not deprive Agurs (D) of a fair trial. Reversed.

DISSENT: (Marshall, J.) The majority defines the category of material evidence too narrowly. The standard of disclosing only evidence that will create a reasonable doubt in the minds of a judge or jury is a high one. It creates little incentive for the prosecution to disclose. The proper standard should be that the withheld evidence had a significant chance of creating reasonable doubt in the minds of the jury.

ANALYSIS

In *United States v. Begley*, 473 U.S. 667 (1985), the Court reformulated the criminal discovery standard. That decision held that evidence is material if there is reasonable probability that had the prosecution disclosed the evidence, the result of the case would have been different. In many states, prosecutors who withhold evidence intentionally from defense counsel may face disciplinary action from the state board of bar overseers.

Quicknotes

EXCULPATORY EVIDENCE A statement or other evidence that tends to excuse, justify, or absolve the defendant from alleged fault or guilt.

MATERIALITY Importance; the degree of relevance or necessity to the particular matter.

Smith v. Cain

Individual convicted of first-degree murder (D) v. State (P)

565 U.S. 73 (2012)

NATURE OF CASE: Appeal from multiple state courts' denial of his petition for postconviction relief.

FACT SUMMARY: After a jury convicted Smith (D) of five counts of first-degree murder, Smith (D) later obtained police records that contained statements from the only witness in the case that were contradictory to the witness's trial testimony.

RULE OF LAW

Evidence is material to a defendant's guilt or innocence when there is a reasonable probability that had the evidence been disclosed, the result of the matter would have been different.

FACTS: At Smith's (D) trial for five counts of first-degree murder, the prosecution presented only one witness, Boatner, who identified Smith (D) as the shooter. No other witnesses or physical evidence connected Smith (D) to the murders. At trial, Boatner testified that he had been face to face with Smith (D) during the robbery and shootings. A jury convicted Smith (D) of five counts of first-degree murder. Smith (D) subsequently sought postconviction relief in the Louisiana state courts. Smith (D) had obtained police files that contained notes of a principal investigator. The notes contained statements from Boatner that directly conflicted with his trial testimony. According to the notes, Boatner could not identify the shooter on the night of the murders and could not describe him as anything more than a Black male. Boatner also stated he could not identify anyone because he could not see any faces. As each judicial level, the Louisiana state courts denied Smith's (D) petition for postconviction relief. The United States Supreme Court granted Smith's (D) petition for review.

ISSUE: Is evidence material to a defendant's guilt or innocence when there is a reasonable probability that had the evidence been disclosed, the result of the matter would have been different?

HOLDING AND DECISION: (Roberts, C.J.) Yes. Evidence is material to a defendant's guilt or innocence when there is a reasonable probability that had the evidence been disclosed, the result of the matter would have been different. A state violates a defendant's right to a fair trial if it withholds evidence that is material to a defendant's guilt or innocence. The reasonable probability that newly disclosed evidence would lead to a different result does not mean that it is more likely than not that the result would be different. Rather, the likelihood of a different result need only be great enough to undermine the confidence in the defendant's conviction. In addition, newly disclosed evidence impeaching an eyewitness may not be material if the state had other, ample evidence to support the conviction. Here, that is not the case. Boatner's identification of Smith (D) as the shooter was the sole evidence the State (P) relied upon to support its case. Boatner's statements to the police investigator directly contradict his trial testimony and are therefore material to Smith's (D) guilt or innocence. Reversed and remanded.

DISSENT: (Thomas, J.) Smith (D) has not shown a reasonable probability that the jury would have decided differently based on the new evidence. The determination of materiality must be based on the entire trial record. Boatner consistently, with a few minor exceptions, described Smith (D) as the shooter. Because the new statements would have had a minimal impeachment impact, the State (P) did not violate Smith's (D) right to a fair trial by not producing Boatner's inconsistent statements.

ANALYSIS

Where the undisclosed evidence is contrary to evidence presented at trial, the likelihood of a decision granting a new trial is higher. State prosecutors typically respond to such motions by arguing that either the new evidence is not material to the case or that the state had ample evidence to convict the defendant in any event.

Quicknotes

MATERIALITY Importance; the degree of relevance or necessity to the particular matter.

Arizona v. Youngblood

State (P) v. Kidnapping suspect (D)

488 U.S. 51 (1988)

NATURE OF CASE: Review of reversal of conviction for kidnap and sexual assault.

FACT SUMMARY: Certain fluid samples removed from a sexual assault victim were improperly stored by the police and could not be examined on behalf of Youngblood (D).

RULE OF LAW

Absent bad faith, failure by the police to preserve potentially exculpatory evidence does not violate due process.

FACTS: A minor was kidnapped and repeatedly assaulted sexually before being released by the perpetrator. His mother then took him to a hospital. A physician diagnosed sexual assault and then took certain evidence in the form of residual body fluids. The evidence was put into storage. Police tests proved inconclusive. Meanwhile, the victim picked out Youngblood's (D) photo from a photo lineup, and he was arrested. Upon being informed of the fluid samples, Youngblood's (D) counsel requested specimens for testing. It turned out that the remaining samples had been improperly stored and could not be used. Youngblood (D) was convicted. The state court of appeals reversed, holding the loss of the evidence to have constituted a due process violation. The United States Supreme Court granted review.

ISSUE: Absent bad faith, does failure by the police to preserve potentially exculpatory evidence violate due process?

HOLDING AND DECISION: (Rehnquist, C.J.) No. Absent bad faith, failure by the police to preserve potentially exculpatory evidence does not violate due process. In the case of evidence that is only potentially exculpatory, courts have the difficult task of divining the import of materials whose significance is unknown and often disputed. To impose a duty on police to preserve all potential evidence creates too great a burden on law enforcement. The better rule is that only intentional, bad-faith destruction of evidence should constitute reversible error. Here, the loss of evidence was at worst negligent, so the court of appeals erred. Reversed and remanded.

CONCURRENCE: (Stevens, J.) There may well be cases in which the defendant is unable to prove that the state acted in bad faith but in which the loss or destruction of evidence is nonetheless so critical to the defense as to make a criminal trial fundamentally unfair. This, however, is not such a case.

DISSENT: (Blackmun, J.) The Constitution requires that a criminal defendant receive a fair trial, not a "good faith" try at a fair trial. When evidence is lost due to police activity, due process has been violated.

ANALYSIS

The tests done by the police department did not include a certain "state of the art" test. Youngblood (D) contended that failure to use this most reliable test was improper. The United States Supreme Court disagreed, noting that a defendant did not have a constitutional right to any particular type of test.

Quicknotes

DUE PROCESS The constitutional mandate requiring the courts to protect and enforce individuals' rights and liberties consistent with prevailing principles of fairness and justice and prohibiting the federal and state governments from such activities that deprive its citizens of life, liberty, or property interest.

EXCULPATORY EVIDENCE A statement or other evidence that tends to excuse, justify, or absolve the defendant from alleged fault or guilt.

Williams v. Florida

Alibi user (D) v. State (P)

399 U.S. 78 (1970)

NATURE OF CASE: Appeal from conviction of robbery.

FACT SUMMARY: Florida law requires that a defendant submit to a limited form of pretrial discovery by the State (P) whenever the defendant intends to rely at trial on the defense of alibi.

RULE OF LAW

The notice-of-alibi rule is not violative of the Fifth and Fourteenth Amendments by compelling a defendant to be a witness against himself.

FACTS: Williams (D) was charged with robbery. Prior to his trial, Williams (D) sought a protective order to be excused from complying with a Florida law that requires a defendant, on written demand of the prosecution, to give notice in advance of trial if the defendant intends to claim an alibi, and to furnish the prosecution with information as to the place he claims to have been and with the names and addresses of the alibi witnesses he intends to use. Williams (D) wanted to declare his intent to use an alibi but objected to further disclosure on the ground that the notice-of-alibi rule would compel him to be a witness against himself in violation of the Fifth and Fourteenth Amendments. The rule also obligated the State (P) to notify a defendant of any rebuttal witnesses to the alibi defense the State (P) will call. Failure to comply, by either side, results in the exclusion of the defendant's alibi evidence or the State's (P) rebuttal evidence. When Williams's (D) motion for the protective order was denied, he complied with the rule. On the morning of his trial, the State (P) interviewed Mrs. Scotty, Williams's (D) chief alibi witness. At trial, Mrs. Scotty gave testimony that contradicted her pretrial statements. The State (P) also furnished a rebuttal witness. Williams (D) was convicted.

ISSUE: Is the notice-of-alibi rule violative of the Fifth and Fourteenth Amendments by compelling a defendant to be a witness against himself?

HOLDING AND DECISION: (White, J.) No. The notice-of-alibi rule is not violative of the Fifth and Fourteenth Amendments by compelling a defendant to be a witness against himself. The rule is fair to both the defendant and the State (P) in permitting liberal discovery. The State (P) has a legitimate interest in protecting itself against eleventh-hour defenses: although based on an adversary system, a trial is not yet a poker game in which players may conceal their cards at will. No pretrial statements of Mrs. Scotty were introduced at trial; her pretrial testimony was used only to find rebuttal witnesses. A defendant is always in a dilemma whether to remain silent or present a defense that may prove disastrous. Nothing in the rule obligates the defendant to rely on an alibi or prevents him from abandoning it as a defense. The rule requires only that a defendant accelerate the timing of his disclosure of information he would have revealed at trial anyway. A defendant is not entitled to await the end of the prosecution's case against him before announcing the nature of his defense any more than he can await the jury's verdict on the State's (P) case before deciding to take the stand himself. Absent the rule, the prosecution would be entitled to a continuance at trial on the grounds of surprise; the rule thus serves to prevent a disrupted trial.

CONCURRENCE AND DISSENT: (Black, J.) Before trial defense counsel can only guess at what the State's (P) case might be. The notice-of-alibi rule thus compels defendants with any thoughts at all of pleading alibi to be forced to disclose their intentions so as to preserve the possibility of later raising the defense—the decision goes to more than just "timing." Pretrial disclosure will adversely affect the defendant who then decides to forgo raising an alibi defense. His alibi witnesses will still help the prosecution to new leads or evidence. The rule is a clear violation of the Fifth Amendment because it requires a defendant to give information to the State (P) that may destroy him. The entire burden of proving criminal activity rests on the State (P): no constitutional provision is designed to make conviction easier. The defendant need not do anything to defend or convict himself. While a criminal trial is in part a search for truth, it also is designed to protect "freedom" by ensuring that the State (P) carries its burden. Efficiency is not a consideration. The majority's decision opens the way to compel complete pretrial discovery of a defendant's case, and any defenses he might raise.

ANALYSIS

At the time *Williams* was decided, 15 states other than Florida had notice-of-alibi requirements of varying kinds. One such rule, in *Wardins v. Oregon,* 412 U.S. 470 (1973), was struck down because it failed to provide reciprocal discovery rights to the defendant. The United States Supreme Court found this omission violative of the Due Process Clause of the Fourteenth Amendment. Because exclusion of the testimony of alibi witnesses is

Continued on next page.

a drastic sanction for failure on the defendant's part to comply with the rule's disclosure requirements, other sanctions have been suggested. These include: (1) granting a continuance to the prosecution; (2) allowing the prosecution or court to comment on the defendant's failure to the jury; (3) placing the defense counsel in contempt when the failure was not in "good faith."

Quicknotes

ALIBI Provable documentation of an individual's activities at the time a criminal offense was committed, thereby relieving the individual of possible guilt.

CONTINUANCE The postponement of a case to a later date.

DUE PROCESS CLAUSE Language in the Fifth and Fourteenth Amendments to the U.S. Constitution, providing that no person shall be deprived of "life, liberty, or property, without due process of law."

PRIVILEGE AGAINST SELF-INCRIMINATION A privilege guaranteed by the Fifth Amendment to the U.S. Constitution in a criminal proceeding for communications made by an accused and protecting an accused or witness from having to give testimony that may incriminate him- or herself.

State v. Reldan

State (P) v. Accused murderer (D)

N.J. Super. Ct., 167 N.J. Super. 595, 401 A.2d 563 (1979)

NATURE OF CASE: Motion to sever trial upon indictment of Reldan (D) for two murders.

FACT SUMMARY: Reldan (D) was charged with the murder of two women and sought separate trials, claiming that the jury would be prejudiced by a joint trial.

RULE OF LAW

More than a mere allegation of prejudice must be offered to warrant an order for separate trials of properly joined offenses.

FACTS: Within two days, two women in their twenties were found strangled to death in New York, in different locations but within the same county. They were both nude and had both died by the unusual method of a fractured hyoid bone in their necks. Reldan (D) was charged with both murders in a single indictment, and moved for separate trials, alleging prejudice.

ISSUE: Must more than a mere allegation of prejudice be offered to warrant an order for separate trials of properly joined offenses?

HOLDING AND DECISION: (Madden, J.) Yes. More than a mere allegation of prejudice must be offered to warrant an order for separate trials of properly joined offenses. Reldan (D) did not proffer that he wished to testify as to one count only; if he made such a proffer at trial, I would then be empowered to decide whether to grant a severance. As to the evidence of one crime being used to infer guilt as to the other, even if the trials were severed, the prosecution would still be able to offer evidence of one crime at the trial for the other to show motive, intent, common scheme, knowledge, absence of mistake, or identity. The evidence here is not so prejudicial as to outweigh its probative value, and the defendant has not made an adequate showing that a jury would be unable to fairly hear the two counts of murder in the same trial. The motion is denied.

ANALYSIS

Judge Madden distinguished a case—*State v. Orlando*, 101 N.J. Super. 390 (App. Div. 1968)—in which the only evidence against the defendant was the testimony of his two victims, and severance was ordered. Madden observed that a joinder in that case would have given the prosecution two witnesses instead of one to overcome the denial of either offense.

Quicknotes

JOINDER The joining of claims or parties in one lawsuit.

PROBATIVE Tending to establish proof.

SEVERANCE Dividing or separating; setting aside one or more claims in a lawsuit to be tried separately.

Barker v. Wingo

Convicted murder suspect (D) v. State (P)

407 U.S. 514 (1972)

NATURE OF CASE: Appeal from affirmances of murder conviction rendered five years after defendant was arrested.

FACT SUMMARY: Although Barker (D) made no objections during the first four years of a five-year delay between his arrest and conviction for murder, he subsequently claimed that his right to a speedy trial had been violated.

RULE OF LAW

The determination of whether a defendant has been deprived of the Sixth Amendment right to a speedy trial must be made on a case-by-case basis by balancing the following four factors: (1) length of delay, (2) reason for delay, (3) the defendant's assertion of the right to a speedy trial, and (4) prejudice to the defendant.

FACTS: On July 20, 1958, an elderly couple was murdered. Shortly afterwards, Silas Manning and Willie Barker (D) were arrested as suspects. They were indicted on September 15, counsel was appointed on September 17, and Barker's (D) trial was set for October 21. However, Barker (D) was not brought to trial for more than five years after his arrest due to numerous continuances by the prosecution. Initially the continuances were for the purpose of first convicting Manning, against whom the Commonwealth (P) had a stronger case, to assure his testimony at Barker's (D) trial (i.e., to eliminate problems of self-incrimination). However, Manning was not convicted until 1962. Afterwards, Barker's (D) trial was delayed another seven months due to the illness of the chief investigating officer in the case. During these continuances, Barker (D) was free for all but ten months in jail, and he made no objections during the first four years of delay. However, Barker (D) objected to the last few continuances, and at his trial he moved for dismissal on the basis that his Sixth Amendment right to a speedy trial had been violated. This motion was denied, and Barker (D) was convicted of murder. Upon appeal to the Kentucky Court of Appeals, the conviction was affirmed. Barker (D) then petitioned for habeas corpus in the U.S. District Court. Upon denial of that petition, he appealed to the Sixth Circuit Court of Appeals. Upon affirmance of his conviction, Barker (D) brought a petition for certiorari to the United States Supreme Court, which was granted.

ISSUE: Must the determination of whether a defendant has been deprived of the Sixth Amendment right to a speedy trial be made on a case-by-case basis by balancing the following four factors: (1) length of delay, (2) reason for delay, (3) the defendant's assertion of the right to a speedy trial, and (4) prejudice to the defendant?

HOLDING AND DECISION: (Powell, J.) Yes. The determination of whether a defendant has been deprived of his Sixth Amendment right to a speedy trial must be made on a case-by-case basis by balancing the following four factors: (1) length of delay, (2) reason for delay, (3) the defendant's assertion of the right to a speedy trial, and (4) prejudice to the defendant. Because the deprivation of the right to a speedy trial does not per se prejudice the ability of an accused to defend himself, it is impossible to state "with precision" when the right has been denied. Each factor, therefore, must be separately analyzed. First, it is true that a long delay before trial is more likely to be justified for a serious, complex crime (e.g., murder) than for a simple one. Here, however, the delay of over five years was extreme by any standard. Second, it is true that a delay in bringing an accused to trial may be justified by a showing of some strong reason for it. Here, however, there was a strong reason for delay (i.e., illness of the chief investigator) for only seven months of the five-year delay. Although some additional delay might also have been necessary to acquire Manning as a witness, over four years was clearly unreasonable. Third, it is true that the failure to assert the right to a speedy trial will not constitute a waiver of that right, unless it is found to be an "intentional relinquishment or abandonment of a known right." Here, however, it is obvious that Barker (D) did not want a trial at all, hoping, rather, that the delays would ultimately result in dismissal of the charges against him. Fourth, it is true that the prejudice that results from a delay of a defendant's trial must be evaluated in light of those interests that a speedy trial was designed to protect (i.e., prevention of "oppressive pretrial incarceration," minimization of anxiety and concern of the accused, and limitation on the possibility that the defense will be "impaired"). Here, however, prejudice was minimal. Although Barker (D) was prejudiced to some extent by spending some time in jail and by living for years under "a cloud of suspicion," none of his witnesses died or became unavailable. Therefore, when assessing these factors together, the facts that Barker (D) did not want a trial and was not prejudiced by the delay outweigh the unjustified length of delay, so that it cannot be said

Continued on next page.

that Barker (D) was unconstitutionally denied a speedy trial. Judgment affirmed.

CONCURRENCE: (White, J.) Had Barker (D) not so clearly acquiesced in the major delays involved in this case, the outcome would have been different. Nonetheless, it is important to emphasize that one of the major purposes of the Constitution's speedy trial provision is to guard against inordinate delay between a public charge and trial, which, wholly aside from possible prejudice to a defense on the merits, may "seriously interfere with the defendant's liberty, whether he is free on bail or not, and that may disrupt his employment, drain his financial resources, curtail his associations, subject him to public obloquy, and create anxiety in him, his family and his friends." *United States v. Marion*, 404 U. S. 307, 404 U. S. 320 (1971). Although these factors will be more serious for some than for others, they are inevitably present in every case to some extent, because every defendant will either be incarcerated pending trial or on bail, subject to substantial restrictions on his liberty.

ANALYSIS

This case illustrates the discretion available (through the balancing test) to the courts in determining when the right to a speedy trial has been violated, and the emphasis on the desire of an accused to have a speedy trial. Note that an accused "waives" the right to a speedy trial if the accused flees the state after arraignment or requests postponement of his trial. Note, also, that the right to a speedy trial attaches only after a person is accused (i.e., indicted or arrested), so that it is not violated by police delay in filing charges. However, if such a delay was purposeful, due process requires dismissal of the charges.

Quicknotes

CERTIORARI A discretionary writ issued by a superior court to an inferior court in order to review the lower court's decisions; the U.S. Supreme Court's writ ordering such review.

CONTINUANCE The postponement of a case to a later date.

SIXTH AMENDMENT Provides the right to a speedy trial by impartial jury, the right to be informed of the accusation, the right to confront witnesses, and the right to have the assistance of counsel in all criminal prosecutions.

CHAPTER 14

The Role of Defense Counsel

Quick Reference Rules of Law

Nix v. Whiteside

Prosecution on appeal (P) v. Murder convict (D)

475 U.S. 157 (1986)

NATURE OF CASE: Appeal from a reversal of denial of habeas corpus following conviction for murder.

FACT SUMMARY: Whiteside (D), who was dissuaded by his attorney from committing perjury, sought habeas corpus relief for ineffective assistance of counsel.

RULE OF LAW

A defendant is not denied effective assistance of counsel if his attorney dissuades him from committing perjury.

FACTS: Whiteside (D) stabbed and killed Love. Prior to the trial, Whiteside (D) told his attorney that he was going to testify that he saw Love holding a gun, something he had earlier stated was not the case. Whiteside's (D) attorney said that he would inform the court of Whiteside's (D) perjury if Whiteside (D) did this, so Whiteside (D) did not make the assertion. Whiteside (D) was convicted, and the conviction was affirmed. A district court denied habeas corpus, but the Eighth Circuit Court of Appeals reversed, holding that Whiteside (D) had been denied effective assistance of counsel.

ISSUE: Is a defendant denied effective assistance of counsel if his attorney dissuades him from committing perjury?

HOLDING AND DECISION: (Burger, C.J.) No. A defendant is not denied effective assistance of counsel if his attorney dissuades him from committing perjury. A defendant is denied effective counsel only if counsel's errors are so serious as to amount to not functioning as counsel. An attorney is under an ethical duty to prevent perjury, and counsel's efforts to dissuade were perfectly in keeping with this duty. A defendant does not have a right to testify falsely, and that is the only "right" that Whiteside (D) could possibly have been denied. Therefore, Whiteside's (D) counsel's acts were perfectly proper. Reversed.

CONCURRENCE: (Brennan, J.) The Court has no authority to establish rules of ethical conduct for lawyers practicing in state courts.

CONCURRENCE: (Stevens, J.) In this case, Whiteside (D) intended to commit perjury, his lawyer knew it, and the lawyer had a duty to take extreme measures to prevent the perjury from occurring. In this task, the lawyer was successful, and it is clear his client, Whiteside (D), suffered no legally cognizable prejudice.

ANALYSIS

The duty of an attorney not to tolerate perjury from his client is time honored. Written guidelines go as far back as 1908, but the tradition goes much further than that. This principle is embodied today in MR 3.3(a)(3) of the Model Rules of Professional Conduct.

Quicknotes

HABEAS CORPUS A proceeding in which a defendant brings a writ to compel a judicial determination of whether he or she is lawfully being held in custody.

INEFFECTIVE ASSISTANCE OF COUNSEL A claim brought by an accused in which it must be determined whether the attorney's rendering of representation was such that the ultimate disposition of the case may not be relied upon as fair.

PERJURY The making of false or misleading statements knowingly and under oath.

Gideon v. Wainwright

Indigent suspect (D) v. State (P)

372 U.S. 335 (1963)

NATURE OF CASE: Felony prosecution.

FACT SUMMARY: Gideon (D) was charged with a felony in a state prosecution. He requested court-appointed counsel but was refused on the basis that state law required appointment of counsel only in capital cases.

RULE OF LAW

The right of an indigent defendant to the assistance of counsel at trial is a fundamental and essential right required to insure a fair trial.

FACTS: Gideon (D) was charged with felony breaking and entering, a violation of state law. He was without funds and requested the court appoint an attorney for him at trial. The request was refused since Florida state law did not require appointment of counsel for indigents except in capital offense cases. Gideon (D) then conducted his own defense and was convicted and sentenced to five years. He filed a writ of habeas corpus based on the denial of counsel at trial.

ISSUE: Is the right of an indigent defendant to the assistance of counsel at trial a fundamental and essential right required to insure a fair trial?

HOLDING AND DECISION: (Black, J.) Yes. The right of an indigent defendant to the assistance of counsel at trial is a fundamental and essential right required to insure a fair trial. This Court first expressed the view that the right to counsel at trial was a fundamental right essential to a fair trial in *Powell v. Alabama,* 287 U.S. 45 (1932). That decision was limited to its facts, however. In *Betts v. Brady,* 316 U.S. 455 (1942), the right to counsel was predicated on a case-by-case examination of the special circumstances of each case to determine if denial of counsel was a denial of a fair trial. But it is evident that every defendant who can afford a lawyer will have one at his criminal trial. It does not appear to be a luxury but is viewed as a necessity. This Court is of the opinion, now, that *Powell v. Alabama* was right in holding that the right to counsel is fundamental to a fair trial and that *Betts v. Brady* was wrong in limiting that right to special circumstances. The Court holds that the right to counsel is a fundamental right for all criminal defendants at trial.

CONCURRENCE: (Harlan, J.) For capital cases the special circumstances rule has been formally abandoned. It is now time when such rule similarly should be abandoned also in noncapital cases, at least in situations in which a substantial prison sentence is a possibility.

ANALYSIS

Upon retrial, with the assistance of appointed counsel, Gideon (D) was acquitted. The *Gideon* decision was read to require counsel in only non-petty (i.e., six months or more imprisonment) cases. However, in a subsequent case, *Argersinger v. Hamlin,* 497 U.S. 25 (1972), the right to appointed counsel was extended to any case where the possibility of imprisonment existed. There was no minimum time specified and so if the judge wishes to imprison the defendant, if convicted, he must have appointed counsel, if indigent. The denial of counsel at trial where imprisonment results is error per se and is not subject to the harmless error rule.

Quicknotes

HARMLESS ERROR An error committed during trial that does not require the reviewing court to overturn or modify the trial court's judgment in that it did not affect the appellant's substantial rights or the disposition of the action.

INDIGENT A person who is poor and thus is unable to obtain counsel to provide defense in a criminal proceeding and for whom counsel must be appointed.

WRIT OF HABEAS CORPUS A proceeding in which a defendant brings a writ to compel a judicial determination of whether he or she is lawfully being held in custody.

Douglas v. California

Indigent convict (D) v. State (P)

372 U.S. 353 (1963)

NATURE OF CASE: Appeal from criminal conviction.

FACT SUMMARY: After his conviction, Douglas (D) was denied appointed counsel for assistance in pursuing his right of first appeal. The denial came after the appellate court had reviewed the transcript of his trial and, pursuant to state law, had determined that counsel would not be of help to the defendant.

RULE OF LAW

An indigent is entitled to appointed counsel to prepare an appellate brief where the appeal pursued is granted as a matter of right to all defendants.

FACTS: Douglas (D) was convicted in a state proceeding and was sentenced. He served notice that he wished to appeal his conviction and that he needed appointed counsel due to indigency. The first appeal after a trial conviction is granted as a matter of right in California (P). However, Douglas (D) was denied the appointment of counsel to prosecute the appeal. The denial came after the appellate court had reviewed the transcript and determined that appointed counsel would not be of help to either Douglas (D) or the court. The decision was in line with a state rule providing for this procedure.

ISSUE: Is an indigent entitled to appointed counsel to prepare an appellate brief where the appeal pursued is granted as a manner of right to all defendants?

HOLDING AND DECISION: (Douglas, J.) Yes. An indigent is entitled to appointed counsel to prepare an appellate brief where the appeal pursued is granted as a matter of right to all defendants. In spite of California's (P) otherwise forward-looking favorable treatment of indigents, the problem presented by this case is the same as that presented by *Griffin v. Illinois,* 351 U.S. 12 (1956) (i.e., discrimination against the indigent). By the system employed, only a defendant affluent enough to retain counsel will obtain a full judicial review of his conviction. The indigent is entitled to no more than a review of the bare transcript by the appellate court. Not all appealable issues will appear on the face of a transcript. While the Fourteenth Amendment does not demand absolute equality, due process cannot be denied by "invidious discrimination." While the rich man can employ counsel to focus on appealable issues and to raise hidden objections to the conduct of the trial, the indigent is denied this same right. Our decision is not directed toward discretionary appeals but toward appeals granted as a matter of right to all defendants. In such an instance, the indigent is entitled to appointed counsel.

DISSENT: (Harlan, J.) The majority appears to rely on both the Equal Protection Clause and the Due Process Clause of the Fourteenth Amendment. I do not think the former is applicable or the latter violated in this case. The Equal Protection Clause prohibits discrimination between rich and poor "as such." The California (P) procedure affords everyone the right to appeal and to transcript of the trial. The difference comes in determining whether appointed counsel is necessary. California (P) has determined appointed counsel is not necessary in nonmeritorious cases. To compel counsel in all cases is to say that the state is obligated to provide absolute equality of all services, which is both an impossibility and not mandated by the Equal Protection Clause. In *Griffin v. Illinois,* this Court, while finding a transcript must be furnished to the indigent appellant, also said the state could find other means of affording adequate and effective appellate review to indigent defendants. This is what California (P) has done and yet the majority strikes down the procedure. California (P) has apparently gone beyond what this Court has recently required for indigents in federal courts, yet it has been found insufficient. A state can legitimately advance its own economic interests in the face of needless expense. That is what California (P) has done. The indigent is not denied appellate review or counsel in a meritorious case, but the state need not fund frivolous appeals.

ANALYSIS

Some commentators have viewed the *Douglas* decision as a precursor to a requirement for appointed counsel whenever retained counsel is permitted. In fact, some lower courts (not a majority) have held that the difference between appeals of right and discretionary appeals is not a barrier to the right to appointive counsel. However, the weight of the commentaries appears to favor viewing the *Douglas* and *Griffin v. Illinois,* 351 U.S. 12 (1956), decisions as interposing the right to counsel only where the lack of such counsel, in relation to retained counsel cases, works an inequality so significant as to amount to fundamental unfairness. On that basis, the right to counsel on a discretionary appeal is not found since such appeals rarely delve into new ground not covered in the first appeal and involve broad policy decisions fully developed in the first appeal.

Continued on next page.

Quicknotes

EQUAL PROTECTION CLAUSE A constitutional provision that each person be guaranteed the same protection of the laws enjoyed by other persons in like circumstances.

INDIGENT A person who is poor and thus is unable to obtain counsel to provide defense in a criminal proceeding and for whom counsel must be appointed.

INVIDIOUS DISCRIMINATION Unequal treatment of a class of persons that is particularly malicious or hostile.

Ross v. Moffitt

Forgery convict (P) v. Court (D)

417 U.S. 600 (1974)

NATURE OF CASE: Appeal of decision granting a writ of habeas corpus.

FACT SUMMARY: Ross (P) wanted the state to provide him an attorney to appeal his convictions to the state supreme court and the United States Supreme Court.

RULE OF LAW

The states are not required to provide a convicted indigent defendant with counsel for appeals beyond the appeal granted as a matter of right by the states.

FACTS: Ross (P) was convicted of forgery in both Mecklenberg County and in Guilford County, North Carolina. He wanted the state to provide him with an attorney to assist him in seeking discretionary review in the state supreme court of the Mecklenberg County conviction, and he also wanted court-appointed counsel to prepare a writ of certiorari to the United States Supreme Court for the Guilford County conviction. Ross (P) was represented by the public defender in the state supreme court in his appeal of the Guilford County conviction. When the state refused to honor his request, he sought a writ of habeas corpus in federal court, claiming the right to have counsel provided for him by the state. North Carolina authorizes appointment of counsel for a convicted defendant appealing to the intermediate court of appeals, but not for a defendant who seeks either discretionary review in the state supreme court or a writ of certiorari in the United States Supreme Court. The U.S. court of appeals ruled that under the rationale of *Douglas v. California,* 372 U.S. 353 (1963), the state was required to provide counsel for Ross (P) in both cases.

ISSUE: Are the states required to provide a convicted indigent defendant with counsel for appeals beyond the appeal granted as a matter of right by the states?

HOLDING AND DECISION: (Rehnquist, J.) No. The Court held that the Due Process and Equal Protection Clauses do not require that the state provide a convicted indigent defendant with counsel for appeals beyond the appeal granted as a matter of right by the states. There is no question that under the Due Process Clause the states must provide an indigent defendant with counsel at his trial, but the nature of appellate review is materially different from the trial court. The convicted defendant is no longer trying to protect himself from having the state prove him guilty of some crime but is trying, instead, to overturn a finding of guilt made by a judge or jury. Just because the state has provided appellate courts does not mean that a state must provide counsel to indigent defendants at every stage of appellate review. The Court stated that the fact that some people have enough money to obtain counsel in making discretionary appeals doesn't mean that the Equal Protection Clause requires that all defendants be provided with the same opportunity. The fact that a particular service might be a benefit to an indigent defendant does not mean that the service is constitutionally required. Ross (P) had counsel in making his appeal to the intermediate court of appeals in the state and the state is not required to provide counsel for any further appeals. The decision of the court of appeals was, therefore, reversed.

DISSENT: (Douglas, J.) The right to seek discretionary review is a substantial right grounded upon concepts of fairness and equality. In discretionary review, an attorney can be of significant assistance to an accused who is indigent.

ANALYSIS

The United States Supreme Court has refused to appoint counsel for persons seeking to file petitions for certiorari with that Court and as pointed out in this case, has refused to require the states to provide counsel for indigents appealing to the Court. Up until this case was decided, it wasn't clear how far the Court was willing to extend the ruling in *Douglas v. California,* 372 U.S. 353 (1963). Many commentators have felt that under the Equal Protection Clause the state was required to provide counsel for indigents in all cases where more affluent defendants had a right to be represented by counsel. This case clearly points out that equal protection doesn't require that poor defendants be treated just like rich defendants in all instances.

Quicknotes

CERTIORARI A discretionary writ issued by a superior court to an inferior court in order to review the lower court's decisions; the U.S. Supreme Court's writ ordering such review.

EQUAL PROTECTION CLAUSE A constitutional provision that each person be guaranteed the same protection of the laws enjoyed by other persons in like circumstances.

Continued on next page.

INDIGENT A person who is poor and thus is unable to obtain counsel to provide defense in a criminal proceeding and for whom counsel must be appointed.

RIGHT TO COUNSEL Right conferred by the Sixth Amendment that the accused shall be provided effective legal assistance in a criminal proceeding.

WRIT OF HABEAS CORPUS A proceeding in which a defendant brings a writ to compel a judicial determination of whether he or she is lawfully being held in custody.

Faretta v. California

Grand theft suspect (D) v. State (P)

422 U.S. 806 (1975)

NATURE OF CASE: Appeal of a conviction for grand theft.

FACT SUMMARY: Faretta (D) was charged with grand theft. Before and during trial, he moved to represent himself. The trial judge refused, and he was convicted.

RULE OF LAW

A state may not constitutionally impose a lawyer on a defendant who wishes to represent himself, so long as the defendant has made a knowing and intelligent waiver of his right to a lawyer.

FACTS: Faretta (D) was charged with grand theft. Several weeks before the date of his trial, Faretta (D) requested that he be permitted to defend himself. The trial judge, in a preliminary ruling, accepted Faretta's (D) waiver of counsel. Several weeks later, but still before trial, the judge held a sua sponte hearing to determine Faretta's (D) ability to conduct his own defense and decided on the basis of Faretta's (D) answers to questions on state law that Faretta (D) had not made a knowing and intelligent waiver of his right to assistance of counsel. The trial judge ruled that Faretta (D) had no constitutional right to conduct his own defense and appointed a public defender to represent him. Faretta (D) was convicted and sentenced to prison. This decision was affirmed by the court of appeals, and the state supreme court refused to hear the case. The United States Supreme Court granted certiorari.

ISSUE: May a state constitutionally impose a lawyer on a defendant who wishes to represent himself, so long as the defendant has made a knowing and intelligent waiver of his right to a lawyer?

HOLDING AND DECISION: (Stewart, J.) No. A state may not constitutionally impose a lawyer on a defendant who wishes to represent himself, so long as the defendant has made a knowing and intelligent waiver of his right to a lawyer. The rationale for this rule lies within the structure of the Sixth Amendment in that it is consistent with the Sixth Amendment's right to make a personal defense. Here, Faretta (D) was literate and competent, and knowingly exercised his free will to make a choice to represent himself. His level of legal knowledge was not relevant to an assessment of his knowing exercise of the right to defend himself. Vacated.

DISSENT: (Burger, C.J.) Society has an interest in ensuring that trials are fair and permitting an ill-advised defendant to represent himself undercuts that interest. Moreover, the "right" recognized here is found nowhere in the Constitution.

DISSENT: (Blackmun, J.) The questions raised today by this Court's opinion as to the standards of waiver by a pro se defendant will haunt the trial of every defendant who seeks to assert the right of self-representation.

ANALYSIS

The right of an accused to proceed pro se is a constitutional right. Moreover, on the federal level, it is a statutory right as well. However, this right is qualified by the requirement that a waiver of counsel is, considering all circumstances, knowingly and intelligently made. The trial judge should ask the accused about the circumstances of the waiver. If a defendant has successfully waived the right to counsel, a written memorial of this should be made. (Wright, Fed. *Prac. & Proc.*, Vol. 3, at 213–216.)

Quicknotes

CERTIORARI A discretionary writ issued by a superior court to an inferior court in order to review the lower court's decisions; the U.S. Supreme Court's writ ordering such review.

KNOWING AND INTELLIGENT WAIVER The intentional or voluntary forfeiture of a recognized right.

PRO SE An individual appearing on his or her own behalf.

SIXTH AMENDMENT Provides the right to a speedy and public trial by impartial jury, the right to be informed of the accusation, the right to confront witnesses, and to the right have the assistance of counsel in all criminal prosecutions.

Strickland v. Washington

Defense attorney (D) v. Criminal defendant (P)

466 U.S. 668 (1984)

NATURE OF CASE: Review of order granting writ of habeas corpus.

FACT SUMMARY: Washington (P), in federal habeas proceeding, contended that, in a capital sentence hearing, he had been denied effective assistance of counsel.

RULE OF LAW

At a capital sentence hearing, a Sixth Amendment violation occurs only if counsel's performance was deficient and such deficiency resulted in actual prejudice.

FACTS: Washington (P) went on a crime spree that resulted in three deaths. He was charged with numerous offenses, including burglary, kidnapping, and murder. Against his attorney's wishes, he confessed. Also, against his attorney's advice, he waived a jury trial. Finally, he pleaded guilty on all counts, again against his attorney's advice. At the sentence hearing, his attorney stressed Washington's (P) absence of a prior criminal record, his generally good character, and alleged mental disturbance due to poor economic circumstances. He did not introduce character witnesses. He also did not introduce psychiatric testimony, as he had not been able to find a mental health professional who would testify that Washington (P) was mentally disturbed. The judge, citing numerous aggravating circumstances due to the gruesome nature of the murders, imposed the death sentence. The Florida Supreme Court affirmed. Washington (P) petitioned for a writ of habeas corpus. The district court denied relief, but the Eleventh Circuit reversed. The United States Supreme Court granted review.

ISSUE: At a capital sentence hearing, does a Sixth Amendment violation occur only if counsel's performance was deficient and such deficiency resulted in actual prejudice?

HOLDING AND DECISION: (O'Connor, J.) Yes. At a capital sentence hearing, a Sixth Amendment violation occurs only if counsel's performance was deficient and such deficiency resulted in actual prejudice. The Sixth Amendment's right to counsel envisions effective assistance of counsel; ineffective assistance is tantamount to no assistance. The purpose of assistance of counsel is to ensure a fair trial. Consequently, ineffectiveness of counsel is that type of ineffectiveness that renders a trial unfair. The proper standard for evaluating effectiveness is that counsel will be considered ineffective if counsel's performance is so deficient that counsel was not functioning as counsel. Further, such deficiency must result in prejudice, as an absence of prejudice removes concerns of trial fairness. Exactly what constitutes a deficient performance by counsel cannot be set out in specific guidelines; rather, counsel's performance must be viewed against professional standards, considering the facts reasonably available to counsel at the time of his tactical decisions. It must be emphasized that counsel's competence is to be presumed, and counsel's performance should not be second-guessed with the benefit of hindsight not available to counsel at the time of his decisions. With respect to prejudice, prejudice will not be presumed in other than a narrow set of circumstances, such as corruption or conflict of interest. Applying the foregoing standards to the present case, it is clear Washington's (P) counsel's performance was far from ineffective. Operating under severe disadvantages, not the least being Washington's (P) habitual rejection of his advice, counsel made certain tactical decisions with respect to evidence and argument that were quite reasonable. Beyond this, the circumstances were so aggravating that it is unlikely that prejudice could have resulted from ineffectiveness even had it occurred. Therefore, no Sixth Amendment violation occurred in this case. Reversed.

CONCURRENCE AND DISSENT: (Brennan, J.) The death penalty is in all circumstances cruel and unusual punishment forbidden by the Eighth and Fourteenth Amendments. Thus, the death sentence here should be vacated, and the case remanded for further proceedings. The standards set forth by the Court in this decision, however, do provide helpful guidance when considering claims of ineffectiveness of counsel, the standard being "that of reasonably effective assistance."

DISSENT: (Marshall, J.) The majority opinion is excessively deferential to counsel in several respects. The standard for competency is too lenient and the level of prejudice that needs to be shown for a Sixth Amendment violation to occur is excessive. Finally, the Court errs in applying the same standard to capital cases as less crucial cases.

ANALYSIS

Prior to the present opinion, lower courts had grappled with the same issue, reaching widely varied results. Both objective and subjective standards of competence had been applied. With respect to prejudice, some

Continued on next page.

courts had employed the "outcome-determinative" test the United States Supreme Court used. Others had held prejudice to be presumed.

Quicknotes

EIGHTH AMENDMENT The Eighth Amendment to the federal Constitution prohibits the imposition of excessive bail, fines, and cruel and unusual punishment.

FOURTEENTH AMENDMENT Declares that no state shall make or enforce any law that shall abridge the privileges and immunities of citizens of the United States. No state shall deny to any person within its jurisdiction the equal protection of the laws.

INEFFECTIVE ASSISTANCE OF COUNSEL A claim brought by an accused in which it must be determined whether the attorney's rendering of representation was such that the ultimate disposition of the case may not be relied upon as fair.

SIXTH AMENDMENT Provides the right to a speedy and public trial by impartial jury, the right to be informed of the accusation, the right to confront witnesses, and the right to have the assistance of counsel in all criminal prosecutions.

WRIT OF HABEAS CORPUS A proceeding in which a defendant brings a writ to compel a judicial determination of whether he or she is lawfully being held in custody.

CHAPTER 15

Plea Bargaining and Guilty Pleas

Quick Reference Rules of Law

Brady v. United States

Convicted kidnapper (D) v. Federal government (P)

397 U.S. 742 (1970)

NATURE OF CASE: Petition for collateral relief attacking conviction of kidnapping.

FACT SUMMARY: Brady (D) claimed that rather than risk trial and a possible death sentence, he pled guilty to kidnapping under 18 U.S.C. § 1201(a), which provided for a maximum penalty of death upon conviction if a jury should so recommend. Brady (D) contended that after the United States Supreme Court ruled in *United States v. Jackson*, 390 U.S. 570 (1968), the "inevitable effect" of the death penalty provision of § 1201(a) was the needless encouragement of pleas of guilty and waivers of jury trial. All guilty pleas entered under that statute had to be invalidated, including his own.

RULE OF LAW

A guilty plea is not per se compelled and invalid under the Fifth Amendment whenever motivated by the defendant's desire to accept the certainty or probability of a lesser penalty rather than face a wider range of possibilities extending from acquittal to conviction and a higher penalty authorized by law for the crime charged, including death, where the guilty plea was intelligently made and voluntarily entered into.

FACTS: In 1959, Brady (D) was charged with kidnapping in violation of 18 U.S.C. § 1201(a). The section provided for a maximum penalty of death upon conviction if the jury should so recommend. At first, Brady (D) elected to plead not guilty and made no serious attempt to waive a jury trial. Upon learning that a co-defendant would be available to testify against him, Brady (D) changed his plea to guilty. His plea was accepted after the trial judge questioned Brady (D) as to its voluntariness. He was ultimately sentenced to 30 years in prison. In 1967, Brady (D) petitioned for collateral postconviction relief, claiming that § 1201(a) operated to coerce his confession. The District Court denied relief, finding that Brady (D) pled guilty only after learning that his co-defendant would plead guilty, not by reason of § 1201(a). The Court of Appeals for the Tenth Circuit affirmed. In 1968, the United States Supreme Court, in *United States v. Jackson*, 390 U.S. 570 (1968), held that § 1201(a) was unconstitutional insofar as its death penalty provision "needlessly penalize[d]" the assertion of the Sixth Amendment right to a jury trial and the Fifth Amendment right not to plead guilty. Brady (D) asserted that *Jackson* required the invalidation of all guilty pleas entered under § 1201(a), including his own. The United States Supreme Court granted certiorari.

ISSUE: Is a guilty plea per se compelled and invalid under the Fifth Amendment whenever motivated by the defendant's desire to accept the certainty or probability of a lesser penalty rather than face a wider range of possibilities extending from acquittal to conviction and a higher penalty authorized by law for the crime charged, including death, where the guilty plea was intelligently made and voluntarily entered into?

HOLDING AND DECISION: (White, J.) No. A guilty plea is not per se compelled and invalid under the Fifth Amendment whenever motivated by the defendant's desire to accept the certainty or probability of a lesser penalty rather than face a wider range of possibilities extending from acquittal to conviction and a higher penalty authorized by law for the crime charged, including death, where the guilty plea was intelligently made and voluntarily entered into. Although *United States v. Jackson*, 390 U.S. 570 (1968), prohibited the imposition of death under 18 U.S.C. § 1201(a), it neither invalidated the rest of that statute nor did it did fashion a new standard to supplant the test that guilty pleas are valid if both "voluntary" and "intelligent." *Jackson* ruled neither that all pleas of guilty encouraged by the fear of a possible death sentence are involuntary pleas nor that such encouraged pleas are invalid whether involuntary or not. Even assuming Brady (D) would not have pled guilty but for the death penalty provision, this does not prove that the entering of the plea was an involuntary act. His guilty plea must be considered by all the circumstances surrounding it. One of these circumstances was the possibility of a heavier sentence following a guilty verdict after a trial. It may be that Brady (D), faced with a strong case against him and recognizing that his chances for acquittal were slight, preferred to plead guilty and thus limit the penalty to life imprisonment rather than to elect a jury trial that could result in a death penalty. However, even assuming that Brady (D) would not have pleaded guilty except for the death penalty provision of § 1201(a), this assumption merely identifies the penalty provision as a "but for" cause of his plea. That the statute caused the plea in this sense does not necessarily prove that the plea was coerced and invalid as an involuntary act. Here, Brady (D) was advised by competent counsel, and there is no claim that Brady's (D) plea was induced by actual or threatened physical harm or by mental coercion or that he did not rationally weigh the advantages of not going to trial. The rule that a plea must be intelligently made

Continued on next page.

to be valid does not require that a plea be vulnerable to later attack if the defendant did not correctly assess every relevant factor entering into his decision. A defendant is not entitled to withdraw his plea merely because he discovers long after the plea has been accepted that his calculus misapprehended the quality of the state's case or the likely penalties attached to alternative courses of action. More particularly, absent misrepresentation or other impermissible conduct by state agents, a voluntary plea of guilty intelligently made in the light of the then applicable law does not become vulnerable because later judicial decisions indicate that the plea rested on a faulty premise.

ANALYSIS

Although the United States Supreme Court was not inclined to expand the scope of the voluntariness standard, it indicated, in *Boykin v. Alabama*, 395 U.S. 238 (1969), a willingness to provide for more controls over the acceptance by the trial court of a "voluntary" plea. The Court held that a guilty plea is not presumed voluntary where the judge does not question the defendant concerning his or her plea, and the defendant does not address the court, and that the trial judge must employ great care in canvassing the plea with the accused to make sure the accused completely understands what the plea connotes and its consequences. In *Brady*, the Court emphasized that Brady (D) was made aware of the nature of the charge against him, that there was nothing to indicate that he was incompetent or otherwise not in control of his mental faculties, and that only once his confederate had pleaded guilty and became available to testify, Brady (D) chose to plead guilty, perhaps to ensure that he would face no more than life imprisonment or a term of years. Also, the Court noted that Brady (D) was aware of precisely what he was doing when he admitted that he had kidnaped the victim and had not released her unharmed. For these reasons, the Court concluded that Brady's (D) plea was intelligent and truthful, and, therefore, not unconstitutionally coerced.

Quicknotes

18 U.S.C. §1201(A) Provides that discretion for assigning the death penalty rests with the jury. This section has been invalidated.

COERCED CONFESSION A statement by a person charged with the commission of a criminal offense acknowledging his or her guilt in respect to the charged offense made when the confessor's free will was overcome as a result of threats, promises, or undue influence, and that is inadmissible at trial.

North Carolina v. Alford

State (P) v. Plea-bargaining murder suspect (D)

400 U.S. 25 (1970)

NATURE OF CASE: Appeal of a conviction for second-degree murder.

FACT SUMMARY: Alford (D), although still claiming his innocence, pleaded guilty, and was convicted of second-degree murder.

RULE OF LAW

An assertion of innocence by a defendant does not, of itself, render a plea of guilty invalid.

FACTS: Faced with strong evidence of guilt and no substantial evidentiary support for the claim of innocence, Alford's (D) attorney recommended that he plead guilty. The prosecutor agreed to accept a plea of guilty to a charge of second-degree murder, and Alford (D) pleaded guilty to the reduced charge. Alford (D), however, maintained that he had not committed the murder but that he was pleading guilty because he faced the threat of the death penalty if he did not do so. The court sentenced Alford (D) to the maximum penalty allowed, and Alford (D) sought post-conviction relief in state court, which was refused. After two unsuccessful petitions for a writ of habeas corpus, the court of appeals reversed the conviction on the ground that Alford's (D) guilty plea was made involuntarily, and the State (P) appealed.

ISSUE: Does an assertion of innocence by a defendant, of itself, render a plea of guilty invalid?

HOLDING AND DECISION: (White, J.) No. An assertion of innocence by a defendant does not, of itself, render a plea of guilty invalid. The Constitution does not bar imposition of a prison sentence upon an accused who is unwilling expressly to admit his guilt but who, faced with grim alternatives, is willing to waive his trial and accept the sentence. The standard remains whether the plea represents a voluntary and intelligent choice among the alternative courses of action open to the defendant. Here, confronted with the choice between a trial for first-degree murder, on the one hand, and a plea of guilty to second-degree murder, on the other, Alford (D) quite reasonably chose the latter and thereby limited the maximum penalty to a 30-year term. That he would not have pleaded except for the opportunity to limit the possible penalty does not necessarily demonstrate that the plea of guilty was not the product of a free and rational choice, especially where the defendant was represented by competent counsel whose advice was that the plea would be to the defendant's advantage.

ANALYSIS

The problem with Alford's (D) assertion of innocence here is that it was not in accord with his actions. According to confirmed testimony, Alford (D) left his home with his gun stating his intention to kill and he later declared that he had carried out his intention.

Quicknotes

SECOND-DEGREE MURDER The unlawful killing of another person, without premeditation, and characterized by either intent to kill or by a reckless disregard for human life.

WRIT OF HABEAS CORPUS A proceeding in which a defendant brings a writ to compel a judicial determination of whether he or she is lawfully being held in custody.

Missouri v. Frye

State (P) v. Convicted individual claiming actionable ineffective assistance of counsel (D)

566 U.S. 134 (2012)

NATURE OF CASE: State's (P) appeal from state appellate court's decision to grant plaintiff postconviction relief.

FACT SUMMARY: Frye's (D) attorney failed to communicate to him a formal plea offer from the prosecution that included more favorable terms than the terms to which Frye (D) eventually pleaded guilty.

RULE OF LAW

Counsel for criminal defendants has the duty to communicate formal offers from the prosecution with terms and conditions that may be favorable to the defendants.

FACTS: In August 2007, Frye (D) was charged with driving with a revoked license. He had been convicted of the same offense on three other occasions. Under Missouri law, the fourth charge allowed the State (P) to charge him with a Class D felony. The felony charge carried a possible four-year prison term. In November, the prosecution sent a formal written plea offer to Frye's (D) counsel with two choices. First, the prosecutor offered a three-year sentence if Frye (D) plead guilty to the felony charge, without a recommendation for probation but a requirement that Frye (D) spend ten days "shock" time in jail. The second offer was to reduce the charge to a misdemeanor and have Frye (D) serve 90 days in jail. The misdemeanor charge had a possible one-year maximum sentence. The letter stated the offer would expire on December 28. Frye's (D) counsel never communicated the offer to him, and the plea offers expired. A week before his preliminary hearing on the August 2007 charge, Frye (D) was again arrested for driving with a revoked license. At a subsequent hearing, Frye (D) eventually pleaded guilty to the felony charge and the trial court sentenced him to three years in prison. Following the conviction, Frye (D) filed for postconviction relief in state court on the grounds his attorney's failure to inform him of the plea offers constituted actionable ineffective assistance of counsel. The state trial court denied his petition, but the Missouri Court of Appeals reversed, finding that Frye (D) received ineffective assistance of counsel and that Frye (D) was prejudiced thereby. The United States Supreme Court granted the State of Missouri's (D) petition for review.

ISSUE: Does counsel for criminal defendants have the duty to communicate formal offers from the prosecution with terms and conditions that may be favorable to the defendants?

HOLDING AND DECISION: (Kennedy, J.) Yes. Counsel for criminal defendants has the duty to communicate formal offers from the prosecution with terms and conditions that may be favorable to the defendants. When a defense counsel fails to communicate a plea offer to his or her client, that failure constitutes actionable ineffective assistance of counsel under the Constitution. This holding is supported by the reality that more than 94 percent of state criminal convictions are the result of guilty pleas. That is only one part of the analysis. The convicted defendant must also show the ineffective assistance of counsel caused him prejudice in the criminal proceedings. To show prejudice when an attorney fails to communicate a plea offer, the defendant must demonstrate a reasonable probability that he would have accepted the earlier plea offer had he been aware of it. Significantly, defendants must also show that the prosecution would not have canceled the plea deal or that the trial court would not have rejected the agreement. This is relevant because some states allow prosecutors the discretion to cancel a plea agreement up to the moment the agreement is accepted by the court. This further showing is also important because a defendant has no constitutional right to be offered a plea agreement and no right the judge must accept the agreement. In the instant case, Frye (D) can show he would have accepted the offer to plead guilty to the lesser misdemeanor charge. However, Frye's (D) subsequent arrest for the same offense one week prior to his hearing complicates matters for him. It is not entirely clear that the prosecution would not have canceled the agreement based on that new arrest. Nor is it clear that the trial court would have agreed to the plea deal. Accordingly, it is appropriate to remand the case to the Missouri Court of Appeals for it to consider whether the prosecution and the trial court would have agreed to the plea offer of the lesser misdemeanor charge in light of Frye's (D) new arrest for the same offense. Vacated and remanded.

DISSENT: (Scalia, J.) The majority improperly constitutionalizes the plea-bargaining process in criminal cases. While it is clear Frye (D) received ineffective assistance of counsel, it is not entirely clear he was prejudiced thereby. The majority's reasonable probability test is nothing more than crystal ball gazing masquerading as legal analysis. There are no cases that discuss the standard for a prosecutor's withdrawal from a plea agreement or

Continued on next page.

a trial court's authority to accept or reject a plea deal. In most states, the trial court has broad discretion to accept or reject such agreements. The judicial branch should not create precedents based upon what prosecutors and judges might have done in the past. State legislatures are better equipped to regulate the plea-bargain process, starting by imposing punishments upon a defense counsel's right to practice when counsel fails to communicate valid plea offers to his or her clients. However, in this case, Frye (D) was not prejudiced because he pled guilty to the felony charge after the usual colloquy with the trial court judge that assured his guilty plea was voluntary and truthful.

ANALYSIS

The majority's decision was based on the prevalent use of plea bargains in criminal prosecutions, both at the state and federal level. In addition to the 94 percent of convictions in state cases resulting from plea bargains, 97 percent of convictions in federal court are similarly the result of plea negotiations. Note that the majority's holding is narrow: where a plea offer is made, the defense counsel must communicate it to his or her clients. The United States Supreme Court refrained from adjudicating on any strategic decisions defense counsel may make during those plea negotiations.

Quicknotes

INEFFECTIVE ASSISTANCE OF COUNSEL A claim brought by an accused in which it must be determined whether the attorney's rendering of representation was such that the ultimate disposition of the case may not be relied upon as fair.

PLEA BARGAIN An agreement between a prosecutor and a criminal defendant that is submitted to the court for approval; it generally involves the defendant's pleading guilty to a lesser charge or count in exchange for a more lenient sentence.

Lafler v. Cooper

State (P) v. Convicted individual seeking relief due to ineffective counsel (D)

566 U.S. 156 (2012)

NATURE OF CASE: State's (P) appeal from Sixth Circuit Court of Appeals' decision upholding plaintiff's postconviction relief.

FACT SUMMARY: After the State (P) charged Anthony Cooper (D) with intent to murder and related charges, the State (P) offered a favorable plea agreement to Cooper (D). Cooper's (D) counsel advised him not to take it and to proceed to trial. A jury convicted Cooper (D), and he received a sentence greater than that offered in the plea agreement.

RULE OF LAW

When claiming ineffective assistance of counsel based on erroneous advice to reject a plea offer, a defendant must show there was a reasonable probability that the court would have accepted the plea agreement and that the conviction and sentence would have been less severe than those that were in fact imposed.

FACTS: On March 25, 2003, Anthony Cooper (D) shot Kali Mundy multiple times, but Mundy survived. The State of Michigan (P) charged Cooper (D) with intent to murder, possession of a firearm by a felon, possession of a firearm in the commission of a felony, and for being a habitual offender. Prior to trial, the prosecution offered to dismiss two of the charges and to recommend a sentence of 51 to 85 months in prison in exchange for a guilty plea. Cooper's (D) counsel advised him to reject the offer because he felt the State (P) would be unable to prove intent at the trial. A jury convicted Cooper (D) of all charges. The trial court sentenced him to 185 to 360 months in prison. Cooper (D) then filed a petition for habeas relief in federal district court. The basis for the petition was that the advice of Cooper's (D) counsel to reject the plea offer constituted ineffective assistance of counsel. The district court granted the writ and ordered the State (P) to impose a sentence consistent with the original plea offer. The Sixth Circuit Court of Appeals affirmed. The United States Supreme Court granted the State's (P) petition for review.

ISSUE: When claiming ineffective assistance of counsel based on erroneous advice to reject a plea offer, must a defendant show there was a reasonable probability that the court would have accepted the plea agreement and that the conviction and sentence would have been less severe than those that were in fact imposed?

HOLDING AND DECISION: (Kennedy, J.) Yes. When claiming ineffective assistance of counsel based on erroneous advice to reject a plea offer, a defendant must show there was a reasonable probability that the court would have accepted the plea agreement and that the conviction and sentence would have been less severe than those that were in fact imposed. In this appeal, all parties agree the advice of Cooper's (D) attorney constituted ineffective assistance of counsel. The issue here is whether that ineffective assistance prejudiced Cooper (D). The State (P) essentially argues that Cooper (D) and his counsel validly rejected the plea offer in the hopes the jury would return a verdict of not guilty. The State (P) argues that Cooper (D) went on to receive a full and fair trial and his subsequent conviction rendered the ineffective assistance of counsel moot. When examining ineffective assistance of counsel claims in the context of plea bargaining, the defendant must show a reasonable probability the court would have accepted the agreement. The defendant must also show the prosecutor would not have withdrawn the offer prior to trial. The State's (P) view of the protections of the Sixth Amendment is too narrow. The Sixth Amendment requires effective assistance of counsel at all critical stages of the criminal proceeding, especially including the plea-bargaining process. If a plea bargain is offered, the defendant has the right to effective counsel when considering whether to accept the offer. Cooper (D) has shown that he did not receive effective assistance of counsel and was prejudiced because he received a greater sentence than the sentence included in the plea offer. The task now is to determine the appropriate remedy. The Sixth Amendment requires that remedies should be tailored to the injuries suffered and should not infringe on competing interests. The remedy should not grant a windfall to the defendant. Essentially, the trial court has the discretion to review the matter and impose the sentence offered as part of the plea agreement or to retain the sentence imposed after the jury verdict. Courts should consider a defendant's willingness or unwillingness to accept responsibility for his or her actions. Here, the State (P) should reoffer the plea agreement to Cooper (D). The court can then exercise its discretion to accept the agreement, retain the sentence imposed postconviction, or do something between those two options. Vacated and remanded.

DISSENT: (Scalia, J.) Cooper (D) received a full and fair trial and received a sentence that the law prescribed. This Court has never held that a defendant is entitled to competent counsel when deciding to reject a plea

Continued on next page.

offer. The Court effectively creates a new constitutional right to effective plea bargaining. Moreover, the Sixth Amendment's focus is to ensure a fair trial. The inquiry is to determine if the ineffective assistance of counsel undermined the adversarial process and failed to produce a just result. Here, the error of Cooper's (D) attorney was unfortunate, but it was not of constitutional significance. The Court's remedy is also absurd. It is extraordinary that a trial judge has discretion to create a remedy where there is a constitutional violation and even more extraordinary that the judge has discretion to issue no remedy at all.

ANALYSIS

This decision expands on the companion case of *Missouri v. Frye*, 566 U.S. 134 (2012). In *Frye*, the United States Supreme Court held that defense counsel has the duty to communicate plea offers to their clients. The *Cooper* decision goes further and essentially constitutionalizes the entire plea-bargaining process. Both decisions are based on the reality that well over ninety percent of convictions in state and federal court are the result of plea bargains.

Quicknotes

INEFFECTIVE ASSISTANCE OF COUNSEL A claim brought by an accused in which it must be determined whether the attorney's rendering of representation was such that the ultimate disposition of the case may not be relied upon as fair.

PLEA BARGAIN An agreement between a prosecutor and a criminal defendant that is submitted to the court for approval; it generally involves the defendant's pleading guilty to a lesser charge or count in exchange for a more lenient sentence.

Bordenkircher v. Hayes

State (P) v. Forgery convict (D)

434 U.S. 357 (1978)

NATURE OF CASE: Appeal of a criminal conviction and penalty enhancement.

FACT SUMMARY: The prosecutor informed Hayes (D) that he would seek an indictment under the Kentucky Habitual Criminal Act if he did not plead guilty to the charge of uttering a forged instrument; Hayes (D) pled innocent, a jury convicted him, and his sentence was enhanced when the prosecutor initiated the Habitual Criminal indictment.

RULE OF LAW

It is constitutionally permissible for a prosecutor to try to influence a defendant to accept a plea bargain by informing him that more severe charges will be brought if the plea bargain is refused.

FACTS: Hayes (D), who was charged with uttering a forged instrument (for $88.30), faced a sentence of two to ten years if convicted. The prosecutor offered a five-year sentence in return for a guilty plea and told Hayes (D) that refusal to take the plea bargain would result in his seeking an additional indictment under the Kentucky Habitual Criminal Act, which makes a life sentence mandatory if there are two prior felony convictions. When Hayes (D) declined the plea bargain, he was subjected to the additional indictment and sentenced to life imprisonment under the Habitual Criminal Act, after having been found guilty of the uttering charge. The two previous felonies in which Hayes (D) was involved had never resulted in his imprisonment; one was a rape charge reduced to a plea of detaining a female, and the other was a robbery conviction resulting in five years in a reformatory. Finding the prosecutor to have acted vindictively in securing the second indictment, the court of appeals reversed Hayes's (D) conviction for violation of due process of law.

ISSUE: Is it constitutionally permissible for a prosecutor to try to influence a defendant to accept a plea bargain by informing him that more severe charges will be brought if the plea bargain is refused?

HOLDING AND DECISION: (Stewart, J.) Yes. It is constitutionally permissible for a prosecutor to try to influence a defendant to accept a plea bargain by informing him that more severe charges will be brought if it is refused. As the constitutionality and utility of plea bargaining have been recognized, there is no bar to the prosecutor's use of the possibility of more severe charges being brought for purposes of persuading a defendant to accept a plea bargain. As long as the defendant is advised that the bringing of additional charges will accompany his refusal to bargain, the situation becomes similar to that where the prosecutor offers to drop a charge as part of the plea bargain. If plea bargaining is a recognized process, neither can be forbidden simply because the charging decision is influenced by what a prosecutor hopes to gain in plea bargaining negotiations. In accepting plea bargaining, it is implicit that there is acceptance of the notion that the prosecutor's interest is to persuade the defendant not to exercise his right to plead not guilty. As long as a prosecutor has probable cause to believe the accused committed the offense, he properly exercises his discretion, and he makes decisions that are not influenced by standards of race, religion, etc., there is no due process violation. Reversed.

DISSENT: (Blackmun, J.) Past cases indicate that prosecutorial vindictiveness resulting from a defendant's exercise of his rights is a constitutionally impermissible basis for discretionary actions. Here, it is admitted that such vindictiveness was the sole reason for the new indictment.

DISSENT: (Powell, J.) Discretion used to deter the exercise of constitutional rights is not constitutionally exercised. The prosecutor's initial failure to charge indicates his own appreciation of the unreasonableness of placing Hayes (D) in jeopardy of life imprisonment when many murderers and rapists face lighter sentences.

ANALYSIS

The case in which the United States Supreme Court first recognized plea bargaining as a legitimate practice was *Brady v. United States*, 397 U.S. 742 (1970). While the majority here suggests that such an acceptance implies sanctioning of prosecutorial use of charging powers to influence a defendant to plead guilty, the *Brady* decision specifically states that it makes no reference to such use by the prosecutor or a similar use by the judge of his sentencing power.

Quicknotes

PLEA BARGAIN An agreement between a prosecutor and a criminal defendant that is submitted to the court for approval; it generally involves the defendant's pleading guilty to a lesser charge or count in exchange for a more lenient sentence.

UTTERING To make something public, or to put something into circulation.

Santobello v. New York

Plea-negotiating convict (D) v. State (P)

404 U.S. 257 (1971)

NATURE OF CASE: Appeal from a felony conviction and one-year prison sentence.

FACT SUMMARY: Santobello (D) challenged his conviction and sentence, based on the breach of a commitment by the prosecutor made in course of plea bargaining.

RULE OF LAW

Where the state fails to keep a commitment concerning the sentence recommendation on a guilty plea, a new trial is required.

FACTS: Indicted on two felony counts, Santobello (D) negotiated with the assistant district attorney and agreed to plead guilty to a lesser included offense, provided the prosecutor agreed to make no recommendation as to the sentence. Following procedural delays between Santobello's (D) conviction and the imposition of sentence, during which time both defense counsel and prosecutor were replaced, the new prosecutor at the sentence hearing requested the maximum sentence of one year. The trial judge imposed the maximum sentence and Santobello (D) appealed.

ISSUE: Where the state fails to keep a commitment concerning the sentence recommendation on a guilty plea, is a new trial required?

HOLDING AND DECISION: (Burger, C.J.) Yes. Where the state fails to keep a commitment concerning the sentence recommendation on a guilty plea, a new trial is required. The disposition of criminal charges by agreement between the prosecutor and the accused, sometimes loosely called "plea bargaining," is an essential component of the administration of justice. Properly administered, it is to be encouraged. It leads to prompt and largely final disposition of most criminal cases. However, these considerations presuppose fairness in securing agreement between an accused and a prosecutor. When a plea rests in any significant degree on a promise or agreement of the prosecutor, so that it can be said to be part of the inducement or consideration, such promise must be fulfilled. Here, on the record Santobello (D) "bargained" and negotiated for a particular plea in order to secure dismissal of more serious charges, but also on condition that no sentence recommendation would be made by the prosecutor. That a breach of agreement was inadvertent does not lessen its impact. We conclude that the interests of justice and appropriate recognition of the duties of the prosecution in relation to promises made in the negotiation of pleas of guilty will be best served by remanding the case to the state courts for further consideration. Judgment vacated and case remanded for reconsideration.

CONCURRENCE: (Douglas, J.) A sentence must be vacated when a prosecutor fails to honor a "plea bargain." Upon such failure, it is then for the state court to determine in view of the facts of each case whether due process requires that there be specific performance of the plea bargain or that the defendant be provided with the option to go to trial on the original charges.

CONCURRENCE AND DISSENT: (Marshall, J.) When a prosecutor breaks a plea bargain, he or she weakens the basis for the waiver of constitutional rights that is implicit in the plea. This provides sufficient reason to rescind the plea.

ANALYSIS

The United States Supreme Court here, in not only the majority but also the concurring and dissenting opinions, affirmed both the constitutionality and the viability of modern plea bargaining. What is noteworthy here is that the Court, per Justice Douglas, applied the common-law principles of contract law, rather than criminal law, in fashioning the "remedies" available to the defendant when the prosecutor "breaches" his or her commitment (i.e., specific performance of the bargain, or rescission of the entire agreement, including the guilty plea).

Quicknotes

PLEA BARGAIN An agreement between a prosecutor and a criminal defendant that is submitted to the court for approval; it generally involves the defendant's pleading guilty to a lesser charge or count in exchange for a more lenient sentence.

McMann v. Richardson

State (P) v. Convicted criminal (D)

397 U.S. 759 (1970)

NATURE OF CASE: Petitions for writ of habeas corpus in federal court collaterally attacking three state court criminal convictions based on guilty pleas.

FACT SUMMARY: In their petitions for writ of habeas corpus in federal court, Richardson (D) and two other convicted criminals, who had been represented by competent counsel and who had pled guilty to state criminal charges, alleged that they would not have pled guilty but for fear that a coerced confession would be introduced into evidence.

RULE OF LAW

A defendant who was represented by reasonably competent counsel, and who pleaded guilty to criminal charges, is not entitled to a hearing on a petition for habeas corpus to impeach the otherwise valid guilty plea merely by alleging, or proving, without more, that the defendant pleaded guilty because of a prior coerced confession.

FACTS: Richardson (D), and two others, on advice of reasonably competent counsel, each entered a guilty plea in the respective criminal case against them. Afterward, they each filed a petition for a writ of habeas corpus in which they alleged that they had pled guilty because they had been afraid a prior coerced confession would be introduced at trial against them. The Court of Appeals for the Second Circuit held that each defendant was entitled to a hearing on their habeas petition. The State (P) sought reversal of each of the Court of Appeals' judgments. The United States Court granted certiorari.

ISSUE: Is a defendant who was represented by reasonably competent counsel, and who pled guilty to criminal charges, entitled to a hearing on a petition for habeas corpus to impeach the otherwise valid guilty plea merely by alleging, or proving, without more, that the defendant pleaded guilty because of a prior coerced confession?

HOLDING AND DECISION: (White, J.) No. A defendant who was represented by reasonably competent counsel, and who pleaded guilty to criminal charges, is not entitled to a hearing on a petition for habeas corpus to impeach the otherwise valid guilty plea merely by alleging, or proving, without more, that the defendant pleaded guilty because of a prior coerced confession. In these cases, as the Second Circuit Court of Appeals recognized, the confession, even if coerced, is not a sufficient factor in the plea to justify relief. Additionally, these cases involve neither an uncounseled defendant nor a coerced confession that taints the plea. These cases involve a defendant who believes his confession is critical to the case against them, and who would go to trial if he thought his chances of acquittal were good. A defendant's decision to plead guilty or not in such a case turns on whether the defendant thinks the law will allow his confession to be used against him. For the defendant who considers his confession involuntary, and hence inadmissible at trial, tendering a plea of guilty would not make sense; the sensible course would be to contest guilt; prevail on the confession claim at trial, on appeal, or, if necessary, in a collateral proceeding; and win acquittal, regardless of how guilty he might be. Under such circumstances, the evidence aside from the confession is presumably weak, so the defendant would have no reason of his own to enter a guilty plea. If the defendant nevertheless enters a guilty plea, it represents nothing less than a refusal to present any federal habeas claims to the state court in the first instance, and a choice to take the benefits, if any, of the guilty plea and then to pursue a coerced-confession claim in collateral proceedings. Such a scenario, however, is unlikely unless the defendant is incompetently advised as to the forum in which the federal claim should first be presented. A more likely explanation for a plea of guilty by a defendant who would go to trial except for the defendant's prior confession is the defendant's prediction that the law will permit the defendant's admissions to be used against the defendant by the trier of fact. At least the probability of the State's (P) being permitted to use the confession as evidence is sufficient to convince the defendant that the State's (P) case is too strong to contest and that a plea of guilty is the most advantageous course. Nothing in this train of events suggests that the defendant's plea, as distinguished from the defendant's confession, is an involuntary act. The defendant's later petition for collateral relief asserting that a coerced confession induced the guilty plea is at most a claim that the admissibility of the confession was mistakenly assessed, and that since the defendant was erroneously advised, either under the then applicable law or under the law later announced, the plea was an unintelligent and voidable act. The Constitution, however, does not render pleas of guilty so vulnerable. In the face of unavoidable uncertainty, the defendant and counsel must make their best judgment as to the weight of the State's (P) case. Counsel must predict how the facts, as counsel understands them, would be viewed by a court. Waiving trial entails the inherent risk that the good-faith evaluations of a reasonably competent attorney will turn out to be mistaken either as to the facts or

Continued on next page.

as to what a court's or jury's judgment might be on given facts. The constitutional requirement that a guilty plea must be intelligently made is not a requirement that all advice offered by the defendant's lawyer withstand retrospective examination in a post-conviction hearing. Thus, a defendant's plea of guilty based on reasonably competent advice is an intelligent plea not open to attack on the ground that counsel may have misjudged the admissibility of the defendant's confession. Whether a plea of guilty is unintelligent, and, therefore, vulnerable when motivated by a confession erroneously thought admissible in evidence depends, as an initial matter, not on whether a court would retrospectively consider counsel's advice to be right or wrong but on whether that advice was within the range of competence demanded of attorneys in criminal cases. Therefore, a defendant who alleges that he pled guilty because of a prior coerced confession is not, without more, entitled to a hearing on his petition for habeas corpus. [Reversed.]

ANALYSIS

The United States Supreme Court, in *Tollett v. Henderson*, 411 U.S. 258 (1973), reiterated its decision in *McMann* by holding that where a defendant pled guilty on advice of counsel, the defendant is not entitled to collateral relief in federal court simply because, unknown to defendant or counsel, the indicting grand jury was unconstitutionally selected. The Court stated that a guilty plea may not be vacated merely because the trial judge failed to advise the defendant of "every conceivable constitutional plea in abatement he might have to the charge, no matter how peripheral such a plea might be to the normal focus of counsel's inquiry [here, a factual one]. . . . Often the interests of the accused are not advanced by challenges that would only delay the inevitable date of prosecution or by contesting all guilt. . . ."

Quicknotes

COERCED CONFESSION A statement of a person charged with the commission of a criminal offense acknowledging his or her guilt in respect to the charged offense made when the confessor's free will was overcome as a result of threats, promises, or undue influence, and that is inadmissible at trial.

PETITION OF HABEAS CORPUS Petition to compel an independent review of whether a prisoner is being lawfully imprisoned.

CHAPTER 16

The Trial Process

Quick Reference Rules of Law

CHAPTER 16

Duncan v. Louisiana

Simple battery convict (D) v. State (P)

391 U.S. 145 (1968)

NATURE OF CASE: Appeal from conviction for simple battery.

FACT SUMMARY: Duncan (D) was convicted without the right to a jury trial of simple battery, a crime punishable by two years' imprisonment and a $300 fine.

RULE OF LAW

The Constitution imposes a duty upon the state to give a jury trial in any criminal case, regardless of the seriousness of the crime or the punishment that may be imposed.

FACTS: Duncan (D), a Black youth, was convicted in Louisiana of simple battery and sentenced to 60 days imprisonment and to pay a fine of $150. Before his trial, Duncan (D) requested a jury trial, but his request was denied. Under Louisiana law, a jury trial is guaranteed only in cases where capital punishment or imprisonment at hard labor may be imposed. Simple battery, however, is a misdemeanor punishable only with up to two years imprisonment and a $300 fine. After his conviction, Duncan (D) appealed on the basis that denial of a jury trial violated his Sixth and Fourteenth Amendment rights. After the Louisiana Supreme Court upheld his conviction, Duncan (D) appealed to the United States Supreme Court.

ISSUE: Does the Constitution impose a duty upon the state to give a jury trial in any criminal case, regardless of the seriousness of the crime or the punishment that may be imposed?

HOLDING AND DECISION: (White, J.) Yes. The Constitution imposes upon the state to give a jury trial in any criminal case, regardless of the seriousness of the crime or the punishment that may be imposed. Fourteenth Amendment due process guarantees a right of jury trial in all state criminal cases that were they to be tried in a federal court, would come within the Sixth Amendment's guarantee. Furthermore, any serious crime tried in a federal court comes within the Sixth Amendment's guarantee of a jury trial. Trial by jury in such serious criminal cases is so fundamental to the American scheme of justice (i.e., as a defense against arbitrary law enforcement) that it cannot be denied by state courts either. Of course, the possible penalty for a particular crime is of major importance in determining if it is serious. Here, however, the Court does not need to settle the exact location of the line between petty offenses and serious crimes. It is sufficient for our purposes to hold that a crime punishable by two years in prison (as here) is, based on past and contemporary standards in this country, a serious crime and not a petty offense. As such, Duncan (D) should have received a jury trial. Reversed.

DISSENT: (Harlan, J.) Due process of law requires nothing more than that a criminal trial be fundamentally fair. Trial by jury is not the only fair means of resolving issues of fact. Even if a jury trial were a fundamental right in some criminal cases, there is no fundamental rule saying that a simple battery is within the category of "jury crimes" rather than "petty crimes."

ANALYSIS

This case illustrates the doctrine of "selective incorporation" of the Bill of Rights into the Fourteenth Amendment Due Process Clause. Under this doctrine, the Bill of Rights is incorporated by the Due Process Clause only to the extent that the United States Supreme Court decides that the protections and rights therein are "so essential to fundamental principles of due process of law, as to be preserved against both federal and state action" (*Bloom v. Illinois*, 391 U.S. 194 (1968)). A minority of the Court's justices (particularly Justices Black and Douglas), however, have argued for "total incorporation." Note that the Court has specifically found only two of the guarantees of the Bill of Rights to be non-fundamental. The first is the Fifth Amendment right to indictment by grand jury (some states permit criminal prosecutions to proceed upon the filing of information only). The second is the Eighth Amendment's guarantees regarding bail and fines.

Quicknotes

DUE PROCESS CLAUSE Language in the Fifth and Fourteenth Amendments to the U.S. Constitution providing that no person shall be deprived of "life, liberty, or property, without due process of law."

MISDEMEANOR Any crime that does not constitute a felony; generally less severe than a felony and results in lesser punishment.

RIGHT TO JURY TRIAL The right guaranteed by the Sixth Amendment to the U.S. Constitution that in all criminal prosecutions the accused has a right to a trial by an impartial jury of the state and district in which the crime was allegedly committed.

Taylor v. Louisiana

Kidnapping convict (P) v. State (D)

419 U.S. 522 (1975)

NATURE OF CASE: Appeal from conviction for aggravated kidnapping.

FACT SUMMARY: Taylor (D), a male who was convicted of aggravated kidnapping, challenged the jury that convicted him on the ground that 53 percent of the eligible jurors in the community were women, but that 90 percent of those in the actual jury pool were men.

RULE OF LAW

Women as a class may not be excluded or given automatic exemptions from jury duty based solely on sex if the consequence is that criminal jury venires are almost totally male.

FACTS: Under Louisiana (P) law women were not selected for jury duty unless they had previously filed a written declaration of desire to serve. Taylor (D), a male, was charged with aggravated kidnapping and moved in the trial court to quash the petit jury venire on the ground that women were systematically excluded from the venire and that this deprived him of his constitutional right to a fair trial by a jury of a representative segment of the community. His motion was denied, and Taylor (D) was subsequently convicted and sentenced to death. The Louisiana Supreme Court affirmed. Taylor (D) appealed, arguing that 53 percent of the eligible jurors in the community were women but that 90 percent of those in the actual jury pool were men.

ISSUE: May women as a class be excluded or given automatic exemptions from jury duty based solely on sex if the consequence is that criminal jury venires are almost totally male?

HOLDING AND DECISION: (White, J.) No. Women as a class may not be excluded or given automatic exemptions from jury duty based solely on sex if the consequence is that criminal jury venires are almost totally male. While the Louisiana (P) jury system did not disqualify women from jury service, in operation its conceded effect was that only a very few women, greatly disproportionate to the number of eligible women, were called for jury service. While Taylor (D) was not a member of the excluded class, he had standing to raise the issue because his claim went to the community makeup of the jury and not just to the exclusion of women. The American concept of the jury trial contemplates a jury drawn from a fair cross section of the community. To exclude a class of persons from the cross section of the community to create a fair jury requires more than just rational grounds; it cannot be argued that it would be too great a hardship on every woman to perform jury service. While petit juries must be drawn from a source fairly representative of the community, petit juries actually chosen need not mirror the community or reflect the various distinctive groups in the population. All that is required is that the jury pool does not systematically exclude distinctive groups in the community so as to be unrepresentative. Reversed.

DISSENT: (Rehnquist, J.) It is not conceivable that the majority's decision is necessary to guard against oppressive or arbitrary law enforcement, or to prevent miscarriages of justice and to assure fair trials, especially when the criminal defendant makes no claims of prejudice or bias. The Court in its decision fails to provide any satisfactory explanation of the mechanism by which the Louisiana system undermines the prophylactic role of the jury, either in general or in this case. The Court's decision "smacks more of mysticism than of law."

ANALYSIS

Justice Marshall wrote: "A state cannot, consistent with due process, subject a defendant to indictment or trial by a jury that has been selected in an arbitrary and discriminatory manner, in violation of the Constitution and the laws of the United States. Illegal and unconstitutional jury selection procedures cast doubt on the integrity of the whole judicial process. They create the appearance of bias. . . .But the exclusion from jury service of a substantial and identifiable class of citizens has a potential impact that is too subtle and too pervasive to admit of confinement to particular issues or particular cases." *Peters v. Kiff,* 407 U.S. 493 (1972).

Quicknotes

RIGHT TO JURY TRIAL The right guaranteed by the Sixth Amendment to the U.S. Constitution that in all criminal prosecutions the accused has a right to a trial by an impartial jury of the state and district in which the crime was allegedly committed.

VENIRE A list of jurors called to serve for a particular term.

Ham v. South Carolina

Drug possession convict (D) v. State (P)

409 U.S. 524 (1973)

NATURE OF CASE: Appeal of a conviction for marijuana possession.

FACT SUMMARY: Ham (D) was convicted of marijuana possession but contended that the trial judge's refusal to examine jurors on voir dire as to possible prejudice against Black people violated Ham's (D) federal constitutional rights.

RULE OF LAW

Where the state creates a framework for the examination of jurors, the Due Process Clause of the Fourteenth Amendment requires that a defendant be permitted to have the jurors interrogated on the issue of racial bias.

FACTS: Ham (D) was convicted of marijuana possession and sentenced to 18 months' confinement. Prior to the trial judge's voir dire examination of prospective jurors, Ham's (D) lawyer requested that the judge ask the jurors four questions—two concerning racial prejudice, one relating to prejudice against beards, and one relating to pretrial publicity. The trial judge refused and, instead, posed questions required by the South Carolina code. These were general questions as to bias, prejudice, and partiality. A divided South Carolina Supreme Court affirmed, and the United States Supreme Court granted certiorari limited to the question of prejudice on voir dire.

ISSUE: Where the state has created a framework for the examination of jurors, does the Due Process Clause of the Fourteenth Amendment require that a defendant be permitted to have the jurors interrogated on the issue of racial bias?

HOLDING AND DECISION: (Rehnquist, J.) Yes. Where the state has created a framework for the examination of jurors, the Due Process Clause of the Fourteenth Amendment requires that a defendant be permitted to have the jurors interrogated on the issue of racial bias. A major purpose in adopting the Fourteenth Amendment was to prevent the states from invidiously discriminating on the basis of race. The Due Process Clause is designed to ensure essential fairness. Therefore, Ham (D) had the right to have the jurors interrogated on the issue of racial bias. However, the Due Process Clause permits a wide discretion as to the form and number of questions, and, thus, Ham's (D) particular questions did not have to be adopted. An inquiry into racial prejudice need not be in any particular form. Ham's (D) request to have a question put forth concerning prejudice against beards does not reach the level of a constitutional violation. Reversed.

CONCURRENCE AND DISSENT: (Douglas, J.) The trial judge was constitutionally compelled to inquire into the possibility of racial prejudice on voir dire. In denying the defendant to probe the prejudices of prospective jurors concerning hair growth, the trial court judge denied the defendant his most effective means of voir dire examination.

ANALYSIS

The United States Supreme Court, in recent years, has cast a stern eye on racial matters in jury selection. Peremptory challenges in particular have been closely scrutinized. The use of peremptory challenges to exclude members of a certain race is, for the most part, not allowed.

Quicknotes

DUE PROCESS CLAUSE Language in the Fifth and Fourteenth Amendments to the U.S. Constitution providing that no person shall be deprived of "life, liberty, or property, without due process of law."

INVIDIOUS DISCRIMINATION Unequal treatment of a class of persons that is particularly malicious or hostile.

PEREMPTORY CHALLENGE A challenge issued by counsel during voir dire proceedings to refuse a jury seat to a prospective juror, for which no reason need be advanced other than the preference of counsel advocating exclusion.

VOIR DIRE A preliminary examination conducted by the court for the purpose of selecting prospective jurors to serve at trial.

People v. Newton

State (P) v. Murder suspect (D)

Cal. Super. Ct., Case No. 41266 (1968)

NATURE OF CASE: Preliminary voir dire for a murder trial.

FACT SUMMARY: [The casebook presents excerpts from a transcript of the voir dire proceedings of the highly publicized and charged trial of murder suspect Huey Newton (D), on the examination of a potential juror, Mr. Strauss, by the trial judge as well as the parties' attorneys.]

RULE OF LAW

[The casebook excerpt from the voir dire transcript does not present any Rule of Law.]

FACTS: Newton (D), a co-founder and Minister of Defense of the highly controversial Black Panther Party, was charged with murdering a White police officer. Because of the controversial nature and notoriety of the Black Panther Party, which, among other things, called for an end to police brutality in Black communities, and advocated for organizing Black self-defense groups to protect Black communities from racist police brutality, as well as the extensive pretrial publicity that followed, the defense was concerned as to whether it could secure an impartial jury. During the course of the voir dire proceedings, the trial judge permitted defense counsel, Mr. Garry, and the prosecution, Mr. Jensen, to question a potential juror, Mr. Strauss, regarding his pretrial biases of Newton's (D) culpability. The juror in question, Mr. Strauss, had a strong belief that Newton (D) was guilty. When defense counsel, Mr. Garry, asked Mr. Strauss if he believed that Newton (D) was innocent of wrongdoing of any kind, Mr. Strauss stated, "No. That I don't believe." The trial judge then informed Mr. Strauss that the system of criminal justice in the United States provides a presumption of innocence until proven guilty. Upon questioning by defense counsel and the prosecution, Mr. Strauss attempted to characterize his opinions as to Newton's (D) guilt as neutral. However, as a consequence of defense counsel's persistent questioning, Mr. Strauss's biases were brought out. Toward the end of the colloquy, Mr. Garry asked Mr. Strauss if he thought Newton (D) was absolutely innocent. Mr. Strauss answered, "Yes." Mr. Garry then asked him, "But you don't believe it, do you?" Mr. Strauss answered, "No." This permitted the court to recognize the defense's challenge for cause and to dismiss Mr. Strauss as a potential juror. Newton (D) was convicted of voluntary manslaughter. His conviction was reversed, but not on grounds related to the jury selection.

ISSUE: [The casebook excerpt from the voir dire transcript does not present any Issue.]

HOLDING AND DECISION: [The casebook excerpt from the voir dire transcript does not present any Holding and Decision.]

ANALYSIS

A challenge for cause and peremptory challenges are used during jury selection to dismiss prospective jurors. However, it is favorable for a party to dismiss a juror based on a challenge for cause as opposed to a peremptory challenge because the latter are limited in number. The primary benefit of a peremptory challenge is that the party making the challenge need not provide a rationale for dismissal, whereas a challenge for cause, to be granted, requires a satisfactory rationale as to the nature of the challenge. Note that since a reason is required, challenges for cause may be exercised whenever the rationale arises.

Quicknotes

CHALLENGE FOR CAUSE The right to refuse a jury seat to a prospective juror where that person possesses bias or other knowledge of the case that would impair the ability to render a fair verdict, predicated upon the showing by counsel of a compelling reason as to why that juror should be dismissed.

PEREMPTORY CHALLENGE A challenge issued by counsel during voir dire proceedings to refuse a jury seat to a prospective juror, for which no reason need be advanced other than the preference of counsel advocating exclusion.

VOIR DIRE A preliminary examination conducted by the court for the purpose of selecting prospective jurors to serve at trial.

United States v. Salamone

Federal government (P) v. Convicted violator of gun registration laws (D)

800 F.2d 1216 (3d Cir. 1986)

NATURE OF CASE: Appeal from conviction on charges of illegal gun possession and failure to register firearms.

FACT SUMMARY: The court granted the Government's (P) motion to dismiss a potential juror for cause on basis of his former membership in the National Rifle Association (NRA).

RULE OF LAW

A potential juror may not be disqualified for cause based on his membership in an organization without an individualized determination by the court as to the potential juror's ability to faithfully and impartially apply the law.

FACTS: During voir dire in Salamone's (D) trial on various charges, including the possession of and failure to register an illegally made machine gun, the court inquired as to each juror's membership in the National Rifle Association (NRA). One potential juror stated that he was a former member of the NRA and supported its principles, and another stated that her husband belonged to it and that she supported its principles. On the motion of the prosecution, the court found that the former member of the NRA was unfit to serve on the jury because of his support of the organization, which has a record of opposition to gun control. The court did not inquire as to whether that potential juror felt he would be able to impartially apply the law to the facts of the case. The other juror who had indicated her support of the NRA was dismissed by a peremptory challenge, and Salamone was convicted.

ISSUE: May a potential juror be disqualified for cause based on his membership in an organization without an individualized determination by the court as to the potential juror's ability to faithfully and impartially apply the law?

HOLDING AND DECISION: (Higginbotham, J.) No. A potential juror may not be disqualified for cause based on his membership in an organization without an individualized determination by the court as to the potential juror's ability to faithfully and impartially apply the law. To allow judges to determine juror eligibility based solely on their perceptions of the external associations of a juror threatens the right of the accused to a fair trial by an impartial jury. Juror bias need not be established with "unmistakable clarity." However, at no time were the excluded jurors questioned about their ability to faithfully and impartially apply the law. Jury competence is an individual rather than a class matter, and such presumed bias is impermissible. The judgment of the district court is reversed.

ANALYSIS

Although Circuit Judge Higginbotham states that no individualized inquiry was made as to the excluded jurors' ability to fairly hear the case, it seems incorrect to say that no individualized inquiry was made. The trial court judge did not merely ask the potential jurors about their membership or former membership in the National Rifle Association, but further asked whether they, personally, supported the principles and policies of the organization. The jurors' positive response was thus in some sense an indication of individual bias, though evidently not sufficient to satisfy the court of appeals.

Quicknotes

CHALLENGE FOR CAUSE The right to refuse a jury seat to a prospective juror where that person possesses bias or other knowledge of the case that would impair the ability to render a fair verdict, predicated upon the showing by counsel of a compelling reason as to why that juror should be dismissed.

PEREMPTORY CHALLENGE A challenge issued by counsel during voir dire proceedings to refuse a jury seat to a prospective juror, for which no reason need be advanced other than the preference of counsel advocating exclusion.

Batson v. Kentucky

Burglary suspect (D) v. State (P)

476 U.S. 79 (1986)

NATURE OF CASE: Appeal of conviction for burglary and receiving stolen goods.

FACT SUMMARY: After the Kentucky (P) prosecutor used peremptory challenges to strike all Black jurors, Batson (D), a Black man, unsuccessfully moved to dismiss the jury on grounds he was denied equal protection.

RULE OF LAW

To establish an equal protection violation for a state's use of peremptory challenges to exclude members of his race from a petit jury, a defendant must make out a prima facie case by showing: (1) he is a member of a cognizable racial group and (2) either that members of his race have not been summoned for jury duty in that jurisdiction for an extended period of time, or that the circumstances of his case raise an inference of purposeful discrimination.

FACTS: At Batson's (D) trial for burglary and receiving stolen goods, the Kentucky (P) prosecutor used peremptory challenges to remove all four Black people from the jury. Batson (D), a Black man, moved to dismiss the jury before it was sworn in, arguing that the state's (P) use of its peremptory challenges violated Batson's (D) Sixth Amendment right to a jury drawn from a fair cross section of the community and his Fourteenth Amendment right to equal protection. The trial judge denied the motion, stating that peremptory challenges could be used to strike anyone. Batson (D) was convicted, and he appealed.

ISSUE: To establish an equal protection violation for a state's use of peremptory challenges to exclude members of his race from a petit jury, must a defendant make out a prima facie case by showing: (1) he is a member of a cognizable racial group and (2) either that members of his race have not been summoned for jury duty in that jurisdiction for an extended period of time, or that the circumstances of his case raise an inference of purposeful discrimination?

HOLDING AND DECISION: (Powell, J.) Yes. To establish an equal protection violation for a state's use of peremptory challenges to exclude members of his race from a petit jury, a defendant must make out a prima facie case by showing: (1) he is a member of a cognizable racial group and (2) either that members of his race have not been summoned for jury duty in that jurisdiction for an extended period of time, or that the circumstances of his case raise an inference of purposeful discrimination. Once a prima facie case has been established, the state must provide a neutral explanation for the exercise of its peremptory challenges or else the defendant's conviction will be overturned. Whether a defendant has made out a prima facie showing based solely on evidence from his own case involves consideration of all relevant circumstances, for example, any "pattern" of strikes against jurors of the defendant's race and any questions and statements made by the prosecutor during voir dire. Once the burden shifts to the state to rebut a prima facie case, the prosecutor's explanation need not rise to the level of justifying a challenge for cause, but a statement that jurors will be partial to members of their own race or a simple denial of discriminatory intent will not suffice. Black people have an equal right to participation on juries, and their discriminatory exclusion impedes the pursuit of equal justice for defendants, excluded jurors, and the entire community. Thus, the Equal Protection Clause extends beyond selection of the jury venire to the petit jury and to the prosecutor's peremptory challenges. While peremptory challenges are important in our judicial system, they are often used to discriminate against Black people, and so a requirement that trial judges be sensitive to the discriminatory use of peremptory challenges strikes a balance between the continued use of peremptory challenges and equal protection. Remanded for further proceedings. If the trial court decides that the facts establish, prima facie, purposeful discrimination and the prosecutor does not come forward with a neutral explanation for his action, our precedents require that petitioner's conviction be reversed.

CONCURRENCE: (Marshall, J.) Peremptory challenges should be completely eliminated because their use cannot be reconciled with the requirements of equal protection. The discriminatory use of peremptory challenges will not be ended by this decision. Defendants cannot attack challenges unless their use is so flagrant as to establish a prima facie case. Even if a prima facie case can be made out, a prosecutor may easily fabricate nondiscriminatory motives, or his "neutral" determination that a juror is, for example, "sullen" or "distant" may be based on unconscious racism. The trial judge will have a difficult time determining the prosecutor's motives, and the judge's decision may be based on his own conscious or unconscious racism.

Continued on next page.

DISSENT: (Rehnquist, J.) The use of peremptory challenges to strike minorities from juries does not violate equal protection so long as challenges are also used to exclude White people in cases involving White defendants.

ANALYSIS

Justice Powell's opinion explicitly left open the issue of whether a criminal defendant can use race-based peremptory challenges. In *Edmonson v. Leesville Concrete Co.,* 500 U.S. 614 (1991), the United States Supreme Court extended the bar against discriminatory peremptory challenges to civil cases involving private litigants. The Court found state action in the discrimination a prerequisite for Equal Protection Clause analysis, since it is the state that empowers the jury and discharges a juror upon the use of a peremptory challenge. This reasoning would seem to extend to the use of peremptory challenges by criminal defendants.

Quicknotes

EQUAL PROTECTION CLAUSE A constitutional provision that each person be guaranteed the same protection of the laws enjoyed by other persons in like circumstances.

PEREMPTORY CHALLENGE A challenge issued by counsel during voir dire proceedings to refuse a jury seat to a prospective juror, for which no reason need be advanced other than the preference of counsel advocating exclusion.

PETIT JURY A trial jury as distinguished from the grand jury.

PRIMA FACIE CASE An action where the plaintiff introduces sufficient evidence to submit the issue to the judge or jury for determination.

VOIR DIRE A preliminary examination conducted by the court for the purpose of selecting prospective jurors to serve at trial.

United States v. Thomas

Federal government (P) v. Convicted drug dealer (D)

116 F.3d 606 (2d Cir. 1997)

NATURE OF CASE: Appeal from conviction under federal narcotics laws.

FACT SUMMARY: After retiring to deliberate, numerous jurors complained about the conduct of one of their number; that juror was dismissed, and a verdict returned.

RULE OF LAW

If there is any indication that the request to discharge a juror is based on that juror's view of the sufficiency of the evidence, the request must be denied.

FACTS: In a trial where all the defendants were Black, a jury was selected with one Black member, identified as Juror No. 5. The prosecution attempted to remove Juror No. 5 by means of a peremptory challenge, but the challenge was denied. During the defense summation, several jurors complained that Juror No. 5 was showing agreement with defense counsel. However, in interviews with each juror, including Juror No. 5, the jurors indicated they would be able to apply the law to the facts as sworn. After the jurors retired to deliberate, several jurors complained again about Juror No. 5, informing the court that he was unyieldingly in favor of acquittal. Several jurors cited various reasons for Juror No. 5's apparent behavior, such as his statements that the defendants were "his people" or were "good people." Other jurors recalled him discussing his opposition to conviction in terms of the evidence and challenging the sufficiency or reliability of the prosecution's witnesses. Juror No. 5 himself, in an interview with the court, said nothing to indicate that he was not making a good-faith effort to apply the law to the facts of the case. Finally, the court dismissed Juror No. 5, and the remaining eleven jurors returned a verdict of conviction.

ISSUE: If there is any indication that the request to discharge a juror is based on that juror's view of the sufficiency of the evidence, must the request be denied?

HOLDING AND DECISION: (Cabranes, J.) Yes. If there is any indication that the request to discharge a juror is based on that juror's view of the sufficiency of the evidence, the request must be denied. If a juror is ignoring the law, the court has the authority to remove that juror. Jurors do not have a right to engage in the practice described as nullification. However, that power must be exercised with great caution. A court may not delve deeply into a juror's motivations because it may not intrude on the secrecy of deliberations. Because there was some evidence here—his own statements, as well as the statements of other jurors—that Juror No. 5 was weighing the evidence and was unconvinced by the government's case, it was inappropriate to dismiss him. Reversed.

ANALYSIS

Judge Cabranes discusses at some length the double-edged sword of jury nullification. On the one hand, he recalls the case of John Peter Zenger, acquitted of criminal libel in 1735 and the acquittals in prosecutions under the fugitive slave laws in the nineteenth century. However, he also notes cases–more numerous and more recent–such as the two hung juries in the prosecution of Byron De La Beckwith for the murder of NAACP secretary Medgar Evers.

Quicknotes

JURY NULLIFICATION Inherent power of a jury to ignore the strength of evidence and override the decision-making authority of the forum, to render a binding verdict acquitting the defendant according to its own impulses.

Maryland v. Craig

State (P) v. Accused child abuser (D)

497 U.S. 836 (1990)

NATURE OF CASE: On certiorari from appellate court judgment overturning conviction.

FACT SUMMARY: Four children were permitted to testify via a one-way closed-circuit television procedure designed to keep the witness from having to look at the defendant.

RULE OF LAW

A state's interest in the physical and psychological well-being of child witnesses may outweigh the right of a defendant to confront his accusers face-to-face.

FACTS: Craig (D) was accused of sexually abusing young children, and expert testimony suggested that the children alleged to have been abused would be unable to testify if required to do so in front of Craig (D). A Maryland statutory procedure was invoked, permitting the child witness and the prosecuting and defense attorneys to retire to a separate room, while the judge, defendant, and jury remained in the courtroom. The defendant remained in communication with counsel by electronic means, and those in the courtroom were able to observe the witness via a one-way, closed-circuit television hookup. The witnesses testified by this means and Craig (D) was convicted; however, the court of appeals concluded the State (P) had not made sufficient showing of the necessity to prevent a face-to-face confrontation and reversed.

ISSUE: May a state's interest in the physical and psychological well-being of child witnesses outweigh the right of a defendant to confront his accusers face-to-face?

HOLDING AND DECISION: (O'Connor, J.) Yes. A state's interest in the physical and psychological well-being of child witnesses may outweigh the right of a defendant to confront his accusers face-to-face. The clear preference of the Confrontation Clause of the Sixth Amendment is for a face-to-face meeting between the defendant and the witnesses testifying against him. We have never held, however, that the right to such a face-to-face confrontation is absolute. The Confrontation Clause serves several purposes: to ensure that a witness's statements are given under oath, to permit cross-examination, and to permit the jury to observe the demeanor of the witness. Maryland's procedure permits all these purposes. To insist upon face-to-face confrontation in every instance would not only make examination of child witnesses in cases such as these difficult, but it would also virtually abrogate every exception to the hearsay rule. The purpose of the Confrontation Clause is to promote the seeking of truth, and we determine that where a procedure such as this is used to protect a young child from trauma, the truth-seeking function of the clause is furthered rather than hindered. The judgment of the court of appeals is reversed.

DISSENT: (Scalia, J.) Constitutional requirements may not be subordinated to currently favored public policy. We are not free to conduct a cost-benefit analysis of clear and explicit constitutional guarantees. The Maryland procedure may be virtually constitutional, but it is not actually constitutional.

ANALYSIS

Justice Scalia, in dissent, states that the defendant's "right, 'to be confronted with the witnesses against him' means always and everywhere, at least what it explicitly says: the 'right to meet face to face all those who appear and give evidence at trial.'" His reading of the phrase "to be confronted," while reasonable, seems interpretive rather than literal; the Constitution simply does not refer anywhere to a "face-to-face" confrontation. Yet the majority opinion did not take issue with Justice Scalia's claim that the text permitted only one "literal reading"; instead, it justified the Maryland procedure wholly on policy grounds.

Quicknotes

ABROGATE Annul; cancel; void.

CONFRONTATION CLAUSE A provision in the Sixth Amendment to the U.S. Constitution that an accused in a criminal action has the right to confront the witnesses against him or her, including the right to attend the trial and to cross-examine witnesses called on behalf of the prosecution.

HEARSAY An out-of-court statement made by a person other than the witness testifying at trial that is offered in order to prove the truth of the matter asserted.

SIXTH AMENDMENT Provides the right to a speedy trial and public trial by impartial jury, the right to be informed of the accusation, the right to confront witnesses, and the right to have the assistance of counsel in all criminal prosecutions.

Crawford v. Washington

Attempted murder convict (D) v. State (P)

541 U.S. 36 (2004)

NATURE OF CASE: Appeal of an attempted murder conviction.

FACT SUMMARY: When at Michael Crawford's (D) trial, the prosecutor played for the jury a witness's prior out-of-court tape-recorded statement to the police, thus providing Crawford (D) with no opportunity for cross-examination, Crawford (D) argued deprivation of his constitutional rights on the grounds that the Sixth Amendment Confrontation Clause applies not only to in-court testimony.

RULE OF LAW

The Sixth Amendment Confrontation Clause applies not only to in-court testimony.

FACTS: Michael Crawford (D) stabbed a man who allegedly tried to rape his wife, Sylvia. At his trial, the prosecutor played for the jury Sylvia's tape-recorded statement to the police describing the stabbing, even though Crawford (D) had no opportunity for cross-examination. Crawford (D) claimed self-defense. Sylvia did not testify at trial because of the state's marital privilege; in Washington, this privilege does not extend to a spouse's out-of-court statements admissible under a hearsay exception. The Washington Supreme Court upheld Crawford's (D) attempted murder conviction after determining that Sylvia's statement was reliable. Crawford (D) appealed to the United States Supreme Court on Confrontation Clause grounds.

ISSUE: Does the Sixth Amendment Confrontation Clause apply only to in-court testimony?

HOLDING AND DECISION: (Scalia, J.) No. The Sixth Amendment Confrontation Clause applies not only to in-court testimony. The history of the Confrontation Clause supports two inferences about its meaning. First, the principal evil at which it was directed was the civil-law mode of criminal procedure, particularly its use of ex parte examinations as evidence against the accused. The Sixth Amendment must be interpreted with this focus in mind. Leaving the regulation of out-of-court statements to the law of evidence would render the Clause powerless to prevent even the most flagrant inquisitional practices. This focus also suggests that not all hearsay implicates the Sixth Amendment's core concerns. An off-hand, overheard remark, for example, might be unreliable evidence and thus a good candidate for exclusion under hearsay rules, but it bears little resemblance to the civil-law abuses the Clause targeted. On the other hand, ex parte examinations might sometimes be admissible under modern hearsay rules, but the Framers certainly would not have condoned them. Statements taken by police officers in the course of investigations, as here, are testimonial evidence under even a narrow standard. Police interrogations bear a striking resemblance to examinations by justices of the police in England; the statements are not sworn testimony, but the absence of oath was not dispositive. In sum, police interrogations fall squarely within the class of statements to which the right of confrontation is historically required. Secondly, the Framers would not have allowed admission of testimonial statements of a witness who did not appear at trial unless unavailable and the defendant had had a prior opportunity for cross-examination. The text of the Sixth Amendment "does not suggest any open-ended exceptions from the confrontation requirement to be developed by the courts." Dispensing with confrontation because testimony is "obviously reliable" is akin to dispensing with jury trial because a defendant is "obviously guilty." Reversed.

CONCURRENCE: (Rehnquist, C.J.) Although the wife's statement should have been excluded, adoption of a new approach in this area is not backed by sufficiently persuasive reasoning to overrule long-established precedent.

ANALYSIS

In *Crawford*, the United States Supreme Court makes clear that where testimonial evidence is involved, the Framers did not intend to leave the Sixth Amendment's protections "to the vagaries of the rules of evidence, much less to amorphous notions of 'reliability.'" Admitting statements deemed reliable by a judge is fundamentally at odds with the right of confrontation. The Confrontation Clause commands not that evidence be reliable but that reliability be assessed in a particular manner: by testing in the crucible of cross-examination.

Quicknotes

CONFRONTATION CLAUSE A provision in the Sixth Amendment to the U.S. Constitution that an accused in a criminal action has the right to confront the witnesses against him or her, including the right to attend the trial and to cross-examine witnesses called on behalf of the prosecution.

HEARSAY EXCEPTION Out-of-court statement made by a person other than the witness testifying at trial that is offered in order to prove the truth of the matter asserted and is admissible at trial notwithstanding the fact that it is hearsay.

Michigan v. Bryant

State (P) v. Murder suspect (D)

562 U.S. 344 (2011)

NATURE OF CASE: Appeal from state court decision reversing conviction of an individual for murder.

FACT SUMMARY: After Bryant (D) shot victim Anthony Covington, Covington made statements before his death to the police implicating Bryant (D) as the shooter.

RULE OF LAW

Where the primary purpose of an interrogation of a witness is to allow police to respond to an ongoing emergency, statements made by a witness will not qualify as testimonial statements and the Confrontation Clause will not bar their admission at trial.

FACTS: Bryant (D) shot Covington. Police responding to a radio call found Covington and asked him what happened. Covington informed police that "Rick" Bryant (D) had shot him 25 minutes earlier through the back door of Bryant's (D) house. The conversation between five police officers and Covington lasted five to ten minutes before an ambulance arrived and transported Covington to a hospital. He died several hours later. Police went to Bryant's (D) house and found blood and a bullet hole in the back door. At trial, the court allowed the police officers to testify as to Covington's statements regarding the identity of Bryant (D). A jury convicted Bryant (D), but the Michigan Supreme Court eventually reversed the conviction because the Confrontation Clause barred the use of Covington's statements, which that court held to be testimonial. The State (P) appealed to the United States Supreme Court.

ISSUE: Where the primary purpose of an interrogation of a witness is to allow police to respond to an ongoing emergency, will statements made by a witness qualify as testimonial statements and will the Confrontation Clause bar their admission at trial?

HOLDING AND DECISION: (Sotomayor, J.) No. Where the primary purpose of an interrogation of a witness is to allow police to respond to an ongoing emergency, statements made by a witness will not qualify as testimonial statements and the Confrontation Clause will not bar their admission at trial. To determine if the primary purpose is to assist the police with an ongoing emergency, courts should analyze the circumstances present and the statements of the parties and their actions. It is an objective test. When an emergency situation is present, statements made to resolve the emergency are given indicia of reliability, thus shielding them from cross-examination usually required by the Confrontation Clause for out-of-court statements. In addition to the circumstances, another factor is the informality of the questioning, including where the questioning took place. A review of both the questions and answers given during the alleged emergency situation is critical. Police officers have a duty to resolve emergency situations and serve as criminal investigators. A victim's statements often have a purpose of protecting themselves, particularly when an armed assailant remains at large. Another factor is the type of dispute. If the dispute is domestic, the level of emergency may be lower. That was not the case here. The police did not know if Covington's shooter was a threat only to Covington at the time. Nor did the police know the location or motive of Bryant (D) during the police officers' questioning of Covington. The questioning was also informal and occurred in a public place. Accordingly, because the primary purpose of Covington's statements was to assist the police in resolving the emergency, the statements were not testimonial and the Confrontation Clause did not bar their admission at trial. Vacated.

CONCURRENCE: (Thomas, J.) Covington's statements were not testimonial because they occurred in an informal setting. The statements did not therefore "bear testimony" against Bryant (D). Analysis of the setting in which the statements were made is more appropriate rather than the majority's primary purpose test.

DISSENT: (Scalia, J.) The majority's decision greatly distorts our prior Confrontation Clause jurisprudence. The focus of the inquiry should be on the intent of the declarant. Here, 25 minutes after the shooting, Covington found himself surrounded by five police officers. These five officers all asked Covington to describe what had happened, what the shooter looked like, and what events led to the shooting. The alleged "emergency situation" had ended 25 minutes earlier. It is unreasonable to think that Bryant (D) would attempt to fire upon Covington again. Covington, aware that the threat had ended, had the sole purpose of identifying his shooter to the police. Even if the perspective of the officers is considered, none of the officers testified that they were in danger of any imminent threat. At a minimum, the questions from the officers became investigative, thus rendering Covington's statements testimonial in nature. The majority's decision greatly expands the definition of emergency situations in violation of the Confrontation Clause. Pursuant to this decision, prosecutors and police may be able to argue that

Continued on next page.

statements given in the hours after an incident but before a suspect is arrested are not testimonial because an ongoing emergency still exists. Finally, the court's reversion to a reliability standard has been previously rejected by this Court. Reliability of a statement does not mean it is testimonial or nontestimonial. Per the Sixth Amendment, the proper analysis is whether the statements are testimonial, not reliable. If they are testimonial, the Confrontation Clause bars the admission of such statements because the defendant has not been given the right to cross-examine.

DISSENT: (Ginsburg, J.) Justice Scalia is correct that Covington's statements were testimonial and that it is the declarant's intent that is relevant. However, this case should have been analyzed under the dying declaration exception to the hearsay rule. The exception arises when statements are made by a person who is aware that he or she is facing imminent death. However, the prosecutor had abandoned this argument in the courts below.

ANALYSIS

The significance of this case is that it deals solely with the Confrontation Clause analysis. The United States Supreme Court remanded the case to the Michigan courts for a determination of whether the statements could be admitted through another hearsay exception, such as a dying declaration or an excited utterance. The *Crawford v. Washington,* 541 U.S. 36 (2004), decision rejected the notion that out-of-court statements were admissible over Confrontation Clause objections if they were shown to be reliable. Justice Scalia's dissent argued that the majority's decision was a return to the improper reliability standard.

Quicknotes

CONFRONTATION CLAUSE A provision in the Sixth Amendment to the U.S. Constitution that an accused in a criminal action has the right to confront the witnesses against him or her, including the right to attend the trial and to cross-examine witnesses called on behalf of the prosecution.

EXCITED UTTERANCE An exception to the hearsay rule for a statement relating to a startling event or condition, made while the declarant was under the stress of excitement that it caused. Fed. R. Evid. 803(2).

Cruz v. New York

Convicted murderer (D) v. State (P)

481 U.S. 186 (1987)

NATURE OF CASE: On certiorari from appellate court judgment affirming murder conviction.

FACT SUMMARY: Testimony concerning Cruz's (D) confession to the murder of a gas station attendant was admitted; his co-defendant's confession was likewise admitted with a limiting instruction.

RULE OF LAW

The Confrontation Clause bars the admission of a nontestifying co-defendant's confession incriminating the defendant at their joint trial, even if the defendant's confession is admitted.

FACTS: Cruz (D), his brother, and two other men robbed a gas station. In the course of the robbery, Cruz's (D) brother shot and killed the gas station attendant. Cruz (D) and his brother were indicted and tried jointly for felony murder. The prosecution called a witness who testified that Cruz (D) had confessed to his participation in the incident. Cruz's (D) brother had confessed in detail to the assistant district attorney and identified Cruz (D) as one of the participants in the robbery-murder. The court, instructing the jury not to consider the confession of Cruz's (D) brother against Cruz (D), admitted the brother's confession.

ISSUE: Does the Confrontation Clause bar the admission of a nontestifying co-defendant's confession incriminating the defendant at their joint trial, even if the defendant's confession is admitted?

HOLDING AND DECISION: (Scalia, J.) Yes. The Confrontation Clause bars the admission of a nontestifying co-defendant's confession incriminating the defendant at their joint trial, even if the defendant's confession is admitted. We have previously held that a nontestifying co-defendant's confession may not be admitted where the defendant seeking to bar admission has not himself confessed. Even a limiting instruction will not cure the Confrontation Clause violation in such an instance. Regardless of such an instruction, the chance that a jury will be unable to ignore the incriminating effect of one co-defendant's statements concerning another is too great, and the stakes too high. Cruz's (D) own confession may have increased the reliability of his brother's confession, but it operated to increase the very risk sought to be avoided by our prior decisions. It seems more likely, once Cruz's (D) confession is admitted, that his brother's confession would be considered by the jury in evaluating Cruz's (D) guilt, regardless of any limiting instruction. Reversed.

DISSENT: (White, J.) It is not even remotely possible that in all cases admission of a defendant's interlocking confession will have devastating effects.

ANALYSIS

Justice White, claiming "common sense" on his side, argued that "interlocking confessions" were more reliable than the confession of a single defendant who might be determined to take his co-defendants down with him. Justice Scalia noted that the dissent missed the point; the nontestifying co-defendant's confession was inadmissible because it was apparently extremely reliable. In fact, Justice Scalia wrote, it might seem so reliable that a jury would be unable to ignore a limiting instruction.

Quicknotes

CONFRONTATION CLAUSE A provision in the Sixth Amendment to the U.S. Constitution that an accused in a criminal action has the right to confront the witnesses against him or her, including the right to attend the trial and to cross-examine witnesses called on behalf of the prosecution.

LIMITING INSTRUCTION Directions given by a judge to the jury prior to deliberation to consider or ignore a piece of evidence; counsel can request the court give a limiting instruction.

Gray v. Maryland

Convicted murderer (D) v. State (P)

523 U.S. 185 (1998)

NATURE OF CASE: Appeal from murder conviction.

FACT SUMMARY: Defendant was convicted of beating a victim to death; he was tried jointly with another alleged participant in the beating.

RULE OF LAW

The prosecution may not introduce the confession of a nontestifying co-defendant where the confession implicates another defendant in their joint trial, even if a blank space or the word "deleted" is inserted wherever the implicated defendant is identified in the confession.

FACTS: Stacy Williams was beaten to death. Anthony Bell confessed to police and named Gray (D) and another man as participants in the beating. The other man subsequently died, but Bell and Gray (D) were jointly tried for murder. Bell's confession was redacted to put the word "deleted" wherever the name of Gray (D) appeared, and the jury was instructed that it was not to consider the confession as evidence against Gray (D). Both Bell and Gray (D) were convicted.

ISSUE: May the prosecution introduce the confession of a nontestifying co-defendant where the confession implicates another defendant in their joint trial, even if a blank space or the word "deleted" is inserted wherever the implicated defendant is identified in the confession?

HOLDING AND DECISION: (Breyer, J.) No. The prosecution may not introduce the confession of a nontestifying co-defendant where the confession implicates another defendant in their joint trial, even if a blank space or the word "deleted" is inserted wherever the implicated defendant is identified in the confession. We have held that such confessions, where one defendant is named in the confession of another who does not testify in their joint trial, are so prejudicial that even a limiting instruction to the jury to consider the statement as evidence against only the confessing defendant will not overcome the prejudice thus created. We hold today that confessions redacted in a manner indicating that other participants were involved in the crime, where the alleged co-participants are being jointly tried, are still highly prejudicial and inadmissible. As Judge Learned Hand wrote in a similar case, "[T]here could not have been the slightest doubt as to whose names had been blacked out," but "even if there had been, that blacking out would have not only laid the doubt but underscored the answer." Vacated and remanded.

DISSENT: (Scalia, J.) We have held that the rule against admitting incriminating confessions of non-testifying jointly tried defendants does not extend to statements that incriminate only by inference from other evidence. The Court concedes that "the jury must use inference to connect the statement in this redacted confession with the defendant." Though the jury may speculate, the statement expressly implicates no one but the speaker.

ANALYSIS

The majority in *Gray* suggested that a confession might be acceptably redacted by eliminating all references to co-participants in the crime. Justice Scalia argued that such redactions would misrepresent the confessing defendant's statement; moreover, he said, a defendant who replied "Me" to the question "Who agreed to beat the victim?" would have an insanity defense.

Quicknotes

LIMITING INSTRUCTION Directions given by a judge to the jury prior to deliberation to consider or ignore a piece of evidence; counsel can request the court give a limiting instruction.

United States v. Burr

Federal government (P) v. Criminal defendant (D)

25 Fed. Cas. 30 (No. 14,692D) (C.C.D. Va. 1807)

NATURE OF CASE: Defense motion in a criminal proceeding for a *subpoena duces tecum*.

FACT SUMMARY: Defense counsel moved for a *subpoena duces tecum* against the President of the United States to obtain letters relevant to the defense of a criminal prosecution.

RULE OF LAW

In a criminal case, a *subpoena duces tecum* may be directed to the President of the United States.

FACTS: In the prosecution of Burr (D), defense counsel moved for a *subpoena duces tecum* to obtain an original letter from General Wilkinson to the President of the United States in relation to Burr (D), together with the President's answer to that letter, as material to the defense.

ISSUE: In a criminal case, may a *subpoena duces tecum* be directed to the President of the United States?

HOLDING AND DECISION: (Marshall, C.J.) Yes. In a criminal case, a *subpoena duces tecum* may be directed to the President of the United States. The Sixth Amendment right must be deemed sacred by the courts and must be so construed as to be something more than a dead letter. In the provision of the Constitution that gives the accused a right to the compulsory process of the court, there is no exception whatsoever. This Court would be very unwilling to say that upon fair construction, the constitutional and legal right to obtain its processes to compel the attendance of witnesses does not extend to their bringing with them such papers as may be material in the defense. Motion granted.

ANALYSIS

In the *Burr* case, Chief Justice Marshall expressed the viewpoint that where documents may be important to the defense of a criminal action, "it would be a blot in the page which records the judicial proceedings of this country" if in such a serious case as the present one, the accused were denied the use of a *subpoena duces tecum.*

Quicknotes

SIXTH AMENDMENT Provides the right to a speedy and public trial by impartial jury, the right to be informed of the accusation, the right to confront witnesses, and the right to have the assistance of counsel in all criminal prosecutions.

SUBPOENA DUCES TECUM A court mandate compelling the production of documents under a witness's control.

Taylor v. Illinois

Criminal defendant (D) v. State (P)

484 U.S. 400 (1988)

NATURE OF CASE: Appeal of criminal conviction.

FACT SUMMARY: Illinois (P) requires pretrial disclosure of all defense witnesses, but Taylor (D), who claimed that an exculpatory witness was not on the list because he could not be located before trial, was not allowed by the trial judge to call the witness to testify.

RULE OF LAW

Where the defense intentionally omits a witness from a required pretrial witness list to gain a tactical advantage, the trial judge may refuse to let the witness testify.

FACTS: Illinois (P) law requires the defense to provide a pretrial list of all witnesses it intends to call. During his trial, Taylor's (D) defense counsel wished to call a witness who was not on the pretrial list. Taylor (D) claimed that the witness could not be located before trial, but the witness admitted at a hearing that defense counsel had visited him the week before trial. The trial judge, concluding that the witness was not credible and that the evidence might be manufactured, did not allow the witness to testify. Taylor (D) appealed, arguing that the Sixth Amendment Compulsory Process Clause bars a judge from precluding the testimony of a surprise witness.

ISSUE: Where the defense intentionally omits a witness from a required pretrial witness list to gain a tactical advantage, may the trial judge refuse to let the witness testify?

HOLDING AND DECISION: (Stevens, J.) Yes. Where the defense intentionally omits a witness from a required pretrial witness list to gain a tactical advantage, the trial judge may refuse to let the witness testify. The Compulsory Process Clause mandates not only that a defendant may compel the presence of a witness but also that the trier of fact must hear the witness. However, where the defendant fails to comply with discovery rules, the defendant's rights must be weighed against the public interest in excluding unreliable or perjured testimony, in avoiding prejudice to the prosecution, and in enforcing rules for the fair and efficient functioning of the adversary process. While there are less drastic sanctions available (granting a continuance or mistrial or disciplining the defendant or defense counsel, for example), in the event a discovery violation is willful only the severest sanction—witness preclusion—may be strong enough to combat the defendant's powerful incentive to present perjured testimony. Finally, unless defense counsel is constitutionally ineffective, the adversary process requires a client to be held responsible for the actions of his attorney. Accordingly, there was no error committed by not allowing Taylor's (D) omitted witness to testify at trial. Affirmed.

DISSENT: (Brennan, J.) Where the defendant is not personally responsible for the discovery violation, alternative sanctions are adequate and avoid the arbitrary and disproportionate sanction of witness preclusion. Unless the defendant is responsible, the Compulsory Process Clause should require a per se rule against discovery sanctions that exclude criminal defense evidence.

ANALYSIS

Under *Wardius v. Oregon*, 412 U.S. 470 (1973), where discovery rules place a particular burden on the defense, due process requires that the defense must have reciprocal discovery rights against the prosecution. Federal Rule of Criminal Procedure 16 provides defendants with a number of discovery and inspection rights, essentially providing the prosecution with reciprocal rights where the defense has chosen to exercise its rights first. The Federal Rules of Criminal Procedure do not require either party to provide a pretrial list of all witnesses, but federal judges have discretion to order the government to provide a witness list.

Quicknotes

DISCOVERY Pretrial procedure during which one party makes certain information available to the other.

PERJURY The making of false or misleading statements knowingly under oath.

Griffin v. California

First-degree murder convict (D) v. State (P)

380 U.S. 609 (1965)

NATURE OF CASE: Certiorari from a murder conviction.

FACT SUMMARY: Griffin (D), during his trial for first-degree murder, did not testify on the issue of his guilt, and both the prosecutor and judge subsequently commented on this failure to the jury before it convicted him.

RULE OF LAW

Comment by a judge or prosecutor on an accused's failure to testify violates the accused's Fifth Amendment privilege against self-incrimination.

FACTS: Griffin (D) refused to testify at his trial for first-degree murder, invoking the Fifth Amendment privilege against self-incrimination. Before the jury deliberated on the issue of guilt, the prosecutor commented on this failure to testify and suggested that guilt should be inferred therefrom. During instructions to the jury, the court stated that if Griffin (D) failed to explain facts within his knowledge that tended to indicate his guilt, then the jury could take that failure as "tending to indicate the truth of such evidence," but that such failure alone does not by itself "warrant an inference of guilt." Upon conviction, and affirmance of that conviction by the California Supreme Court, Griffin (D) brought a petition for certiorari to the United States Supreme Court.

ISSUE: Does comment by a judge or prosecutor on an accused's failure to testify violate the accused's Fifth Amendment privilege against self-incrimination?

HOLDING AND DECISION: (Douglas, J.) Yes. Comment by a judge or prosecutor on an accused's failure to testify violates the accused's Fifth Amendment privilege against self-incrimination. The Fifth Amendment Self-Incrimination Clause forbids comment by the prosecution on an accused's failure to testify or instructions by the court that such failure is evidence of guilt. Such comment by the prosecution or court is a "remnant of the inquisitorial system of criminal justice which the Fifth Amendment protects against." Such comment penalizes the exercise of a constitutional privilege to refrain from self-incrimination and, as such, cannot be allowed. It may be true that there is a natural inference of guilt from a failure to testify as to facts within the knowledge of an accused, but the jury must make this inference on its own without comment from the court. Here, therefore, Griffin's (D) conviction must be reversed.

CONCURRENCE: (Harlan, J.) Since within the federal system the Fifth Amendment bars adverse comments by federal prosecutors and judges on a defendant's failure to take the stand in a criminal trial, there is no legitimate escape from today's decision. Unfortunately, the decision exemplifies the creeping paralysis with which the Supreme Court "incorporation" doctrine is infecting the operation of the federal system.

DISSENT: (Stewart, J.) In examining whether an accused's privilege against self-incrimination has been violated, "compulsion" is the focus of inquiry (i.e., such privilege has been violated only if the accused was "compelled to be a witness against himself"). The Court, however, fails to identify any such compulsion in the comments of the court and prosecutor. First, such comments do not compel an accused's testimony by creating awareness in the jury of his failure to testify, since that failure is obvious by itself. Second, no compulsion may be assumed on the grounds that the inferences drawn by the jury that has heard such comments will be detrimental to an accused, especially where the Court has carefully controlled its comments. The trial court here carefully instructed the jury that Griffin's (D) failure to testify "does not by itself warrant an inference of guilt." It is doubtful that a jury without such instructions would have observed such a limitation. The comment in this case was a means of articulating and rationally discussing a fact that is necessarily impressed on the jury's consciousness (i.e., the failure to testify). The State (P) has an important interest in such discussion, which should not arbitrarily be cut off.

ANALYSIS

This case illustrates the rule applicable to "direct comment" on an accused's failure to "testify." Note, however, that it does not prevent a prosecutor from commenting on an accused's "failure to offer evidence" on critical aspects of the case. It has been held that a court's comment that an accused's "failure to explain" possession of recently stolen property should be considered in determining whether he knew the goods were stolen does not violate *Griffin* (*Barnes v. United States,* 412 U.S. 837 (1973)). Of course, what is considered permissible depends upon the wording of the prosecutor's comments. If he emphasizes an accused's failure to present other evidence instead of the fact that he "personally"

Continued on next page.

offered no explanation, there is probably no violation of *Griffin.* Note further that *Griffin* does not prevent a prosecutor from commenting to a jury upon an accused's "refusal to submit to reasonable tests or examinations," the results of which would have been admissible on the issue of guilt or innocence. Note, finally, that *Griffin* does prevent counsel for one of several co-defendants from commenting on the failure of other co-defendants to testify.

Quicknotes

CERTIORARI A discretionary writ issued by a superior court to an inferior court in order to review the lower court's decisions; the U.S. Supreme Court's writ ordering such review.

FIRST-DEGREE MURDER The willful killing of another person with deliberation and premeditation; first-degree murder also encompasses those situations in which a person is killed within the perpetration of, or attempt to perpetrate, specified felonies.

PRIVILEGE AGAINST SELF-INCRIMINATION A privilege guaranteed by the Fifth Amendment to the U.S. Constitution in a criminal proceeding for communications made by an accused and protecting an accused or witness from having to give testimony that may incriminate him- or herself.

CHAPTER 17

Sentencing

Quick Reference Rules of Law

Mistretta v. United States

Criminal defendant (P) v. Federal government (D)

488 U.S. 361 (1989)

NATURE OF CASE: Challenge to the constitutionality of the Sentencing Commission. [Implied from casebook excerpt.]

FACT SUMMARY: [Facts not stated in casebook excerpt.]

RULE OF LAW

The Sentencing Commission is constitutional. [Implied from casebook excerpt.]

FACTS: [Facts not stated in casebook excerpt.]

ISSUE: Is the Sentencing Commission constitutional? [Implied from casebook excerpt.]

HOLDING AND DECISION: (Blackmun, J.) Yes. The Sentencing Commission is constitutional. [Implied from casebook excerpt.]

Congress enacted specific guidelines that were meant to establish a range of determinate sentences for categories of offenses and defendants according to various specified factors, "among others." The maximum of the range ordinarily may not exceed the minimum by more than the greater of 25 percent or six months, and each sentence is to be within the limit provided by existing law. The Sentencing Commission was established "as an independent commission in the judicial branch of the United States." In addition to the duty the Commission has to promulgate determinative-sentence guidelines, it is under an obligation periodically to "review and revise" the guidelines. It is to "consult with authorities on, and individual and institutional representatives of, various aspects of the Federal criminal justice system." It must report to Congress "any amendments of the guidelines." It is to make recommendations to Congress whether the grades or maximum penalties should be modified. It must submit to Congress at least annually an analysis of the operation of the guidelines. It is to issue "general policy statements" regarding their application. And it has the power to "establish general policies . . . as are necessary to carry out the purposes" of the legislation; to "monitor the performance of probation officers" with respect to the guidelines; to "devise and conduct periodic training programs of instruction in sentencing techniques for judicial and probation personnel and others; and to perform such other functions as are required to permit federal courts to meet their responsibilities" as to sentencing. [Constitutionality of the Sentencing Commission is implied from the casebook excerpt.]

ANALYSIS

The *Mistretta* Court noted that before settling on a mandatory guideline system, Congress considered other competing proposals for sentencing reform. It rejected strict determinate sentencing because it concluded that a guideline system would be successful in reducing sentence disparities while retaining the flexibility needed to adjust for unanticipated factors arising in a particular case. The Judiciary Committee rejected a proposal that would have made the sentencing guidelines only advisory.

Williams v. New York

Death row convict (P) v. State (D)

337 U.S. 241 (1949)

NATURE OF CASE: Appeal of a conviction for murder.

FACT SUMMARY: Following a conviction for murder, the trial judge sentenced Williams (P) to death using out-of-court records and reports to reach his decision.

RULE OF LAW

The use of additional out-of-court records and reports by a trial judge in sentencing does not violate the Due Process Clause.

FACTS: Williams (P) was tried for first-degree murder. The evidence proved a wholly indefensible murder committed by a person engaged in a burglary. The jury returned a verdict of guilty with a recommendation for life sentence. The judge imposed the death penalty, stating that the presentence investigation of Williams's (P) past criminal record and psychiatric reports revealed that he was a menace to society. Consideration of this additional information was pursuant to the New York Criminal Code. The court of appeals affirmed the conviction and sentence over Williams's (P) contention that the statute as construed violated the Due Process Clause of the Fourteenth Amendment in that the information was supplied by witnesses with whom Williams (P) had not been confronted and had no opportunity to cross-examine. Williams (P) appealed.

ISSUE: Does the use of additional out-of-court information by a trial judge in sentencing violate the Due Process Clause?

HOLDING AND DECISION: (Black, J.) No. The use of additional out-of-court information by a trial judge in sentencing does not violate the Due Process Clause. The procedural policy grounded in the Due Process Clause of the Fourteenth Amendment provides in part that no person shall be tried and convicted of an offense unless he is given reasonable notice of the charges against him and is afforded an opportunity to confront and examine adverse witnesses. That the Due Process Clause does provide these protections where the question is the guilt of a defendant is clear. However, a sentencing judge is not confined to the narrow issue of guilt. Essential to his selection of an appropriate sentence is the possession of the fullest information possible concerning a defendant's life and characteristics. Williams (P) was found guilty after a fairly conducted trial. His sentence followed a hearing conducted by the judge in which Williams (P) testified as to his sentence. The case went to the highest state court, which affirmed the sentence. Williams (P) was not denied due process of law. Affirmed.

DISSENT: (Murphy, J.) Here, the judge exercised his discretion to deprive a man of his life in reliance on material made available to him in a probation report, consisting almost entirely of evidence that would have been inadmissible at the trial. In a capital case, against the unanimous recommendation of a jury, when the report would concededly not have been admissible at the trial, and was not subject to examination by the defendant, the high commands of due process were not obeyed. Due process of law includes at least the idea that a person accused of crime shall be accorded a fair hearing through all the stages of the proceedings against him.

ANALYSIS

In *Gardner v. Florida,* 430 U.S. 349 (1977), the United States Supreme Court held that a sentence of death imposed at least in part on basis of information in a presentence report that the defendant had no opportunity to contest was unconstitutional. Distinguishing its holding in *Williams,* the Court said that the death penalty had now been recognized by majority of the Court as "a different kind of punishment than any other that may be imposed in this country."

Quicknotes

FOURTEENTH AMENDMENT DUE PROCESS CLAUSE Provides that protections mandated by the U.S. Constitution and observed by the federal government are equally applicable, and therefore must be observed by the states.

McMillan v. Pennsylvania

Felony convict (D) v. State (P)

477 U.S. 79 (1986)

NATURE OF CASE: Appeal of sentence imposed upon conviction.

FACT SUMMARY: McMillan (D) was sentenced under a Pennsylvania law that required a minimum sentence of five years for certain felonies if the sentencing judge finds by a preponderance of the evidence that the offender was in "visible possession of a firearm" during commission of the crime.

RULE OF LAW

Due process does not require a sentencing court to find any facts used in sentencing to be proven beyond a reasonable doubt, by clear and convincing evidence, by a preponderance of the evidence, or by any other burden of proof.

FACTS: McMillan (D) was sentenced under a Pennsylvania law that required a minimum sentence of five years for certain felonies if the sentencing judge finds by a preponderance of the evidence that the offender was in "visible possession of a firearm" during commission of the crime. McMillan (D) appealed his sentence, arguing that due process requires "visible possession of a firearm" to be proven by at least clear and convincing evidence.

ISSUE: Does due process require a sentencing court to find any facts used in sentencing to be proven beyond a reasonable doubt, by clear and convincing evidence, by a preponderance of the evidence, or by other burden of proof?

HOLDING AND DECISION: (Rehnquist, J.) No. Due process does not require a sentencing court to find any facts used in sentencing to be proven beyond a reasonable doubt, by clear and convincing evidence, by a preponderance of the evidence, or by any other burden of proof. Sentencing courts traditionally have heard evidence and found facts without any burden of proof at all. So long as the fact to be proven is not an element of the offense, as here, no burden of proof need be imposed simply because the fact concerns the crime, as opposed to the background or character of the offender. Thus, McMillan (D) was properly sentenced. Affirmed.

DISSENT: (Stevens, J.) There must be some constitutional limits on the power of a state to define the elements of criminal offenses. A high standard of proof is required because of the immense importance of the individual interest in avoiding both the loss of liberty and the stigma that results from a criminal conviction. It follows that if a state provides that a specific component of a prohibited transaction shall give rise to both a special stigma and to a special punishment, that component must be treated as a fact necessary to constitute the crime. Here, the constitutional significance of the special sanction cannot be avoided by the cavalier observation that it merely "ups the ante" for the defendant.

ANALYSIS

The defense in *McMillan* pointed to prior United States Supreme Court decisions holding that due process required proof by at least clear and convincing evidence in involuntary commitment procedures and procedures to terminate parental rights. However, the Court distinguished sentencing procedures from those types of cases, because where an offender is being sentenced, he or she has already been proven guilty of a crime beyond a reasonable doubt. The Court also held that the aggravating factor of visible possession of a firearm can constitutionally be treated as a sentencing consideration as opposed to an element of the charged offense.

Quicknotes

BURDEN OF PROOF The duty of a party to introduce evidence to support a fact that is in dispute in an action.

DUE PROCESS The constitutional mandate requiring the courts to protect and enforce individuals' rights and liberties consistent with prevailing principles of fairness and justice and prohibiting the federal and state governments from such activities that deprive its citizens of life, liberty, or property interest.

FELONY A criminal offense of greater seriousness than a misdemeanor; felonies are generally defined pursuant to statute as any crime that is punishable by death or by a term of imprisonment exceeding one year.

Apprendi v. New Jersey

Hate crime convict (D) v. State (P)

530 U.S. 466 (2000)

NATURE OF CASE: Appeal from conviction under state hate crime statute.

FACT SUMMARY: Apprendi (D) fired shots into the home of an African-American family because he allegedly did not want the occupants of the home in the neighborhood because of their race.

RULE OF LAW

Any fact that increases the penalty for a crime beyond the statutory minimum, other than the fact of a prior conviction, must be submitted to a jury and proven beyond a reasonable doubt.

FACTS: Apprendi (D) fired shots into the home of an African-American family. When he was arrested, he stated that he did not want the family in the neighborhood because of their race. He was indicted on 23 counts, none of which referred to the New Jersey hate crime statute or alleged that Apprendi (D) acted with a racially motivated purpose. After an evidentiary hearing on the issue of Apprendi's (D) motive for the shooting, the judge concluded that the crime was motivated by racial bias, and he was sentenced to 12 years to run consecutively with his other sentences. Apprendi (D) appealed.

ISSUE: Must any fact that increases the penalty for a crime beyond the statutory minimum, other than the fact of a prior conviction, be submitted to a jury and proven beyond a reasonable doubt?

HOLDING AND DECISION: (Stevens, J.) Yes. Any fact that increases the penalty for a crime beyond the statutory minimum, other than the fact of a prior conviction, must be submitted to a jury and proven beyond a reasonable doubt. Here the issue is whether the Due Process Clause of the Fourteenth Amendment requires that a factual determination authorizing an increase in the maximum prison sentence for an offense from 10 to 20 years be made by a jury on basis of proof beyond a reasonable doubt. In *Jones v. United States*, 526 U.S. 227 (1999), under the Due Process Clause of the Fifth Amendment and the notice and jury trial guarantees of the Sixth Amendment, any fact increasing the maximum penalty for a crime must be charged in an indictment, submitted to a jury, and proven beyond a reasonable doubt. The Fourteenth Amendment requires the same conclusion in this case. [Here, the constitutional proscription against deprivation of liberty without due process of law and the guarantee that in all criminal prosecutions the accused enjoy the right to a speedy and public trial by an impartial jury.] While traditionally judges were bound to the sentence proscribed by statute, judges have been accorded wide latitude in sentencing so long as such discretion is limited to the range of sentencing options prescribed by the legislature. While trial practice procedures may change, they must at least adhere to the basic principles of trying to a jury all facts necessary to constitute the offense and proving such facts beyond a reasonable doubt. Prosecution subjects a criminal defendant both to the risk that he will lose his liberty and that he will face stigmatization. Thus, the standard of reasonable doubt is imposed to ensure that he will not be subject to such deprivation erroneously. Constitutional limits exist to states' authority to eliminate facts necessary to constitute a criminal offense. State statutory schemes that keep from the jury facts that may expose defendants to greater or additional punishment raise serious constitutional issues. Here the statutory scheme in issue allows a jury to convict a defendant of a second-degree offense based on a finding beyond a reasonable doubt that he unlawfully possessed a weapon, and then allows a judge to impose punishment, following a second and subsequent hearing, equal to crimes of the first degree based on a finding by the preponderance of the evidence that defendant's purpose was intimidation of the victim based on a particular characteristic the victim possessed. This practice cannot stand. Reversed and remanded.

CONCURRENCE: (Scalia, J.) The founders of the republic were not prepared to leave criminal justice to the states, which is why the jury-trial guarantee was one of the least controversial provisions of the Bill of Rights. Furthermore, as a guarantee of fairness, an individual's guilt will be determined beyond a reasonable doubt by the unanimous vote of twelve fellow citizens, and a criminal will never get more punishment than he bargained for when he did the crime. To allow a single employee of the state to determine the length of a sentence is not the system envisioned by a constitution that guarantees trial by jury. In addition, the guarantee that "[i]n all criminal prosecutions, the accused shall enjoy the right to . . . trial, by an impartial jury" has no intelligible content unless it means that all the facts that must exist in order to subject the defendant to a legally prescribed punishment must be found by the jury.

CONCURRENCE: (Thomas, J.) The Constitution requires a broader rule than adopted by the Court here. A "crime" includes every fact that is by law a basis for imposing or increasing punishment. If the legislature

Continued on next page.

defines some core crime and then provides for increasing punishment of that crime upon a finding of some aggravating fact, then the two constitute an aggravated crime and the aggravated fact is an element of the aggravated crime.

DISSENT: (O'Connor, J.) The Court has long recognized that not every fact that bears on a defendant's punishment need be charged in an indictment, submitted to a jury, and proven beyond a reasonable doubt. Instead this Court has held that the legislature's definition of the elements is usually dispositive, and courts proceed with caution before deciding that a certain fact must be treated as an offense element despite the legislature's decision not to characterize it as such. The Court's rule is unsupported by history and case law.

DISSENT: (Breyer, J.) The majority's rule promotes an ideal that juries determine the existence of those facts upon which punishment turns. There are practically speaking too many sentencing factors for all of them to be submitted to a jury. The solution lies not in prohibiting the legislature from enacting sentencing factors, but in sentencing rules that determine punishment on basis of properly defined relevant conduct, with procedural and Due Process safeguards.

ANALYSIS

Here the United States Supreme Court annunciates a broad rule with the effect of precluding the state and federal government from invoking sentence enhancements in order to increase a maximum sentence.

Quicknotes

BILL OF RIGHTS The first ten Amendments to the U.S. Constitution, setting forth individual rights and liberties.

DUE PROCESS CLAUSE Language in the Fifth and Fourteenth Amendments to the U.S. Constitution, providing that no person shall be deprived of "life, liberty, or property, without due process of law."

Blakely v. Washington

Convicted kidnapper (D) v. State (P)

542 U.S. 296 (2004)

NATURE OF CASE: Appeal from a conviction for kidnapping.

FACT SUMMARY: When Blakely (D) was sentenced by a judge to more than three years beyond the statutory maximum for the crime to which he had pleaded guilty (because of a statutory enhancement based on a fact not included within the guilty plea), he argued that a sentencing procedure which deprives a defendant of the right to a jury determination of all facts essential to the sentence violates the Sixth Amendment.

RULE OF LAW

A sentencing procedure that deprives the defendant of the right to a jury determination of all facts essential to the sentence violates the Sixth Amendment.

FACTS: The State (P) charged Blakely (D) with first-degree kidnapping. Upon reaching a plea agreement, however, the State (P) reduced the charge to second-degree kidnapping involving domestic violence and use of a firearm. Blakely (D) entered a guilty plea admitting the elements of the second-degree kidnapping and the domestic violence and firearm allegations, but no other relevant facts. The case proceeded to sentencing. The facts of his plea, standing alone, supported a maximum sentence of 53 months. Pursuant to state law, however, the judge imposed an "exceptional" sentence of 90 months after making a judicial determination that Blakely (D) had acted with "deliberate cruelty." Faced with an unexpected increase of more than three years in his sentence, Blakely (D) argued that since the State's (P) sentencing procedure deprived him of the right to a jury determination of all facts essential to the sentence, his Sixth Amendment rights were violated. The state court of appeals affirmed the conviction, and the Washington Supreme Court denied discretionary review. Blakely (D) appealed to the United States Supreme Court.

ISSUE: Does a sentencing procedure that deprives the defendant of the right to a jury determination of all facts essential to the sentence violate the Sixth Amendment?

HOLDING AND DECISION: (Scalia, J.) Yes. A sentencing procedure that deprives the defendant of the right to a jury determination of all facts essential to the sentence violates the Sixth Amendment. Blakely (D) was sentenced to prison for more than three years beyond what the law allowed for the crime to which he confessed, on the basis of a disputed finding that he had acted with "deliberate cruelty." The Framers would not have thought it too much to demand that, before depriving a person of three more years of liberty, the state should suffer the "modest inconvenience" of submitting its accusation to the unanimous suffrage of twelve of the accused's equals and neighbors, rather than a lone employee of the state. Here, the facts supporting the finding of "deliberate cruelty" were neither admitted by Blakely (D) nor found by a jury. The statutory maximum a judge may constitutionally impose must be based solely on the basis of the facts reflected in the jury verdict or admitted by the defendant. In other words, the relevant statutory maximum is not the maximum sentence a judge may impose after finding additional facts, but the maximum he or she may impose "without any additional findings." Finally, whether the judge's authority to impose an enhanced sentence depends on finding a specified fact, one of several specified facts, or an aggravating fact, it remains the case that the jury's verdict alone does not authorize the sentence. Reversed.

DISSENT: (O'Connor, J.) The effect of today's decision will be greater judicial discretion and less uniformity in sentencing. It is implausible that the Framers would have considered such a result to be required by the Due Process Clause or the Sixth Amendment. Prior to Washington's sentencing reform legislation, the state's unguided discretion inevitably resulted in severe disparities in sentencing received and served by defendants committing the same offense and having similar criminal histories. Because of today's decision, over 20 years of sentencing reform are all but lost, and tens of thousands of criminal judgments are in jeopardy.

DISSENT: (Breyer, J.) As a result of the majority's ruling, sentencing must now take one of three forms, each of which risks impracticality, unfairness, or harm to the jury trial right the majority purports to strengthen. This circumstance reveals that the majority's Sixth Amendment interpretation cannot be correct. First, creating a "determinate" sentencing system, although assuring uniformity, it would do so at an intolerable cost by imposing identical punishments on people who committed their crimes in very different ways. Second, "indeterminate" sentencing systems in which the sentence is entirely discretionary with the judge may produce unfair disparities in the punishments of similarity situated defendants, the so-called "what the judge ate for breakfast" on the day of sentencing test. Third, the "structured" sentencing system contains so many complexities and difficult choices for

Continued on next page.

the defendant as to make it unworkable and provides an unreasonable extent to which a prosecutor can control the outcome through what charges might be brought for the same offense. Hence, the majority today ignores the adverse consequences inherent in its conclusion. While there are many faults to the guidelines systems, they will be better cured through legislation with reasoned input from the criminal justice community than by an unchangeable decision of the Court.

ANALYSIS

As the United States Supreme Court stresses in *Blakely*, the need to provide intelligible content to the right of jury trial is no mere procedural formality but a fundamental reservation of power in our constitutional structure. The *Blakely* case was not about whether determinate sentencing is constitutional but only about how it can be implemented in a way that respects the Sixth Amendment.

Quicknotes

SIXTH AMENDMENT Provides the right to a speedy and public trial by impartial jury, the right to be informed of the accusation, the right to confront witnesses, and the right to have the assistance of counsel in all criminal prosecutions.

North Carolina v. Pearce

State (P) v. Retried rapist (D)

395 U.S. 711 (1969)

NATURE OF CASE: Petitions for writs of habeas corpus.

FACT SUMMARY: Pearce (D) obtained a reversal of his conviction. Upon retrial, he was sentenced to eight years in prison which, when added to the time he had already served, amounted to a longer total sentence than that originally imposed. Rice (D) also obtained a reversal of his conviction. Upon retrial, he was sentenced to a harsher sentence than his original sentence, and no credit was given for the time he had already served.

RULE OF LAW

The Double Jeopardy Clause does not prohibit, upon a reconviction, imposition of a harsher sentence than imposed after the first conviction so long as the court's reasons affirmatively appear.

FACTS: Pearce (D) was sentenced to 12 to 15 years in prison for assault with intent to rape. He obtained a reversal of his conviction. Upon retrial, he was convicted and sentenced to eight years, which, when added to the time he had already served, amounted to a longer sentence than that originally imposed. Rice (D) was sentenced to ten years in prison after pleading guilty to burglary. He obtained a reversal of his conviction. Upon his retrial, he was convicted upon three of the original four counts and sentenced to a term totaling 25 years. No credit was given for the time he had already served. Pearce (D) was granted habeas corpus on the grounds that the longer sentence was unconstitutional. Rice (D) was also granted habeas corpus as it was found that the state was punishing him for his having exercised his postconviction right of review.

ISSUE: Does the Double Jeopardy Clause prohibit, upon a reconviction, imposition of a harsher sentence than imposed after the first conviction so long as the court's reasons affirmatively appear?

HOLDING AND DECISION: (Stewart, J.) No. The Double Jeopardy Clause does not prohibit, upon a reconviction, imposition of a harsher sentence than imposed after the first conviction so long as the court's reasons affirmatively appear. The guarantee against double jeopardy does not include restrictions upon length of a sentence imposed upon reconviction since the original conviction has, at the defendant's request, been nullified. Nevertheless, an accused may not be punished for exercising the constitutional right to appeal and have a tainted sentence set aside. Accordingly, to ensure absence of a retaliatory motivation on the part of the judge who performs the second sentencing, the reasons for a harsher second conviction must affirmatively be set forth. Furthermore, the Double Jeopardy Clause protects against multiple punishments as well as multiple prosecutions, hence any punishment already exacted must be fully credited in imposing sentence upon a new conviction for the same offense. In both the *Pearce* and *Rice* cases the state did not justify the harsher sentences imposed, which violates the Due Process Clause. Reversed.

CONCURRENCE: (White, J.) The Court should authorize an increased sentence on retrial based on any objective, identifiable factual data not known to the trial judge at the time of the original sentencing proceeding.

ANALYSIS

In *Green v. U.S.*, 355 U.S. 184 (1957), mentioned in one of the concurring opinions, the defendant had originally been charged with first-degree murder but was convicted of second-degree murder. His appeal resulted in the reversal of his conviction, and he was retried on the original charge. The second jury convicted him of first-degree murder. The United States Supreme Court held that double jeopardy barred conviction on that charge, since Green had already been in peril of being convicted and punished for first-degree murder at his first trial. In *Tucker v. Peyton*, 357 F.2d 115 (4th Cir. 1956), it was held that where a prisoner serving consecutive sentences succeeded in having one of the sentences invalidated after it had been fully or partially served, the state must give credit on the sentence remaining for the time served. In *Miller v. Cox*, 443 F.2d 1019 (4th Cir. 1971), it was held that a defendant who had served 21 years on a void conviction was not entitled to credit against subsequently committed felonies.

Quicknotes

DOUBLE JEOPARDY A prohibition against a second prosecution for the same offense after an acquittal or conviction for that offense in a prior proceeding or against multiple punishments for the same offense.

REVERSAL The annulment of a trial court decision by a reviewing court.

WRIT OF HABEAS CORPUS A proceeding in which a defendant brings a writ to compel a judicial determination of whether he or she is lawfully being held in custody.

CHAPTER 18

Double Jeopardy

Quick Reference Rules of Law

Blockburger v. United States

Drug convict (D) v. Federal government (P)

284 U.S. 299 (1932)

NATURE OF CASE: Appeal from a conviction for violation of the Harrison Narcotic Act.

FACT SUMMARY: Blockburger (D) was charged with several different crimes arising from the same essential transaction.

RULE OF LAW

(1) Each of several successive sales under the Harrison Narcotic Act constitutes a distinct offense, however closely they follow each other.

(2) The sale of morphine hydrochloride not in or from the original stamped package, and without a written order, constitutes two separate offenses, although the transaction was the same.

FACTS: Blockburger (D) was charged in a five-count indictment with violating provisions of the Harrison Narcotic Act. He was found guilty on three of the counts that charged him with a sale of morphine hydrochloride to the same purchaser on consecutive days. The judgment was affirmed on appeal, and Blockburger (D) appealed to the United States Supreme Court.

ISSUE:

(1) Does each of several successive sales under the Harrison Narcotic Act constitute a distinct offense, however closely they follow each other?

(2) Does the sale of morphine hydrochloride not in or from the original stamped package, and without a written order, constitute two separate offenses, although the transaction was the same?

HOLDING AND DECISION: (Sutherland, J.)

(1) Yes. Each of several successive sales of narcotics without compliance with the Harrison Narcotic Act constitutes a distinct offense, however closely the sales may follow each other. Here, the sales, although made to the same person, were distinct and separate sales made at different times. The question is: Are the sales two individual acts or are they one course of action? If the former, then each act is punishable separately; if the latter, there can be but one penalty. Here, the first transaction, resulting in a sale, had come to an end. The next sale was not the result of the original impulse, but of a fresh one, namely, of a new bargain.

(2) Yes. The sale of morphine hydrochloride not in or from the original stamped package, and without a written order, constitutes two separate offenses, although the transaction was the same. The face of the statute creates two distinct offenses. Here, each of the offenses created required proof of a different element. When the same act or transaction constitutes a violation of two distinct statutory provisions, the test to be applied to determine whether there are two offenses or only one is whether each provision requires proof of an additional fact that the other does not. Affirmed.

ANALYSIS

In *Blockburger*, the United States Supreme Court noted that the Narcotic Act was not aimed at sales of the forbidden drugs qua sales, a matter entirely beyond the authority of Congress, but at sales of such drugs in violation of the requirements set forth in sections 1 and 2, enacted as aids to the enforcement of the stamp tax imposed by the act.

Brown v. Ohio

Convicted car thief (D) v. State (P)

432 U.S. 161 (1977)

NATURE OF CASE: On certiorari from appellate court judgment upholding Brown's (D) auto theft conviction.

FACT SUMMARY: After serving his sentence for a joyriding conviction, Brown (D) was tried and convicted of auto theft.

RULE OF LAW

Successive prosecutions for the same offense and course of conduct may not be brought merely by dividing the conduct into different segments of time.

FACTS: Brown (D) was convicted of "joyriding"—taking or operating a vehicle without the owner's consent. The date charged in the complaint was December 8, 1973, the date he was apprehended. After serving a jail term, Brown (D) was indicted for auto theft arising out of the same taking; the indictment specified that the vehicle had been stolen on or about November 29, 1973.

ISSUE: May successive prosecutions for the same offense and course of conduct be brought merely by dividing the conduct into different segments of time?

HOLDING AND DECISION: (Powell, J.) No. Successive prosecutions for the same offense and course of conduct may not be brought merely by dividing the conduct into different segments of time. For purposes of the Double Jeopardy Clause, the two crimes charged constitute the same offense, as joyriding is a lesser included offense of auto theft. Joyriding requires proof of the unauthorized taking of a vehicle, but not proof of intent to permanently deprive the owner of his property. The prosecutor who proves auto theft has established all the elements of joyriding. However, we disagree with the court of appeals that Brown (D) may be prosecuted twice merely by focusing on different aspects of his nine-day joyride. Under Ohio law, the theft and operation of a single car is a single offense. The judgment of the court of appeals is reversed.

CONCURRENCE: (Brennan, J.) The Double Jeopardy Clause, except in extremely limited circumstances not-present here, requires the prosecution of all charges in a single proceeding that grow out of a single criminal act. The "single-transaction" test applies, even if the offenses may be viewed as discrete for charging purposes.

DISSENT: (Blackmun, J.) Nine days elapsed between the two incidents that are the basis of Brown's (D) convictions. The time must have come when he stopped driving the car. When he operated it again in a different community, the Ohio courts could find that the acts were sufficiently distinct to justify a second prosecution.

ANALYSIS

The "same offense" test used by the United States Supreme Court to bar the successive prosecution of a statutory offense as well as a lesser included offense was enunciated in *Blockberger v. United States*, 284 U.S. 299 (1932). Some commentators have criticized *Blockberger* for being too generous, saying that "the same offense" means exactly that. Others have said the *Blockberger* rule is not generous enough, allowing multiple prosecutions under statutes that overlap substantially, where neither is wholly included in the other.

Quicknotes

DOUBLE JEOPARDY A prohibition against a second prosecution for the same offense after an acquittal or conviction for that offense in a prior proceeding or against multiple punishments for the same offense.

LESSER INCLUDED OFFENSE One that is necessarily established by proof of the greater offense; the greater offense requires proof of all the elements of the lesser offense in order to sustain a conviction.

Missouri v. Hunter

State (P) v. Convicted robber (D)

459 U.S. 359 (1983)

NATURE OF CASE: On certiorari from state supreme court judgment setting aside conviction for armed criminal action.

FACT SUMMARY: Hunter (D) was convicted, in the same trial, for first-degree robbery and for the crime of armed criminal action, and sentenced for each.

RULE OF LAW

Where a legislature specifically authorizes punishment under two statutes, regardless of whether one is a lesser included offense of the other, the court may impose cumulative punishment.

FACTS: Hunter (D) was convicted under a Missouri (P) statute of first-degree robbery. He was also convicted in the same trial for the crime of armed criminal action. The latter crime requires proof of a felony committed with the use of a dangerous or deadly weapon. The statute proscribing armed criminal action specifies that punishment under the statute shall be administered in addition to the punishment for the underlying offense.

ISSUE: Where a legislature specifically authorizes punishment under two statutes, regardless of whether one is a lesser included offense of the other, may the court impose cumulative punishment?

HOLDING AND DECISION: (Burger, C.J.) Yes. Where a legislature specifically authorizes punishment under two statutes, regardless of whether one is a lesser included offense of the other, the court may impose cumulative punishment. Legislatures, not courts, proscribe the scope of punishment. With respect to cumulative sentences imposed in a single trial, the Double Jeopardy Clause does no more than prevent the sentencing court from imposing greater punishment than the legislature intended. The Missouri Supreme Court recognized that the Missouri (P) legislature intended that punishment for these statutes be cumulative. The judgment of the Missouri Supreme Court is reversed and Hunter's (D) sentence is upheld.

DISSENT: (Marshall, J.) A scheme that permits the prosecution to obtain two convictions and two sentences for the same is not equivalent to a single conviction, even if the one conviction carries a sentence of equal severity to the two separate convictions. Each of the two convictions imposes an additional stigma and does additional damage to the defendant's reputation. Such multiple convictions are thus not permitted by the Double Jeopardy Clause.

ANALYSIS

The dissent stated that in the context of multiple prosecutions, prosecutions for an offense and a lesser included offense arising out of the same conduct violated the Double Jeopardy Clause, regardless of legislative intent. Justice Marshall was prepared to apply the same rationale to the single-prosecution context; however, the majority deferred to the legislature where the case involved multiple punishments arising out of a single criminal act.

Quicknotes

CUMULATIVE PUNISHMENT Consecutive penalties imposed on the same person.

DOUBLE JEOPARDY A prohibition against a second prosecution for the same offense after an acquittal or conviction for that offense in a prior proceeding or against multiple punishments for the same offense.

LESSER INCLUDED OFFENSE One that is necessarily established by proof of the greater offense; the greater offense requires proof of all the elements of the lesser offense in order to sustain a conviction.

Fong Foo v. United States

Corporation and its employees (D) v. Federal government (P)

369 U.S. 141 (1962)

NATURE OF CASE: On certiorari from writ of mandamus vacating an acquittal in federal district court.

FACT SUMMARY: A corporation and two of its employees (D) were tried before a jury on an indictment charging conspiracy and concealment of material facts. After seven days of testimony, the district judge ordered a directed verdict of acquittal as to all the defendants. The record shows that the judge's action was based on supposed improper action by the prosecutor, an assistant United States attorney, and upon a supposed lack of credibility in the testimony of one of the Government's (P) witnesses.

RULE OF LAW

A verdict of acquittal may not be reviewed without putting the defendant twice in jeopardy.

FACTS: A corporation and two of its employees (D) were indicted on charges of conspiracy and concealment of material facts. They were tried before a jury in federal district court. After several witnesses for the prosecution testified, the judge directed a verdict of acquittal to all defendants. The order was based on the supposed improper conduct of the prosecutor and the supposed lack of credibility in the testimony of one of the witnesses who had testified for the Government (P). On appeal, the court of appeals reversed the acquittal and ordered a new trial.

ISSUE: May a verdict of acquittal be reviewed without putting the defendant twice in jeopardy?

HOLDING AND DECISION: (Per curiam) No. A verdict of acquittal may not be reviewed without putting the defendant twice in jeopardy. Although the court of appeals thought, not without reason, that the acquittal was based on an egregiously erroneous foundation, the acquittal was final and could not be reviewed without violating the Double Jeopardy Clause of the Constitution. The judgment of the court of appeals is reversed.

CONCURRENCE: (Harlan, J.) Retrial of petitioners should be permitted if the acquittal was clearly based solely on the exercise of a power the trial judge unquestionably did not have. However, the record fails to indicate that the district court judge based his order solely on the exercise of a nonexistent judicial power.

DISSENT: (Clark, J.) The trial judge clearly had no power to direct a verdict of acquittal. The word "acquittal" is no magic "open sesame;" in this case, the judgment of acquittal was null and void.

ANALYSIS

Federal law prohibits an appeal from an acquittal, even to clarify a point of law, because of the "case and controversy" requirement of Article III. In some states, the government may appeal an acquittal to seek clarification of the law; however, the acquittal will stand even if the state prevails on the point of law.

Quicknotes

CONSPIRACY Concerted action by two or more persons to accomplish some unlawful purpose.

DIRECTED VERDICT A verdict ordered by the court in a jury trial.

PER CURIAM Denotes a decision that represents the opinion of the entire court.

WRIT OF MANDAMUS A court order issued commanding a public or private entity, or an official thereof, to perform a duty required by law.

Ashe v. Swenson

Convicted robber (P) v. State official (D)

397 U.S. 436 (1970)

NATURE OF CASE: Petition for writ of habeas corpus after conviction of robbery.

FACT SUMMARY: Three or four men robbed six men who had been playing poker and stole and fled in the car of one of the victims. Each alleged robber was charged with seven separate offenses. Ashe (P) was acquitted on the robbery charge as to one of the victims. At that trial, the State's (D) proof that the robbery had occurred and that the alleged victim was one of the victims was unassailable, but the evidence that Ashe (P) was one of the robbers was weak. At a second trial for the robbery of a second victim, Ashe (P) was convicted. Ashe (P) contended that collateral estoppel was one of the elements of the Fifth Amendment guarantee against double jeopardy, so that his conviction at the second trial was unconstitutional.

RULE OF LAW

The doctrine of collateral estoppel is embodied in the Fifth Amendment guarantee against double jeopardy, so that an acquittal based on a factual issue that is also presented as an essential element of a second charge bars trial on that charge.

FACTS: Three or four men robbed six men who were playing poker and stole and fled in the car of one of the victims. (It was never clear whether there were three or four robbers.) Three men were arrested near the abandoned stolen car. Ashe (P) was arrested separately some distance away. Each of the four was charged with six robbery counts and the theft of the car. At Ashe's (P) trial for the robbery of Knight, the proof that the armed robbery had occurred and that Knight had been a victim was unassailable. However, the State's (D) evidence that Ashe (P) had been one of the robbers was weak, and the jury found Ashe (P) not guilty. Six weeks later, Ashe (P) was brought to trial for the robbery of Roberts. Ashe (P) moved to dismiss, but his motion was not granted. The witnesses at the second trial were for the most part the same as those at the first trial, but their testimony on Ashe's (P) identification was much stronger. The victim whose identification testimony had been negative at the first trial was not called at the second trial. The jury found Ashe (P) guilty, and he was sentenced to 35 years. Ashe (P) then brought a habeas corpus proceeding in federal court on the ground that the second trial had violated his constitutional right not to be twice put in jeopardy. The United States Supreme Court granted certiorari.

ISSUE: Is the doctrine of collateral estoppel embodied in the Fifth Amendment guarantee against double jeopardy, so that an acquittal based on a factual issue that is also presented as an essential element of a second charge bars trial on that charge?

HOLDING AND DECISION: (Stewart, J.) Yes. The doctrine of collateral estoppel is embodied in the Fifth Amendment guarantee against double jeopardy, so that an acquittal based on a factual issue that is also presented as an essential element of a second charge bars trial on that charge. Collateral estoppel means that when an issue of ultimate facts has once been determined by a valid and final judgment, that issue cannot be litigated again between the same parties in any future lawsuit. Although first developed in civil litigation, the doctrine has long been held applicable in criminal cases. Where a previous judgment of acquittal was based upon a general verdict, as is usually the case, the court must examine the records of the prior proceedings to determine whether a rational jury could have grounded its verdict upon any issue other than the one that the defendant seeks to foreclose from consideration. Typically, this requires the court to take into account the pleadings, evidence, charge, and other relevant matters, and conclude whether a rational jury could have grounded its verdict on an issue other than that which the defendant seeks to foreclose from consideration. The inquiry must be set in a practical frame and viewed with an eye to all the circumstances of the proceedings. Looking to the record here, there is no indication that the first jury could have rationally based its verdict on a finding that the robbery did not occur or that Knight had not been a victim. The only rationally conceivable issue in dispute before the jury was whether Ashe (P) had been one of the robbers. The jury, by its verdict, found that he had not. The federal rule of law, therefore, would make a second prosecution for the robbery of Roberts wholly impermissible. The ultimate question, then, is whether this established federal rule is an element of the Fifth Amendment's guarantee against double jeopardy. It is clear that the State (D) would be precluded from bringing Ashe (P) to a second trial for Knight's robbery. From a constitutional perspective, the situation is no different even though Ashe (P) was brought to trial for the robbery of Roberts, because the name of the victim has no bearing on whether Ashe (P) was one of the robbers. Accordingly, the doctrine of collateral estoppel

Continued on next page.

is embodied in the Fifth Amendment guarantee against double jeopardy. [Reversed.]

DISSENT: (Burger, C.J.) Nothing in the language or any of the gloss previously placed on the Double Jeopardy Clause remotely justifies the majority's treatment of the collateral estoppel doctrine. The majority rests its holding in part on a series of cases that did not involve constitutional double jeopardy but applied collateral estoppel as developed in civil litigation to federal criminal prosecutions as a matter of the Court's supervisory power over the federal court system. Doing so, the majority comes to find an element of the Fifth Amendment that other judges did not find for over two centuries. Moreover, the collateral estoppel doctrine developed in civil cases as a way to conserve judicial resources as well as those of the parties to the actions. It also was justified as a way of providing finality. In criminal cases, however, these concerns are not as great, and the doctrine would not apply to both parties, as is true in civil cases. The majority's rationale seems to also rest on the desire to prevent harassment of suspects. They say that Ashe (P) has "run the gantlet" once before. However, that is not the way that phrase was originally used. The full phrase is "run the gantlet once on that charge." Here, there were multiple crimes against multiple victims. By misapplying the phrase, and using it incorrectly, the majority renders the decision "by slogan." Finally, the majority violates its own stated direction that the rule of collateral estoppel in criminal cases not be applied with the hypertechnical and archaic approach, because that is precisely what the majority does.

ANALYSIS

Ashe deprives the prosecution of a major tactical advantage in trying separately, closely related offenses arising from a single transaction. The effect of the collateral estoppel doctrine is to prevent the prosecutor from "treating the first trial as no more than a dry run for a second prosecution" on a second charge. With this tactic eliminated, the prosecutor may find less advantage in separate prosecutions in such situations. In *Harris v. Washington*, 404 U.S. 55 (1971), the United States Supreme Court held that the constitutional guarantee applies, irrespective of whether the jury considered all relevant evidence, and irrespective of the state's good faith in bringing successive prosecutions. There a bomb sent through the mail killed Burdick and the defendant's son. After his acquittal on a charge of murdering Burdick, the defendant was charged with murdering his son. It was contended that the issue of identity had not been fully litigated because the trial judge had wrongly excluded a threatening letter written by the defendant.

Quicknotes

COLLATERAL ESTOPPEL A doctrine whereby issues litigated and determined in a prior proceeding are binding upon all subsequent litigation between the parties regarding that issue.

DOUBLE JEOPARDY A prohibition against a second prosecution for the same offense after an acquittal or conviction for that offense in a prior proceeding or against multiple punishments for the same offense.

FIFTH AMENDMENT Provides that no person shall be compelled to serve as a witness against him- or herself, be subject to trial for the same offense twice, or be deprived of life, liberty, or property without due process of law.

Downum v. United States

Defendant (D) v. Federal government (P)

372 U.S. 734 (1963)

NATURE OF CASE: On certiorari from conviction in state court.

FACT SUMMARY: Two days after discharge of the jury, a second jury was impaneled and Downum (D) was tried and convicted.

RULE OF LAW

Where the prosecution allows a jury to be selected despite the absence of a key prosecution witness, jeopardy may attach as soon as the jury is sworn.

FACTS: A jury was selected and sworn to try Downum (D) on seven counts. The prosecution then asked that the jury be discharged because a key witness on two counts was absent. Over Downum's (D) motion to dismiss those two counts and proceed on the rest of the charges, the judge discharged the jury. A second jury was impaneled two days later; over Downum's (D) plea of double jeopardy, he was tried and convicted.

ISSUE: Where the prosecution allows a jury to be selected despite the absence of a key prosecution witness, may jeopardy attach as soon as the jury is sworn?

HOLDING AND DECISION: (Douglas, J.) Yes. Where the prosecution allows a jury to be selected despite the absence of a key prosecution witness, jeopardy may attach as soon as the jury is sworn. The Double Jeopardy Clause must be broadly construed; its prohibition is not against being twice punished but against twice being put in jeopardy. We resolve any doubt in favor of the liberty of the citizen. Each case must be judged on its facts—here, the prosecution opposed Downum's (D) motion to proceed with the trial on the counts unaffected by the absence of the witness. The conviction is reversed.

DISSENT: (Clark, J.) The circumstances in which the prosecutor found himself resulted from excusable oversight rather than any deliberate action. Downum (D) was never formally arraigned by the first jury, it heard no evidence, and he was not prejudiced in any way. The "ends of public justice" require that the government have an opportunity to present its case.

ANALYSIS

There are some situations in which a second trial may be had after a jury is discharged without reaching a verdict. The most common of these is the hung jury, where the jurors are discharged because they are unable to agree.

Quicknotes

DOUBLE JEOPARDY A prohibition against a second prosecution for the same offense after an acquittal or conviction for that offense in a prior proceeding or against multiple punishments for the same offense.

HUNG JURY The failure of a jury to reach agreement on a verdict resulting in a mistrial.

IMPANEL Select and assign a jury for a case.

MOTION TO DISMISS Motion to terminate an action based on the adequacy of the pleadings, improper service or venue, etc.

Bartkus v. Illinois

Accused robber (D) v. State (P)

359 U.S. 121 (1959)

NATURE OF CASE: On certiorari from state court conviction for robbery.

FACT SUMMARY: Bartkus (D) was tried and acquitted in federal district court; he was then tried and convicted in state court for the same conduct.

RULE OF LAW

(1) Prosecution in a state court following acquittal for the same conduct in a federal court does not place a defendant twice in jeopardy.
(2) Prosecution in a state court following acquittal for the same conduct in a federal court is not necessarily a violation of due process.

FACTS: Bartkus (D) was tried and acquitted by a jury in a federal district court for the robbery of a federally insured savings and loan. He was then tried on robbery charges in a state court and was sentenced to life imprisonment. The prosecutions were conducted independently although there were some connections; for example, the federal investigator turned all the evidence he had gathered over to state prosecutors.

ISSUE:
(1) Does prosecution in a state court following acquittal for the same conduct in a federal court place a defendant twice in jeopardy?
(2) Is prosecution in a state court following acquittal for the same conduct in a federal court necessarily a violation of due process?

HOLDING AND DECISION: (Frankfurter, J.)
(1) No. Prosecution in a state court following acquittal for the same conduct in a federal court does not place a defendant twice in jeopardy. We have repeatedly held in this Court that a defendant may be punished for the same conduct in successive state and federal prosecutions. A citizen of the United States is also a citizen of a state and may be held accountable by both sovereigns.
(2) No. Prosecution in a state court following acquittal for the same conduct in a federal court is not necessarily a violation of due process. Several states have enacted laws barring or limiting such successive prosecutions. We believe that the individual state legislatures are more competent to deal with this issue and thus develop a rational, integrated body of criminal law. The conviction is upheld.

DISSENT: (Black, J.) The Court takes the position that a second trial is less offensive if one is conducted by the federal government and the other by the state. This distinction is too subtle for me to grasp. Whether by two "sovereigns" or one, in either case a man is forced to face danger twice for the same conduct.

ANALYSIS

Justice Brennan, joined by two other justices, voted to set aside the conviction on factual grounds alone, criticizing the conduct of the federal prosecutors. In his view, the participation by federal prosecutors in the state trial was so great that the state prosecution was "actually a second federal prosecution of Bartkus" and thus impermissible.

Quicknotes

ACQUITTAL The discharge of an accused individual from suspicion of guilt for a particular crime and from further prosecution for that offense.

CERTIORARI A discretionary writ issued by a superior court to an inferior court in order to review the lower court's decisions; the U.S. Supreme Court's writ ordering such review.

CHAPTER 19

Post-Trial Process: Correcting Erroneous Verdicts

Quick Reference Rules of Law

Jackson v. Virginia

Convicted murderer (D) v. State (P)

443 U.S. 307 (1979)

NATURE OF CASE: On habeas corpus from court of appeals decision upholding murder conviction.

FACT SUMMARY: Jackson (D) was convicted of first-degree murder.

RULE OF LAW

In reviewing a habeas corpus challenge to the sufficiency of the evidence, an appellate court must do more than determine whether any quantum of the slightest record evidence supported the charges.

FACTS: Jackson (D) appealed his first-degree murder conviction in federal court, then petitioned the court of appeals for review in a habeas corpus proceeding. The court of appeals, considering Jackson's (D) argument that the evidence was insufficient to permit a rational factfinder to conclude that the killing was premeditated, noted that there was some evidence in the record to support that conclusion, and upheld the conviction.

ISSUE: In reviewing a habeas corpus challenge to the sufficiency of the evidence, must an appellate court do more than determine whether any quantum of the slightest record evidence supported the charges?

HOLDING AND DECISION: (Stewart, J.) Yes. In reviewing a habeas corpus challenge to the sufficiency of the evidence, an appellate court must do more than determine whether any quantum of the slightest record evidence supported the charges. In *Thompson v. Louisville*, 362 U.S. 199 (1960), this Court stated that we could "find no evidence whatever in the record to support these charges." This statement has been wrongly interpreted by the courts of appeals in habeas corpus proceedings to stand for the proposition that the presence of the merest modicum of evidence in the record supporting each element of the crime is all that is needed to deny a challenge to the sufficiency of the evidence. The correct test is for the reviewing court to consider all the evidence from the record in the light most favorable to the prosecution, and to inquire whether any rational factfinder, aware of the requirement of proof beyond a reasonable doubt, could have reached a verdict of guilty on the basis of the evidence so viewed. The judgment of the court of appeals is reversed.

CONCURRENCE: (Stevens, J.) The Supreme Court, in its majority opinion, does not require the reviewing court to view just the evidence most favorable to the prosecution and then to decide whether that evidence convinced it beyond a reasonable doubt, nor whether, based on the entire record, rational triers of fact could be convinced of guilt beyond a reasonable doubt. Instead, and without explanation, it chooses a still narrower standard that merely asks whether, "after viewing the evidence in the light most favorable to the prosecution, any rational trier of fact could have found the essential elements of the crime beyond a reasonable doubt." It seems to me that if logic allows this choice after *In re Winship*, 397 U.S. 358 (1970), it should also allow the presumption that the Court has rejected—that trial judges and juries will act rationally and honestly in applying the reasonable-doubt standard, at least so long as the trial is free of procedural error and the record contains evidence tending to prove each of the elements of the offense. Time may prove that the rule the Court has adopted today is the wisest compromise between one extreme that maximizes the protection against the risk that innocent persons will be erroneously convicted and the other extreme that places the greatest faith in the ability of fair procedures to produce just verdicts. But the Court's opinion should not obscure the fact that its new rule is not logically compelled by the analysis or the holding in *Winship* or in any other precedent, or that the rule reflects a new policy choice rather than the application of a pre-existing rule of law.

ANALYSIS

Justice Stevens described the majority holding as an unnecessary encroachment upon the guarantee of substantive fairness heretofore left almost entirely to the trial courts. Stevens criticized the decision as inappropriately diminishing the power of the trial courts to determine the sufficiency of the evidence.

Quicknotes

HABEAS CORPUS COLLATERAL REVIEW An independent review of whether a prisoner is being lawfully imprisoned.

PROOF BEYOND A REASONABLE DOUBT Standard of proof necessary to convict a defendant, requiring the absence of evidence that would cause a reasonable person to hesitate in making an important decision in his or her personal affairs.

QUANTUM An essential amount; a modicum of the required degree.

Arizona v. Fulminante

State (P) v. Confessing first-degree murderer (D)

499 U.S. 279 (1991)

NATURE OF CASE: Appeal from grant of motion to suppress confessions.

FACT SUMMARY: In Arizona's (P) criminal action against Fulminante (D) for first-degree murder, the Arizona Supreme Court, reversing the trial court's ruling, granted Fulminate's (D) motion to suppress two confessions he allegedly made in respect to the murder.

RULE OF LAW

Admission of a coerced confession may be harmless if it appears beyond a reasonable doubt that its admission did not contribute to the verdict obtained.

FACTS: After his incarceration for federal charges relating to possession of a firearm, Fulminante (D) allegedly confessed to one Sarivola, an undercover Federal Bureau of Investigation agent, that he sexually assaulted and murdered his daughter prior to his incarceration. Nearly one year after this alleged confession and after his release from prison on the firearms charge, Fulminante (D) allegedly made another confession to Sarivola's fiancee regarding the same incident. As a result of these confessions, Fulminante (D) was charged with the first-degree murder of his daughter, leading to his eventual conviction and a death sentence despite his pretrial motion to suppress the alleged confessions, which the trial court denied. On appeal, however, the Arizona Supreme Court granted Fulminante's (D) motion, holding that Fulminante's (D) alleged confessions were coerced and, thus, inadmissible, and ruling that the harmless error analysis was not applicable to coerced confessions. Arizona (P) appealed.

ISSUE: May admission of a coerced confession be harmless if it appears beyond a reasonable doubt that its admission did not contribute to the verdict obtained?

HOLDING AND DECISION: (White, J.) Yes. Admission of a coerced confession may be harmless if it appears beyond a reasonable doubt that its admission did not contribute to the verdict obtained. This rule merely applies the rule as laid down in *Chapman v. California*, 386 U.S. 18 (1967), which made clear that federal constitutional error may be held harmless if it is declared harmless beyond a reasonable doubt. In applying *Chapman's* rule to confessions, it is especially noteworthy that confessions are probably the most probative and damaging evidence that can be admitted against a defendant. Indeed, a full confession in which the defendant discloses the motive for and means of the crime may tempt the jury to rely upon that evidence alone in reaching its verdict. Accordingly, a reviewing court must exercise extreme caution before determining that the admission of a confession at trial was harmless. In the instant case, since the transcript discloses that a successful prosecution depended on the jury believing the two confessions, that both confessions were impeachable standing alone, and that the admission of the first confession led to the admission of other evidence prejudicial to Fulminante (D), Arizona (P) has failed to prove beyond a reasonable doubt that the admission of the coerced confessions was harmless. Fulminante's (D) motion to suppress the confessions was properly granted. Affirmed.

CONCURRENCE: (Kennedy, J.) Although having reservations about the involuntariness of Fulminante's (D) confessions, the majority's holding that the confessions were coerced, inadmissible and, therefore, its admission did not constitute harmless error, is acceptable.

DISSENT: (Rehnquist, C.J.) When reviewing the erroneous admission of an involuntary confession, an appellate court must simply review the remainder of the evidence against the defendant to determine whether its admission was harmless beyond a reasonable doubt. In such event, a harmless error analysis is appropriate, and the instant case constitutes a classic example of harmless error. Here, a second confession providing even more details of the crime was in fact properly admitted into evidence.

ANALYSIS

By opening the door to harmless error analysis, the above case creates the risk of erroneous harmless error determinations, and erroneous determinations are most likely to take place in cases in which there is strong independent evidence of a defendant's guilt. Thus, the above case may lead in practice, if not in rhetoric, to a harmless error standard for involuntary confessions that is similar to the lax standard rejected in *Payne v. Arkansas*, 356 U.S. 560 (1958).

Quicknotes

COERCED CONFESSION A statement of a person charged with the commission of a criminal offense acknowledging his or her guilt in respect to the charged offense made when the confessor's free will was overcome as a result

Continued on next page.

of threats, promises, or undue influence, and that is inadmissible at trial.

HARMLESS ERROR An error committed during trial that does not require the reviewing court to overturn or modify the trial court's judgment in that it did not affect the appellant's substantial rights or the disposition of the action.

Teague v. Lane

Robbery convict (P) v. Prosecution (D)

489 U.S. 288 (1989)

NATURE OF CASE: Review of denial of habeas corpus.

FACT SUMMARY: Teague (P) argued in habeas proceeding that a post-conviction judicial decision had rendered his conviction invalid.

RULE OF LAW

Except in special circumstances, case law will not be retroactively applied in collateral review.

FACTS: Teague (P) was charged with various felonies. An all-White jury convicted Teague (P), a Black man, of attempted murder, robbery, and battery. The prosecution had used all its peremptory challenges to exclude Black people from the jury. Teague (P) appealed, contending that this denied him due process. On appeal the conviction was upheld. Teague (P) subsequently petitioned for habeas corpus, contending that he had been entitled to a jury consisting of a cross section of the community. The district court denied his petition on the merits, as did the court of appeals. The United States Supreme Court granted review.

ISSUE: Except in special circumstances, will case law be retroactively applied in collateral review?

HOLDING AND DECISION: (O'Connor, J.) No. Except in special circumstances, case law will not be retroactively applied in collateral review. Habeas corpus provides an avenue for upsetting judgments that otherwise would be final. It is not intended to be a substitute for direct review. Both the state and criminal defendants have an interest in leaving concluded litigation in a state of repose. If new rules of constitutional law were to be applied retroactively, any litigation might be reopened if the new rule were to be applicable. Further, the purpose of habeas is that its presence creates an incentive for trial and appellate judges to conduct their proceedings in a manner consistent with established constitutional principles. To apply new principles retroactively would actually subvert this purpose. Therefore, the Court concludes that, unless the post-conviction rule announced is so fundamental to the concept of ordered liberty that it would be unconscionable not to retroactively apply it, retroactive application will not be given. A necessary corollary to this rule is that no new rule of constitutional criminal procedure should be announced in a habeas proceeding. Here, to rule as Teague (P) urges would amount to that. Therefore, without ruling on the merits of the claim, the denial of habeas must be affirmed.

DISSENT: (Brennan, J.) When collateral review challenges have merit, the plurality's decision would prevent vindication of constitutional rights, hence denying a check against further violations until the same claim is presented on direct review. The plurality's adherence to treating similar cases alike, amounts to "letting the tail wag the dog" when it stymies the resolution of substantial constitutional questions. Uniform treatment of habeas petitioners is not worth the price the plurality is willing to pay.

ANALYSIS

The opinion in fact announces two rules, the first being that stated above and the second being that new constitutional issues cannot be announced in a habeas proceeding. The latter rule is potentially much more significant than the first. It is important to note, however, that only four justices joined the section announcing that rule, which limits its precedential value.

Quicknotes

PEREMPTORY CHALLENGE A challenge issued by counsel during voir dire proceedings to refuse a jury seat to a prospective juror, for which no reason need be advanced other than the preference of counsel advocating exclusion.

WRIT OF HABEAS CORPUS A proceeding in which a defendant brings a writ to compel a judicial determination of whether he or she is lawfully being held in custody.

Wainwright v. Sykes

Court (P) v. Intoxicated homicide suspect (D)

433 U.S. 72 (1977)

NATURE OF CASE: Habeas corpus challenge to a murder conviction.

FACT SUMMARY: Sykes (D) sought a review of his murder conviction via a habeas corpus proceeding, but he had failed to comply with state procedural rules in not raising the underlying claim at trial.

RULE OF LAW

One who did not comply with state procedural rules by not raising his federal claim at trial cannot obtain federal habeas corpus review of his state criminal conviction unless he shows "cause" for noncompliance and shows "prejudice" as a result of the claimed error in the original proceeding.

FACTS: Sykes (D) violated a state procedural rule by not raising at trial his claim that the incriminating statements admitted against him were involuntary because he did not understand the *Miranda* warnings that he had been given. When he was convicted in state court for murder, Sykes (D) then presented a federal habeas corpus challenge to that conviction based on the aforementioned contention. Opposing such action, Wainwright (P) argued that the rule in *Francis v. Henderson*, 425 U.S. 536 (1976), should be extended to cover this case. That rule was that federal habeas corpus review was barred absent a showing of "cause" and "prejudice" where the challenge was to the makeup of a grand jury. Sykes (D) argued that *Fay v. Noia*, 372 U.S. 391 (1963), had laid down an all-inclusive rule rendering state timely-objection rules ineffective to bar review of underlying federal claims in federal habeas corpus proceedings absent a showing of "knowing waiver" or a "deliberate bypass" of the right to so object.

ISSUE: In order to obtain federal habeas corpus review of his state criminal conviction, must one who did not comply with state procedural rules in raising his federal claim at trial show "cause" for noncompliance and show "prejudice" resulting from the claimed error in the original proceeding?

HOLDING AND DECISION: (Rehnquist, J.) Yes. One who did not comply with state procedural law by raising his federal claim at trial cannot obtain federal habeas corpus review of his state criminal conviction unless he shows "cause" for noncompliance and shows "prejudice" as a result of the claimed error in the original proceeding. A state's contemporaneous objection rule is designed to ensure that constitutional claims are heard when they are fresh, not years later in a federal habeas corpus proceeding. Furthermore, to apply the "knowing waiver" or "deliberate bypass" standard, the more lenient of those suggested, would encourage "sandbagging" by lawyers who would take their chances on a not guilty verdict at trial with the intent to raise their constitutional claims in a federal habeas corpus court if their initial gamble does not pay off. The "cause" and "prejudice" rule herein adopted attempts to make the state trial on the merits the "main event" rather than a "tryout on the road." In this case, the required showing of cause was not made. Remanded with instructions to dismiss the petition for a writ of habeas corpus.

DISSENT: (Brennan, J.) The Court is not justified in imposing a stricter standard than the deliberate bypass test. It is the harshest test possible that still distinguishes between intentional and inadvertent noncompliance by counsel with procedural rules. Most procedural defaults are born of the inadvertence, negligence, inexperience, or incompetence of trial counsel, and it is unfair to make the criminal defendant accountable for the naked errors of his attorney. The mistakes of a trial attorney should be visited on the head of a federal habeas corpus applicant only when this Court is convinced that the lawyer actually exercised his expertise and judgment in his client's service, and with his client's knowing and intelligent participation where possible.

ANALYSIS

One possible result of this case may be that defendants are pushed into making more claims based on ineffectiveness of counsel to fulfill the requirement that they show "cause." That is, a particular procedural default will simply be cited as an example of general incompetence of counsel. The effect would be merely to transform the old claims alleging deprivation of constitutional rights to new claims alleging ineffectiveness of counsel, with all the attendant problems which that will engender.

Quicknotes

WRIT OF HABEAS CORPUS A proceeding in which a defendant brings a writ to compel a judicial determination of whether he or she is lawfully being held in custody.

Smith v. Murray

Convicted murderer-rapist (D) v. Government official (P)

477 U.S. 527 (1986)

NATURE OF CASE: On certiorari from denial of habeas corpus petition.

FACT SUMMARY: Smith (D) was convicted of rape and murder; a psychiatrist testified under cross-examination by the prosecutor to the content of statements made by Smith (D) during the course of his examination.

RULE OF LAW

A tactical decision by defense counsel not to pursue an objection on appeal does not provide a basis for reviving the issue under the rubric of an ineffective assistance of counsel claim.

FACTS: Smith (D) raped a woman at knifepoint near his home. He then murdered her by means of choking, drowning, and stabbing. At his trial on rape and murder charges, Smith's (D) appointed counsel requested that a psychiatrist be appointed to examine Smith (D). On cross-examination, the prosecutor elicited damaging information from the psychiatrist, including the fact that Smith (D) told the psychiatrist during the examination that he had come close to raping a schoolgirl on a bus and had torn off the girl's clothes before abandoning the attack. On appeal, Smith (D) did not raise the issue of the inadmissibility of the psychiatrist's testimony under the Fifth and Fourteenth Amendments' prohibition against self-incrimination. He later petitioned for writ of habeas corpus, which was denied on the grounds Smith (D) had forfeited the claim by failing to press it in earlier proceedings. Smith (D) argued that the issue was preserved because his attorney's failure to raise the claim constituted ineffective assistance of counsel and thus provided cause for not pursuing the claim on appeal. This petition was denied.

ISSUE: Does a tactical decision by defense counsel not to pursue an objection on appeal provide a basis for reviving the issue under the rubric of an ineffective assistance of counsel claim?

HOLDING AND DECISION: (O'Connor, J.) No. A tactical decision by defense counsel not to pursue an objection on appeal does not provide a basis for reviving the issue under the rubric of an ineffective assistance of counsel claim. The process of winnowing out weaker arguments on appeal and focusing on those more likely to prevail, far from being evidence of incompetence, is the hallmark of effective appellate advocacy. The decision not to pursue an objection to the admission of the psychiatrist's testimony fell well within the wide range of professionally competent assistance. The decision of the district court to deny the writ of habeas corpus is upheld.

DISSENT: (Stevens, J.) To the extent there has been a procedural "default," it is exceedingly minor. The Court has lost its way in a procedural maze of its own creation and grossly misevaluated the federal court's statutory mission under the federal habeas corpus statute.

ANALYSIS

The dissent raises an issue of sharp concern: that because of failure to adhere to the finer points of procedure, whether "excusable" under the standards of post-conviction review, a legally innocent defendant might be put to death. The issue becomes even more significant when a claim of factual innocence is maintained. There is an "actual innocence" exception to the rule barring revival of defaulted claims. However, a defendant seeking to show that the defaulted claim deprived the factfinder of exculpatory evidence must show it is more likely than not that no reasonable juror would have convicted him or her in light of the new evidence.

Quicknotes

EXCULPATORY EVIDENCE A statement or other evidence that tends to excuse, justify, or absolve the defendant from alleged fault or guilt.

HABEAS CORPUS A proceeding in which a defendant brings a writ to compel a judicial determination of whether he or she is lawfully being held in custody.

PRIVILEGE AGAINST SELF-INCRIMINATION A privilege guaranteed by the Fifth Amendment to the U.S. Constitution in a criminal proceeding for communications made by an accused and protecting an accused or witness from having to give testimony that may incriminate him- or herself.

Glossary

Common Latin Words and Phrases Encountered in the Law

A FORTIORI: Because one fact exists or has been proven, therefore a second fact that is related to the first fact must also exist.

A PRIORI: From the cause to the effect. A term of logic used to denote that when one generally accepted truth is shown to be a cause, another particular effect must necessarily follow.

AB INITIO: From the beginning; a condition that has existed throughout, as in a marriage that was void ab initio.

ACTUS REUS: The wrongful act; in criminal law, such action as is sufficient to trigger criminal liability.

AD VALOREM: According to value; an ad valorem tax is imposed upon an item located within the taxing jurisdiction calculated by the value of such item.

AMICUS CURIAE: Friend of the court. Its most common usage takes the form of an amicus curiae brief, filed by a person who is not a party to an action but is nonetheless allowed to offer an argument supporting his or her legal interests.

ARGUENDO: In arguing. A statement, possibly hypothetical, made for the purpose of argument.

BILL QUIA TIMET: A bill to quiet title (establish ownership) to real property.

BONA FIDE: True, honest, or genuine. May refer to a person's legal position based on good faith or lacking notice of fraud (such as a bona fide purchaser for value) or to the authenticity of a particular document (such as a bona fide last will and testament).

CAUSA MORTIS: With approaching death in mind. A gift causa mortis is a gift given by a party who feels certain that death is imminent.

CAVEAT EMPTOR: Let the buyer beware. This maxim is reflected in the rule of law that a buyer purchases at his or her own risk because it is the buyer's responsibility to examine, judge, test, and otherwise inspect what he or she is buying.

CERTIORARI: A writ of review. Petitions for review of a case by the United States Supreme Court are most often done by means of a writ of certiorari.

CONTRA: On the other hand. Opposite. Contrary to.

CORAM NOBIS: Before us; a writ of error directed to the court that originally rendered the judgment.

CORAM VOBIS: Before you; a writ of error directed by an appellate court to a lower court to correct a factual error.

CORPUS DELICTI: The body of the crime; the requisite elements of a crime amounting to objective proof that a crime has been committed.

CUM TESTAMENTO ANNEXO, ADMINISTRATOR (ADMINISTRATOR C.T.A.): With will annexed; an administrator c.t.a. settles an estate pursuant to a will in which he or she is not appointed.

DE BONIS NON, ADMINISTRATOR (ADMINISTRATOR D.B.N.): Of goods not administered; an administrator d.b.n. settles a partially settled estate.

DE FACTO: In fact; in reality; actually. Existing in fact but not officially approved or engendered.

DE JURE: By right; lawful. Describes a condition that is legitimate "as a matter of law," in contrast to the term "de facto," which connotes something existing in fact but not legally sanctioned or authorized. For example, de facto segregation refers to segregation brought about by housing patterns, etc., whereas de jure segregation refers to segregation created by law.

DE MINIMUS: Of minimal importance; insignificant; a trifle; not worth bothering about.

DE NOVO: Anew; a second time; afresh. A trial de novo is a new trial held at the appellate level as if the case originated there and the trial at a lower level had not taken place.

DICTA: Generally used as an abbreviated form of obiter dicta, a term describing those portions of a judicial opinion incidental or not necessary to resolution of the specific question before the court. Such nonessential statements and remarks are not considered to be binding precedent.

DUCES TECUM: Refers to a particular type of writ or subpoena requesting a party or organization to produce certain documents in their possession.

EN BANC: Full bench. Where a court sits with all justices present rather than the usual quorum.

EX PARTE: For one side or one party only. An ex parte proceeding is one undertaken for the benefit of only one party, without notice to, or an appearance by, an adverse party.

EX POST FACTO: After the fact. An ex post facto law is a law that retroactively changes the consequences of a prior act.

EX REL.: Abbreviated form of the term "ex relatione," meaning upon relation or information. When the state brings an action in which it has no interest against an individual at the instigation of one who has a private interest in the matter.

FORUM NON CONVENIENS: Inconvenient forum. Although a court may have jurisdiction over the case, the action should be tried in a more conveniently located court, one to which parties and witnesses may more easily travel, for example.

GUARDIAN AD LITEM: A guardian appointed by the court to represent a minor or incompetent person in a legal action.

HABEAS CORPUS: You have the body. The modern writ of habeas corpus is a writ directing that a person (body) being detained (such as a prisoner) be brought before the court so that the legality of his or her detention can be judicially ascertained.

IN CAMERA: In private, in chambers. When a hearing is held before a judge in his or her chambers or when all spectators are excluded from the courtroom.

IN FORMA PAUPERIS: In the manner of a pauper. A party who proceeds in forma pauperis because of his or her poverty is one who is allowed to bring suit without liability for costs.

INFRA: Below, under. A word referring the reader to a later part of a book. (The opposite of supra.)

IN LOCO PARENTIS: In the place of a parent.

IN PARI DELICTO: Equally wrong; a court of equity will not grant requested relief to an applicant who is in pari delicto, or as much at fault in the transactions giving rise to the controversy as is the opponent of the applicant.

IN PARI MATERIA: On like subject matter or upon the same matter. Statutes relating to the same person or things are said to be in pari materia. It is a general rule of statutory construction that such statutes should be construed together, i.e., looked at as if they together constituted one law.

IN PERSONAM: Against the person. Jurisdiction over the person of an individual.

IN RE: In the matter of. Used to designate a proceeding involving an estate or other property.

IN REM: Signifies an action against the res, or thing. An action in rem is basically one that is taken directly against property, as distinguished from an action in personam, i.e., against the person.

INTER ALIA: Among other things. Used to show that the whole of a statement, pleading, list, statute, etc., has not been set forth in its entirety.

INTER PARTES: Between the parties. May refer to contracts, conveyances, or other transactions having legal significance.

INTER VIVOS: Between the living. An inter vivos gift is a gift made by a living grantor, as distinguished from bequests contained in a will, which pass upon the death of the testator.

IPSO FACTO: By the mere fact itself.

JUS: Law or the entire body of law.

LEX LOCI: The law of the place; the notion that the rights of parties to a legal proceeding are governed by the law of the place where those rights arose.

MALUM IN SE: Evil or wrong in and of itself; inherently wrong. Describes an act that is wrong by its very nature, as opposed to one which would not be wrong but for the fact that there is a specific legal prohibition against it (malum prohibitum).

MALUM PROHIBITUM: Wrong because prohibited, but not inherently evil. Describes something that is wrong because it is expressly forbidden by law but that is not in and of itself evil, e.g., speeding.

MANDAMUS: We command. A writ directing an official to take a certain action.

MENS REA: A guilty mind; a criminal intent. A term used to signify the mental state that accompanies a crime or other prohibited act. Some crimes require only a general mens rea (general intent to do the prohibited act), but others, like assault with intent to murder, require the existence of a specific mens rea.

MODUS OPERANDI: Method of operating; generally refers to the manner or style of a criminal in committing crimes, admissible in appropriate cases as evidence of the identity of a defendant.

NEXUS: A connection to.

NISI PRIUS: A court of first impression. A nisi prius court is one where issues of fact are tried before a judge or jury.

N.O.V. (NON OBSTANTE VEREDICTO): Notwithstanding the verdict. A judgment n.o.v. is a judgment given in favor of one party despite the fact that a verdict was returned in favor of the other party, the justification being that the verdict either had no reasonable support in fact or was contrary to law.

NUNC PRO TUNC: Now for then. This phrase refers to actions that may be taken and will then have full retroactive effect.

PENDENTE LITE: Pending the suit; pending litigation underway.

PER CAPITA: By head; beneficiaries of an estate, if they take in equal shares, take per capita.

PER CURIAM: By the court; signifies an opinion ostensibly written "by the whole court" and with no identified author.

PER SE: By itself, in itself; inherently.

PER STIRPES: By representation. Used primarily in the law of wills to describe the method of distribution where a person, generally because of death, is unable to take that which is left to him or her by the will of another, and therefore his or her heirs divide such property between them rather than take under the will individually.

PRIMA FACIE: On its face, at first sight. A prima facie case is one that is sufficient on its face, meaning that the evidence supporting it is adequate to establish the case until contradicted or overcome by other evidence.

PRO TANTO: For so much; as far as it goes. Often used in eminent domain cases when a property owner receives partial payment for his or her land without prejudice to his or her right to bring suit for the full amount he or she claims the land to be worth.

QUANTUM MERUIT: As much as the party deserves. Refers to recovery based on the doctrine of unjust enrichment in those cases in which a party has rendered valuable services or furnished materials that were accepted and enjoyed by another under circumstances that would reasonably notify the recipient that the rendering party expected to be paid. In essence, the law implies a contract to pay the reasonable value of the services or materials furnished.

QUASI: Almost like; as if; nearly. Essentially used to signify that one subject or thing is almost analogous to another but that material differences between them do exist. For example, a quasi-criminal proceeding is one that is not strictly criminal but shares enough of the same characteristics to require some of the same safeguards (e.g., procedural due process must be followed in a parole hearing).

QUID PRO QUO: Something for something. In contract law, the consideration, something of value, passed between the parties to render the contract binding.

RES GESTAE: Things done. In evidence law, this principle justifies the admission of a statement that would otherwise be hearsay when it is made so closely to the event in question as to be said to be a part of it, or with such spontaneity as not to have the possibility of falsehood.

RES IPSA LOQUITUR: The thing speaks for itself. This doctrine gives rise to a rebuttable presumption of negligence when the instrumentality causing the injury was within the exclusive control of the defendant, and the injury was one that does not normally occur unless a person has been negligent.

RES JUDICATA: A matter adjudged. Doctrine that provides that once a court of competent jurisdiction has rendered a final judgment or decree on the merits, that judgment or decree is conclusive upon the parties to the case and prevents them from engaging in any other litigation on the points and issues determined therein.

RESPONDEAT SUPERIOR: Let the master reply. This doctrine holds the master liable for the wrongful acts of his or her servant (or the principal for his or her agent) in those cases in which the servant (or agent) was acting within the scope of his or her authority at the time of the injury.

STARE DECISIS: To stand by or adhere to that which has been decided. The common-law doctrine of stare decisis attempts to give security and certainty to the law by following the policy that once a principle of law as applicable to a certain set of facts has been set forth in a decision, it forms a precedent that will subsequently be followed, even though a different decision might be made were it the first time the question had arisen. Of course, stare decisis is not an inviolable principle and is departed from in instances where there is good cause (e.g., considerations of public policy led the Supreme Court to disregard prior decisions sanctioning segregation).

SUPRA: Above. A word referring a reader to an earlier part of a book. (The opposite of infra.)

ULTRA VIRES: Beyond the power. This phrase is most commonly used to refer to actions taken by a corporation that are beyond the power or legal authority of the corporation.

Addendum of French Derivatives

CHATTEL: Tangible personal property.

CY PRES: Doctrine permitting courts to apply trust funds to purposes not expressed in the trust but necessary to carry out the settlor's intent.

IN PAIS: Not pursuant to legal proceedings.

PER AUTRE VIE: For another's life; during another's life. In property law, an estate may be granted that will terminate upon the death of someone other than the grantee.

PROFIT A PRENDRE: A license to remove minerals or other produce from land.

VOIR DIRE: Process of questioning jurors as to their predispositions about the case or parties to a proceeding in order to identify those jurors displaying bias or prejudice.

